China's Conservative Revolution

In this ambitious examination of the complex political culture of China under Guomindang rule, Brian Tsui interweaves political ideologies, intellectual trends, social movements and diplomatic maneuvers to demonstrate how the Chinese revolution became conservative after the anti-Communist coup of 1927. Dismissing violent struggles for class equality as incompatible with nationalist goals, Chiang Kai-shek's government should, Tsui argues, be understood in the context of the global ascendance of radical right-wing movements during the interwar period. The Guomindang's revolutionary nation-building and modernization project struck a chord with China's reformist liberal elite, who were wary of mob rule, while its obsession with Eastern spirituality appealed to Indian nationalists fighting Western colonialism. The Nationalist vision was defined by the party-state's hostility to communist challenges as much as by its ability to coopt liberalism and Pan-Asianist anticolonialism. Tsui's revisionist reading revisits the peculiarities of the Guomindang's revolutionary enterprise, resituating Nationalist China in the moment of global radical right ascendancy.

Brian Tsui is Assistant Professor at The Hong Kong Polytechnic University. His works on Guomindang ideology, China–India relations and the Cold War have appeared in journals such as *Modern China*, *Twentieth-Century China* and *positions: asia critique*.

D1596482

Studies of the Weatherhead East Asian Institute, Columbia University

The Studies of the Weatherhead East Asian Institute of Columbia University were inaugurated in 1962 to bring to a wider public the results of significant new research on modern and contemporary East Asia.

China's Conservative Revolution

The Quest for a New Order, 1927–1949

Brian Tsui

The Hong Kong Polytechnic University

CAMBRIDGE
UNIVERSITY PRESS

CAMBRIDGE
UNIVERSITY PRESS

University Printing House, Cambridge CB2 8BS, United Kingdom

One Liberty Plaza, 20th Floor, New York, NY 10006, USA

477 Williamstown Road, Port Melbourne, VIC 3207, Australia

314-321, 3rd Floor, Plot 3, Splendor Forum, Jasola District Centre, New Delhi - 110025, India

79 Anson Road, #06-04/06, Singapore 079906

Cambridge University Press is part of the University of Cambridge.

It furthers the University's mission by disseminating knowledge in the pursuit of
education, learning and research at the highest international levels of excellence.

www.cambridge.org
Information on this title: www.cambridge.org/9781316647226
DOI: 10.1017/9781108164610

First published 2018
First paperback edition 2019

A catalogue record for this publication is available from the British Library

ISBN 978-1-107-19623-0 Hardback
ISBN 978-1-316-64722-6 Paperback

Contents

Figures

Acknowledgments

It would be presumptuous of me to pretend that this book is a collective enterprise, but I could never have managed to link random jottings into prose, let alone a full monograph, without the generous help and contributions of many individuals and institutions. In New York City, where this work all began, I benefited from a community of dedicated scholars at Columbia University and beyond. My deepest gratitude goes to Eugenia Lean for her gentle encouragements and admirable open-mindedness as I meandered along the intellectual path. Her influence on me was by no means confined to this book. Mentors including Madeleine Zelin, Lydia Liu, Victoria De Grazia, Kim Brandt and Dorothy Ko helped me sharpen sensitivity to texts and arguments at different critical stages in the journey. Rebecca Karl and Vijay Prashad provided invaluable comments and models of intellectual creativity. It is a privilege to count as my fellow travelers Buyun Chen, Arunabh Ghosh, Gal Gvili, Ho Han-peng, Liza Lawrence, Li Pei-ting, Lin Shing-ting, Andy Liu, Chelsea Schieder, Shim Mi-ryong, Annie Shing and Tim Yang. I thank in particular Daniel Asen, Reto Hofmann, Then Siew Fung, Zhong Yurou and the late Chang Yi-hsiang, who guided me out of the darker alleyways with their camaraderie.

In Canberra, Geremie Barmé provided a stimulating sanctuary for me to refine and substantiate the work. I can only look up to his breadth of knowledge and command of languages. Benjamin Penny was a most caring senior colleague. Other scholars at the Australian National University, including Tomoko Akami, Duncan Campbell, Hyaeweol Choi, Richard Rigby, David Brophy, Sue Chen, Huang Hsuan-ying, Olivier Krischer, Elisa Nesossi, Tsai Tsan-huang, Shuge Wei, Qian Ying, Nathan Woolley, Zhang Yinghong, Zhu Yayun and Zhu Yujie, never hesitated to share acumen, food and company. At The Hong Kong Polytechnic University, I am fortunate to be mentored by Chak Chi-shing, King-fai Tam and Han Xiaorong, who are ever supportive in my development as a scholar and teacher. I thank my dean Chu Hung-lam for giving me the opportunity to contribute to my hometown and Ho Koon-wan for easing my transition to a full-fledged faculty position. Colleagues at the Department of Chinese Culture, particularly Wicky Tse, Leung Shuk Man, Chien Li-kuei and Pan Lu, have been supportive. Hu Nan, my research assistant, is a paragon of patience and detail-mindedness.

Many scholars have graciously provided me with opportunities to present parts of this book in their various stages of development. I especially thank Prasenjit Duara and Tansen Sen for introducing me to the study of China–India interactions. John Carroll, Angela Leung, Chen Kuan-hsing, Madhavi Thampi and Max Ward made it possible for this work to reach larger audiences. Gratitude is due to interlocutors who raised stimulating questions and sustained my interest in intellectual pursuits, particularly Chen Yunqian, Hon Tze-ki, Lai Chi-kong, Fabio Lanza, Lin Shaoyang, Pan Kwang-che, Dan Vukovich, Wang Yuan-yi, Philip Wickeri, Yen Hsiao-pei, Peter Zarrow and the late Arif Dirlik. Maggie Clinton, whose scholarship I greatly admire, is most generous in sharing her insights. I thank Alfred Lin, my teacher at the University of Hong Kong, for keeping an interest in my career. The friendship of Calvin Hui, Kelvin Ng and Lorraine Wong, whom I have known from my high school or undergraduate days, has been invaluable. I thank Charles and Loretta Matthews, Li Hoi Hung and Eliza Sainsbury for welcoming me to their homes in New Jersey and Sydney and nudging me away from the computer screen.

A postdoctoral fellowship from the Australian Centre on China in the World has afforded this project the luxury of time to take shape. Start-up funding for new staff members from the Dean's Reserve of the Faculty of Humanities, The Hong Kong Polytechnic University allowed me to incorporate new materials and substantiate this book's argument. In its former incarnation as a doctoral dissertation, this project was supported financially by the Columbia University Graduate School of Arts and Sciences, the Weatherhead East Asian Institute, Columbia University, the Consortium for Intellectual and Cultural History and the Chiang Ching-kuo Foundation for International Scholarly Exchange. I thank all these organizations for their generosity. No less critical, for a work of history, is the help of staff members at Academia Historica, the Kuomintang Party History Institute, the Second Historical Archives of China, the Guangdong Provincial Archives, Nehru Memorial Museum and Library, the Academia Sinica library system, the Peking University Library, the National Library of China, the C. V. Starr East Asian Library at Columbia University, the University of Hong Kong Libraries and the Pao Yue-kong Library at The Hong Kong Polytechnic University.

Lucy Rhymer at Cambridge University Press has been a joy to work with. I thank her and Ross Yelsey at the Weatherhead East Asian

Institute, Columbia University for their enthusiasm for this project. I was most fortunate to be able to enlist the expertise of Glenda Browne, who prepared a detailed and user-friendly index. Two anonymous readers read the entire manuscript and their generous but exacting comments helped me to fill gaps and avoid embarrassing mistakes.

Portions of Chapter 2 are reproduced from "Class Politics and the Entrenchment of the Party-State in Modern China," in Lion Koenig and Bidisha Chaudhuri, eds., *Politics of the Other in India and China: Western Concepts in Non-Western Contexts* (London: Routledge, 2016), 115–26, with permission from Taylor & Francis. An earlier version of Chapter 6 appears as "The Plea for Asia – Tan Yunshan, Pan-Asianism, and Sino-Indian Relations," which was originally published in *China Report*, vol. 46, no. 4 Copyright 2010 © Institute of Chinese Studies, New Delhi. All rights reserved. Reproduced with the permission of the copyright holders and the publishers, Sage Publications India Pvt. Ltd, New Delhi.

My parents, Tsui King Wah and Tam Oi Ling, my grandmother Cheng Mei Hing and my grand aunt Lau Wai Sok have nurtured me in many more ways than I can begin to enumerate. I cannot ask for a more faithful companion than Agnes Pau. To them I gratefully dedicate this book.

A Note on Romanization

This book adopts the *pinyin* system for transliterating Chinese names and terms.

Exceptions are made for historical figures who are no strangers to general English readers, most notably Sun Yat-sen and Chiang Kai-shek, and scholars of Chinese descent who publish under their personal names. Places and institutions, including those outside mainland China, are rendered in their official transliterations. For the Chinese Nationalist Party, this book uses Guomindang (GMD) or the party's name in English translation to refer to the subject under study and Kuomintang in connection with the archives maintained by the party now headquartered in Taipei.

1   Introduction

Chinese citizens who persevered into the tail end of the war of resistance against Japan were given, albeit not for the first time, an intimate glimpse of their leader. Chiang Kai-shek (1887–1975) set for his compatriots an example of efficiency in organizing one's everyday life in a time of crisis. According to a slim volume published by the main organ of the Nationalist Party, the leader maintained strict discipline and regularity, getting up at five in the morning and retiring to bed at eleven in the evening.[1] Chiang's incredible industriousness allowed the chairman of the Nationalist government to preside over a vast bureaucratic machine, all the while taking meals and exercises at regular hours through the day. After completing official business at six and before dinner at half past seven, the head of China's state, party and military establishments even found the time to take his Methodist wife, Song Meiling (1898–2003), to Chongqing's suburbs for walks. On his drive to the wartime capital's outskirts, Chiang would take mental notes of military or police officers who did not wear proper uniforms or of other inadequacies in the city's appearance. The leader billed to deliver his country from Japanese enslavement had superhuman stamina, but was also perfectly ordinary, piously keeping to a work–leisure routine and enjoying quality time with his family. This blend of the grandiose and the everyday is well encapsulated in the title of the volume, which promised insights into the elevated figure's private life and his teachings on everyday life.

What messages can readers take away from this carefully curated publication? More charitable observers would see Chiang's fastidious obsession with order and punctuality as testament to his military background and Neo-Confucian upbringing.

They might take comfort in the Japanese-educated officer's regular evocations, as indeed seen in his calligraphy in the book, of propriety (*li*), righteousness (*yi*), rectitude (*lian*) and a sense of shame (*chi*).

---

[1] Tao Baichuan, ed., *Jiang zhuxi de shenghuo he shenghuo guan* [*Chairman Chiang's Daily Life and His Outlook on Daily Life*] (Chongqing: Zhongzhou chubanshe, 1944).

1

Detractors might associate the authoritarian leader's puritanism with a witty Shanghailander slight: "There's a Methodism in his madness," an allusion to his sudden but zealous conversion to the Protestant faith.[2] Like many a colorful twentieth-century leader, Chiang's mediated persona drew admiration and contempt, awe and ridicule.

But no personality cult worthy of its name is just about the politician. The political leader's putative qualities also revealed much about the state over which he presided and its enemies. In the case of the Guomindang (GMD, the Chinese Nationalist Party or Kuomintang), stage-managed adoration for Chiang, who was far from the undisputed leader throughout its history as China's ruling party, betrayed the state's aspiration to build a modern, salubrious and orderly society. Chiang's attachment to his spouse could be intended to compensate for his notoriety as a womanizer, but it was equally plausible that the family man persona served as a counterpoint to the lax personal life many of the GMD's detractors led. Chiang's Spartan daily routine contrasted sharply with the Communist leaders' peripatetic and supposedly loose lifestyle. His clockwork discipline sent a message to workers and students who slacked off their duties, indulged in consumerist pleasures or, worse, disrupted production and social order by joining strikes and boycotts. Bureaucrats were warned not to get too comfortable in their positions as their superiors were keeping a constant eye on them. The Nationalist chief personified the vision of a hierarchical, efficient community where members knew their places, toiled meekly and conscientiously, maintained good health and went about their daily life with military-like precision. The aspiration to turn China into a well-oiled social machine free of class conflicts, held even more dearly in such times of vast displacement and precariousness as the Second Sino–Japanese War, was the hallmark of Nationalist rule. Chiang's daily routine was, in this sense, a shorthand for the GMD's *raison d'être*.

The Nationalist government was the product of a revolution. The GMD party-state claimed custody of the incomplete national revolution (*guomin geming*) Sun Yat-sen launched in 1924. Founded in Guangzhou, and settling into Nanjing in April 1927 after deposing the warlord-led Beiyang regime, the Chinese Nationalist Party presided over the first government that had brought unity, albeit tentative, to China since the end of dynastic rule. At the same time, the Nationalists governed in contention with elements of the very revolution they claimed to inherit. Sun Yat-sen never envisaged a communist China, but he countenanced Soviet assistance and participation of Chinese

[2] James Burke, *My Father in China* (New York: Farrar and Rinehart, 1942), 347.

Communists in his enterprise.[3] As such, the Communist movement gathered strength and prestige among workers and peasants with whom it engaged as the national revolution gathered steam. Despite substantial differences among themselves, Chiang and his colleagues devoted their careers to neutralizing whatever gains the Chinese Communist Party (CCP) achieved in the three years during which it acted as the GMD's revolutionary partner. Their political careers were inseparable from the bloody crackdown against Communists and labor unionists on April 12, 1927.

For the next decades, the one leitmotif that underpinned the Nationalist administration that lasted for almost half a century was responding to the threat of revolutionary socialism. This response took on board the rhetoric and methods of the radical left but committed itself to consolidating, rather than eradicating, unequal social relations. Hailing the nation-state as the only legitimate organizing principle of social life, it promised social development by managing capitalism and neutering modernity's disorienting effects on social norms and culture. Confrontations between classes and radical anti-imperialism, Nationalists charged, would derail China's political and economic revival. If the coupling of the nationalist and social revolutions defined Chinese Communism, the GMD led a nationalist revolution that had decidedly conservative socioeconomic goals. It demanded, just as radical right activists elsewhere did or still do, capitalism without capitalism.[4]

China's conservative revolution, like any revolution, entailed both destruction and consolidation. The April 12 purge, multiple encirclement campaigns in the 1930s and the doomed "bandit suppression" (*jiaofei*) campaign from 1946 until the early 1950s were the GMD's most obvious responses to the Communist threat. Censorship of the media and limitations on political freedom also attested to the party-state's unease with its left-wing opposition. Yet Chiang's national revolution was also a proactive program; it set out to form a social bloc, focusing on intellectuals and the urban middle class, in contention with proletarian politics. It worked assiduously to channel popular and elite sympathy away from left-wing or class politics and to cultivate social movements

---

[3] In this book, "Communist" refers to the Chinese political movement that was founded in 1921, while "communist" denotes political ideologies that aspired to a classless social order, which also inspired, but not always defined, the Chinese Communist Party's agendas throughout its existence. The same distinction applies to "Fascist" the Italian party and "fascist" the ideology.

[4] Slavoj Žižek, *Welcome to the Desert of the Real! Five Essays on September 11 and Related Dates* (London: Verso, 2002), 131. "Capitalism without capitalism" is, of course, Žižek's definition of fascism.

and an everyday culture that engaged the masses in renovation of the spirit, rather than realignment of property relations. Suppression of political activism accompanied carefully choreographed expressions of civic enthusiasm. Deploying the political machinery of a radical revolutionary party, the GMD embraced industrial capitalism, but rejected Western materialism and imperialism. It sought an ethno-communal solution to China's semi-colonial status. Instead of confronting the capitalist system, it appealed to the nation and, by extension, Eastern civilization as aestheticized communions in which acute class tensions were imagined away, citizens worked harmoniously under an apparently apolitical state's tutelage and China's independence was achieved through alliances that, in rhetoric but not in substance, transcended the international liberal order.

Placing China's Conservative Revolution in Global History

By characterizing the national revolution since 1927 as a conservative one, this book situates a core period in China's modern experience within the context of global history. At stake is how to understand the Chinese revolution's nature. Rather than seeing China's revolutionary process as one of continuous state-building presided over by successive regimes, I highlight dimensions of the Nationalist experiment that set it apart from the Communist movement it fought against. The Nationalists as described in the following pages shared resemblances not primarily with their domestic nemesis but with international counterparts that valorized the nation – defined as a hierarchal, spiritual and productive community – as the primary subject of history. The GMD differed from the Chinese Communists not because it proved much less successful in maintaining an effective, centralized state but because Nationalists saw confrontational class politics as the ultimate threat to national rejuvenation and social health.

Of course, placing the Nationalist government under a comparative light is no new strategy, even though past scholarship has tended to see China as epiphenomenal to the radical right-wing ascendency in the interwar world. An earlier generation of historians debated on the GMD's fascist nature, considering the regime's connections with its right-wing counterparts in Germany and Italy. They homed in on Nationalist leaders' fascination with fascist experiments in Europe, particularly the efforts of such party groupings as the Blue Shirts or Lixingshe to emulate the organization, trappings and ideological dispositions of the Nazi Party in the 1930s.[5] Despite similarities between the ruling parties of China, Germany and Italy, historians tended to see the GMD's right-wing politics as superficial. Lloyd Eastman, credited for revealing the GMD's fascist tendencies, believes the party that governed China from 1927 to 1937 lacked ideological identity and those who looked to Continental Europe for inspiration on how to mobilize the disaffected populace were at the margins of an ossified bureaucratic behemoth.[6] The GMD could lay claim not to a conservative revolution, but to an *aborted* one. William Kirby, a specialist in twentieth-century Sino–German relations, argues that "there was no 'fascist movement' in China but rather a vogue that coincided with the emergence of a close Sino–German friendship." Nationalists were attracted to national socialism for diverse reasons, and such interest did not translate into concrete action. The same allegedly applies in the case of Italian Fascism insofar as China's relationships with Italy and the Vatican became increasingly cordial, with anticommunism as the common denominator.[7] Chinese admiration of fascist movements was thus ephemeral, superficial and lacking in historical significance. It follows from this line of argument that the global ascendance of the radical right had cosmetic effects on China's development, just as the GMD's prolonged campaign against its erstwhile revolutionary partners was a domestic matter that had little relevance to political developments beyond Chinese borders.

In returning Nationalist China's crusade against Chinese Communists to the interwar moment, I stress the ideological import of a revolution that not just imitated but shared qualities manifest in fascist movements that raged from Tokyo to Buenos Aires.[8] These affinities were not confined to the paraphernalia – adoption of Nazi military drills, interfusion between

---

[5] Lloyd E. Eastman, *Abortive Revolution: China under Nationalist Rule, 1927–1937* (Cambridge, MA: Harvard University Press, 1974), chap. 2; Frederic Wakeman argues that contemporary and historiographical accounts often confused the Lixingshe with the Blue Shirts, which were in fact two distinct organizations (*Spymaster: Dai Li and the Chinese Secret Service* [Berkeley: University of California Press, 2003], 63). For an alternative viewpoint on the Blue Shirts, see Maria Hsia Chang, *The Chinese Blue Shirt Society: Fascism and Developmental Nationalism* (Berkeley: Institute of East Asian Studies, University of California, 1985).

[6] Eastman, *Abortive Revolution*, 83–4, 303–6.

[7] William C. Kirby, *Germany and Republican China* (Stanford, CA: Stanford University Press, 1984), 175; Michele Fatica, "The Beginning and the End of the Idyllic Relations between Mussolini's Italy and Chiang Kai-shek's China (1930–1937)," in *Italy's Encounters with Modern China: Imperial Dreams, Strategic Ambitions*, eds. Maurizio Marinelli and Giovanni B. Andornino (New York: Palgrave Macmillan, 2014), 89–115.

[8] Recent major book-length studies of the radical right beyond Europe include Reto Hofmann, *The Fascist Effect: Japan and Italy, 1915–1952* (Ithaca, NY: Cornell University Press, 2015); Federico Finchelstein, *Transatlantic Fascism: Ideology, Violence,*

left-wing and right-wing aesthetics in cultural products such as films and literary writings or even the proliferation of cult-like, secret sects that answered directly to the Leader.[9] Instead, they struck at the very core of the right's approach to the reigning sociopolitical order and were internal to China's own history. Margherita Zanasi's pioneering study of Nationalist economic thoughts argues that China confronted the same political and economic crises that plagued interwar Europe. The currency autarky, corporatism and military industrialization enjoyed among Nationalist leaders cumulated in a "brand of state fascism" in 1930s China. They were tools anticommunist nationalists took from Fascist Italy and Nazi Germany to resist foreign imperialism.[10] This book builds on Zanasi's insight but shows that fascist tendencies in China needed no borrowing from abroad. Instead, they were intrinsic to the country's experience of what historical sociologist Giovanni Arrighi called the "long twentieth century" – the convergence of territorial and capitalist expansionism that propelled established colonial empires and more recent predators such as Germany, Italy and Japan.[11] For economically backward and (semi)colonized societies like China, the choice was one between joining the capitalist interstate system and, as in the case of the 1917 Revolution in Russia, challenging the premises of property and imperialist hegemony. What made the conservative revolution distinct in modern Chinese history and typical of contemporaneous radical right movements is the promise to overcome capitalism and its deleterious effects on the national community without challenging its structural foundation.

Nationalism and Opposition to Class Struggle

There were two core dimensions to the conservative revolution: nationalism and an obsession with the aesthetics of mass society. Nationalism lay at the heart of radical right attempts to offset the alienating effects of

and the Sacred in Argentina and Italy, 1919–1945 (Durham, NC: Duke University Press, 2010).

[9] Robert Culp, Articulating Citizenship: Civic Education and Student Politics in Southeastern China, 1912–1940 (Cambridge, MA: Harvard University Asia Center, 2007), 197–206; Liu Jihui [Joyce C. H. Liu], Xin de bianyi: xiandaixing de jingshen xingshi [Perverted Heart: The Psychic Forms of Modernity] (Taipei: Maitian chuban, 2004), chap. 7; Wakeman, Spymaster, chaps. 7–8.

[10] Margherita Zanasi, Saving the Nation: Economic Modernity in Republican China (Chicago: University of Chicago Press, 2006), 14–15.

[11] Giovanni Arrighi, The Long Twentieth Century: Money, Power and the Origins of Our Times (New York: Verso, 1994), 60–6. See also Karatani Kojin, The Structure of World History: From Modes of Production to Modes of Exchange, trans. Michael K. Bourdaghs (Durham, NC: Duke University Press, 2014), 170–5.

capitalist modernity. Cultural historians of Europe have emphasized populist nationalism as the basis of fascist mobilization. Fascist agitators appealed to emotions, brandished the nation's mythic qualities and promised rebirth out of collective malaise while embracing industrial modernization. They claimed to have brought about a synthesis of conservatism and socialism, energizing the populace to challenge a skewed international order without damaging social cohesion.[12] For example, Benito Mussolini found in the nation a substitute for class, identifying Italy as one proletarian collective to be saved from international bourgeois domination. The former socialist participated in a wider intellectual trend in late industrializing Europe, prevalent since the Great War, that valorized the ethnic community as the oppressed group while jettisoning class politics.[13] Suppression of communist and liberal opposition, building a dirigiste economy and crafting mass rituals and monumental architecture all contributed to the radical redefinition of the state's role in commanding social and political processes.

Investing in the nation-state's transformative potential was characteristic not only of fascists but also noncommunist revolutionaries and reformers with ambiguous socialist sympathies. The illusion that the nation was an affective, organic community where each citizen could be taken care of informed those politicians who were fed up with the crumbling liberal global order. Despite their jarringly different reputation and policy outcomes, progressives such as Franklin D. Roosevelt shared with the radical right on the European Continent belief in the nation-state's ability to bring meaning, order and succor to a crisis-ridden and demoralized populace.[14] The displacement of class politics by appealing to an underprivileged national community, which characterized Mussolini's position, resonated with Sun Yat-sen's (1866–1925) Principle of Livelihood (*minsheng zhuyi*). Rejecting Marxism, the *minsheng* theory posited that all Chinese people partook in the nation's poverty. "Since China's largest capitalists are poor men out in the world," Sun argued,

---

[12] Prominent examples include Roger Griffin, *The Nature of Fascism* (New York: St. Martin's Press, 1991); George L. Mosse, *The Fascist Revolution: Toward a General Theory of Fascism* (New York: Howard Fertig, 1999); Zeev Sternhell, *The Birth of Fascist Ideology: From Cultural Rebellion to Political Revolution* (Princeton, NJ: Princeton University Press, 1994).

[13] Mark Neocleous, *Fascism* (Minneapolis: University of Minnesota Press, 1997), 21.

[14] Wolfgang Schivelbusch, *Three New Deals: Reflections on Roosevelt's America, Mussolini's Italy, and Hitler's Germany, 1933–1939*, trans. Jefferson Chase (New York: Metropolitan Books, 2006).

"then all the Chinese people must be counted as poor."[15] The revolutionary leader went on to lay out strategies conceived to prevent class divisions as the country industrialized. Sun's lament of China as a proletarian nation caught up in a world dominated by imperialist powers anticipated his anti-Communist followers' rejection of class confrontations as the bases of political action.

While nationalism had inspired all major modern Chinese political movements one way or another, the Guomindang's conservative revolution was unique in seeing the nation as an end in itself and irreconcilable with social revolution. Nationalism and statism, Peter Zarrow observes, undergirded modern China's participation in the international system, as the Qing empire transformed into a "people." Yet the nation-state was not consistently the ultimate ideal of the Chinese revolution; Mao Zedong (1893–1976), for one, was famously ambivalent about the party-state throughout his long political career.[16] To the contrary, the regime Mao's Communists replaced was singularly committed to the nation. GMD luminaries such as Dai Jitao (1891–1949) and Hu Hanmin (1879–1936) promoted national revival to counter proletarian internationalism. While nationalist goals were shared across the political divide, an appeal to the nation as an ideal community inherently incompatible with communism and social revolution was peculiar to conservative revolutionaries around the globe.

The GMD's unique brand of nationalism set the conservative revolution apart from the governments that preceded and succeeded it. It is, therefore, misleading to argue that the GMD had nothing specific to it but was only a stage in China's strengthening authoritarianism and departure from liberal democratic ideals. Narratives of the Nationalist period from the 1990s and the turn of the twenty-first century, produced against the background of the Communist state's political consolidation and economic liberalization in the People's Republic, situate the GMD state in the *longue durée* of modern nation-state formation and downplay its particularities. Characterizing the Nationalist regime as a case of "Confucian fascism," Frederic Wakeman notes Chiang Kai-shek's attraction to Germany, Italy and Turkey as ascendant interwar powers.

---

[15] Sun Yat-sen, *Sanmin zhuyi* (Taipei: Zhengzhong shuju, 1954), 210. Translation taken from Sun, *San Min Chu I: The Three Principles of the People*, trans. Frank W. Price (Taipei: China Publishing Co., n.d.), 173.

[16] Peter Zarrow, *After Empire: The Conceptual Transformation of the Chinese State, 1885–1924* (Stanford, CA: Stanford University Press, 2012), 4, 288–9. As Alain Badiou observes, Mao's Cultural Revolution was a "revolution within – and largely against – a socialist state," in line with the communist commitment to the state's eventual demise (Badiou and Jean-Claude Milner, *Controversies: A Dialogue on the Politics and Philosophy of Our Times* [Cambridge: Polity, 2014], 46).

However, while the GMD party-state embraced the latest fascist organizational form, Chiang's "nativist" Confucian moralism "lent a fussy air to his imitative fascism," indebted not to Hitler and Mussolini but to China's dynastic past. Its defining features were comparable much less to Continental Europe's latest political fad than fidelity to imperial China's reigning ideology.[17] Taking as his points of comparison revolutionary movements, A. James Gregor posits that the radical right was no different from its left-wing nemesis. Defining fascism as a mix of "nationalism and Marxist revolutionary syndicalism," Gregor lumps Sun Yat-sen and Mao Zedong together with figures as diverse as Mussolini, Lenin and Stalin as redemptive nationalists committed to developmentalism and an aggrandized state. As for Chiang's GMD, Gregor offers the following:

> It was not Italian Fascism or German National Socialism, *per se*, that Chiang Kai-shek or the Blue Shirts recommended to the revolutionaries of China. What the Blue Shirts found admirable in Italian Fascism and German National Socialism was the same thing they and Sun Yat-sen found attractive in Bolshevism. All these movements had succeeded in restoring dignity to their respective national communities.[18]

From this line of argument, one infers that all Chinese political movements were merely nationalist and statist, rendering the radical right indistinguishable from revolutionary socialists. Of course, Gregor's intervention concerns not only China but all revolutions, which he saw as inherently antidemocratic and united in opposition to liberal democracy. This typology, drawn from totalitarian theorists prevalent in Cold War political science, erased fundamental differences between communist and right-wing approaches to revolution.

Making a Conservative Revolution

The GMD's nationalist revolution, like other movements on the radical right, was conservative. Yet, to the extent that it intersected with state politics, Chinese conservatism as an intellectual position was only partially aligned with the GMD. Historians have drawn attention to Republican conservatives' elevation of traditional culture as central to their nationalism but have stressed their varied and ambiguous relationship with the governing regime. Scholars also wrestle with the apparent

---

[17] Frederic Wakeman, "A Revisionist View of the Nanjing Decade: Confucian Fascism," *China Quarterly*, no. 150 (1997): 395–432.

[18] A. James Gregor, *A Place in the Sun: Marxism and Fascism in China's Long Revolution* (Boulder, CO: Westview Press, 2000), 15–16, 80; Gregor, *The Faces of Janus: Marxism and Fascism in the Twentieth Century* (New Haven, CT: Yale University Press, 2000).

paradox of China's modern elite espousing a conservative agenda. Benjamin Schwartz believes that China had no conservative tradition in the Euro-American sense. His example is none other than Chiang Kaishek, who was a "conservative modernizer" and did not hold onto the political status quo. For Schwartz, therefore, conservatism in China was a cultural position, not a political one that called for the conservation of existing state institutions. For Guy Alitto, conservatism in China was similar to those of societies outside the "Western European cradle of modernization" in presupposing the binary between the national spirit and material modernity. While the latter was necessary, it was the former that lent meaning to social life. Conservatism in China, for Edmund Fung, was likewise part of the global questioning of Enlightenment rationality and progress.[19] Even as it did inform politics, conservatism, in these accounts, describes an intellectual disposition on national traditions that ran parallel to or tempered the modernizing thrust of twentieth-century Chinese society.

Nationalist revolutionaries' conservatism was not a cultural temperament but a form of political activism that was self-consciously modern. GMD ideologues were future-oriented because and not in spite of their espousal of national essence (*guocui*) and its relevance to modernity. Their cultural nationalism was articulated with the party's alacrity in leveraging an expanding state to build new social hierarchies and alliances to neuter challenges to unequal production relations.[20] Like fascism in general, conservative revolutionaries appealed to precapitalist and archaic forces not to conserve an idealized past but to create it for the first time. While claiming to recover what many Nationalists called China's "primordial traditions" (*guyou chuantong*), they joined radical right-wing activists around the interwar world in mobilizing popular sentiments and imagination through industrial-scale spectacles and political

---

[19] Charlotte Furth, "Culture and Politics in Modern Chinese Conservativism," in *The Limits of Change: Essays on Conservative Alternatives in Republican China*, ed. Charlotte Furth (Cambridge, MA: Harvard University Press, 1976), 38–9; Edmund S. K. Fung, *The Intellectual Foundations of Chinese Modernity: Cultural and Political Thought in the Republican Era* (Cambridge: Cambridge University Press, 2010), 65, 96–127; Benjamin Schwartz, "Notes on Conservatism in General and in China in Particular," in *The Limits of Change: Essays on Conservative Alternatives in Republican China*, 16–19; Guy S. Alitto, *The Last Confucian: Liang Shu-ming and the Chinese Dilemma of Modernity*, 2nd edn. (Berkeley: University of California Press, 1986), 9–12.

[20] GMD theoreticians' fascination with national essence as they charted a course for China's future mirrored that of early twentieth-century revolutionaries such as Liu Shipei and Zhang Taiyan. See Tze-ki Hon, *Revolution as Restoration: Guocui xuebao and China's Path to Modernity, 1905–1911* (Leiden: Brill, 2013).

pageantry, often deploying the Leninist state form copied from the communists. Dai Jitao, the anticommunist theorist who lent intellectual weight to the April 1927 purge, took on board the conservative adoration of the nation as defined by its cultural, particularly Confucian, traditions. At the same time, he and other radical right Nationalists celebrated youthful vigor and a militant revolutionary vanguard that prized activist intervention. In their forward-looking vision, conservative revolutionaries shared formal elements with their socialist adversaries.[21] Dai, critical of imperialism, identified the GMD's mission as one that relieved China's modernizing economy from foreign grip on capital flow and urban industries. To serve nationalist ends, he argued as late as 1925 that alliance with the Soviet Union and incorporation of selected socialist principles were desirable.[22] Out of the party's interaction with Chinese Communists emerged a strategy that appropriated the organizational form and anti-capitalist sentiments of Bolshevism. The GMD's radicalism was channeled, however, away from everything that formed the core of a communist movement. Class struggle and the overthrow of private property were deemed incompatible with the goals of building a virile national community, a self-contained economy and contented, productive workers under state coordination. This approach to shaping society represented a conservative alternative to Chinese Communist visions of revolution-making.

Opposition to social revolution, as much as commitment to national rebirth, undergirded the conservatism of the GMD's revolutionary project. Modern China was of course not the only society that hosted insurgencies targeting systematic changes. Reactionary movements worldwide since the French Revolution had sought to violently re-impose hierarchal order, industrialize the economy and mobilize the state and the populace to suppress class war. When the phrase "conservative revolution" was coined in 1848, Frederick Engels used it to characterize the 1830 Polish insurrection against direct Russian rule at which the Polish aristocracy sought to defend its own class interests by returning to the *status quo ante* of relative autonomy under the czar. "The insurrection of 1830," Engels declared, "was neither a national revolution ... nor a social or a political revolution; it changed nothing in

---

[21] Peter Osborne, *The Politics of Time: Modernity and Avant-garde* (London: Verso, 1995), 164–6; Corey Robin, *The Reactionary Mind: Conservatism from Edmund Burke to Sarah Palin* (New York: Oxford University Press, 2011), 42–55.

[22] Dai Jitao, *Guomin geming yu Zhongguo Guomindang* [*The Nationalist Revolution and the Guomindang*] (1925; reprint, Shanghai: n.p., 1928), 70–2 (page citations are to the reprint edition); Dai, *Zhongguo duli yundong de jidian* [*The Basis of China's Independence Movement*] (Guangzhou: Minzhi shuju, 1925), 18–30.

the internal condition of the people; it was a conservative revolution."
These aristocrats posed no threat to Russian colonialism, the post-
Napoleonic international order that stripped Poland of its independence
or a social system that dispossessed peasants and Jews.[23] In interwar
Germany, conservative revolution came to encompass mass movements
and paramilitary squads on the far right of the political spectrum. With
their modernist and avant-gardist sensibility, intellectuals such as
Martin Heidegger embraced "a form of revolutionary reaction" radicalized by Nazism into an ultranationalist, highly disciplined mass
movement.[24] Yet, despite the Germans' radical veneer, they shared
with Polish conservative revolutionaries an unwillingness to challenge
the structures of power that underwrote unequal relations between the
privileged and the dispossessed. Fascists sought an "*alternative* to social
revolution." Conservative revolutionaries targeted not capitalist
economics but its paraphernalia, in particular financiers, consumerism
and what Karl Polanyi calls anarchistic sovereignty under *laissez-faire*
international economics.[25] Compensating for social dislocation and
chaos would be the wholesome, organic community that was the nation.

In exorcising Sun Yat-sen's national revolution of communist
elements, the GMD aggressively expanded state command over society
but ultimately constricted the transformative potential of politics. As Dai
Jitao stated, "not having developed our own country and rejuvenated our
nation, there could be no talk of world revolution."[26] The nation-state
was, for the theoretician, not an agent for systemic transformation but an
institution managing, consolidating and tweaking hierarchal power
relations. In practice, as Joseph Fewsmith put it, the GMD state set out
"to *administer* (rather than restructure) class relations."[27] That the GMD
was as ready to lash out at capitalists as it was quick to suppress workers,
intellectuals and students derived from the party's ideal of a state-
coordinated capitalist economy. Its two competing modes of economic

---

[23] Karl Marx and Frederick Engels, "On the Polish Question," in *Collected Works* (London: Lawrence & Wishart, 1976), 6:550.

[24] Roger Woods, *The Conservative Revolution in the Weimar Republic* (New York: St. Martin's Press, 1996), 3; Osborne, *Politics of Time*, 164.

[25] Neocleous, *Fascism*, 43–4, 56; Karl Polanyi, *The Great Transformation: The Political and Economic Origins of Our Time*, 2nd paperback edn. (Boston, MA: Beacon Press, 2001), 261.

[26] Dai Jitao, *Dai Jitao zuijin yanlun* [*Dai Jitao's Latest Remarks*], 2nd edn. (N.p.: Shangwu yinshuguan, 1928), 8.

[27] Joseph Fewsmith, *Party, State, and Local Elites in Republican China: Merchant Organizations and Politics in Shanghai* (Honolulu: University of Hawaii Press, 1985), 181; see also Parks M. Coble Jr., *The Shanghai Capitalists and the Nationalist Government, 1927–1937* (Cambridge, MA: Council on East Asian Studies, Harvard University, 1980), 268.

planning, drawn from Nazi Germany and Fascist Italy, respectively, both allocated a domineering role for a technocratic state. Wang Jingwei's (1883–1944) economic nationalism, derived from Sun Yat-sen's Three People's Principles, called for Italian-style corporativism to ride out capitalist crises. Antonio Gramsci described this approach as a "passive revolution," in which the capitalist economy came under state control through reformist methods.[28] But despite its identity as the vanguard of a postliberal, omnipotent nation-state, the GMD elite was ever cautious to bring state machinery to bear on global capitalism. While Germany, Italy and Japan responded to the Great Depression of 1929 by delinking themselves from the international financial order, China remained wedded to it at the expense of the state's capacity to bring relief to the struggling industrial and agricultural sectors.[29]

China's conservative revolution brought a great deal of changes and action, but they related not to the social structure or the systemic conditions that relegated the country to the receiving end of the global economic order. The state's meekness in transforming political economy stood in jarring contrast with the revolutionary elite's radical self-identity and ambition to deliver China from capitalist imperialism. At stake was not only what Prasenjit Duara famously calls "involution," a process by which a state's expansion led to a lower capacity in bringing meaningful social changes.[30] The GMD's quagmire also highlighted the different functions played by nation and state, two distinct but entwined formations, in radical right-wing politics. As Fewsmith observes, the GMD's claim that it represented the interests of all classes meant collusion with capital at the expense of labor.[31] In essence, corporativism and economic nationalism represented the "union of state and capital," as the state sought to manage an increasingly privatized, domesticated bourgeoisie.[32] While the state's convergence with industrial capitalism proceeded at full steam, the nation disguised the disorienting effects and disparities that attended the hegemonic social order. The latter afforded an imaginary space for which desires for harmony and cooperation could be projected. As a locus of solidarity, it offered a sentimental outlet to

---

[28] Zanasi, *Saving the Nation;* Antonio Gramsci, *The Gramsci Reader: Selected Writings 1916–1935,* ed. David Forgacs (New York: New York University Press, 2000), 265.

[29] Tomoko Shiroyama, *China during the Great Depression: Market, State, and the World Economy, 1929–1937* (Cambridge, MA: Harvard University Asia Center, 2008), 234–7.

[30] Prasenjit Duara, *Culture, Power, and the State: Rural North China, 1900–1942* (Stanford, CA: Stanford University Press, 1988), 251–5. Only the Chinese Communists, the author notes, were able to revert involution because its state-building program was coupled with meaningful social changes from the bottom up.

[31] Fewsmith, *Party, State, and Local Elites in Republican China,* 181.

[32] Karatani, *Structure of World History,* 172–3.

offset capitalism's profit logic by appealing to shared customs and spiritual traditions. Yet the nation was no more than an aestheticized response to social inequalities and offered opposition to neither the state nor capital. It "[took] on the guise of socialism" and sought to transcend state and capital through imagination.[33] Simply put, as an anti-Marxist alternative to capitalism, conservative revolutionaries offered an illusion of social solidarity while shielding the system of private property from political intervention.

Aestheticization of Politics

In practice, the conservative revolution involved meticulous management of emotions and sentiments to conceal social dislocation and compensate for political polarization. The GMD deployed tools from a range of traditions to inscribe its top-down corporate vision into the "minutiae of subjective experience," such that unequal power relations became internalized by the masses. This process of aestheticization followed on the heels of the violent anticommunist coup.[34] In the 1930s, the Leninist party-state, Eugenia Lean shows, was shrewd in exploiting print media-induced frenzy, channeling populist sympathy for apparently apolitical criminal cases for nationalist purposes.[35] As the following pages reveal, agitators of the anticommunist insurrection like Dai Jitao cherry-picked institutions and ideas from across the ideological spectrum to encode contented, docile and efficient production in citizens' habits, customs and pieties. From scouting typical of treaty-port semi-colonialism and total war mobilization to seemingly apolitical celebration of personal cultivation and Pan-Asianism, conservative revolutionaries infused their particular political vision in everyday experiences and articulated it with the nation's idealist, mythic core. A community of selfless and obedient workers became entwined with the ideal of a spiritually fecund nation-state that challenged Western modernity.

By deploying mass spectacles and appropriating preexisting institutions, the GMD countered the threat of class struggle by making citizens embrace a fixed cultural identity, behave as sleek, voluntaristic parts in the social machine and, in other ways, know their place. Class

---

[33] Ibid., 220, 258.
[34] For the relationship between aestheticization and conservative politics, see Terry Eagleton, *The Ideology of the Aesthetic* (Oxford: Basil Blackwell, 1990), 20; Daniel Woodley, *Fascism and Political Theory: Critical Perspectives on Fascist Ideology* (London: Routledge, 2010), 18.
[35] Eugenia Lean, *Public Passions: The Trial of Shi Jianqiao and the Rise of Popular Sympathy in Republican China* (Berkeley: University of California Press, 2007), 150–62.

struggle, prevalent among young urbanites influenced by radical ideas such as historical materialism, was equated to cultural rootlessness and ethical insouciance. A Nationalist by the name of Shiyong, for example, wrote to Dai in 1927 and accused Chinese Communists of enticing urban youths with faint promises of vanity, money and sexual pleasure.[36] The cadre echoed Oswald Spengler by lumping together ideological unorthodoxy, material desire and moral failure, albeit in a less theoretically sophisticated fashion. The German philosopher wrote some eight years before Shiyong that a materialist vision of history, with its emphasis on relations of production, wrenched cosmopolitan urban intellectuals off from religion and traditional values.[37] Marxism must be resisted for it represented a foreign-inspired affront to the ethnos. In a hostile global environment where the nation survived in contention with predatory imperialist powers, communism was a threat to ethnic cohesion and a symptom of modern decadence.

The GMD's aestheticized politics camouflaged capitalist dislocations and diverted citizens' attention away from political actions that led to social revolution. Rather than agitate for equality and material uplift, citizens were exhorted to revamp their own selves as parts of the national collective. The party's revised revolutionary theory targeted historical materialist critique of China's political economy to neuter radical challenges to power relations. Dai's interpretation of the *minsheng* principle in the run-up to the April 12 coup shifted Sun's examination of his compatriots' well-being from material concerns such as food, clothing, shelter and transportation to spiritual cultivation (*yu*) and enjoyment (*le*). The GMD's focus on managing prosaic details of the people's daily routine – hygienic practices, leisure activities, diet, sleeping habits etc. – signaled an individualist turn of political practice. That the individual became a prime battleground in the GMD's revolutionary crusade meant beautification of personal behaviors was a highly mediated matter, as Chiang Kai-shek's wartime exemplary life cited in the beginning of this book shows. Nationalist leaders including Chiang projected their own immaculate bodies and habits, in contrast to "filthy" Communists, as foci of public discussion and models for the multitude to emulate.[38] How citizens consumed, leisured and carried themselves was misrecognized as

[36] Shiyong to Dai Jitao, 1927, *wubu*, 1339, Kuomintang Archives.
[37] Oswald Spengler, *Preußentum und Sozialismus* [*Prussiandom and Socialism*], in *Politische schriften* (Munich and Berlin: Beck, 1933), 83–5, cited in Woods, *The Conservative Revolution in the Weimar Republic*, 66.
[38] Sean Hsiang-lin Lei [Lei Xianglin], "Xiguan cheng siwei: Xin shenghuo yundong yu fei jiehe yufang zhong de lunli, jiating yu shenti [Habituating the Four Virtues: Ethics, Family and the Body in Anti-tuberculosis Campaigns and the New Life Movement]," *Jindai shi yanjiusuo jikan*, no. 74 (2011): 169–70.

determinants of society's vitality and competitiveness. Politics, by extension, became a matter of taming one's own self instead of changing social relations.

Such concern for the superficial phenomena of everyday life was in tune with general conservative responses to China's freewheeling urban culture. Under the New Culture Movement in the 1910s, student activists coalesced around university dormitories, libraries and classrooms into an unfettered community that rejected social hierarchy. New ways of thinking about and organizing one's personal and social life thrived from the bottom up and fed into May Fourth political radicalism.[39] As patent signs of a new and, for some, threatening urban culture, individuals' mundane manners and habits became important social issues. Through the 1920s, the flourishing print media called on the state to intervene in student activism, romance between men and women and increasing commercialization in urban life.[40] GMD ideologues took this plea fully on board by collapsing politics with personal lifestyle, equating sexual laxity with communism and with challenges to a patriarchal social order that was touted as the essence of the Confucian moral universe.[41] This puritanism served not only to forge a docile, laborious community but also to strip oppositional groups of political reason by reducing them to moral failures.

This blend of the high-minded and the prosaic allowed conservative revolutionaries to project their own political project as a nonpartisan program that chimed in with intellectuals beyond the GMD, domestically and abroad. Intellectuals who were unenthusiastic about the party's authoritarianism or vanguardist approach to state-building could, out of liberal inclinations, nonetheless identify with the GMD's determination to perfect the hearts and minds of the citizenry. Like conservative revolutionaries, liberal intellectuals saw private individuals as composites of society in which structures such as class relations were secondary. A Confucian-inflected idea of spiritual self-introspection also formed the basis of the GMD's ideological affinity with India, where anti-colonialist resistance took on strong spiritual significance. Chinese

---

[39] Fabio Lanza, *Behind the Gates: Inventing Students in Beijing* (New York: Columbia University, 2010), 48–50.

[40] Rebecca E. Karl, "Journalism, Social Value and a Philosophy of the Everyday in 1920s China," *Positions: East Asia Cultures Critique* 16 (2008): 540–2.

[41] Maggie Clinton, *Revolutionary Nativism: Fascism and Culture in China, 1925–1937* (Durham, NC: Duke University Press, 2017), 100. As Clinton observes, GMD fascists "addressed Communist insurrection with similar forms of military and epistemological violence" as a colonial state, seeing the revolutionary left as debased fanatics incapable of meaningful action. Communists were simple yet poisonously harmful miscreants, and did not constitute a political opposition with a rational agenda.

conservative revolutionaries, despite their lack of organizational similarities with the Indian National Congress, could claim solidarity with the likes of Mohandas Gandhi and Rabindranath Tagore by forging civilizational opposition to a Euro-American modernity obsessed with material interests.

Consensus-Building

As a response to May Fourth culture and in opposition to communist politics, the GMD's conservative revolution was internal to China's development and played to a domestic and international audience. The GMD embraced China's emergent mass society and devised a strategy to retain engagement with it while denying students and workers who took to the street since the late 1910s independent political agency. This form of non-antagonistic civic mobilization, unlike labor strikes and class boycotts, held attraction for urban middle and intellectual classes who craved stability and individual advancement. It appealed to liberals who viewed revolutionary violence as socially disruptive. Constitutionalist Zhang Junmai (1897–1969) lamented that Communists perverted society's spiritual cohesion; some foreign observers, even as they derided Chiang Kai-shek's conversion to Christianity, were effusive in their praise for Song Meiling's reform of wayward radical activists into humble laborers working away day in and day out making shoes or umbrellas.[42] That the Chinese social democrat and Western Christian missionaries found the Nationalists preferable to communist insurgents was no isolated examples. For Chinese and foreign elite concerned with mob rule, there was nothing less laudable than transforming youthful rebels into cogs in the wheel of the nation's moral and political economy. Imposing a salubrious routine onto citizens, insofar as it defanged their political radicalism, allowed Nationalists to make unnatural bedfellows with those who inhabited

---

[42] The centerpiece of Song's reformism, the New Life Movement, has been receiving a lot of attention lately. Examples include Lei, "Xiguan cheng siwei," 133–77; Clinton, *Revolutionary Nativism*, chap. 4; Hsiao-pei Yen, "Body Politics, Modernity, and National Salvation: The Modern Girl and the New Life Movement," *Asian Studies Review* 29 (2005): 165–86; Frederica Ferlanti, "The New Life Movement in Jiangxi Province, 1934–1938," *Modern Asian Studies* 44 (2010): 961–1000; Ferlanti, "The New Life Movement at War: Wartime Mobilisation and State Control in Chongqing and Chengdu, 1938–1942," *European Journal of East Asian Studies* 11 (2012): 187–12; Wennan Liu, "Redefining the Moral and Legal Roles of the State in Everyday Life: The New Life Movement in China in the Mid-1930s," *Cross-Currents: East Asian History and Culture Review*, no. 7 (2013): 30–59. For a classic examination, see Arif Dirlik, "The Ideological Foundations of the New Life Movement: A Study in Counterrevolution," *Journal of Asian Studies* 34 (1975): 945–80.

other ends of the ideological spectrum. Indeed, as this book shows, the conservative revolution enjoyed some success reaching out to liberals and traditionalists in China and abroad. Scout leaders, writers and anti-colonialists – particularly Pan-Asianists who saw both capitalism and communism as symptoms of Western materialist decadence – partook in the GMD's taming of youth activism, mobilization of wartime loyalties for Chiang Kai-shek and cultivation of an international anti-colonial alliance that stressed Asian spiritual values and excluded class revolution.

The GMD's ability to bring altogether constituents beyond party cadres in some form of consensus was critical to the conservative revolution's viability; it reigned over China since the April 12 coup for more than twenty years, holding attraction for moderate nationalists at home and in Asian societies such as India. Conservative revolutionaries within the GMD confronted the challenge of transforming their insurrection against their communist and left-leaning allies prowess in 1927 into a self-perpetuating regime. As it settled into the seat of power, the Nationalist Party saw its radical self-image clash with its new administrative role. It was reluctant to follow through with even limited campaigns against private property and to make good on its promise not to play heed to sectarian interests.[43] The claim to represent the entire nation and manage capitalism in the benefit of all classes, Karatani Kojin observes, marked the process whereby fascist movements evolved from insurrections into sovereigns of a postliberal domestic and international order. This ambition was by its very nature illusionary.[44] Aside from bureaucratic ossification and inability to bring fundamental changes to the political economy, the Nationalists had at their disposal a much weaker state than fascist regimes in Germany, Italy and Japan. Chiang Kai-shek, despite his dictatorial tendency, never managed to govern the whole of China due to the Communist military presence in the interior, inability to eradicate regional warlords, Japanese invasion and splits within the party leadership. Chiang's disputes with Hu Hanmin (1879–1936) resulted in a rival government based in the southern city of Guangzhou during the 1930s, while those with Wang Jingwei led first to the brief Wuhan government in 1927 and then to the Japanese-sponsored collaborationist regime from 1940 to 1945. The GMD's fractured rule, conspired with its ideological ambiguity, meant that conservative revolutionaries often sought support from far and wide.

[43] Fewsmith, *Party, State, and Local Elites in Republican China*, 183.
[44] Karatani, *History and Repetition*, 35–42.

Taking nationalism, anticommunism and emphasis on a hierarchal order as common denominators, conservative revolutionaries were eclectic in whom they included in their struggle for a new order. Recent studies have pointed to the relative catholicity of radical right-wing politics. Alan Tansman, writing on interwar Japan, describes a broad consensus among anticommunist politicians and intellectuals who saw in aestheticizing the everyday and fetishizing the nation a solution to modern social ills. Germinating from the bottom up was "fascism in cultural (or political) work that [did] not speak fascism's name."[45] Lacking an ideological straitjacket, China's conservative revolution was likewise all things to all people upset with the cultural dislocation, political chaos and social upheaval brought about by capitalism and left-wing activism. The GMD's dictatorial manners and occasional resort to terror might have been objectionable, but Communist revolutionary violence was even less appetizing. To traditionalists and some liberals, left-wing culture and politics were symptoms of an atrophic, frivolous urban society and associated with the privileged and the undesirable – naïve students, bohemians, Russophile thinkers etc. – who were unpatriotic, disruptive and parasitic. Desire for an orderly, industrious community that respected authority and rejected consumerist decadence compensated for the GMD's failure to lay down coherent agendas. It provided the conditions for liberals and traditionalists to rally behind an otherwise authoritarian regime that insisted on its Leninist revolutionary role.

Popular and intellectual consensus that legitimated GMD rule could and did easily unravel. Co-option of scouting by conservative revolutionaries instilled voluntarism, self-discipline and respect for hierarchy among urban youths but failed to create a generation of nimble, loyal workers. Aggressive drive to mobilize mass sentiments in support of resistance against Japanese invasion from 1937 to 1945 did not coagulate into a sustainable order beyond the war. Liberal and even conservative intellectuals who rallied around the GMD in the struggle against Japan soon withdrew their support; most of them refused to follow the Nationalists' retreat to Taiwan in 1949. Appeal to genteel good sense, fear of violent upheaval, patriotism and pan-Asian ethical pieties backfired when conservative revolutionaries guaranteed neither order, economic development nor national independence toward the late 1940s with rampant inflation, accompanied by intensified state terror and the

[45] Alan Tansman, "Introduction: The Culture of Japanese Fascism," in *The Culture of Japanese Fascism*, ed. Alan Tansman (Durham, NC: Duke University Press, 2009), 17.

GMD's submission to US demands.[46] With Taipei's dependence on Washington's patronage, the GMD's solidarity with the Indian National Congress, based on anti-colonialism and celebration of Eastern morality, proved hollow. As an extension of the GMD's anticommunist, aesthetic nationalism, Pan-Asianism appealed to Chinese and Indian suspicion against revolutionary socialism but was theoretically too flimsy to allow for a common response to the changing terms in which imperialist hegemony exerted itself in the early Cold War order of the late 1940s.

Chapter Overview

This book reconstructs the conservative revolution by grappling with its ideological articulations and organizational initiatives. The following five chapters trace the origins of the conservative revolution in the GMD right's reaction against Sun's alliance with Chinese Communists, assess its proficiency in mass politics in peacetime and at war, and piece together short-lived domestic and intra-Asian alliances. Together they reveal the multifaceted strategy by which conservative revolutionaries constructed a distinctive, if still inchoate, alternative to communism. This alternative shared many similarities with the revolution it sought to suppress – a Leninist organization, investment in mass mobilization, anti-colonialism and an international outlook, and sensitivity to the undesirable impacts on society attendant to China's uneven capitalist development. Yet, the GMD, unlike its left-wing nemesis, aimed not to overthrow capitalism and private property but to bypass its alienating effects by appealing to the nation and Eastern civilizational ideals. The goal was to drive capitalist development through heavy-handed state command while deploying the nation as an imagined community endowed with virility, harmony, full sovereignty and spiritual superiority to decadent Western imperialists.

Chapter 2, "Orthodoxy: Purifying the Revolution," reveals how anticommunist Nationalists coalesced into an ideological force that laid the foundation for the coup of April 1927. Known among Nationalists as "party purification," the violent purge gave ideological and institutional shape to the conservative revolution. It ended the GMD's four-year cooperation with Chinese Communists and divorced the goal of national independence from empowerment of workers and peasants.

---

[46] Nonpartisan forces were increasingly betting on the communist, not the conservative, revolution for sustaining a viable society. Thomas D. Lutze, *China's Inevitable Revolution: Rethinking America's Loss to the Communists* (New York: Palgrave Macmillan, 2007).

Party theoreticians – Dai Jitao (1891–1949), Hu Hanmin (1879–1936) and Li Shizeng (1881–1973) – who set the tenor of the coup were versed in socialism and met Communist foes on their own ground. They saw Sun Yat-sen's Three People's Principles as the only true formula for building an ethical, cooperative *gemeinschaft* that would put an end to the moral agnosticism of both capitalism and communism. Although Dai was keen to draw a genealogy that tied Sun with Confucianism, the purge signified not nostalgia for a decrepit imperial system but a futuristic vision of classless harmony where altruistic factory owners and contented workers joined together in the communion of labor under party supervision. It put forward a third way to securing modernization that competed with predatory capitalism and revolutionary socialism. Treatises that denounced the GMD's erstwhile coziness to Chinese Communists and their Soviet sponsors anticipated concerns that preoccupied the Nationalist government for the next two decades. These include searching for ethical norms that naturalized hierarchy and order, rationalizing and beautifying work and leisure and the obsession with youth as a crucial but potentially disruptive social category. The paramount objective of conservative revolutionaries was to turn the vanguard party into a potent machine to suppress class struggle and bring order to the national community.

Chapter 3, "The Masses: A Youth Movement for the Conservative Revolution," takes the story of the conservative revolution up to the early years of the Second Sino–Japanese War (1937–45), focusing on the re-channeling of mass politics from agitation to collaboration. Despite its anti-colonial and traditionalist rhetoric, the GMD appropriated reformist institutions and ideals that grew out of industrializing treaty ports. The scout movement was a paragon of convergence between a vanguard revolutionary party and a youth organization with colonial origins and liberal aspirations. The GMD subsumed the existing scout units under a malleable umbrella body rather than replacing it with a party youth wing. The Scouts of China General Association, set up in 1934, enlisted original leaders who brought along ideas and methods that characterized scouting as a treaty-port program. These practices appealed to party cadres because they formed a nonconfrontational alternative to students' and labor unions. Scout training privileged hierarchy over egalitarianism, discipline over rebellion, self-cultivation over demands for wider social change. It encouraged the right form of cosmopolitanism – well-behaved, hardworking, apolitical and middle-class – while leaving ample room for projection of statist and militaristic might in its rituals and training activities. Scouting as a mass movement anticipated and coincided with the New Life Movement in placing the burden of collective progress on individuals young and old, tying their everyday chores with the nation's strength and development.

Chapter 4, "State Comes First: Wartime Spiritual Revolution," extends the story of mass engagement under the GMD by considering the dialectic of politicization and depoliticization during the Second Sino–Japanese War. While Japanese aggression forced the GMD and much of the intellectual elite from the relatively industrialized coastal regions into the impoverished hinterland, the contingency of total war presented an opportunity for the state to remodel the masses into a cohesive population undivided by ideological and class differences. Since the Mukden Incident of 1931, which resulted in the Japanese occupation of Manchuria, "emergency period" and "national mobilization" circulated widely in popular discourse. Inspired by parallel developments in Germany, the United States and particularly Japan, GMD and nonpartisan intellectuals billed the War of Resistance as an opportunity for a fresh round of nation-building. Full-scale military conflict unified the nation as one community around one government. Blurred distinction between trenches and the home front also served to refocus the revolution on the people's mentality, desires and bodies. The National Spiritual Mobilization Movement, launched in 1939, aimed both to suppress ideological dissent and reform mass morality. "Stray branches," as communism and other unorthodox political beliefs were called, became ever more eminent as targets of attack. Military discipline reined in frivolous entertainment, restricted import of luxury products, enhanced productive capacity, fought corruption, encouraged donations to the country, and promoted hygienic practices and physical training. War against Japan provided the GMD a unique opportunity to reconstruct the national community with a new militaristic everyday culture that delegitimized political contention and sanctified the party-state's stewardship of the Chinese people.

Chapter 5, "Convergence: Liberal Sentimentalities and the Conservative Revolution," explores how intellectuals outside the GMD converged with the conservative revolutionary agenda in their views on mass politics, culture and the social role of the elite. Writers and academics of liberal persuasion often found common ground with the party-state. Even though they might not endorse the party's authoritarian excesses and bureaucratic corruption, intellectuals were attracted to such putatively "nonpartisan" goals as restoring a stable cultural order, maintaining the elite's self-identity as conveyors of civilization and checking philistinism and savagery. In particular, both the state and liberal intellectuals were anxious to tame the masses, whether they coalesced as protesters on the street, consumers indulging in seedy pleasures or individuals complaining excessively about social wrongs. By focusing on aesthetician Zhu Guangqian (1897–1986), I show how his short stint writing for the party organ *Central Weekly* during the Second Sino–Japanese War was a logical development of, not aberration from, liberal fear of mob rule. Experiences of beauty, as Zhu defined them in his writings before and during the war, became integral to a self-disciplinary regime that tasked individuals with refining their own lives despite social crises, corrupt bureaucrats and extended warfare. Like scout training and the National Spiritual Mobilization Movement, Zhu's prescription for readers turned mass politics on its head. Rather than more equal social relations, national revival hinged on enthusiastic participation of salubrious individuals in the common moral, sublime project that was China's war against Japan. The state, alongside the intellectual elite, served as an ethical agent that guided the masses along in this endeavor.

Chapter 6, "World Revolution: China, Pan-Asianism and India," argues that the appeal to ethics and culture was characteristic of not only domestic politics under Nationalist China but also its international relations. GMD theoreticians like Dai Jitao and his associates understood their revolution as having a regional, if not global, significance. It provided an alternative to Moscow's proletariat internationalism and anticipated a form of moral existence superior to the West's materialism and plundering of other countries. Nationalist China presented itself as the leader of an Asia-wide bloc that upheld Eastern civilizational virtues for heralding a new order freed of capitalist colonialism and social alienation. While China initially considered Japan its natural Pan-Asianist ally, military conflicts from the 1930s forced the former to turn its attention to other Asian societies, particularly India. Buddhist academic Tan Yunshan (1898–1983), although not a cadre, served as the GMD's major institutional and intellectual link to Indian nationalism. Having joined the faculty of Visva-Bharati, a college founded by Rabindranath Tagore (1861–1941), Tan partook in the Nobel laureate's hope that a revived spiritual Asia would overcome the banality of mass culture, instrumental reason and bourgeois modernity. He managed to attract Nationalist funding for the sinological institute Cheena Bhavana, which became the locus of an idealistic and Buddhist-inflected concept of a unified Asia based in Visva Bharati. During the Pacific War, the ideal of a decolonized, conflict-free Eastern civilization became the rhetorical basis for Chiang's outreach to the Indian National Congress, with Tan playing an intermediary role between the two nationalist movements. Yet this apolitical Asianist vision ran into conflict with China's failure to call for an immediate end of British colonial rule in 1942 and quickly

Figure 1.1 Cover of *Chairman Chiang's Daily Life and His Outlook on Daily Life*

unraveled with the onset of Cold War politics as left-wing Third Worldism replaced civilizational discourse as the main driver bringing together decolonizing societies in the region.

This book ends with a brief discussion of the conservative revolution's afterlife as part of the Cold War anticommunist crusade in 1950s Taiwan.

2   Orthodoxy
Purifying the Revolution

China's conservative revolution began as a return to orthodoxy – Sun Yat-sen's revolutionary legacy before its perversion in Communist hands. In the early morning of April 12, 1927, Chiang Kai-shek, with the support of southern-based military strongman Bai Chongxi (1893–1966) and Shanghai gang leaders like Du Yuesheng (1888–1951), launched a brutal crackdown on Communists and labor unionists. As a participant in the Nationalists' military expedition against the Beiyang regime and its affiliated warlords, the Communist-led labor movement had just wrested control of China's industrial and financial hub away from its enemies. The unionists subsequently set up a provisional municipal government that alarmed industrialists and foreign powers who held the economic reins of the metropolis. The coup catapulted Chiang and his right-wing coterie to the leadership of the GMD and the national revolution (*guomin geming*) the party was conducting with its erstwhile Communist allies. After a brief split with Wang Jingwei and other Wuhan-based Nationalists who continued cooperation with the Communists, the party-state that Chiang headed and transplanted to Nanjing became the internationally recognized government of China. It billed the violent dissolution of the revolutionary coalition Sun Yat-sen had forged three years prior as a new beginning, a purification of the nation-building quest the late leader launched as an anti-Manchu activist.

This chapter reconsiders the April 12 coup as an extended intellectual moment that gave birth to the conservative revolution and its attendant state formation based in Nanjing. It reconstructs an anticommunist approach to capitalism, social management and mass politics embraced by key GMD intellectuals involved in the coup, basing their activism on particular readings of Sun Yat-sen's principle of people's livelihood (*minsheng zhuyi*). To be sure, there was nothing new in the view that "party purification" (*qingdang*) was a product of ideological struggle. The left has long considered the coup a counterrevolution. For Song Qingling (1893–1981), Sun Yat-sen's widow, the attack on Communists amounted to apostasy. She chided her former comrades in August 1927 for "allowing the new militarist clique in the Yangtze to capture and utilize the Kuomintang," alluding to Chiang's military background and power base.[1] Party cadres in charge of the Nanjing-based government, on the other hand, touted the coup as a necessary reorientation of the revolution's objectives. Core features of this reorientation – emphases on China's independence and cultural distinctiveness from the West, the state's potential to command capitalist modernization, a modern citizenry that was Spartan in everyday habits and devoted to the national community – defined not only the GMD's identity but also how it engaged with the masses, related to the liberal elite and garnered foreign sympathies.

While political violence marking the beginning of the conservative revolution began in 1927, the coup was the culmination of longer-term ideological labor. Before the GMD started incorporating the militant Communist-affiliated labor movement into docile party and gangster-run "yellow" unions, intellectual assault against class struggle and Marxism was well under way. Dai Jitao, the most prolific apologist of the ascendant GMD right, began writing anticommunist diatribes soon after Sun's death in 1925 and exerted considerable influence on Chiang's ideology. The accomplished writer, as Communist general secretary Chen Duxiu (1879–1942) complained, lent theoretical foil to those engaging in political shenanigans against the united front.[2] Mass activism, for Dai, must continue unabated after the coup, but its priorities must change. Praising workers for constituting the national revolution's vanguard, Dai urged them in May 1927 to work cooperatively for industrial development instead of holding strikes and fighting for class interests. The imperialist threat China faced rendered delusionary the working-class internationalism of the Communists and anarchists, whom Dai branded as "reactionary elements" (*fandong fenzi*). The nationalist imperative required workers to impose bitter discipline (*woxin changdan*) on themselves. Only by raising productivity could the state support cooperatives, schools and insurance for the laboring masses.[3] If Sun had tolerated confrontational class politics, it must no longer be allowed lest the national revolution be compromised.

---

[1] Song Qingling, "Statement before Leaving for Moscow," in *The Struggle for New China* (Peking: Foreign Languages Press, 1953), 9.

[2] Chen Duxiu, "Gei Dai Jitao de yifeng xin [A letter to Dai Jitao]," *Xiangdao zhoubao*, no. 129 (1925): 4.

[3] Dai Jitao, "Gongren jiuguo de renwu you shi da youdian jiangci [A Speech on the Ten Items That Workers Should Do for the Sake of National Salvation]," *Dai Jitao xiansheng wencun* [*Collected Works of Dai Jitao*, hereafter *DJTXSWC*], 399–402.

Decoupling Two Revolutions

Dai's separation of the social revolution from the national meant that the April 12 coup had both an ideological and a *realpolitik* dimension. To be sure, party purification (*qingdang*) was a calculated move orchestrated by hard-nosed politicians vying for state power. Machiavellian machinations, as archives and personal diaries opened since the easing of tensions across the Taiwan Strait demonstrate, doomed the GMD–CCP coalition. As Taiwan-based historian Yu Miin-ling explains, historians could do worse than "lay ideology aside and . . . see Chiang [Kai-shek] not as a hero or a villain but as a human being" worried about being outcompeted by the Comintern and the (CCP).[4] In the People's Republic, Yang Kuisong's majestic study of Nationalist policy on the CCP sheds important light on the simmering ideological rifts between the two allies. Yet it still tends to see the collapse of the united front more as a result of raw power struggles between organizations and political figures than fundamental ideological differences.[5] Rather than neat dogmatic confrontations, messy contingencies and personal motivations now occupy the pride of place in many recent studies on the united front and its demise.

This emphasis on intrigues over ideas chimes in with works that point to the organizational similarities, particularly vanguardism and discomfort with social diversity, that the two parties shared. Common Leninist heritage, they argue, overshadowed ideological differences. The national revolution was thus the first stage in China's modern authoritarianism. As John Fitzgerald's influential account of the united front suggests, Sun Yat-sen's GMD–CCP coalition turned its back on the republican ideals that once fueled the antimonarchist movement. It used class politics as a ploy to outmaneuver liberal opponents and regional elites, all the while privileging nationalist and social cohesion. Acknowledging that the Communists believed, unlike the GMD, that national unity set the stage for a proletariat-led socialist revolution, Fitzgerald nonetheless maintains that it is easy to exaggerate the differences between the one-time partners. Sun and his Nationalist disciples fed on a staple of Bolshevik literature, partaking with the Communists in the goal of expanding state power, eliminating sectarian interests and mobilizing the masses by applying party discipline. A direct lineage linked Sun

---

[4] Yu Miin-ling, "A Reassessment of Chiang Kaishek and the Policy of Alliance with the Soviet Union, 1923–1927," in *The Chinese Revolution in the 1920s*, eds. Mechthild Leutner et al. (New York: RoutledgeCurzon, 2002), 98–9, 118–19.

[5] Yang Kuisong, Guomindang de "lian-Gong" yu "fan-Gong" [Kuomintang: Unity with "Communists" and "anti-Communism"] (Beijing: Shehui kexue wenxian chubanshe, 2008), 61–174.

through Mao Zedong, who was once at the helm of the GMD's propaganda department, in the party-state's opposition to liberal values.[6] The argument that the GMD's was the first installment of an extended statist project also features in Michael Tsin's study of Nationalist mobilization in mid-1920s Guangzhou. The imperative of modern governance, for Tsin, was to forge an organic "society-and-nation" by categorizing the populace into neat, discrete classes. While class mobilization empowered the hitherto marginalized, it simultaneously suppressed society's "infinite plurality of activities."[7] Overarching narratives of China's nation-state-building process, by stressing its functional impact on social diversity and aversion to liberal constitutionalism, downplay the ruptures in the country's revolutionary history. Like scholarship that focuses on personalities and intrigues, the ideological schisms between the left and the right were noted but promptly cast aside.

The approaches discussed earlier, despite their different politics, converge with Cold War totalitarianism theory in depicting the radical right and the revolutionary right as evil twins. An absence of meaningful social conflicts in revisionist accounts blinds us to the historical significance of the national revolution since the anticommunist purge. To the extent that struggle for state power did not necessarily reflect spontaneous social processes, there is nothing in the works of Fitzgerald and Tsin to which I take exception. They demonstrate clearly that the CCP did not mechanically reflect the aspirations of a rising proletariat, nor did the GMD act solely for compradors or the bourgeoisie. What these narratives do not account for, however, are the specificities of the GMD's nationalism and social vision or the party's affinities with interwar fascist regimes outside China. Tsin aptly points out that while the GMD saw classes as constitutive of a coherent social body, the Communists believed relations between classes were confrontational in nature. He nonetheless maintains that this difference was marginal to the logic of modern governance.[8] In fact, divergence in how the two Leninist parties viewed class politics was of critical importance as the national revolution's *raison d'être* was at stake.

By highlighting the GMD's distinct approach to capitalism and mass activism, this chapter shows that the united front's dissolution resulted from disagreements among Chinese revolutionaries on how a late industrializing, semi-colonized society could not only recover its political

---

[6] John Fitzgerald, *Awakening China: Politics, Culture, and Class in the Nationalist Revolution* (Stanford, CA: Stanford University Press, 1996), 175–7.

[7] Michael Tsin, *Nation, Governance and Modernity in China: Canton, 1900–1927* (Stanford, CA: Stanford University Press, 1999), 14, 171, 181.

[8] Ibid., 181.

sovereignty from imperialism but also overcome social and cultural dislocations brought about by uneven capitalist development. The key question was whether the national revolution entailed a social revolution or if the two were mutually exclusive. Despite its association with radicalism in contemporary usage, the Chinese-character compound *geming* has been ambiguous in meaning; the term has not always lent itself, as the *Great Chinese Word Dictionary* (*Hanyu da cidian*) glosses it, to "oppressed classes wresting control over the state through violence, destroying old social systems and production relations while creating new ones."[9] In imperial China, *geming* referenced the cosmological theory of the Mandate of Heaven and was concerned, therefore, not with social relations per se, but with their legitimate overseers. It was only by the late nineteenth century that the character compound acquired distinctly modern significance with the rise of nationalist politics. Drawing from their observations on the French and Japanese nation-states, figures like Sun Yat-sen and Liang Qichao (1873–1929) oscillated between advocating violent struggle against the Qing state and prescribing gradualist social reforms.[10] *Geming*, in late Qing reckoning, took as its objects the dynastic system and Manchu rulers.

With the Qing government's demise, *geming* began to acquire additional meanings beyond the constitution of the state and began to involve the populace. Political instability in the center and China's participation in the calamitous Great War sensitized intellectuals to wider malaise in capitalist modernity beyond the republic's fragile institutions. Drastic overhaul of social system and norms, domestically and sometimes globally, featured prominently on the intellectual agenda in the New Culture Movement, with transformation and enlightenment of the people identified as its keys. Revolution began to encompass literature and eventually urban students, youths and workers. Academics and writers became revolutionary agents, soon joining Nationalist and Communist agitators in organizing the masses as the united front bridged cultural experimentations and street politics. United in their concern for mass culture, liberals and communists differed nonetheless in their thinking on class. Liberal intellectuals like Hu Shi (1891–1962) and Gu Jiegang (1893–1980) celebrated folk culture in order to displace classical Chinese as the medium of elite writing, not class distinctions or the

---

[9] *Hanyu da cidian*, s.v. "geming."

[10] Jianhua Chen, "Chinese 'Revolution' in the Syntax of World Revolution," in *Tokens of Exchange: The Problem of Translation in Global Circulations*, ed. Lydia H. Liu (Durham, NC: Duke University Press, 1999), 361–70.

existence of social classes.[11] For leftists committed to a broader alliance, transforming mass culture was inseparable from not only nationalist goals but proletarian politics. How to deal with class disparities thus underpinned political divides among intellectuals and activists committed to the revolutionary project. Did national independence hinge on a global revolution against capitalist imperialism or must the nation take precedence over internationalist allegiances, whether they took Communist or Wilsonian liberal guise? Were nationalist aspirations compatible with or even contingent on fundamental changes to social relations or would the nation underwrite a hierarchal communion of contented producers playing their allocated roles? These were points of contention over which the Nationalists traded epithets with their Communist colleagues as they had important bearing on the revolutionary party's composition. Dai Jitaoism (*Dai Jitao zhuyi*), Communist theoretician Qu Qiubai complained, was a reactionary pretext for liquidating proletarian agency and consolidating elite domination of the GMD. The mass-based national revolution would become an "aristocratic" (*guizu*) one.[12] For Dai, however, suppressing class struggle and celebrating the nation's traditional culture were means to not only sideline Chinese Communists but also discipline radical young activists who threatened the party's cross-class, popular nature.[13] Concerns over the party-state's organization and the desire to eliminate ideological heterodoxy informed each other.

Rivalries between the GMD and the CCP were not simple extensions of class struggle, but neither were they campaigns for crude power with no social basis. Perry Anderson observes that "secular struggle between classes is ultimately resolved at the *political* – not at the economic or cultural – level of society. In other words, it is the construction and destruction of States which seal the basic shifts in the relations of production, so long as classes subsist."[14] By excluding the Communists, the Nationalists made clear the national revolution was to be decoupled from social revolution. In dramatic and violent fashion, the April 12 coup kept the fundamentals of China's socioeconomic edifice at bay from the interventionist state. Under Chiang Kai-shek and other anticommunists, the revolution continued to mobilize the populace, edify mass culture and,

---

[11] Li Hsiao-t'i, "Making a Name and a Culture for the Masses in Modern China," *Positions: East Asia Cultures Critique* 9 (2001): 44–5.

[12] Qu Qiubai, "Zhongguo guomin geming yu Dai Jitao zhuyi [China's National Revolution and Dai Jitaoism]," *Qu Qiubai wenji – zhengzhi lilun bian* (Beijing: Renmin wenxue chubanshe, 1989), 3:321.

[13] Dai, *Guomn geming yu Zhongguo Guomindang*, 64–6.

[14] Perry Anderson, *Lineages of the Absolutist State* (London: NLB, 1974), 11.

most importantly, pursue China's independence and anti-colonial politics with Asian allies. The revolution became *conservative* in its resolute opposition to insurrectionary attacks on social hierarchies and inequalities, but remained *revolutionary* in its desire to transcend the Euro-American "materialist" order and investment in mass politics as the harbinger of a future community free from problems inherent in capitalist modernity.

Meeting Communism on Its Own Ground

Like radical right activists internationally, Nationalist conservative revolutionaries internalized the organizational form of the left, celebrating mass vigor and a vanguardist party while channeling political energies away from inequalities among classes.[15] Rather than a return to the elite politics of the late Qing or early Republican incarnations, the GMD remained committed to the Bolshevik model of engagement with mass society through professional revolutionaries. When Sun Yat-sen reorganized the GMD into an ideologically uniform body along Soviet lines in 1919, he was not only endowing his party with stronger discipline but also recalibrating the purview of politics itself. Mirroring May Fourth intellectual culture, politics was not confined to formal state institutions that hosted unstable cabinets, military strongmen and parliamentarians prone to compromises. Instead, political struggle was to rally behind the national revolution newly ascendant social forces like urban workers and students, whose attacks on traditions and attraction to anarchist and socialist ideals alarmed the incumbent Republican elite.[16] For Sun, the abject state of the Chinese Revolution was due in no small part to his comrades' misguided understanding of politics. In October 1923, he told cadres at a convention of the GMD branch in Guangdong that

there was a spurious saying at the time of China's retrocession [from Manchu to Han rule in 1911] that "the revolutionary party was to be disbanded at the very moment the revolutionary army successfully rose up" (*geming jun qi, geming dang xiao*). This idea was attributable to a certain bureaucrat who enthusiastically supported the revolution and echoed by party members like Huang Xing, Song Jiaoren and Zhang Taiyan. At that time, it was taken as a truism. After [the Revolutionary Alliance] was reorganized into the Guomindang [in 1912], the party was thoroughly transformed into a political party (*zhengdang*) and depleted of revolutionary spirit.[17]

---

[15] Robin, *Reactionary Mind*, 53; Neocleous, *Fascism*, 43.
[16] Fitzgerald, *Awakening China*, 191–4.
[17] Sun Yat-sen, "Jiantao dangwu buzhen zhi yin, yu xiaofa Eren yidang zhi guo [Reviewing the Reasons Contributing to the Party's Lackluster Performance and Learning from the

Indeed, under Song Jiaoren (1882–1913), the Revolutionary Alliance diluted its socialist, anti-imperialist rhetoric as well as support for women's rights in order to merge with more conservative parties to form the GMD, positioning itself as a contender in a representative system of government. The bloc went on to win a majority at the 1912 election at the expense of its ideological identity, only to be crushed by militarist Yuan Shikai.[18] Sorry fates awaited revolutionaries willing to disarm and resign themselves to the parliamentary chamber.

While Sun mentioned the army in particular, he was warning cadres not about the party's forfeiture of its military wing per se, but about the idea that party politics should be confined to state-building once the imperial system had been overthrown. The party must maintain its hegemonic role in the larger society and its cadres must remain vigilant mobilizers, not state functionaries or elected officials. By exhorting his followers to learn from Soviet Russia, Sun acknowledged the laboring masses' ascendency in nationalist movements, a phenomenon Westernized nationalist elites in other colonized and semi-colonized societies also faced due to interwar urbanization and industrialization.[19] At the same Guangdong gathering where he lamented the revolution's premature end, Sun argued that what the country needed was an armed mass party unified under an ideology. One ploy Yuan used to liquidate the revolution and pave the way for monarchial restoration, Sun charged, was to prohibit army officers from joining the GMD. Instead of separating the party from state institutions, the Nationalist Party must govern the state (*yidang zhiguo*).[20] Sun stressed, however, that one-party rule did not mean taking over the existing state apparatus. Instead, the GMD state would play a prophetic role and

Russians the Strategy of Governing the State with the Party]," *Sun Wen xuanji* (Guangzhou: Guangdong renmin chubanshe, 2007), 3:274–5.

[18] Ibid., 3:275; David Strand, *An Unfinished Republic: Leading by Word and Deed in Republican China* (Berkeley: University of California Press, 2011), 39–41. In a rhetorical sleight of hand, Communist general secretary Chen Duxiu lumped Sun's comrades who called for the revolutionary party's dissolution in the early days of the Republic and Nationalists who opposed the united front into the "right" ("Guomindang youpai zhi guoqu xianzai ji jianglai [The Past, Present and Future of the Guomindang Right]," *Xiangdao*, no. 148 [1926]: 2–3).

Conservative revolutions, as we shall see, took pains to distinguish their anticommunism from anti-revolutionaries'.

[19] Beverly J. Silver and Eric Slater, "The Social Origins of World Hegemonies," in *Chaos and Governance in the Modern World System*, eds. Giovanni Arrighi and Beverly Silver (Minneapolis: University of Minnesota Press, 1999), 198–201.

[20] Sun, "Dangyuan yao ren'ge gaoshang bing zhuzhong xuanchuan caineng de xinren [Cadres Need to Be of Impeccable Character and Pay Attention to Propaganda in Order to Win Hearts]" and "Jiantao dangwu buzhen zhi yin, yu xiaofa Eren yidang zhi guo," *Sun Wen xuanji*, 3:265–76.

convert the entire people into the Three People's Principles. Cadres should be prepared to risk their lives spreading the revolutionary gospel, not expect to form a bureaucratic class or *nomenklatura*. The First United Front, formalized in January 1924, opened the GMD's doors to Chinese Communists. CCP cadres, who maintained a distinct identity under the GMD umbrella, pressed ahead with the organization of workers and peasants into political agents. The national revolution became a mass movement at the expense of the GMD's erstwhile liberal supporters, whom Sun ridiculed as careerists with their sights set on nothing other than lucrative positions in a Nationalist-dominated government.

The Bolshevik model of party-building and mass mobilization survived the April 12 coup. Organizational vitality and ideological piety, the two concerns that underlay Sun Yat-sen's fascination with democratic centralism, remained relevant after the expulsion of Communists from the revolutionary state. The national revolution was not over and Chiang Kai-shek's GMD regime still confronted problems shared by other national liberation movements elsewhere inspired by the new Soviet Union and its commitment to world revolution: national independence and the global anti-imperialist struggle, engagement of workers and peasants and the dialectic between vanguardism and the spontaneity of mass activism. GMD ideological and social praxis after 1927 had to reconcile the party's claim to lead a popular struggle against imperialism on one hand, and its animosity toward any collective action that challenged reigning social hierarchies on the other.

Another result of the GMD's metamorphosis with which cadres grappled was socialism. Like many radical rightists in other countries, GMD cadres who sought to command mass politics and put it to the service of conservative social agendas were initially attracted to left-wing ideas. Various strands of socialism formed the shared political vocabulary among Nationalists. Sun became impressed by strikes against foreign capitalists and their governments in Shanghai and Guangzhou during the 1910s and 1920s. Dai Jitao (1891–1949), Hu Hanmin (1879–1936) and Li Shizeng (1881–1973), who would emerge as ideologues of the radical right, were radicalized much earlier and contributed to the early debates on left-wing politics before the fall of the Qing. The French-educated Li was among China's first anarchists and joined Sun Yat-sen's Revolutionary Alliance in 1906 as an ardent advocate of mutual aid. In the 1910s and 1920s, he worked to bring young Chinese students to France on a work-study program, in which many future Communists had their first experience of industrial labor. As Chinese students and workers became politically active in the late 1910s, Dai and Hu were attracted to

Marxism as they mused on the potential prowess of urban workers in furthering nationalist objectives in light of Lenin's Bolshevik Revolution in 1917.[21] While never a Marxist, Chiang Kai-shek had been part of a left-leaning community since he was a student in early twentieth-century Tokyo, where he befriended Dai and admired the polemicist's patriotism. In Japan, the future Nationalist chief regularly read the Revolutionary Alliance organ *People's News (Minbao)*, in which Hu and Wang Jingwei (1883–1944) published articles calling for nationalization of land and solidarity with revolutionary movements outside China.[22]

Due to their left-leaning origins, ideologues who were most earnest in providing the theoretical justifications for the rightward shift of China's national revolution were initially reluctant to drive the Communists out entirely from the GMD. Dai and Li, in particular, held highly ambivalent attitudes toward GMD elders who met in Western Hills, Beijing in late 1925 to condemn the pro-Communist stance held by Wang Jingwei and the Guangzhou-based Nationalist government he had led since Sun's death in March. Chiang was downright critical of the elders' "corrosive jealousies." Future conservative revolutionaries' initial hesitation to adopt a hawkish stance against communism was partly attributable to their desire to maintain unity among Nationalists. Eventually, however, they coalesced around Chiang in the months leading up to the April 12 coup. Dai, along with Chen Lifu and his brother Guofu, enthusiastically backed the purge Chiang launched in Shanghai.[23] In his memoir, Chen Lifu singled out the support of prominent anarchists including Li for the purge's success.[24] Joining the anarchists was Hu Hanmin who, while eventually falling out with Chiang in 1931 over constitutional matters and the latter's Japan policy, backed the new Nationalist state after the coup and penned numerous anti-Communist treatises. Cadres who lent their intellectual weight to the new Nanjing regime distinguished themselves from their left-wing and liberal critics on one hand, and anti-Manchu veterans on the other. Their prescription for the national revolution combined animosity against challenges to unequal social relations and obsession with order and discipline with a desire to perfect a revolutionary polity modeled on the GMD's former Soviet ally. It underwrote Chiang's China by reconciling the regime's claim to

---

[21] Herman William Mast III, "An Intellectual Biography of Tai Chi-t'ao from 1891 to 1928" (PhD diss., University of Illinois, 1970), 66–72.

[22] Jay Taylor, *The Generalissimo: Chiang Kai-shek and the Struggle for Modern China* (Cambridge, MA: Belknap Press, 2009), 18–19.

[23] Yang, *Guomindang de "lian-Gong" yu "fan-Gong,"* 90–6; Mast, "Intellectual Biography of Tai Chi-t'ao," 320; Taylor, *The Generalissimo*, 53–4, 66.

[24] Chen Lifu, *The Storm Clouds Clear over China: The Memoir of Ch'en Li-fu* (Stanford, CA: Hoover Institution, 1994), 62.

being revolutionary with its unwillingness to empower the society's lower classes against the propertied elite.

Given the GMD's ingrained radical culture, Nationalists' critiques of communism echoed those of social democrats and disillusioned communists internationally. Dai and Hu were both fluent in Marxian analyses of capitalist society and, in the immediate days after the right-wing seizure of Shanghai, deployed anti-Bolshevik strains within socialist thought to criticize the CCP and the Soviet Union. They republished Karl Kautsky's *The Economic Doctrines of Karl Marx* (1887), which Dai first translated from Takabatake Motoyuki's Japanese rendition from 1919 to 1920.[25] Dai argued in one of the prefaces to his Chinese rendition of Kautsky, a German Marxist critical of Lenin, that many young activists were ignorant of Marx's writings. They failed, therefore, to discern the imperialist ambitions of the Comintern, subscribing blindly to the fallacious mission of world revolution with no concern for China's own survival.[26] Elsewhere, in a more provocative speech, Dai accused the CCP of sacrificing the "completely uneducated, utterly feeble and undisciplined" Chinese masses to the global struggle between imperialism and world communism. Without subscribing to strict discipline and organization under Sun Yat-senism, he warned, the nation and its people would never recover from their plight. To prevent talented youths from falling in droves to the Communist embrace, "faithful leaders" of the party had no choice but to impose dictatorship, expressed in the namesake Chinese neologism *diketuiduo*, on the Nationalist mass movement.[27]

Drawing from debates within the left allowed Nationalists to hold onto their revolutionary identity. It differentiated conservative revolutionaries from ultranationalists and liberal politicians committed to the constitutional order of the northern-based Beiyang warlord government against which the GMD was launching a military expedition. "The Chinese Nationalist Party," Hu stated brusquely, "does not sit about parliament and give flowery speeches, score applauses or cast votes." Its mission was to smash the existing order so that a new one guided by Sun's Three

---

[25] Dai and Hu Hanmin, trans., *Ziben lun jieshuo* (Shanghai: Minzhi shuju, 1927). The Chinese title drew directly from the Japanese version *Shihon ron kaisetsu*, literally *Explication of Capital*. Paralleling the political trajectories of his Chinese translators, Takabatake Motoyuki (1886–1928) was a Japanese Marxist who became an ardent advocate of national socialism, claiming to have reconciled Marxism with the supposedly indigenous values of a corporatist national polity embodied by the emperor (Germaine A. Hoston, "Marxism and National Socialism in Taishô Japan: The Thought of Takabatake Motoyuki," *Journal of Asian Studies* 44 [1984]: 46.)
[26] Dai, "Xu yi [Preface One]," *Ziben lun jieshuo*, 2.   [27] Dai, *Dai Jitao zuijin yanlun*, 5–7.

People's Principles could be built.[28] They saw themselves as agents of pure revolutionary fervor working to displace both the inertia of the party elite and Communist adventurism. Li the anarchist, on the other hand, accused Marxism and Marxist–Leninism of being historically regressive and claimed what he called the revolution of people's livelihood or *minsheng* as more compatible with the latest advances in human civilization. Conservative revolutionaries saw themselves as working against the part-warlord and part-parliamentary establishment, promising to lead a mass political movement toward a new order that was neither liberal capitalist nor state socialist as practiced by imperialist powers in Euro-America or the Soviet Union.

The *minsheng* revolution promised not only national independence but a new, salubrious form of moral and social existence. Purged of Marxist influences, GMD rule would prove superior to Soviet-style communism by eventually eliminating, at least in the distant future, all forms of "materialist" struggles that had been a feature of human civilization since the beginning of history. Instead of classes and their malicious conflicts, conservative revolutionaries in China valorized the nation as a corporatist whole. Not unlike European conservatives, the GMD government sought to avoid class struggle by neutralizing working-class antagonism against the reigning power bloc. It sought, to borrow Ernesto Laclau's formulation, to "disarticulate" popular, autonomous political activism by claiming to work for the Chinese people as a whole.[29] The Nanjing state, Michael Tsin notes, deployed various social movements to "manage and police" society since the 1927 purge. Reliance on popular mobilization, a hallmark of the united front period, continued apace despite Chiang's "putative conservative direction."[30] Yet, rather than making the post-coup GMD's conservatism suspect or its anticommunism a cover, the party-state's mass politics – which aimed to put workers and students in their place – was critical to consolidating the nation's pecking order and countered materialist class struggle.

Depoliticizing *Minsheng*

The corporatist ideal served to rebuke the key communist premise – that relationships between individuals were mediated primarily through ownership of the means of production, not national affiliation. The state's role

---

[28] Hu Hanmin, "Qingdang zhi yiyi [The Significance of Party Purifications]," in *Geming yu fan geming*, Lang Xingshi (Shanghai: Minzhi shudian, 1928), 158.
[29] Ernesto Laclau, *Politics and Ideology in Marxist Theory: Capitalism, Fascism, Populism* (London: NLB, 1977), 115–16.
[30] Tsin, *Nation, Governance, and Modernity in China*, 173–4.

under corporatism was, akin to what Wang Hui characterized in a slightly different context, "depoliticized"; it posed as an overseer balancing competing claims to resources and wealth. The state's pretension to neutrality rested on the notion that a technocratic elite was to handle the economy without answering to mass political demands. Rather than taking a leadership role in popular mobilization for changes in social relations, the revolutionary party morphed into an institution in a "depoliticized political order" defending the private property system, managing labor–capital tensions and diverting public sentiments toward the national community.[31] Communists, conservative revolutionaries charged, proffered the wrong prescription for China's malaise. Low levels of industrial development, not capitalist imperialism, was the ultimate reason for the country's plight and patient reforms, not disruptive strikes and class boycotts, were key to national salvation.

In concrete terms, conservative revolutionaries rebuked communism by depoliticizing Sun's ideas. Among them, Dai Jitao, whose theoretical contributions anchored on *minsheng*, was the most controversial. In the summer of 1925, Dai published two influential polemics, *Philosophical Foundations of Sun Yat-senism* (*Sun Wen zhuyi zhi zhexue de jichu*) and *China's National Revolution and the Guomindang* (*Guomin geming yu Zhongguo Guomindang*). The pamphlets became so influential among politically aware readers that they were compared to Chen Duxiu's (1879–1942) famed magazine *New Youth* (*Xin qingnian*). The GMD Central Executive Committee in Guangzhou, then still committed to the united front, censured *China's National Revolution*. Chiang was initially dismayed by Dai's diatribes; he saw Chinese Communists and their Soviet advisers as accomplished mobilizers on whom the GMD must rely if military campaigns against the warlord government were to enjoy popular support. Yet the nation's future leader soon embraced Dai's intellectual insights, through which he studied Sun's writings systematically in late 1925 and early 1926, as they were at one on their animosity toward Russian Bolsheviks and class struggle. *Philosophical Foundations of Sun Yat-senism* defined Chiang's understanding of Sun's intellectual legacy. It helped also that Dai was a thinker through and through who had no designs on Chiang's grip on power.[32]

---

[31] Wang Hui, *The End of the Revolution: China and the Limits of Modernity* (London: Verso, 2009), 11–13.
[32] Taylor, *Generalissimo*, 54; Mast, "Intellectual Biography of Tai Chi-t'ao," 285, 343–4; Kirby, *Germany and Republican China*, 179; Circular No. 209, October 17, 1925, Hankou Collection, 163.7, Kuomintang Archives.

Marxism, Dai argued in the two tracts, was philosophically too simple-minded, being premised on a materialist reading of history. He observed in *Philosophical Foundations* that Marxist politics was concerned only with the economic life of the people.[33] This lopsided understanding of humanity informed Chinese Communists' flawed internationalism and neglect of the nation. It was pure "wishful thinking," Dai declared in *China's National Revolution*, that the competition between nations for survival would be overcome "once the economic structure was changed and capitalism eradicated."[34] While claiming to remain unequivocal in his opposition to the infamous unequal treaties, Dai warned his country not to take part in a full-scale political struggle against imperialism, particularly any Comintern-led global initiative. China needed economic development (*jianshe*) and imports from industrially advanced countries such as German science and American machines. A resolute stance against imperialism had to wait until the all-important national "self-confidence" (*zixin li*) and "awakening" (*juewu*) were attained, which were in turn contingent on the development of the citizenry's material well-being (*wuzhi de jianshe*) with the input of global capital and technology.[35] Playing with the slippages inherent in the compound *geming*, Dai's national revolution was a plea for reformism even as it alluded to an end to capitalist hegemony and a world revolution against imperialism in the indeterminate future.

In contradistinction to Marxist myopia on production relations, GMD conservative revolutionaries claimed to offer a vision for humanity in its wholeness, taking proper account of nation-building as a key revolutionary goal. Hu Hanmin touted Sun as the premier theoretician of a total, instead of a narrowly materialist, revolution. Marx, he asserted, "did not appreciate nationalism" and his disciples at the Comintern were working to annihilate Eastern national consciousness through imperialistic means.[36] Sun, by contrast, had unlocked the basis of human evolution, and superseded European social theorists. Western theorists, for Hu, misidentified particular episodes in history – struggles between church and monarchy in the Renaissance period, monarchy and civil rights leading up to the French Revolution, proletarians and the bourgeoisie in the twentieth century etc. – as universal and timeless. Sun's unique insight was to home in on humans' tendency to struggle against one

---

[33] Dai, *Sun Wen zhuyi zhi zhexue de jichu* (1925; reprint, Taipei: Zhongyang gaizao weiyuan hui wenwu gongying chu, 1951), 15 (page citations are to the reprint edition).

[34] Dai, *Guomin geming yu Zhongguo Guomindang*, 68–9.

[35] Dai, *Dai Jitao zuijin yanlun*, 8–10.

[36] Hu, "Sanmin zhuyi zhi renshi [Understanding the Three People's Principles]," in *Geming yu fan geming*, 150.

another. An exclusive focus on rearranging political institutions or economic interests would not bring long-lasting solutions to world conflicts. Only the Three People's Principles – with their equal attention to the interlocked nature of nationhood, political structures and economics – could address the totality of human life.[37] Only Sun's all-rounded revolutionary formula (*zhengge de geming zhuyi*) could put an end to conflicts between peoples by preventing the degeneration of healthy nationalism into expansionary imperialism, developing a noncapitalist modern economy, and safeguarding genuine democracy from "hypocritical bourgeois democratic politics." The crucial and imminent task for Nationalists was to realize the limitations of Marxism and acknowledge that the Three People's Principles alone provided inspirations for a threefold national-political-social revolution.[38]

While Hu was cautious in emphasizing Sun's three-pronged approach to revolution, Dai performed a more creative reading of his mentor's ideas, identifying *minsheng* as the core of revolution. The principle of *minsheng*, rendered literally as "people's livelihood" or sometimes more provocatively as "socialism," was the most controversial aspect of Sun's political theory that was contested by both right-wing Nationalists and Communists as vindication of their social visions. Dai made two important interventions that not only put daylight between the Sunist project from revolutionary socialism but also steered the revolution's focus away from the political economy. First, he subsumed the other two core elements of the Three People's Principles, nationalism and democracy, under the *minsheng* principle. He argued that the fight for an independent nation-state and empowerment of the citizenry, including disenfranchised workers and peasants, was in the broadest sense part of a coherent endeavor to transform people's livelihood.[39] *Minsheng* was thus the ultimate goal of national and political revolution, covering aspects of human life that went far beyond the constitutional infrastructure of a national polity.

Having established the centrality of *minsheng*, Dai then went about redrawing the remit of people's livelihood so that it would not lend itself to calls for changes in the socioeconomic structure. He was helped by the incoherent manner in which Sun explicated what *minsheng* entailed, in particular vis-à-vis communism. Sun did state that the principle of people's livelihood was the same as socialism or communism. Yet he was also adamant that the GMD only foresaw communism being realized in the indeterminate future, that socialism and communism be subsumed under the *minsheng* doctrine and that he did not endorse the nationalization of

---

[37] Ibid., 142–4.   [38] Ibid., 146, 154.   [39] Dai, *Sun Wen zhuyi*, 10–14.

private property as advocated by socialists in the West.[40] More significantly, while Hu suggested that the principle of people's livelihood incorporated social revolution in a much wider vision, Sun had something different in mind.[41] The late leader declared in 1923 that the *minsheng* program was devised to preempt (*yufang*) the prospect of the disgruntled poor rising up against the rich due to wealth inequalities.[42] The aim of his land reform proposal was to reduce rent, not liquidate landlords. Sun's was a corporatist solution whereby members of society harmoniously sync their assigned productive roles, not fight for ownership of the means of production. His suggestion for suppressing the soaring price of rice in Guangzhou, for example, was that workers and peasants emulate their British and Russian counterparts and form cooperatives so that urbanites would barter the tools they produced for the crop the latter grew.[43] Such mechanisms would bypass predatory merchants who profited by hiking the price of the staple food. Despite the antibusiness rhetoric, Sun's musings on people's livelihood did not subvert existing social relations.

Dai took as his creative license the fact that Sun's more systematic consideration of *minsheng*, as opposed to the principles of nationalism and democracy, was incomplete. While acknowledging Sun died without delivering all his lectures on the people's livelihood, the faithful interpreter of Sunism did not shy away from building on what he saw as the revered revolutionary's inchoate theoretical impulses. Publicized lectures on *minsheng*, as Dai explained, covered the breadth of the people's everyday life with emphasis on material aspects such as clothing (*yi*), food (*shi*), housing (*zhu*) and transportation (*xing*). They covered the concrete needs of a poverty-stricken population – particularly workers and peasants – struggling in a nation where free trade and the wage labor system were imperialist impositions.[44] They were, for Sun, sites for reformist interventions such as land reform and state, instead of private, ownership of major industries. In this sense, *minsheng* was the primary interface between the revolutionary state and the masses on a day-to-day basis. For Dai, however, this interface encompassed not only material well-being but also aesthetic uplift. Unlike communism, *minsheng* addressed only economic livelihood and did not encompass the full spectrum of social life. The theoretician highlighted one important category

[40] Sun Yat-sen, *Sanmin zhuyi* (Taipei: Zhengzhong shuju, 1954), 182, 218; Sun, "Guanyu minsheng zhuyi zhi shuoming [Explanations on the Principle of Livelihood]," *Sun Wen xuanji*, 3:397.
[41] Hu, "Sanmin zhuyi zhi renshi," 143–4.
[42] Sun, "Yaoyong Sanmin zhuyi dapo jiu sixiang huifu geming zhaoqi [Banish Antiquated Thoughts and Revive Revolutionary Zeal with the Three People's Principles]," *Sun Wen xuanji*, 3:327.
[43] Ibid., 3:374. [44] Dai, *Sun Wen zhuyi*, 10–11; Dai, *Guomin geming*, 7–9.

that effectively revised the mundane materialism of *minsheng*.
Claiming privileged access to Sun's handwritten notes and private conversations with his wife, Dai argued that the late leader was preoccupied
with yu – the reproduction (*shengyu*), cultivation (*yangyu*) and education
(jiaoyu) of the populace. Unfortunately, Sun did not have the chance to
discuss the concept in public and left faithful disciples like Dai to complete the task.

Dai's play on *yu* purged *minsheng* of whatever subversive designs the
principle could inspire on socioeconomic arrangements. His interpretation of *minsheng* endowed the state with the depoliticized political function of spearheading productive capacity and diverting mass activism
away from the economic sphere to the affective. Dai glossed *yu* as the
state's responsibility to sustain the living (*yangsheng*) and dispose of the
dead (*songsi*). This new category was concerned as much with rebuilding
a ritualistic order as fulfilling citizens' economic needs. Combined with *le*
(happiness), another dimension Dai introduced with *yu* to complete
Sun's theory of *minsheng*, the national revolution became a campaign to
create for the national community "beautiful and elegant enjoyment"
(*youmei gaoshang de xiangle*). Sun's socialist-sounding principle was transformed under Dai's formulation into a principle of aesthetics.[45] In the
chapters that follow, it will become obvious that "enjoyment" under the
conservative revolutionaries meant moral uplift and a disciplined lifestyle
under the close watch of the state.

Cultivation and happiness, the two categories added to *minsheng*, allegedly surpassed the epistemological naiveté (*danchun*) of communism and
its exclusive focus on material life. This insight had significant bearing on
the conservative revolution's conduct and appeal to non-GMD constituents beyond anticommunist violence. Dai's new orthodoxy legitimated
bold promises to transform the entire nation's collective psychological
makeup. Economic production was critical to the nation's survival, but
precisely due to its importance, it must be tackled through "state planning, coordination and management" untampered by ideological
polemics. On development (*jianshe*), "the *minsheng* principle was not
a theory (*zhuyi*) but merely a social policy." Politics – sweeping critiques
of capitalism, in particular – must be set aside and make way for technocratic deliberations.[46] In its emphasis on the citizenry's ethical and
aesthetic uplift, Dai's interpretation of the Sunist program anticipated
the GMD's social engagement after its break with the Communists.
Slavoj Žižek points out forcefully that the ultimate degeneration of revolutionary movements, particularly those on the radical left, lies in the

---

[45] Dai, *Sun Wen zhuyi*, 11.   [46] Ibid., 15, 21.

displacement of the political struggle from changing the economic order to aesthetic phenomena. Failing to disrupt fundamental social relations, Bolsheviks in the 1920s sought recourse in reorganization of daily rituals, marriage and funeral ceremonies and interaction of workers on the factory floor.[47] Such obsession with the quotidian was evident in Dai's reconstruction of Sunist revolutionary theory and, as we see in the next two chapters, GMD's management of mass organizations in the following decades. This "depoliticized politics" also enjoyed popularity with activists and intellectuals in civil society. These figures treasured their independence from a violent and illiberal regime, but saw their own agendas, producing a new generation of voluntaristic citizens or forging cultural camaraderie between China and other Asian societies, as compatible with a stable order under which citizens lived in sentimental harmony rather than agitated for social emancipation.

Resetting the Agenda: A Revolution of Aesthetics

The yawning gap between Dai's radical intervention into the national psyche and technocratic gradualism in economic development betrayed a worldview in which culture, like politics, operated in abstraction from socioeconomic relations. His approach is also one that, despite its claim of offering China a more thorough solution to overcoming capitalism, confined the national revolution to the narrow realm of collective behaviors, emotions and consciousness.[48] The aim of political mobilization was to make Spartan consumers, harness their productive power and enhance communal devotion to an apotheosized national spirit. The latter was particularly pertinent in the context of looming hostilities with Japan since the early 1930s, as shared cultural traditions were wielded as a unifying force for the nation and formed a far worthier revolutionary focus than the Chinese Communists' alleged sectarian economic interests. The aesthetic, hence, was pitched against the material. Ironically, Dai was among the first senior GMD cadres who coupled transformation of aesthetic experience with reflections on cultural reification under the capitalist economy. In his younger, more left-leaning days, the intricate ties between politics, economics and morality were brought to

---

[47] Slavoj Žižek, *In Defense of Lost Causes* (London: Verso, 2009), 174–5.

[48] Ban Wang has argued persuasively for careful consideration of ways in which, through modern Chinese history and particularly during the Communist era, politics could "feel like art" and be "fleshed out as a form of art and symbolic activity" (*The Sublime Figure of History: Aesthetics and Politics in Twentieth-Century China* [Stanford, CA: Stanford University Press, 1997], 15). What was distinct to GMD politics was not, one cannot stress enough, that the party-state appealed to the intimate and sensuous but that it did so in order to re-channel mass energy from targeting the property system.

bear under a critique on bourgeois culture and commodification of mass entertainment.

In "Drama and the Common People" (*Yanxi yu pingmin*), a now obscure essay that appeared in a special edition of the party organ *Republican Daily* (*Minguo ribao*) marking the alliance between the GMD and the CCP, Dai reminisced about the pure bliss to which the masses were treated by drama troupes during temple fairs and other local festivals when he was a child in his native Sichuan province. China's belated encounter with modern consumerism meant that such carnivalesque scenes in which people freely put on colorful costumes and munched on their noodles while sitting randomly to soak in the free performance had become all but memories in just a few decades, even as this form of popular entertainment had been the norm for generations. In glittering Shanghai, one could only find exclusive theaters in which prices were carefully calibrated and set prohibitively high for most common people.[49] The rowdy but authentic happiness of folk entertainment was transformed into the genteel philistinism of urban consumer society. Far from sentimental nostalgia for an irrecoverable past, Dai's childhood memory provided the impetus for a revolutionary future. "What is the purpose of revolution?" Dai posed rhetorically. "It is," he continued:

> to wrest the new culture which destroyed our old culture away from the minority so that the common people as a whole can reclaim the privileged position (*xingfu de diwei*) where they can partake of that new culture. Our goal is not excessive, for our ancestors had always possessed such privilege. In places where the encounter with modern civilization (*jindai wenming*) came somewhat late, even a man in his thirties like myself can recall the beauty of human sentiments and happiness of the common people.[50]

Given Dai's mature career as a traditionalist, the call to arms targeted at GMD cadres for the construction of a new national culture was all the more striking, considering how it implied not a return to "old culture" but a desire for the new. Dai tasked organized nationalism with creating an egalitarian everyday culture in which gratification would no longer be stemmed by consumerist activities.

Indeed, in 1919, amidst the excitement of the May Fourth Movement, he wrote precisely that the rise of private property and the commodification of social relations, which resulted in the displacement of workers from agrarian society, meant that Confucian ethics had become obsolete. Rather than seeking a return to antiquity, the imminent task facing the

---

[49] Dai, "Yanxi yu pingmin," in *Zhongguo Guomindang gaizu jinian Mingguo ribao tekan* (Guangzhou: Guangzhou Minguo ribao she, 1924), 52–6.
[50] Ibid., 56.

nation was the creation of a new ethics that would address the inadequacies of capitalist social relations. He singled out in particular the compartmentalization of morality into distinct public (*gongde*) and private (*side*) realms, a recent phenomenon that emerged from the ashes of an agrarian, family-centered economy.[51] Dai called for a socialist (*shehui zhuyi de*) ethics befitting a modern industrial society.[52] This new ethics entailed an ideal of benevolence (*ren'ai*) and fraternity (*you'ai*) based on which the young and the old would be taken care of by the social collective as a whole and all members of the community would treat each other as their own kin.[53] It served to overcome bourgeoisie, individualist selfishness on one hand, and Confucian filial piety to one's immediate lineages in an increasingly mobile socioeconomic landscape on the other. In these early days, the revolutionary state as an agent for moral change had yet to enter Dai's horizon. What is palpable, however, is that even in his most radical phase, Dai understood bourgeois society more as a moral failure than as a systematic exploitation.

Six years later, when such key concepts as benevolence acquired conservative Confucian connotations in Dai's reinterpretation of the Three People's Principles, the nation was privileged as the agent and embodiment of a redress to the ethical depravation that was capitalism. This contrasted with Sun's emphasis on economic life in his *minsheng* principle and Communist insistence on the transformation of production relations as the foundation of any revolutionary enterprise. Political praxis was brought to bear only on the symptoms of capitalism – breakdown of old filial ties, disorienting changes in people's habits etc. – not its structural foundation. The man who wrote in 1919 that Confucius was hopelessly harking back to ancient ideals that had lost relevance to the crumbling social order even during the philosopher's own lifetime now argued that noncompliance with Confucian tenets, the "foundation of peace and happiness," was to blame for all the chaos and carnage China had experienced since the Warring States period (475–221 BCE).[54] He went on to observe that Sun Yat-sen had inherited the moral enterprise of the ancient Chinese thinker that was in sharp contrast to the alleged moral agnosticism of Karl Marx and Vladimir I. Lenin. "The basis of nationalism," Dai declared in allusion to the Three People's Principles, "is the ethics of filial piety (*xiaoci*). The basis of democracy is the ethics of trust and righteousness (*xinyi*). The basis of people's livelihood is the ethics of

---

[51] Dai, "Jiu lunli de benghuai yu xin lunli de jianshe [The Collapse of Old Ethics and the Development of a New One]," parts 1 and 2, *Xingqi pinglun*, no. 25 (1919): 2.

[52] Ibid., no. 20 (1919): 1.   [53] Ibid., no. 25 (1919): 2.

[54] Ibid., no. 20 (1919): 1; Dai, *Dai Jitao zuijin yanlun*, 15.

benevolence and peace (ren'ai heping)."[55] Whereas lamentations on frayed filial piety were once criticized as "subjective talk" no longer in sync with objective reality, a Confucianized Sunist doctrine called for the restoration of ancient values as keys to China's future.[56]

The GMD claimed to represent the unique Chinese moral ideals that Sun Yat-sen inherited from Confucius and his disciples. Dai's reduction of Confucian universalist pretensions to the core of state-sanctioned national spirit (Zhongguo minzu de jingshen) served to establish what Antonio Gramsci calls "the autonomous, educative and moral activity of the secular State." Unlike the cosmopolitan aloofness of premodern states run by an intellectual or ecclesiastical caste, Gramsci argues that modern political formations actively shape mass moral norms to serve the interests of the ruling classes.[57] The late imperial Chinese state, to be sure, was not laissez-faire. The Qing court at the height of its power deployed community compacts (xiangyue), which began as spontaneous experiments at local governance, to instill moral norms across the empire. Yet what defined moral economy was much less official Neo-Confucianism as promoted by the court in Beijing than clan relations and local values of mutual help. Neo-Confucianism remained a literati ideology and the extent to which even the literati should be mobilized politically remained a vexed issue throughout dynastic rule.[58]

In any case, Dai's interest in Confucianism, which anticipated the Nationalist state's in the 1930s and beyond, betrayed not commitments to the imperial court's universalism but deployment of China's distinct moral traditions for mass mobilization. Like many in his generation, Dai began his education in the Confucian canons. Yet, even before the abolition of the civil examination system in 1905, Dai had already switched to modern learning, eventually traveling to Japan to study law.[59] Classical concepts such as benevolence and fraternity (bo'ai), just as minsheng itself, acquired new meanings as they were inducted into the political culture of the modern nation-state. In his intellectual biography of Dai, Chiu-chun

[55] Dai, Dai Jitao zuijin yanlun, 15.
[56] Dai, "Jiu lunli de benghuai yu xin lunli de jianshe," Xingqi pinglun, no. 25 (1919): 3.
[57] Antonio Gramsci, Selections from the Prison Notebooks, trans. Quintin Hoare and Geoffrey Smith (New York: International Publishers, 1971), 258–62. Joseph Levenson has identified the nationalist celebration of Confucianism, characteristic of the GMD in the 1930s, as signifying the final demise of its universalism. The hollowing of Confucianism's philosophical heft coincided with the romantic yearning for a Confucian culture peculiar to the Chinese nation (Confucian China and Its Modern Fate: A Trilogy [Berkeley: University of California Press, 1968], 1:107–8.)
[58] Mizoguchi Yuzo, Zhongguo de chongji /China's Impact/, trans. Wang Ruigen (Beijing: Shenghuo, dushu, xinzhi sanlian shudian, 2011), 137–46; Philip A. Kuhn, Origins of the Modern Chinese State (Stanford, CA: Stanford University Press, 2002).
[59] Mast, "Intellectual Biography of Tai Chi-t'ao," 4–11.

Lee draws attention to the ideologue's identification of the nation and its history as balancing devices against the disorienting effect of global modernity. The result was a "neoconservative culture" that bound anomic individual interests together under a holistic society encompassed by the nation.[60] The nation expressed a moral economy that could supposedly insulate China from the universalizing reach of capitalist civilization. Reviving China's "national ethics," Dai claimed, was Sun's answer to predatory militarism and capitalism. Individualism and class struggle, endemic in a European-dominated international order, would be overcome by an altruistic, humane politics inspired by *The Doctrine of the Mean* (*Zhongyong*): reviving extinct lineages and states, restoring order and supporting the imperiled, treating strangers generously while expecting little in return.[61]

Such idealist desire to overcome capitalism by replacing class struggle with a nationalist ethics was not peculiar to China, but a running thread in global radical right politics. Extending Benedict Anderson's famous thesis of the modern nation as an "imagined community," Karatani Kojin traces how the nation-state embodied the French revolutionary ideal of fraternity and co-opted romantic discontent with capitalist modernity. Unlike the two other principles driving the French Revolution, liberty and equality, fraternity appealed to intimate and communal feelings instead of rationally held ideological beliefs. More specifically, it evoked affective solidarity beyond one's immediate family, clan and even ethnicity, thus contributing significantly to the rise of nationalism in Europe since the mid-eighteenth century. As a regime of sentiments, fraternity was not inherent to humanity but rather a product of a specific post-Enlightenment moment.[62] The modern origins of fraternity are echoed in Sun's evocation of fraternity/*bo'ai*. Speaking to military officers in

---

[60] Chiu-chun Lee, "From Liberal to Nationalist: Tai Chi-t'ao's Pursuit of a New World Order" (PhD diss., University of Chicago, 1993), 275–6. Celebrated Japanese Sinologist Takeuchi Yoshimi (1910–77) made a similar argument in a sympathetic reading of Dai's career, seeing his rejection of communism in the 1920s not as a simple rightist gesture but as prioritization of the nation over the facile internationalist world revolution as dominated by Moscow. The indigenization (*dochaku-ka*) and nationalization (*minzoku-ka*) of communism under Mao Zedong decades later, Takeuchi curiously argued, were akin to Dai's insistence that China remain master of its own revolutionary course free from undue foreign influences ("Tai Kitô no 'Nihon ron,'" in *Riben lun*, trans. Ichikawa Hiroshi [Tokyo: Shakai shisôsha, 1972], 228–30.)

[61] Dai, *Sun Wen zhuyi*, 29. Dai cited, in paraphrase, from chapter 20 of *The Doctrine of the Mean*. James Legge's translation reads: "To restore families whose line of succession has been broken, and to revive States that have been extinguished; to reduce to order States that are in confusion, and support those which are in peril; … to send [envoys] away after liberal treatment, and welcome their coming with small contributions" (*Chinese Classics*, vol. 1, *Confucius* [New York: John B. Alden, 1883], 136).

[62] Karatani, *Structure of World History*, 212–13.

1921, Sun cited Tang-dynasty essayist-cum-political philosopher Han Yu (768–824) and glossed benevolence (ren) as *bo'ai*, adding that both signified a love for the common instead of the parochial self. He also resorted to Mencius to explain the magnanimity that allowed the legendary sage-king Yu to relate to his people suffering under flood and famine. However, the anti-Manchu activist was quick to add that benevolence/*ren* and fraternity/*bo'ai* must mean something very different to his audience than to past generations of literati. Whereas readers of Mencius and Han Yu lived under an "autocratic state that was the monarch's private property," military officers in modern China served "a republic where [sovereignty] belonged to the entire citizenry."[63] Despite its classical connotations, fraternity was a doctrine for an emerging twentieth-century nation.

Sun's ostensible backward reach for a fraternal economy was a reaction to the social crises attendant to capitalism. As one practical manifestation of *ren*, the *minsheng* principle called on the nation-state to preempt bourgeois class hegemony not by abolishing the private property system but by developing state-owned industries and moderating land prices.[64] Sun and his successors' allusion to Confucian orthodoxy was akin to Romanticist critiques of industrial civilization at its early stage of development in late eighteenth- and nineteenth-century Europe. Since the May Fourth Movement, Confucianism in China had become an intellectual discourse that, mediated through the idealist strain in Western philosophy, prized emotions, feelings and aesthetics as spheres of human existence independent of social production.[65] By themselves, culturalist critiques of modernity were morality-centered and did not take on its structural core. Fraternal solidarity, including socialist derivatives like the Proudhonian ideal of mutual aid, oftentimes existed only in the realm of emotions and imagination. More significantly, the state emerged as the only body that could underwrite the ethics of fraternity and deliver uplift to the national community. Thus, rather than reversing the tide of capitalist modernization, fraternity became institutionalized in the nation-state; it provided aesthetic sublation of social

---

[63] Sun, "Junren jingshen jiaoyu [Spiritual Education for Military Personnel]," *Sun Wen xuanji*, 3:108.

[64] Ibid., 3:112–13.

[65] Wang, *End of the Revolution*, 152–4. Joseph Levenson made a similar remark on the association of Confucianism, stripped of any social meaning, with the authentic spiritual core of the Chinese nation (*Confucian China and Its Modern Fate*, 2:15). The intellectual search for inner spiritual sanctity was also a common thread of elitist nationalist resistance against Western colonial modernity in other Third World societies like India (Partha Chatterjee, *The Nation and Its Fragments: Colonial and Postcolonial Histories* [Princeton, NJ: Princeton University Press, 1993], 6).

contradictions by appealing to communal feelings. Fraternity as constitutive of modern nationalism, Karatani observes, was a core appeal of
counterrevolutionaries such as Louis Bonaparte, Benito Mussolini and
Konoe Fumimaro.[66]

Karatani's insight on fraternity is germane to our understanding of the
GMD's conservative revolution. Dai was keen to stress that benevolence
would triumph over the self-interested individualist ethos that fused
capitalism. Confucian morality was supposed to convert the bourgeoisie
and landlords to the workers and peasants' cause so that only a cross-class
revolution conformed to Sunist thought. National identity (*guomin xing*)
was likened to the munificence inherent to humanity and pitched against
the bestiality of sectarian class affiliations (*jieji xing*).[67] To be sure, belief
in altruistic compassion as an antidote to both capitalist greed and confrontational class politics was not in itself Confucian. Among supporters
of the April 12 coup were Chinese anarchists indebted to the
Proudhonian tradition that Karatani identifies as a Romanticist revolt
against modernity. Like other GMD members, anticommunist Chinese
anarchists saw the national revolution as an ethical project threatened by
the hunger for material power that underscored both capitalism and class
struggle.

Theorizing Revolutionary Vanguardism

For conservative revolutionaries, therefore, the national revolution was
a morally transformative enterprise that harnessed popular energy
against opponents of a new "benevolent" order, particularly Beiyang
warlords and divisive Communists. What remained in question was the
mechanism that governed how the national revolution was to be executed. This brings our attention back to Sun's adopted Leninism and
its relevance in a country where Marxism had become anathema.
The GMD had attracted anarchists since the Revolutionary Alliance
days. At the first party congress in 1924, three anarchists were elected
to the Central Supervisory Committee. The involvement of Li Shizeng,
Wu Zhihui and Zhang Ji in a party increasingly beholden to the Soviet
state-building model belied the recalibration of anarchist priorities
since the May Fourth Movement. While anarchists and Communists
were ostensibly partners in the United Front, the former were vacating
the political left as they reneged on their enthusiasm for social

[66] Karatani, *Structure of World History*, 234–6; Karatani, *History and Repetition* (New York: Columbia University Press, 2012), 17, 23.
[67] Dai, *Sun Wen zhuyi*, 34–6.

revolution. Anarchists had, as Peter Zarrow puts it, "learned the value of order" and come to favor gradual cultural change and moral uplift.[68] They criticized Marxism for its reliance on the state and envisaged fundamental progress taking place within university campuses, domestic household and local councils. Improvements in China's everyday culture, however, required a stable polity that apparently only the GMD could provide.

The thirst for stability stood in tension with anarchists' anti-state impulse but also endeared them to the Nationalist state. The standard Proudhonian vision, which posited a decentralized, local and participatory mode of government, could not be further removed from a one-party state run by professional revolutionaries. Li Shizeng tried to bridge the jarring gap between anarchist ideals and a party-state engaged in violent internal power struggles in his contribution to the GMD's ideological struggle against communism. The Sorbonne biology graduate adopted an evolutionary notion of history and tied Pierre-Joseph Proudhon's notion of human freedom to Sun's *minsheng* revolution, touting both as expressions of the latest stage of civilizational progress. He attacked communism for its economism and statism, the latter Li glossed in French as *statisme* or *etatisme*, and ridiculed dictatorship of the proletariat as a pretext for an authoritarian polity (*zhuanzhi zhengti*) and the Third International as a virulent form of imperialistic overreach. The best antidote to such revolutionary despotism was Proudhonism – class reconciliation (*quanmin zhuyi/reconciliation des classes*), universal harmony (*datong zhuyi/conciliation universelle*), decentralization, anarcho-syndicalism etc. "If what are better and new belong to the left and what are mediocre and old belong to the right," Li quipped, "then it is obvious that Proudhonists are leftists and Marxists rightists."[69] In what might be best described as vivid anticipation of Cold War ideological moralism, Li contextualized the struggle between the Three People's Principles and what he called pseudo-communism as the global final battle between freedom and authoritarianism. He made the observation, twenty years before Hannah Arendt when the horrors of fascism were yet to fully manifest themselves, that Soviet communism and Italian fascism were different in name only.[70] "Should such a gigantic authoritarian country as Soviet Russia have its way and fulfill its ambition of establishing the universal authoritarian state that exists in the minds of a great many

[68] Peter Zarrow, *Anarchism and Chinese Political Culture* (New York: Columbia University Press, 1990), 207. See also Arif Dirlik, *Anarchism in the Chinese Revolution* (Berkeley: University of California Press, 1991).
[69] Li, "Xianjin geming zhi yiyi (yi)," in *Geming yu fan geming*, 3–6.
[70] Li, "Xianjin geming zhi yiyi (er)," in *Geming yu fan geming*, 12–14.

dreamers," Li warned ominously, "the result would be no less disastrous than Shi Huangdi." Recalling to the imagination the maligned first emperor (259–210 BCE) of the Qin dynasty who maintained iron-fisted control over a vast territory by suppressing intellectual activities, a much more powerful twentieth-century Soviet empire, Li declared, could only mean "the end of human freedom."[71] Fear over the specter of a modern Qin empire writ large barely disguised the anarchist desire for a new civilization in which the coercive functions of the state machinery would be safely consigned to the dustbin of history.

All of this would have constituted a cogent and even prescient critique of the failings of Stalinism if Li had not been, at the same time, trying to present the GMD as compatible with the quest for personal freedom, participatory democracy and internationalism. His dubious labeling of the Soviet bureaucracy as the latest installment of Oriental despotism aside, Li's contemporary observation that the disciplinary power of both state socialism and fascism rested in their combination of organizational might and ability to demand unwavering political faith from activists was a tremendous insight.[72] Li was more equivocal, however, when he attempted to establish the link between the GMD's right-wing coup and an anarchist program. He claimed that the GMD, like Proudhon, was conducting a political and social revolution based on the ideal of universal harmony, a program that was historically more advanced than economic revolutions and the simple competition for control over the state machinery. While Sun Yat-sen and his Shanghai-based successors were working to construct a new political and even world order, Soviet Russia was myopically obsessed with class struggle and the usurpation of state power, which Li dismissed as "court revolt" (*gongting geming*).[73]

Having catapulted Sun's *minsheng* revolution into the pantheon of revolutionary politics and evolutionary progress, Li backtracked slightly in his identification of the GMD with what he called the Proudhonian revolution (*Pu pai geming*). Li declared that "China's fourth-order revolution," a more evolved form of activism compared with class, political and court revolutions, "is a revolution for the entire populace (*quanmin geming*) adapted to the complex demands of the situation."[74] Proudhon favored absolute freedom, to which he conceded the GMD was not committed. Yet the strength of the *minsheng* principle lay precisely in its ambiguity, thus allowing the Three People's Principles as a whole to absorb various revolutionary ideas from abroad when circumstances so

[71] Ibid., 12.   [72] Ibid., 12–15, 19n7.   [73] Li, "Xianjin geming zhi yiyi (yi)," 2–4.
[74] Ibid., 6.

required. The catholicity of the Three People's Principles meant it was ultimately compatible with anarchism. More specifically, Li argued that being a revolution for the entire populace – precisely that Sun's expansive notions of nationhood and political right were not contingent on an analysis of class conflicts – the GMD movement was a good enough approximation of Proudhon's *reconciliation des classes*. As Li concluded almost apologetically, "Although there are differences in the nature [of the two political perspectives, they] at least can co-exist, do not contradict each other and are not mutually exclusive. This is totally unlike the despotism (*zhuanheng*) and cruelness (*yanku*) of Marxists and the Communist Party." The affinity between anarchism and the Chiang's GMD derived less from their inherent similarities than their shared irreconcilability with communism, either at the theoretical level or in Bolshevik revolutionary practices.

While Li's attack on Marxist–Leninism displayed unmistakable anarchist suspicion of state tyranny, it afforded the GMD generous benefit of the doubt. Li acknowledged, for example, that detractors had accused Sun of promoting a strong central state, an objective also attributed to the CCP. Federalists like southern warlord Chen Jiongming (1878–1933) and liberals within the GMD complained of the late leader's increasingly top-down approach to maintaining authority within the party and beyond.[75] Citing the *Outline for Nation-Building (Guomin zhengfu jianguo dagang)*, Li argued, however, that Sun and his followers, in particular Dai Jitao, actually called for a form of local government far superior to federalism. In this system, individual self-governing counties would cooperate to form a polity based on mutual aid (*fenzhi hezuo*).[76] To reclaim the elusive anarchist credentials of the GMD, Li even offered to concede that Sun might have preferred a centralized authoritarian state, "just as a family might rely on the parents to maintain unity." He was quick to add, however, that now that the irreplaceable "father" had died, the

---

[75] Fitzgerald, *Awakening China*, 186–9. For an impassioned account of the struggle between the Sunist camp and the federalist agenda embodied by Chen Jiongming, see Leslie H. Chen, *Chen Jiongming and the Federalist Movement: Regional Leadership and Nation Building in Early Republican China* (Ann Arbor: Center for Chinese Studies, University of Michigan, 2000).

[76] Li, "Fenzhi hezuo wenti [The Problem of Cooperative Self-Governance]," in *Geming yu fan geming*, 20. The *Outline for Nation-Building of the Nationalist Government (Guomin zhengfu jianguo dagang)*, which Sun penned in April 1924 shortly after the founding of the GMD–CCP united front, laid the theoretical foundation for an extended period of political tutelage (*xunzheng shiqi*), during which the GMD maintained absolute power over government. Among other things, the document provides for centrally appointed heads of local governments at the provincial and county levels until citizens in individual counties are deemed sufficiently coached in exercising their political rights and ready to elect their own representatives.

"siblings" who constituted the nation had no choice but to take charge of their own affairs and work together in a spontaneous fashion. "Even if Sun did not support federalism before," Li continued convolutedly, "it is wrong to construe that he would oppose cooperative self-governance in his death." Such optimism was not extended to the other side of the political divide. The lone figure within and without the GMD resolutely opposed to local self-governance was one Chen Duxiu, the general secretary of the authoritarian CCP.[77]

By shedding communist impurities, the GMD could set China back to its destined transformation into a participatory polity. Li's labored projection of anarchist desires onto the anticommunist purge ignored how solidly democratic centralism (*minzhu zhuyi de jituan zhidu*) was embedded in Nationalist political culture. The first party congress in 1924 formalized the GMD's alliance with the Communists and the structure to which it aspired. Hu Hanmin explained in clear terms that "a party without proper organization was but an anarchist club, not a vanguard of the people."[78] The 1927 purge resoundingly rejected Marxism, but GMD cadres like Dai and Hu did not intend to abandon vanguardism, the Bolshevik party model that Sun so admired. Not unlike Leninists who complained of left communism, Dai disdained the political dilettantism of anarchists and dismissed their animosity against the state. For Dai, anarchism was an instance of hollow Enlightenment idealism that took no account of conditions on the ground. Dai charged, "Although their sentiments are most beautiful, their ideals lofty and their actions free from bounds, anarchists are always prone to compromises when confronted with the present conjuncture."[79] In the past, he added, those who adopted China's traditional disdain for social discipline and religious negation of reality might have become Daoists and led a secluded life away from humanity. In the twentieth century, one should not be surprised to find such withdrawal syndrome among anarchists in cosmopolitan Shanghai – "connoisseurs of leisure literature (*xiaoxian wenxue*) and enthusiasts of religious ideas among aristocratic playboys."[80] A combination of decadent aestheticism, antisocial religiosity and infantile utopianism was naturally no recipe for a sustainable revolutionary regime. Cavalier libertarianism was a recipe for disaster.

The problem with the national revolution so far, therefore, was that the GMD allowed for too much anarchism, not too little. If it were not for the

[77] Ibid., 21–3.
[78] Zhongguo di'er lishi dang'an guan, *Zhongguo Guomindang diyi, di'er ci quanguo daibiao dahui huiyi shiliao* [*Historical Materials on the First and Second National Congresses of the Guomindang*] ([Nanjing?]: Jiangsu guji chubanshe, 1986), 28.
[79] Dai, *Guomin geming yu Zhongguo Guomindang*, 14.   [80] Ibid., 14–15.

party's failure to rein in its cadres, the Communists would long have been absorbed into one political bloc as Sun envisioned and not become such a headache. For Dai, only a disciplined, ideologically committed vanguard would lead China toward economic modernization, independence from imperialist domination and cultural renaissance. To mobilize the intellectually wanting laboring masses, and more crucially, to ensure they did not insist on their own interests at others' expense, the elite would have to first submit to one doctrine and one central leadership.[81] Dai's prescription for an efficient revolutionary organization was in line with Hu's description of the dialectical relationship between the state and the party in 1924. The party must, Hu explained, strive to exert control over and sideline rival claimants to state power. In places where GMD authority was established, however, it was the state apparatus that must be wielded to whip party cadres in line. The inability of the two organs to take one another to account was a sign that "the party and the state were not one."[82] This sorry situation was to be rectified as the revolutionary coalition aligned party and state as one sleek organization and brought other parts of China under its fold.

Dai definitely had little appetite for a return to the ambiguous ideological identity and lax discipline that characterized the Nationalists in the immediate aftermath of the 1911 Revolution. To him, trench warfare between contradictory viewpoints perverted the party's health. He put the primacy of the Three People's Principles in the scientific and biomedical language popular among intellectuals both within and beyond the GMD. "There is," Dai admonished:

no basis of unity in a political party other than ideology (*zhuyi*). Ideology is the nerve system of a party. Ideology also constitutes the blood veins of a party. Without a nerve system and blood veins, an animal could no longer be an animal. Without ideology, a party could no longer be a party.[83]

The party was an organic entity, a life-form that could be brought to an abrupt end should its core element – ideological discipline – be taken away. We have an opportunity to examine in greater detail the entanglement between physical virility and the health of the social body in anticommunist discourse after the coup in the next chapter. Suffice it to say that Dai, who was under such immense pressure in 1922 when he traveled to Sichuan province to exert Sun's influence over rival regional strongmen, descended into mental disorder and threw himself into the

[81] Mast, "Intellectual Biography of Tai Chi-t'ao," 142.
[82] Zhongguo di'er lishi dang'an guan, *Zhongguo Guomindang diyi, di'er ci quanguo daibiao dahui*, 28.
[83] Dai, *Guomin geming yu Zhongguo Guomindang*, 25.

river. The idea that intraparty ideological bickering was pathological was therefore a deeply felt one for Dai. Both right-wing and left-wing deviations were virulent diseases (*bing*) attacking the body of the party to be cleansed by single-minded devotion to the Three People's Principles. The CCP was anathema not because, as Li suggested, it was despotic but because it resembled too much the disciplined, ideologically whole body that remained elusive for the GMD.[84]

Pursuing his body metaphor further, Dai argued that any organization was exclusive in nature. The existence of a tightly knit Communist caucus was a parasite on the GMD's carcass (*quke*). The admission of Communists into the GMD was like "a large body (*quanti*) enveloping a smaller one." Yet:

as the small body work[s] to organize itself and manifest its exclusivity, the old cells [in the larger body] lose their vitality. Meanwhile, the small body feeds vociferously on the fresh nutrients, making the deformed [larger] body unable to maintain and rejuvenate itself.[85]

Straying from the overall tenor of his treatise, Dai added that he was concerned not with ideological incompatibilities but with a political parasite sucking on the organizational potency of its senior partner from within. In 1925, Dai was making a last-ditch attempt to bring Communists fully under the Nationalist fold and neutralize their ideological identity. He urged them to show unqualified loyalty toward the party, just as members of the clandestine Revolutionary Alliance had worked under a single organization in spite of their varying ideological persuasions.[86] A proper vanguard party could ill afford the space for a bloc within.

The Body/Machine of the Party

The conservative revolutionary vision of the political party combined imageries of the sensual and natural on one hand, and the impersonal and mechanical on the other. We have seen how the economic and the aesthetic were compartmentalized in Dai's reinterpretation of *minsheng*. Whereas economic planning was to be cautiously managed in a rational and technocratic fashion, everyday culture was the realm of dynamism and action. The latter was the site where the revolution provided the masses gratification, cleansed them of unseemly thoughts and made them into self-reliant producers and authority-abiding citizens. These tasks required a political instrument that was distinct from the liberal

[84] Ibid., 1, 30–1.   [85] Ibid., 57–8.   [86] Ibid., 59.

constitutional order the likes of Song Jiaoren desired. Building on Sun's insistence that the revolutionary regime must continue apace after the Nationalist seizure of power, Dai envisioned the party bringing about a superhuman agency by collecting individual dynamism. He began *Nationalist Revolution* with a cryptic, metaphysical account of life that evokes vitalist philosopher Henri Bergson's celebration of creative irrational instincts. "Survival," he mused:

> is simultaneously the original and ultimate goal of human life. Whenever the act of survival is frustrated, the impulse of life (*sheng de chongdong*) brings out in humans a strong lust for survival (*shengcun de yuwang*). Thanks to the differing abilities within humankind and changing milieu of historical time, the lust for survival expresses itself in varying intensity and modes ... These different manifestations of the same lust are self-aggrandizing (*duzhan*) and exclusionary (*paita*) in nature, while possessing at the same time the tendency to unify and dominate ... The actual contents of the lust for survival constitute the enabler and origins of life, the necessary basis on which maintenance of life depends.[87]

Dai located this potent will to life not in individual subjects but in the collective (*tuanti*) that embodied and synthesized the impulses and instincts of human existence. That collective was the party, the reigning ideological orthodoxy of which unified human urges. As ideology was the realization of raw instincts, it required not reason and logic but simple faith (*xinyang*) and devotion (*xinfeng*).[88] The privileging of moral sentiments in Dai's *minsheng* doctrine lent credence to demands on the populace for pious, feverish devotion rather than careful, dispassionate endorsement. The vision of the GMD commandeering irrational but authentic popular emotions was, not unlike those of contemporary fascist movements abroad, a powerful metaphorical rendering of the mobilized masses as a mighty body whose vitality had to be both unleashed and reined in. In the fascist celebration of political violence in interwar France, to take one particularly vivid example, the "bodies" of grand muscular sculptures visualized the larger-than-life icons from ancient Greece.[89]

---

[87] Dai, *Guomin geming yu Zhongguo Guomindang*, i.   [88] Ibid., 2–4.

[89] Mark Antliff, "Classical Violence: Thierry Maulnier, French Fascist Aesthetics and the 1937 Paris World's Fair," *Modernism/modernity* 15 (2008): 55–8. Some Chinese anarchists, informed by Henri Bergson, also romanticized the explosive and unmediated upsurge of mass emotions as ideal revolutionary practice. One example was Zhu Qianzhi (1899–1972), a May Fourth activist who shared with Dai an interest in Buddhism (Tie Xiao, "In the Name of the Masses: Conceptualizations and Representations of the Crowd in Early Twentieth-Century China" [PhD diss., University of Chicago, 2011], chap. 2).

The revolutionary vanguard featured also as a ruthlessly efficient modern machine that rationalized and smoothed out the idiosyncrasies of its functionaries in Dai's formulation. While the comingling of the biological and the mechanical might seem paradoxical, Dai took his cue from Sun's ideal modern society. Sun, a surgeon by training, deployed an entomological analogy to illustrate how the labor process and the reproduction of social relations should operate in an industrializing society. Human community was likened to an ant colony or a beehive, where each individual knew his or her place in the chain of command. A hive is headed by the queen bee but built, maintained and defended by numerous worker bees, just as a nation is ruled by government officials and guarded by soldiers. Honey bees' "natural dispositions" (*tianxing*), purportedly shared by humans, were conducive not only to common defense but also to proper division of labor. Bees meekly "attended to their assigned chores" (*gesi qishi*) – collecting food, making honey, ensuring communal safety – in deference to their queen. Chinese work-ers, likewise, should reach out to peasants and exchange products of their labor instead of exerting exorbitant demands on factory owners.[90] It was workers' bound duty to grease industrial production and the reproduction of the larger social organism.

Dai echoed Sun in arguing that modernity required a tightly knit, standardized structure of top-down administration. "In today's industrial civilization where science is the norm," he observed, "all social organiza-tions operate under the principle by which labor works with a unified purpose but is assigned separately to individual tasks. A party is also a society and it, of course, cannot afford to deviate from this principle."[91] Dai's promise to bring the latest management technologies of the mundane modern factory floor to bear on the organic revolutionary body might sound like a contradiction in terms. Yet the Taylorist doctrine of instrumental rationality is not necessarily antithetical to the political sublimation of the primordial life impulses. Modern political culture, as Zygmunt Bauman observes, is a garden culture. The health, vitality and continuous growth of a society-as-garden require meticulous manage-ment, whereby elements deemed incompatible with the utopia of beauty were brutally and unsentimentally "weeded."[92] A similar notion of society as an organic, corporatist entity underwrote the fascist promise

<hr/>

[90] Sun, "Zhuzhong xuanchuan yi zaocheng qunli [Pay Attention to Propaganda Work and Use It to Harness Social Force]," *Sun Wen xuanji*, 3:367–74.
[91] Dai, *Guomin geming yu Zhongguo Guomindang*, 43–4.
[92] Zygmunt Bauman, *Modernity and the Holocaust* (Ithaca, NY: Cornell University Press, 1989), 92.

to re-inject life into a national body plagued by the illnesses of "mechanistic" communism and liberalism.[93]

Pseudo-biological and scientific vocabulary punctured Chiang Kaishek's writings, underscoring the ideological stake of the 1927 coup. Not satisfied with being "parasitic" (*jisheng*), Chiang complained in an article inaugurating Nanjing as the nation's capital that the Communist Party had penetrated into the Nationalist system (*xitong*) and, like a cicada shedding off its golden shell (*jinchan tuoke*), sought to fully control the GMD party-state. Yet the anticommunist purge was not just about raw power; it stemmed from conservative revolutionaries' fear of flagging and misplaced political fervor. In the same piece that denounced the Communist scheme of turning the GMD's economic uplift efforts into divisive peasant and worker struggles, Chiang urged his compatriots to leave their collective numbness (*mamu*) and actively contribute to the nation's vitality (*shengji*).[94] The April 12 coup was as much about weeding communist influence as it was about stimulating appetite for revolution among conservative Nationalists. Dai, while taking aim at the Communists, was anxious to prevent the purge from becoming a license for the spread of the "rightist disease" (*youqing bing*). For the GMD elder, the Communists' formidable strength within his party contributed considerably to the inertia of Nationalist cadres, which contrasted sharply with the CCP's dynamism. Developments that pervaded the GMD rank and file resembled those confronting revolutionary movements that had become too accustomed to holding the reins of state power and lost interest in attacking the status quo. Addressing elite university students who could soon join the party-state apparatus, Dai chided bureaucrats who monopolized day-to-day functioning of government for not attending to political theories and lacking a proper understanding of the GMD platform. All they knew were narrow managerial chores and a smattering of political slogans that they perfunctorily brandished at mass rallies. Worse still, there were those for whom anticommunism meant a rejection of revolutionary activism itself. These people, who "failed to oppose imperialism, warlordism and bureaucratization, and who refused to join the masses," were pandering to the anticommunism of such hideous counterrevolutionary figures as Manchurian warlord Zhang Zuolin (1875–1928). The distinctions and, indeed, commonalities between communism and the Three People's

---

[93] Mark Neocleous, *Imagining the State* (Maidenhead: Open University Press, 2003), 29.
[94] Chiang Kai-shek, "Jiandu Nanjing gao quanguo tongbao shu [Letter to Compatriots on the Inauguration of Nanjing as the National Capital]," *Xian zongtong Jiang gong sixiang yanlun zongji* (Taipei: Zhongguo Guomindang zhongyang weiyuanhui dangshi weiyuanhui, 1984), 30:35–45.

Principles were naturally beyond the grasp of these foot soldiers of warlords and bureaucrats.[95] For Dai, rightist deviation – the degeneration of the GMD *nomenklatura* – was as virulent a cancer as the malicious Communist caucus on the already fragile body of the mass party.

Here lies a core distinction between the conservative revolutionaries and other anticommunists within and beyond the GMD. Dai's highly ambivalent attitude toward formal political institutions, shared by Hu, no doubt inherited Sun's investment in a party-led mass movement and dissatisfaction with liberal constitutionalism. Dai attacked those who saw changes in the constitutional order of the state as the ultimate goal of political activism. While nationalists obsessed with taking revenge on the Manchus failed to understand the political and cultural innovations necessary for nation-building, those who fetishized representative democracy were also incapable of effecting wider changes in social organization. Dai acknowledged the critical role constitutional monarchists and the late Qing bureaucratic elite played in the Sichuan railway dispute that eventually culminated in the 1911 Revolution. However, their "formalism" (*xingshi zhuyi*) – the wishful idea that "changing the political structure into a constitutional polity and turning the state into a republic alone would lead to prosperity" – disabled them from making further contributions to the revolution once the Qing court was toppled and a Republican parliament was founded.[96] Worse still, parliamentary politics, which cohabitated with the warlord-dominated executive in Beijing, became a playground for corrupt politicians. These politicians, including former anti-Qing revolutionaries who had long lost their sense of ideological purpose, were merrily making compromises with militarists, bureaucrats and social notables from the old order, even as they retained a pathetic sense of superiority as parliamentarians of the Republic.[97] Dai saw a timid GMD party bureaucracy, planted within the civil service and the military, reinforced by political careerists (*zhengke*) too comfortably ensconced in the parliamentary chamber. He had little sympathy for the anticommunists of this new Republican establishment. He noted sarcastically of cadres whose grasp of revolutionary theory was shaky that "if it were not for the admission of the Communists into the GMD, I am afraid these gentlemen would not even remember to feel confused or befuddled."[98]

More than a nihilistic power struggle, party purification was a campaign to remake the lethargic GMD into a dynamic machine and robust body fit for true revolutionary politics. It aimed to cleanse elements

---

[95] Dai, *Qingnian zhi lu* [*The Way for Youth*] (Shanghai: Minzhi shuju, 1928), 61–2. The collection, which appeared after the April 12 coup, was derived from a series of speeches he gave as president of the Guangzhou-based institution.

[96] Dai, *Guomin geming yu Zhongguo Guomindang*, 13–14.   [97] Ibid., 18.   [98] Ibid., 54.

within the revolutionary bloc that mistook acquisition of state power for nation-building. It was simultaneously a full-frontal attack on communist ideologies and an internal insurgency against the GMD *nomenklatura* of which Dai was a part. Such animosity toward bureaucratism anticipated a recurring theme in twentieth-century China, expressed most rigorously by Mao Zedong in the 1960s, that saw a newly entrenched state apparatus lock horns with the revolutionary zeal that was supposed to drive the party. Dai saw within the Communist Party the strength of ideological faith that remained elusive to the GMD.[99] The CCP might be numerically weak, but it compelled its cadres to subscribe firmly to a common platform. If the Communists were just a "ruble party" (*lubu dang*) thirsty for Russian money, Dai quipped, the brute force of dictatorship would be quite enough to eradicate it. But dictatorial violence, which could presumably be more effectively applied to self-serving state bureaucrats who constituted the GMD mainstay than to Communists, could not guarantee a conversion in ideological piety.[100]

To ensure mass devotion to the GMD-led national revolution, the imminent task for Nationalists was to create new social norms and values that permeated everyday culture. The party's influence had to extend beyond political institutions. In a move that again evokes Gramsci's insight on the state's entanglement with civil society, Dai advanced the argument that more than monopolizing the coercive apparatus of state power, winning hegemony in such ideological arenas as religion and aesthetics required specific attention to commanding faith and artistic production.[101] "If we consign party purification only to political power," he warned, "I can say for certain that it would be impossible to achieve a clean sweep (*chedi chengqing*)" against communism.[102] The state had the important task of overseeing the renewal of the nation's culture (*wenhua*), an expansive nexus that incorporated "the people's way of living, society's existence, citizens' economic well-being, and the life of the masses."[103] Dai lamented that Sun Yat-sen's revolutionary coalition failed to play a leadership role in creating a new national popular culture. He complained that most revolutionaries – "stubborn and inadequate" in thinking – refused to support Chinese language reform in 1914, leaving the important task five years later to such nonparty intellectuals as liberal

---

[99] Ibid., 2.   [100] Dai, *Qingnian zhi lu*, 64.
[101] Gramsci described the transition, although never complete under bourgeois capitalist rule, of a modern state identified purely with the coercive dimension of governmental power to one that organized and embodied the collective consciousness of civil society. He noted further that the centrality of cultural planning in sustaining the hegemony of the reigning socioeconomic order distinguished modern secular nation-states from premodern ecclesiastical regimes (*Selections from the Prison Notebooks*, 259, 262–4).
[102] Dai, *Qingnian zhi lu*, 64–5.   [103] Dai, *Sun Wen zhuyi zhi zhexue de jichu*, 40.

Hu Shi (1891–1962) and Communist Chen Duxiu.[104] Without securing hegemony in the cultural sphere, the goal of fashioning a national revolution free from communist inflections would forever be elusive. This was because communism, a more malicious tumor infecting the GMD's nerve system than corruption, was an ideological malaise that wreaked havoc on those lacking piety toward the Three People's Principle. Dai complained that radicalized youths, yet to be fully formed in their sap and vigor (*xueqi weiding*), were dancing to the tune of the CCP as if possessed by evil spirits (*zhong le fengmo*).[105] The strong communist cultural influence on young minds and bodies was particularly worrisome as the future vitality of the national revolution depended ever more on a new generation of committed GMD cadres who were not fixated on securing stable government positions.

Reclaiming the Youthful Masses

In competing with the Communists for revolutionary authority, the GMD simultaneously resisted the routinization of politics that threatened its ability to mobilize and shape the populace. Compared with disciplined and enthusiastic Communists, devotees of parliamentary institutions among Sun Yat-sen's followers appeared inept and anachronistic to the radical young generation. Parliamentarians, along with self-serving party-state functionaries and militarists running the Beiyang regime, were tainted with warlordism and the failure of the early Republican experiment. As was the case in interwar Europe, liberal politics in China was associated with a weak and irrelevant establishment. In Mussolini's Italy, Fascists promised to rejuvenate the nation by replacing an older generation of liberal custodians of the corrupt regime with a youthful, forward-looking party elite. The Fascist elite could then build a new economic and moral order that was simultaneously antisocialist and anti-liberal, putting in place a corporatism that would resist the spread of bourgeois social atomization while retaining the capitalist system.[106] In China, where the liberal tradition was even weaker than in Italy, constitutional democracy was thoroughly implicated in the social chaos, inept foreign policy and reactionary behaviors attributed to the Beiyang warlord regime.

---

[104] Dai, *Guomin geming yu Zhongguo Guomindang*, 46–7.   [105] Ibid., 50.
[106] Ruth Ben-Ghiat, *Fascist Modernities: Italy, 1922–1945* (Berkeley: University of California Press, 2001), 93–8. Intellectuals in other European countries who contributed to fascism, from Carl Schmitt and George Sorel, likewise called for a state that would eliminate both liberal political institutions and rescue capitalist economics from popular democratic interventions and a weak bourgeois class (Ishay Landa, *The Apprentice's Sorcerer: Liberal Tradition and Fascism* [Leiden: Brill, 2010], 173–86, 197–8).

Conservative revolutionaries like Dai had no doubt that the liberal experiment Sun instituted in 1912 had already run its course. Decadent parliamentarians, all "childish old citizens" (*youzhi de lao guomin*), were incapable of providing the rigorous discipline needed of a mass revolutionary party.[107] Constitutionalism was at once puerile and senile, and could hardly compete with communism in energizing idealistic youth.

China's political evolution was likened to an incomplete *bildungsroman*, in which the "old" inertia of parliamentarianism conspired with "youthful" leftist nihilism to suppress the national revolution from fully coming of age. Here again, one sees early echoes of the easily disturbed balance between senile inaction and puerile adventurism that gave rise to recurring debates in China's revolutionary history.[108] In a poignant autobiographical mode, Dai recalled that he and his fellow revolutionaries were once as romantically minded as today's radical youths. Looking back, the adolescent excesses he and his colleagues committed were most regrettable because they enervated an entire generation of revolutionaries and in turn undermined China's rejuvenation enterprise itself. Dai's poor health and the weak spirit of the revolutionary elite were understood to have an actual adverse impact on the nation's strength. Embattled China contrasted sharply with Japan, where the Meiji oligarchs maintained both youthful stamina and mature discipline throughout their long lives. The oligarchs' sound health – many of them remained active into their seventies whereas Dai, at thirty-six, and his peers were already becoming feeble – explained the spectacular success of the Meiji Restoration. He warned of the detriments of frivolous (*erxi*) revolutionary activism and claimed that the chaos resulting from the destruction of China's existing social order could be worse than that of the late Ming period, which concluded with the founding of the "alien" Manchu empire. The crux of GMD anticommunism was to punish debauched (*zongyu*) youths who threatened the moral fabric of society, the licentious playboys who doubled as left-wing activists.[109] Young Chinese Communists embraced "the hedonism that resulted from nihilist philosophy popular in Russia some seventy or eighty years ago and the permissive ambience in cosmopolitan cities."[110] Dai's ideal revolutionary youth was someone like mining engineer Chen Lifu, who was prompted to join the party in 1925 not by any dilettantish fantasy but by his fervent

[107] Dai, *Guomin geming yu Zhongguo Guomindang*, 45.
[108] For investment in "new youth" as a revolutionary subject in the New Culture Movement and the inherent tensions between transgression and discipline, see Mingwei Song, *Young China: National Rejuvenation and the Bildungsroman, 1900–1959* (Cambridge, MA: Harvard University Asia Center, 2015), chap. 3.
[109] Dai, *Qingnian zhi lu*, vi–x.   [110] Dai, *Dai Jitao zuijin yanlun*, 14.

commitment to industrial modernity – the railways, highways, coastal ports and industrial enterprises promised in Sun's nation-building blueprint.[111] Only when both bureaucratic inertia and juvenile indiscipline were fully purged could the GMD get on with the strenuous work of modernizing China.

China's future lay with the awakened masses who exuded youthful *élan* but fully submitted themselves to the rigor of modern production. Workers and peasants were to be the new subject of the revolutionary process, not military officers, entrepreneurs or liberal politicians. Adopting strong populist language, Dai accused the right of failing to recognize that workers and peasants' well-being was the core of the quest for national liberation. He declared that like all modern revolutions, the Chinese revolution was one in which the peasants and proletariat, aroused from their collective stupor, strived to reclaim their own fate. The Republican establishment, on the other hand, was no better than a crop of self-serving officeholders, corrupt magistrates and exploitative factory managers who failed to keep up with the demands of the post-Manchu situation. They were middle-aged men who missed party branch meetings and alienated young intellectuals and activists.[112] The failure of the GMD machine to inspire and mobilize youths gave those with ulterior motives an opportunity to pursue their own selfish agenda. Alluding to the Communist penchant for class struggle, Dai chided those who reaped political benefits by engaging youths and the masses in destructive political campaigns.[113] Indeed, the youth often stood in for the entire masses (*minzhong*), whose lack of education and political training presented the greatest challenge for the nation's self-anointed custodian. The working class and the peasantry were, like impulsive but idealistic youths, crucial for the national revolution but must first be checked in case they began to organize themselves.

Thus, even as the laboring masses were supposed to form the prime agent of national revolution, they were subsumed under a nebulous community of life (*gongtong shenghuo*).[114] While Dai acknowledged that modern revolution was unthinkable without the working class, capitalist social relations – wage labor and surplus value – were the norm in the industrialized West only.[115] In China, labor (*gongzuo*) for Dai was a transhistorical, inherent human ability to transform nature to satisfy human's material and spiritual needs. It was embedded in reciprocal moral relationships (*lunchang*) that had underpinned society and state

[111] Chen, *The Storm Clouds Clear over China*, 18.
[112] Dai, *Guomin geming yu Zhongguo Guomindang*, 36–43.   [113] Dai, *Qingnian zhi lu*, ii.
[114] Dai, *Sun Wen zhuyi zhi zhexue de jichu*, 40.
[115] Dai, *Guomin geming yu Zhongguo Guomindang*, 8–9.

since antiquity. Conceding that the class identities of both the fledging bourgeoisie and the urban proletariat were sharpened by the growth of Chinese-owned modern industries during the May Fourth Movement, Dai insisted nonetheless that industrial development and capitalism in China were still in their nascent stage. He argued further that there were no inherent contradictions between the interests of China's small bour-geoisie and the goals of national revolution, thus rejecting any program aimed at liquidating the capitalist class. Indeed, he attributed the hostility of a small section of the national bourgeoisie toward the revolution to imperialist treachery and "unrealistic" Communist demands.[116] Chiang echoed this view speaking at the Shanghai Chamber of Commerce in July 1927, arguing that what China needed was an economy free from imperialist, not capitalist, exploitation. He told his audience that "all of you knew full well that you were merchants (*shangren*), not capi-talists (*ziben jia*)." The Chinese revolution was a political one, i.e., with national independence as its goal, not socioeconomic.[117]

With class struggle delegitimized as an option and industrial develop-ment held as the key to revolutionary success, the Communist mobiliza-tion of the working masses was deemed counterproductive and self-serving. Dai criticized the CCP for its instrumentalist relationship with the masses, in which the people were nonchalantly sacrificed for its sole benefit. Truly symbiotic working-class politics would see the party van-guard pursue the "real interests" of the masses and re-channel their ignorant impulses. For example, if workers wanted to call a strike, vision-ary union leaders would discern the heavy price that such action could entail and persuade their less knowledgeable compatriots to hold off on such a destructive campaign. Rather than riding on the tide of sponta-neous workers' action, top union officials must resist "dangerous mob psychology" (*weixian de qunzhong xinli*) and exert authority over the masses. All revolutionary organization and propaganda were to tie the party-led mass movement (*qunzhong yundong*) under the sole aim of safeguarding the national collective. Workers, businesspeople and intel-lectuals were, Chiang exhorted, to set sectarian interests aside and con-tribute to the "enterprise of development" (*jianshe de gongzuo*).[118] Socioeconomic struggle led by workers had no place in the post-purge revolutionary vision.

---

[116] Dai, *Sun Wen zhuyi zhi zhexue de jichu*, 19–20, 39–40.
[117] Chiang, "Guomin geming yu jingji de guanxi [The Relationship between the National Revolution and the Economy]," *Xian zongtong Jiang gong sixiang yanlun zongji*, 10: 274–7.
[118] Dai, *Qingnian zhi lu*, 139; Chiang, "Jiandu Nanjing gao quanguo tongbao shu," 39.

Class politics under the GMD was conceived to prohibit workers, peasants and sympathetic intellectuals from taking matters into their own hands. Despite his occasional nods to Marxist language, Dai's ultimate concern was not to give organized expression to the inchoate instincts of the proletariat and peasantry as political subjects in their own right. Capitalism was to be surgically "aborted."[119] Economic management drew from mass impulses, but experts must be in the driver's seat. In a way that recalls Sun Yat-sen's views on labor in the early 1920s, Dai subsumed working-class activism under the vision of a national society unified in a common struggle against foreign domination. The GMD's politics of class did not allow for class conflicts.[120] Quoting from Sun's 1919 treatise on psychological reconstruction, Dai credited the late revolutionary's privileging of direct action over deep knowledge as the key to harnessing the power of the ignorant and heteronomous populace. Like architecture in which division of labor dictated that construction workers dutifully take heed of the technical intelligentsia, future political campaigns would not see a meeting of minds between activists – a strategy proved inconsequential in the 1913 Second Revolution as most GMD parliamentarians refused to rally behind Sun in his military insurrection against Yuan Shikai. Instead, humble masses would faithfully execute directives from the messianic party leadership. For a populace stuck in their intellectual stupor, it was far easier to blindly perform the revolution than to make full sense of its theoretical basis. Even if Sun's intellectual breakthroughs remained forever elusive for the party's clueless rank and file, they could just play cogs in the wheels of the revolutionary machine. Those who possessed intellect (*zhi*) should of course lead the task of implementing the GMD program. Those who did not have the intellect must still join the action (*xing*).[121]

Such celebration of the working class while denying the need for class struggle differentiated Dai from Marxist revolutionaries. For Lenin, up-and-coming Chinese Communist organizer Mao Zedong and Italian contemporary Gramsci, the party's pedagogical and agitational capabilities were wielded to interpellate a coherent, organized political subject out of the agricultural and urban masses. The goal of national liberation movements was to make the subalterns aware of the totality of social structure and their critical role in the creation of a new political and economic order. Whether through representation by the party or a more dialectical process between cadres and social experiences, the subalterns

[119] Dai, *Sun Wen zhuyi zhi zhexue de jichu*, 19.
[120] Tsin, *Nation, Governance and Modernity in China*, 81–2.
[121] Dai, *Sun Wen zhuyi zhi zhexue de jichu*, 4–5.

were placed on the center stage of the socialist revolution.[122] For the GMD, on the other hand, inadequate political consciousness among the populace was accepted ontologically as a symptom of national weakness. To liberate the masses from the nation's plight, the subalterns had to submit themselves to the dictates of an enlightened elite, the gifted minority who possessed the intellect to set themselves apart from the rest. Whereas communism promised to place workers and peasants in the revolutionary vanguard, conservative revolutionaries envisioned them as humble underlings of the party leadership.

Victory for the Conservative Revolutionaries

At the most fundamental level, one thread tied the ideological eclecticism of Hu Hanmin, Li Shizeng and Dai Jitao – an unwillingness to pursue social revolution. While the April 1927 coup brutally clamped down on the Communist workers' movement, its champions called for benevolence and cooperation among classes with unequal access to power and wealth. In their quest to neutralize the CCP's claim to the revolutionary high ground, conservative revolutionaries held ever more jealously to the party's stewardship over mass politics. Reacting against the revolutionary fatigue of the apparatchiks and committed to suppressing proletarian political subjectivity, they were united in the desire for an anticommunist, nationalist activism. The goal was to craft a path to industrial modernity for a nation-state struggling to reclaim its sovereignty from capitalist imperialism while resisting fundamental changes to nascent capitalist social relations. This contradictory attitude toward handling China's predicament was itself a defining element of this revolutionary identity.

Nationalists vowed to bring the revolution forward. Whether in the form of Dai's state capitalism or Li's anarcho-syndicalism, conservative revolutionaries shared with their left-wing nemeses an impatience with institutional procedures and preference for concrete action. The GMD encouraged mass participation but, unlike Communists, allowed no challenges to the structure of socio-economic power. Nationalists celebrated the virile energy of the masses, but were alarmed that the latter could join the radical left. They acknowledged workers' political potential, but were quick to marginalize class as the basis of political action by placing it under a strictly cross-class national framework. While

---

[122] For similarities and differences between the three Marxist revolutionaries, see Arif Dirlik, "The Predicament of Marxist Revolutionary Consciousness: Mao Zedong, Antonio Gramsci and the Reformulation of Marxist Revolutionary Theory," *Modern China* 9 (1983): 205–7.

uncomfortable with social anomie and the ideological lethargy of government officials, the national revolution tasked the state to consolidate the modern capitalist economy that underpinned cultural commodification and bureaucratism. The ideal result of the GMD's approach to global capitalism and its communist alternative would see the state mediated between a bourgeoisie answering to the nation's developmentalist goals and workers and peasants content with their subservient roles.

Out of party purification emerged a political ethics that claimed to transcend the liberal capitalist pursuit of self-interest and the economism of Marxist materialism. The *minsheng* principle laid claim to superiority as an all-round philosophy that enjoined the people to pursue both economic welfare and spiritual fullness as members of the Chinese national community. In practice, the Nationalist state undertook aesthetic tinkering of quotidian phenomena while leaving structural production relations untouched. It strived to disarm the political demands of the laboring masses and reduce them to problems of aesthetics and mentalities. Labor in China, as Dai would have it, had since antiquity belonged to the realm of culture and had little to do with interactions between workers and capitalists. Social alienation, urban worker militancy and political inertia were attributed to the lack of a refined and civic-minded communal lifestyle among the masses. Communism was branded as a symptom of mental derangement and physical perversion that threatened the nation like a plague. The youth, whom GMD leaders most wanted to reclaim for the national revolution, were particularly targeted by state-sponsored mobilization campaigns. These initiatives, as we see in the next two chapters, offered opportunities for the populace to take part in social movements while containing their political ambitions within the state's confines. The minutiae of everyday experience – what individuals consumed, how they spent their time, their behaviors in public and at home – took the place of social structures as prized objects of revolutionary realigning. Schoolchildren joined scouting and learned to perfect their bodies and minds, pledging obedience to authority and readying themselves for a life of docile production. The war of resistance against Japan presented an opportunity for the entire populace to be molded into one laboring body bound by pious devotion to the nation-state. Yet even as the GMD defined the ultimate goal of the national revolution in the language of spiritual rejuvenation, the very concrete political imperative of suppressing Communism always featured prominently on the conservative revolutionary agenda.

3 The Masses
A Youth Movement for the Conservative Revolution

After the party purification movement in April 1927, the conservative revolutionary vision was no longer an internal insurgency against party inertia and tolerance for communism. It became the *raison d'être* of the Nationalist state. Yet GMD leaders in Nanjing could take little comfort in their command over the national revolution. Chiang Kai-shek warned members of the Central Executive Committee in February 1928 that even though the Nationalist Party had excommunicated Chinese Communists, it "inherited their theory." The purge, the Nationalist leader put in a typical biological metaphor, "merely brought relief to the skin while the vitals (*gaohuang*) were increasingly jeopardized." Of particular concern for Chiang were organizations that engaged with workers, peasants, students and merchants. Communist agents could still be lurking under-cover in these bodies, preying on naïve cadres and inciting citizens to subvert the new establishment. Mass politics, instead of contributing to economic development, remained potentially insurrectionary.[1] For the moment, political violence put down enemies, both external and internal, but a sustainable order over which conservative revolutionaries could exercise hegemony was nowhere in sight.

As far as winning over hearts and minds was concerned, Chiang and his allies' authority was being challenged by both Communists from without the GMD and Wang Jingwei's so-called left faction from within. Warlords continued to run various provinces, although these military strongmen were less adept than Chiang's ideological foes at mobilizing the masses. Wang, whose Wuhan-based government had held on to the alliance with Chinese Communists until the summer of 1927, led an institutionalized clique that competed with Chiang for legitimacy and control.[2] Wang too

---

[1] Chiang Kai-shek, *Jiang Zhongzheng zongtong dang'an: shilüe gaoben* [*Chiang Kai-shek Collections: The Chronological Events*] (Xindian, Taipei County: Academia Historica, 2003–13), 2:316–18.

[2] Treatments of the Wang Jingwei faction include Wai-chor So, *The Kuomintang Left in the National Revolution, 1924–1931* (Hong Kong: Oxford University Press, 1991) and the more recent Zanasi, *Saving the Nation*.

shared with Chiang and Dai deep uneasiness about the continuing influence of communism on the polity. He warned in late 1927 that the CCP
was re-coalescing as an embryo hidden beneath a GMD shell, waiting to be
hatched when the national revolution came to fruition. Communist ideas,
in addition, still enjoyed currency among the masses, particularly in organizations catering to peasants, workers, merchants and students.[3]
Cleansing ideological deviance among the populace, not the political
class, was crucial to the continued hegemony for the right kind of revolutionaries. Sun's partnership with Communists bequeathed to the GMD
a double-edged sword. On one hand, cadres had already acquired experience organizing different social constituents. On the other hand, as leaders
came to realize, mass political demands could cause headaches for the
revolutionary elite. Workers, for example, could be cynically manipulated
to take control of factories, even though the CCP should have known that
similar experiments in Italy and the Soviet Union ended in failure.[4]
The masses represented a potent but unpredictable force that could both
fuse and derail the Nationalist project.

The key challenge for conservative revolutionaries, then, particularly in
urban centers like Shanghai and Guangzhou where social activism was
concentrated, was to tame student and labor militancy without alienating
nationalist sentiments that bolstered Nanjing's quest to bring the entire
nation under its control. The new regime had to sustain and discipline
urban youths' *élan* while channeling it to activities that reinforced the
social order and beautified communal life. In the days leading up to
the April 12 coup, Chiang's functionaries acted to develop alternatives
to the Communist-dominated GMD-affiliated student movement and its
equivalents for peasants and workers. Radical right figures determined to
exterminate their political enemies took a leaf out of what Chen Lifu
(1900–2001), then Chiang's secretary, recalled as a "favorite trick of the
Communists" – forming clandestine party cells within students' and labor
unions to influence and eventually take over larger organizations.[5]
The aggressive mobilization of young citizens seemed to have petered
out as soon as the Nanjing regime consolidated power over its rivals to the
left. Emphasis was directed back to frustrating Communist infiltration
into these same organizations.

At the core of the state-engineered transition from agitational to colla-
borative mass politics was to change the way it functioned at the everyday
level. Huang Jianli suggests that the consensus within the GMD

---

[3] Wang Jingwei, "Fen-Gong yihou [After Separating with Communists]," in *Geming yu fan geming*, 576–8.
[4] Ibid., 246.   [5] Chen, *Storm Clouds Clear over China*, 58.

mainstream by the end of 1927 was to confine young people to the class-room. The party-state demobilized inter-school student unions, substi-tuting them with self-governing associations (*zizhi hui*) based at individual campuses and barring them from participating in school administration.[6] Tapping into the all-powerful but fickle energy of young urbanites was a formidable task for senior Nationalists, who were not favorably disposed to students' judgment. Young people, as the previous chapter demonstrates, were seen as politically unreliable, intel-lectually naïve, emotionally unstable and waiting to be exploited and sacrificed by unscrupulous politicians. Even as Dai Jitao celebrated youthful spirit as a regenerative mechanism for the Nationalist move-ment, it must be institutionally and spatially conscribed. Mass politics under the United Front, Dai reminisced in his first major collection of essays following the 1927 coup, was a disaster. *The Way for Youth* (*Qingnian zhi lu*) depicted a society where government authority lapsed and mob justice reigned supreme. Student unions meted out punishment with impunity by "bundling and parading teenagers on the streets." The Nationalists were supposed to be in command, but law and order were nonexistent as revolutionaries "talked revolution, reforming (*gaizao*) politics, fighting for people's interests and organizing the masses day in and day out" without getting down to concrete state-building tasks.[7] Revolution under Communist influence, Wang Jingwei added, became a pretext for students to excuse themselves from studying as the intelligentsia fell foul of fashionable theories. Instead of "bringing down" (*dadao*) enemies, the national revolution must adopt "building up" (*jianshe qilai*) as its new slogan.[8]

It was imperative on the Nationalist state to haul young people back to the classroom, the factory floor and the field. The conservative revolution's main tenet was to refocus popular enthusiasm on development. The GMD's mobilization of youth, and mass politics in general, was exemplified by the scouting movement, which Dai managed as its vice president. Scouting offered a means to contain and ritualize youth activism, domesticating disruptive street politics into a lifestyle of obedience and voluntarism. It also brought the locus of solidarity from class to the nation. Introduced during the earliest days of Republican China as a new means to engage youngsters, scout troops quickly spread across missionary and secular schools in treaty ports such as Guangzhou, Shanghai, Ningbo, Wuhan and Nanjing. Despite the association of scouting with the British

---

[6] Huang Jianli, *The Politics of Depoliticization in Republican China: Guomindang Policy towards Student Political Activism* (Bern: Peter Lang, 1996), 182.

[7] Dai Jitao, *Qingnian zhi lu* [*The Way for Youth*] (Shanghai: Minzhi shuju, 1928), 144–5.

[8] Wang, "Fen-Gong yihou," 587–8.

Empire and Western presence in China, the GMD set up its own scout troops in 1926 and unified all scouting organizations in the country under one national body in 1927. While intensifying control over the leadership and curriculum of the scouting movement, the GMD absorbed rather than replaced the personnel and international network of the former civic organizations. Until it was subsumed under the Three People's Youth Corps in 1940, the GMD resisted turning the Scouts of China into a full-fledged youth wing of the party.

In its training methods, ideological contents and aesthetic manifestations, scouting exhibited two modes of molding mass society. First, it served to build individual character and instill civic consciousness that was removed from insurrectionary politics. The movement was part of an everyday culture that promoted submission to authority over political dissent, technical knowhow over bookish contemplation and obligatory happiness over discontent. Its nonconfrontational nature was prized by the Nationalists and the liberal-leaning, urban educators who valued order, self-development and apolitical voluntarism. Second, scouting also made room for cultivating a militant spirit fit for the national revolution's future vanguard. Tensions were built into youth mobilization under the GMD, but, at a fundamental level, the two occasional conflicting approaches to mass engagement complemented one another as the new state attempted to win consent among upwardly mobile urban dwellers while preserving its propensity for action as a disciplined movement. Scouting answered Nationalist leaders' priority of bringing students, along with the rest of the masses, back to productive labor. As Chiang Kai-shek made clear, mass movements under the GMD must replace nihilistic destruction under the United Front with attention to economic considerations, educational value and actual benefits (*shiji liyi*) to the national community.[9]

Mass Organizations and Chiang Kai-shek's GMD

Traditionally, the GMD has been cast as a reluctant player in mass politics. Historians point to an in-built ambiguity that had underscored the party's relationship with the people since the May Fourth Movement. Party leaders since Sun Yat-sen had wanted to capitalize on popular fervor, but could never bring themselves to fully endorse it, particularly when the loyalty of students' and other mass organizations was far from guaranteed.[10] Indeed, party leaders demonstrated a clear disinclination

---

[9] Chiang, *Jiang Zhongzheng zongtong dang'an*, 2:325.
[10] Huang, *Politics of Depoliticization*, 188–92; Lu Fang-shang, *Cong xuesheng yundong dao yundong xuesheng: Minguo ba nian zhi shiba nian* [*From Student Movements to Mobilizing*

toward students' participation in national politics after 1927. Nationwide, students' unions were dissolved by Dai Jitao and University Council (*Daxue yuan*) president Cai Yuanpei (1868–1940), and students' role in mass movements was severely limited and defined by individual school authorities. Like most ruling parties, the GMD right was less eager to engage the people directly in the political process after it secured state power. To the contrary, it tried assiduously to suppress protests organized by both workers and capitalists, lest industrial productivity be affected.[11] Arif Dirlik suggests, however, that the GMD's failure to embrace the masses was indicative of not just incumbency but also a deeper dilemma that plagued the party's revolutionary ideology. He argues that some party leaders, including Wang Jingwei, had as late as 1930 hoped that the GMD could maintain an active mass policy to distinguish the party from the burgeoning bureaucratic infrastructure. Yet even cadres who appreciated the need to sustain grassroots enthusiasm feared that it could embolden "particularistic" demands and threaten interclass unity, putatively the prime objective of the *minsheng* program.[12] In sharp contrast to communist and fascist parties abroad, which identified strongly with politicized youths, the impulse of the conservative GMD leadership was to tame mass enthusiasm, including that of party loyalists.[13]

The portrayal of the post-1927 GMD as a cautious, ossified establishment estranged from the populace obscures the ways in which the regime continued to engage the masses, harnessing, cultivating and disciplining youth activism after the end of party purification. After all, a core priority of conservative revolutionaries like Dai Jitao was precisely to cleanse bureaucratic inertia and assert the party as a popular political force.

Students in China, 1919–29] (Taipei: Institute of Modern History, Academia Sinica, 1994), 395–417.

[11] Wang Qisheng, *Dangyuan, dangquan yu dangzheng: 1924–1949 nian Zhongguo Guomindang de zuzhi xingtai* [*Party Cadres, Power and Conflict: The Guomindang's Organizational Patterns, 1924–1949*] (Shanghai: Shanghai shudian chubanshe, 2003), 144–5. For standard accounts of how the GMD distanced itself from both capitalists and workers and balanced their competing class interests, see Parks M. Coble Jr., *The Shanghai Capitalists and the Nationalist Government, 1927–1937* (Cambridge, MA: Council on East Asian Studies, Harvard University, 1980), and Fewsmith, *Party, State and Local Elites in Republican China.*

[12] Arif Dirlik, "Mass Movements and the Left Kuomintang," *Modern China* 1 (1975): 64–72.

[13] Chiang quickly grew disillusioned with the Lixingshe, a secret organization inaugurated by the Leader himself in February 1932. Chiang's former pupils at the Whampoa Military Academy who staffed the clique and its front groups were faulted for their naiveté, sectarian zeal and high ego (Wakeman, *Spymaster*, 79; Lincoln Li, *Student Nationalism in China, 1924–1949* [Albany: State University of New York Press, 1994], 73–4).

Admittedly, the GMD did not have the equivalent of the paramilitary, ideologically driven Hitler Youth that prepared future National Socialist cadres, but tapping into mass energy in overtly political campaigns was not necessarily the norm among radical right-wing movements in the interwar period, particularly after they came to power. Worker and youth organizations in Fascist Italy, even as they became integral parts of Mussolini's party-state, were primarily engaged in managing recreational programs like sports, mass outings and widening access to such commercial entertainments as theater and radio. Grouped according to sex, age and activity, Fascist associations were, as Victoria De Grazia aptly suggests, truly *mass* organizations set up to counter class-based political consciousness. Instead of developing campaigns that prized strong partisan commitments, Italian Fascists' outreach to the people emphasized the subtle neutralization of antagonistic popular demands by embedding an elaborate network of social services and leisure-time management initiatives in the everyday life of the masses. By channeling citizens' expectations to focus on individual consumption, the Fascist establishment worked to avoid class tensions from coalescing into proletarian agitations for changes in social relations. The Italian fascist state co-opted local networks, the Roman Catholic Church and, most significantly, an emerging consumer market to organize consent for a corporatist economic order.[14]

The concept of consent facilitates a reexamination of GMD youth mobilization strategy, for it focuses attention beyond institutions like students' unions, paramilitary organizations and party-affiliated secret societies. Consent, as De Grazia borrows from Gramsci, emphasizes the subtle and often unarticulated dispositions in popular consciousness that lend legitimacy to the ruling bloc. It evokes Dai's insight that a revolution in people's livelihood must deliver a new national popular culture that infuses public and private life, from a modernized common language to affordable drama performances. Cultural and ideological maneuvers that apparently had no significant political bearing were in fact critical in sustaining state hegemony and diverting popular quest for participation in the polity to nonthreatening modes of activism. By realizing how quotidian experience was integral to the efficacy of social orders, we begin to unveil the ideological mechanism that allowed a new conservative revolutionary regime to transition from a revolutionary movement that mobilized cadres for the seizure of state power to a dynamic order that organized active consent from

---

[14] Victoria De Grazia, *The Culture of Consent: Mass Organization of Culture in Fascist Italy* (New York: Cambridge University Press, 1981), 14–16, 33–44.

a much broader constituency.[15] The state's interface with society necessarily had to expand beyond strictly political activists to encompass a vast array of communities and networks.

The quest for consent did not mean GMD gave up using violence to suppress political dissent. As Dai realized, however, dictatorial power alone could not produce ideological loyalty among the governed. Triumph in internecine rivalries among political activists must be translated into popular, enduring assumptions and routines that lent credence to sociopolitical arrangements. The challenge was not simply to eliminate communist propaganda and incitement of mass protests. The very structure of national life had to be recalibrated from the ground up. Chiang Kai-shek implored in Beiping in mid-1928, long before the New Life Movement, that each of the four billion Chinese citizens must keep time, abide by discipline and unify thoughts (*tongyi sixiang*) under the Three People's Principles. Taylorizing citizens' quotidian deportment – attending meetings on time, completing tasks promptly, not whiling away hours on card games and small talk – was the sure antidote to Communist-inspired strikes, class boycotts and talk on personal freedom.[16] Given that the national salvation rested on how individuals managed their own lives, the Nationalist state took active steps to study and structure the political, spiritual and occupational experiences of its citizenry. A national census was launched in July 1928 that, in its pursuit for precision and details, reflected the regime's "new hunger for meticulous information about the social habits, body, and life of each individual." This ambitious undertaking was followed by regular campaigns against what authorities considered superstitious beliefs and practices.[17] In order to pioneer a modern secular culture, the GMD laid claim to the New Culture ideal of the nuclear family, tapping into the juridical, symbolic and widespread sentimental investment in an emerging institution associated with the urban petit-bourgeoisie.[18] Young women were to "cultivate peaceful, kindly and wholesome maternal instinct." Schools became spaces where a new form of social existence, particularly womanhood, and hence

[15] Mabel Bezerin, *Making the Fascist Self: The Political Culture of Interwar Italy* (Ithaca, NY: Cornell University Press, 1997), 13–14.

[16] Chiang, "Zhongguo jianshe zhi tujing [The Way to Develop China]," *Xian zongtong Jiang gong sixiang yanlun zongji*, 10:324–6. By terming the campaign an exercise in Taylorized modernity, Maggie Clinton aptly homes in on the emphasis on efficiency, cutting waste and factory floor discipline that characterized the New Life Movement (*Revolutionary Nativism*, chap. 4).

[17] Tong Lam, *A Passion for Facts: Social Surveys and the Construction of the Chinese Nation-State, 1900–1949* (Berkeley: University of California Press, 2011), 127–9.

[18] Susan Glosser, *Chinese Visions of Family and State, 1915–1953* (Berkeley: University of California Press, 2003), 78–9, 86, 132.

a virile nation were nurtured. Girls were to be separated from boys to put an end to "shared life between the two sexes that encouraged selfish dilettantism, inflamed sensual pleasure, and jeopardized the race."[19] During the New Life Movement, the state further seized on film, literature, sensational media events and urban planning to craft a new paradigm in moral activism.[20]

Conservative revolutionaries, therefore, concerned themselves not only with the political loyalties of the populace. More fundamentally, they sought to reorganize the ways in which young Chinese labored, studied, relaxed and experienced intimacy. Scouting was enlisted by the GMD to cultivate mass consent from before the April 12 coup, through the New Life Movement, and right up to the Second Sino–Japanese War and beyond. It was one vessel with which the revolution became integral to the work and leisure regime of the masses, albeit limited in penetration into rural areas, as Nationalist rule was being consolidated. Mass vitality, Dai stressed, must have "solid basis in everyday living" (jianshi de shenghuo jichu). The masses must lead decent lives if they, like a well-supplied military, were to add fighting prowess to the national revolution. Unlike formal armed forces, which the state funded, civilians had to fend for themselves. Mass movements must stop struggles (douzheng) that disrupted the people's livelihood and focus on building the national economy.[21] Instead of simply withdrawing itself from the masses, the party-state deployed more subtle tools to motivate popular sentiments as it pressed ahead with campaigns against the Communist challenge and more protean threats like modern consumerism, unhygienic customs and tardiness. The stake of rectifying young people's character, hardened as it was by three years of political adventurism and moral degradation, was high; the nation's lifeblood (minggen) was on the line.[22] Wayward youths – attracted to voguish ideas, lifestyles and goods on offer in cities and even abroad – embodied both political dissent and moral breakdown, posing a grave threat to the body politic. Youth deviance and ideological defection, in this sense, were two faces of the same challenge to conservative revolutionary hegemony.

---

[19] Dai, "Weichi jiaoyu jiuji qingnian an [Proposal for Furthering Education and Bringing Salvation to Youths]," DJTXSWC, 430–1.
[20] Lean, Public Passions, 155–8; Federica Ferlanti, "City-Building, New Life and the 'Making of Citizen' in 1930s Nanchang," in New Narratives of Urban Space in Republican Chinese Cities: Emerging Social, Legal and Governance Orders, eds. Billy K. L. So and Madeleine Zelin (Leiden: Brill, 2013), 59–63; Liu, Xin de bianyi, chap. 7. Liu observes that GMD cadres and even left-wing intellectuals in the 1930s shared with German national socialists an idealist investment in the irrational collective will.
[21] Dai, Qingnian zhilu, 140–1.   [22] Ibid., 1–2.

Youth Problem

The previous chapter has delved into the ambivalence conservative revolutionaries attached to youth as a metaphor of the masses. Youthful *élan*, while necessary for the national revolution, could easily become a grave threat as Communists took advantage of impressionable activists. Worse still, subversive ideology was inseparable from a cosmopolitan, urban intemperance that inflamed juvenile rejection of authority and traditions. Taking youth as what literary scholar Kristin Ross calls a "hypostatic sociological category," conservative revolutionaries considered attachment to unorthodox ideologies less as conscious political defiance as abnormal behaviors due to tender age and wayward hormones.[23] In an article first published in the GMD journal *Central Bi-monthly* (*Zhongyang ban yuekan*), Hu Hanmin attempted a socio-psychological exploration into the allure of left-wing activism. He began this long article by pointing out that young Chinese were in a collective state of depression (*fanmen*). "Youths are at their most intense stage of physiological development. Their sap is full, muscles plump, mind nimble. Physiological growth opens them constantly to various impulses (*chongdong*), which are directionless, harmless and unavoidable." Paralleling these physical changes was an outburst of desires – mainly the lust for knowledge, sex, possession and control – which could not be properly fulfilled in a China where "old society had yet to be reformed." Mass politics provided an opportunity for youths to vent their frustration. But rather than carefully managing the desires of the youthful masses, the CCP let them run amok. It proposed a flawed revolutionary formula to impressionable youths, created a youth wing for vainglorious activists seeking leadership positions and encouraged self-serving cadres to amass a fortune by exploiting their positions in peasants' associations and labor unions.

Communism for Hu was a cocktail of toxic drugs, sexual permissiveness and foreign ideas that inflamed lusts (*zongyu*) to the detriment of individuals who had yet to attain maturity. It provided the exact opposite of "beautiful and elegant enjoyment," new elements to Dai's definition of the *minsheng* principle, and its anti-traditionalism was an affront to national cohesion. Echoing Hu's fear that youthful desires were running wild, Dai too saw taming puerile impulses as central to post-coup youth mobilization. Continuing with his creative interpretation of Sunism since 1925, *The Way of Youth* argued that the *minsheng* program had clear moral messages. Sun's policy of equalization of land, brought to bear on private behaviors (*siren xingwei*), called on citizens to be hardworking and ready

---

[23] Kristin Ross, *May '68 and Its Afterlives* (Chicago: University of Chicago Press, 2002), 206.

to sacrifice personal interests for the common good. Regulation of capital entailed regulating desires (*jiezhi yuwang*) – what one ate and drank and "particularly relationships between men and women" – in order to maintain a healthy lifestyle.[24] Hu and Dai's slippages from the biological or moral to the political in their overview of China's twentieth-century transformation underlined Nationalist anxiety that unorthodox personal lifestyles could jeopardize the nation's foundation. They chimed in with intellectual and popular association of sexual prowess with national strength. Intellectuals like Lu Xun and the widely read sociologist Zhang Jingsheng saw a link between Western imperialist intrusion into China's body politic and compromised vigor of Chinese (mostly male) bodies.[25] What was particular to conservative revolutionaries was not their obsession with the people's virility but the proposition that political dissent was morally corrupt and harmed the health of both the national collective and its members. Thus, Zhang, who was no communist, was accused of harboring communist sympathies due to his explicit depictions of sexual customs. Dai named Zhang's *Sex Histories* (*Xingshi*) as a publication that "harmed the physical and mental health of youths and jeopardized the nation's survival." The 1926 book should be banned while

criminal behaviors such as abortion and infanticide must be prohibited. The psychological reason for brutal behaviors committed by Communists like murder and arson is twofold: encouragement of carnal desires among youths and corruption of political society. If social discipline is not carefully maintained, young sex perverts (*seqing kuang*) will become serial murderers. The result will not be much better than the chaos during the twilight of the Ming dynasty. So-called Communists in China today are just sex perverts under the guise of communist ideology ... If we just punish Communists but not clamp down on inhuman thoughts and behaviors, we can never rescue the nation and society from morbid danger.[26]

By tarring the ideology with the erotic and grotesque, Dai rendered communism into a plight suffered by hedonistic and psychologically imbalanced youths.

Conservative revolutionaries painted Communist threat to morality and public order in concrete, individualistic terms. Such portrayal of the enemy put to relief the nature of *minsheng* as a program targeting personal sentiments rather than socioeconomic structures. Indeed, the

---

[24] Dai, *Qingnian zhilu*, 4. The two socialist policies Sun outlined were, in Frank W. Price's GMD-backed translation, "equalization of land" (*pingjun diquan*) and "regulation of capital" (*jiezhi ziben*).

[25] Hugh Shapiro, "The Puzzle of Spermatorrhea in Republican China," *Positions: East Asia Cultures Critique* 6 (1998): 575–6.

[26] Dai, "Weichi jiaoyu jiuji qingnian an," 431.

sins attributed to Communists read like the exploits of rogue playboys, in sharp contrast to the puritan Chiang and his dignified wife brandished in Nationalist media outlets. The CCP and its youth wing nurtured deracinated enclaves cut loose from familial obligations and traditional moral constraints. Urban philistines would look forward to nude protests and men and women bathing together. At the Moscow Sun Yat-sen University, a former student who subsequently converted to the GMD alleged, Russian "red imperialists" enticed gullible men with female cadres while women were approached by other charismatic women or flirted (*diao bangzi*) with by men. At the Comintern-run institution, where only 20 percent of the 500 Chinese students were female, women were "extremely loose and enjoyed romantic love with men as much as they wanted." For example, by report, female cadre Tan Guofu (1908–37) regularly "entertained" (*yingchou*) Qu Jingbai (1906–29), the brother of CCP general secretary Qu Qiubai (1899–1935), despite her supposedly committed relationship with Xia Xi (1901–36). A certain Zhu Hanjie took the dubious honor of "having sexual intercourse with the largest number of men" on campus, boasting that she had slept with some fifteen or sixteen men. Men treated women as prostitutes and "some female fellow-students, not entirely satisfied with Chinese flavor (*Zhongguo wei*), even had sex with Russians." Everywhere on campus from sports grounds and reading rooms "pairs of men and women could be seen engaged in bestial sexual intercourse."[27] Promiscuity, decadence and lust for the exotic were integral to a political and youth culture that turned its back on the Chinese civilizational virtues on which Nationalist rule was supposedly premised.

The results of such escapades were disastrous. Hu derided Qu Qiubai (1899–1935) and propaganda chief Cai Hesen (1895–1931), both "sex enthusiasts," for catching life-threatening tuberculosis. Another CCP propaganda chief, Shen Zemin (1900–33), was confined to his deathbed after being betrayed by his coquettish wife, Zhang Qinqiu (1904–68), a "red modern girl."[28] The indulgence of young Communist revolutionaries in carnal excitement not only served to highlight their frivolousness and hypocrisy as individuals. It also played into the fear that future generations of Chinese would capitulate to an ideology that tore apart the fundamentals of lived experience: family, community and physical

---

[27] Liu Zhipan, "Mosike Zhongshan daxue shouhua zhi jishi [A Veritable Record of Bestialization at Moscow Sun Yat-sen University], *Anhui jiaoyu xingzheng zhoukan* 2, no. 9 (1929): 5–6.

[28] Wu Weimin, "Zhang Qinqiu yu Shen Zemin – feiqu jianwen [Zhang Qinqiu and Shen Zemin – Eyewitness Accounts from Bandit Areas]," in *Hubei fanxing yuan tekan*, ed. Hubei fanxing yuan (Wuchang, 1935), miscellaneous section, 9–10.

vigor. "Even if [the Communists] manage to sacrifice half of all China's youths and bring in the dictatorship of the proletariat," Hu chided in a tongue-in-cheek manner, "they will just end up with a dictatorship of tuberculosis patients!" Communism was for the GMD elder analogous to a youth problem that dispatched the nation to its grave along with pleasure-seeking individuals.

Mass Disciplinary Tool

If communism was ultimately an issue of youth delinquency, it was only natural that the Nationalist state saw high political stakes in the quotidian and the pedestrian. Scouting was one among an array of tools at conservative revolutionaries' disposal to drill values into the youthful masses, form characters, impose behavioral norms and ultimately make laborious, politically docile patriots. Dai's active role in building up the movement suggests that scouting was particularly illustrative of evolving GMD thinking on youth engagement. The changes that mass politics would undergo under the conservative revolution as detailed in Dai's writings – from insurrections to production, from striving for equality and social enfranchisement to pursuit of beauty, physical health and moral rectitude, from socialist commitments to nationalist pieties – were all palpable in the Scouts of China. Through the theorist's intervention, conservative revolutionary ideals infused the movement from its organizational structure to the motto, promise and songs that structured individual experiences of scouting. Yet scouting originated neither from Sun Yat-sen's revolutionary nor from the Soviet experience. Instead, its institutions, rituals and pedagogical practices betrayed an unmistakable liberal concept of social participation. Founded by British general Robert Baden-Powell in 1907, scouting was, moreover, a product of imperialism. A celebrated career soldier with stints in India, Malta and Africa, Baden-Powell received inspiration for the organizing and training of boys from his experience fighting the indigenous Matabele population in Rhodesia in 1896 and setting up the South African Constabulary from 1900 to 1902.[29] The new youth program, invested with a romantic attachment to the outdoors as an allegory for imperial adventurism, fused mid-Victorian bourgeois values such as individual responsibility with more immediate anxieties over foreign threats, socialist politics and the pernicious effects of modern life in Britain. The idea was "to produce efficient recruits for the empire" through a mass movement that revitalized the martial quality

---

[29] Tammy M. Proctor, "'A Separate Path': Scouting and Guiding in Interwar South Africa," *Comparative Studies in Society and History* 42 (2000): 607–8.

of an urbanized, effete and debauched young citizenry in the metropole. Scouting spread across British colonies in North America, Africa and South Asia in the early twentieth century, adopting a "dual guise" as both an expression of imperial commonwealth and a vehicle for promoting sociopolitical cohesion through personal service and brotherhood.[30] While undoubtedly steeped in imperial ideology as *Pax Britannica* began to unravel, scouting caught on in the colonies as industrialization outside the metropole produced a small but powerful urban middle class among the indigenous populations.

The two faces of scouting coexisted in tension as the practice was introduced to semi-colonial China in 1912 around the time when the republic was founded. China's first scout groups, whether attributed to Wuchang-based missionary schoolteacher Yan Jialin or institutions operated by the municipal administration of Shanghai's British-dominated International Settlement, were strongly tied to the cultural and military might of the West. Scout leaders and scouts who wrote about their experiences at Shanghai Municipal Council schools recalled the alien and exotic allure of the activity, from the English verbal commands to the distinct navy blue jacket and khaki shorts that participants wore.[31] The association of scouting with Western imperialist presence was reinforced by suggestions that Shanghai's International Settlement community led a nascent nationwide scouting movement. G. S. F. Kemp, principal of the Public School for Chinese, declared in a 1917 issue of *New Youth* (*Xin qingnian*) that his Boy Scouts Association of China, founded in April 1913, was to "spread the Scout Movement over China," leading a unified organ comprising not only troops in Shanghai, but also local associations in Hankou, Guangzhou, Suzhou, Tianjin, Beijing and Nanjing. Appealing to "the gentry of China" for financial support, Kemp emphasized the apolitical dimension of the movement he putatively led. "Scouting is not intended to make soldiers of boys," Kemp assured his potential Chinese sponsors, "nor is it intended to lead youths to interfere in the government of the country."

---

[30] Michael Rosenthal, *The Character Factory: Baden-Powell and the Origins of the Boy Scout Movement* (New York: Pantheon Books, 1986), 3–6; Allen Warren, "Citizens of the Empire: Baden-Powell, Scouts and Guides and an Imperial Ideal," in *Imperialism and Popular Culture*, ed. John M. Mackenzie (Manchester: Manchester University Press, 1986), 238–41.

[31] Wang Youqian, "Wo suo zhidao de tongzijun [The Scouts of China According to My Knowledge]," in *Zhenjiang wenshi ziliao*, ed. Zhongguo renmin zhengzhi xieshang huiyi Jiangsu sheng Zhenjiang shi weiyuanhui wenshi ziliao yanjiu weiyuanhui, no. 25 (Zhenjiang: Jiangsu sheng Zhenjiang shi zhengxie, 1993), 169; Shen Lumin, "Wo suo zhidao de Shanghai tongzijun [Scouting in Shanghai According to My Knowledge]," in *Shanghai wenshi ziliao cungao huibian*, ed. Shanghai shi zhengxie wenshi ziliao weiyuanhui (Shanghai: Shanghai guji chubanshe, 2001), 11:154.

He highlighted how scouting was a potent tool to structure the quotidian routine of pampered, ill-disciplined youths. Instead of "dawdling about the streets and alleys" and being waited on by servants, boys filled "every moment" of their leisure time with open air, healthy habits, lively music and physical labor.[32] One of Kemp's Chinese collaborators, Li Qifan of the Shanghai-based Young Men's Christian Association (YMCA), was quoted by *Education Review* (*Jiaoyu zazhi*) as saying that the practice was being localized for the interior, devising sets of Chinese verbal commands and replacing the expensive woolen uniform with cotton.[33] Adapting to local sensibilities, scouting was presented as a timely innovation designed to rescue urban China from the malaises already plaguing industrialized society in the West – wastefulness, juvenile restlessness and declining moral standards.

Aside from its foreignness, early Chinese observers writing during the Great War saw scouting as a form of military preparation. In the same issue of *Education Review* that published Li Qifan's plan for popularizing the youth program in the hinterland, an article that investigated scouting in the United States compared the Anglo-American initiatives in their "militarism" (*junguo zhuyi*) to the systematic training of German youths since the end of the Franco–Prussian War. Identifying the origins of boy scouts in Baden-Powell's military background, the article emphasized the mobilization of youths as members of the wider settler community against indigenous Zulu insurgents. Scouting, rendered by the author as "young volunteer corps" (*shaonian yiyong tuan*) in Chinese, was a device to prepare a reserve force.[34] Scouting's inherent ambiguity as an avowedly nonmilitary venture with military origins and army-like uniforms, hierarchies and drills reflected the blurring of demarcations between the trenches and civilian populations in modern European warfare. It also held resonance among Republican educators toward the end of the First World War as they moved China's physical culture away from an emphasis on military citizenship through rigid calisthenics popular during the late Qing to competitive sports that contributed more directly to individual cultivation.[35] The 1917 curriculum adopted in the city of Wuxi for scouts, who ranged from twelve to more than twenty years of age, placed knowledge of the military ranks, ceremonies and hierarchies and such

[32] G. S. K. Kemp, "Boy Scouts Association of China," *Xin qingnian* 2, no. 5 (1917): 1–2.
[33] Xisan, "Tongzijun zhi taolun [A Dialogue on Scouting]," *Jiaoyu zazhi* 8, no. 5 (1916): 12.
[34] Tianmin, "Meiguo shaonian yiyong tuan [Scouting in the United States]," *Jiaoyu zazhi* 8, no. 5 (1916): 40–1.
[35] Andrew D. Morris, *Marrow of the Nation: A History of Sport and Physical Culture in Republican China* (Berkeley: University of California Press, 2004), 38–9.

quasi-military skills as weaponry and cartography among a wide list of optional subjects ranging from swimming, hiking and survival in the wild to translation, music and horticulture. Indeed, one recent amendment to the curriculum was to relegate military training from a core to an optional subject so as to avoid the impression that scouting was a cadet program for the armed forces.[36] Scouting thus subsumed military training under a broader program that cultivated a range of capabilities and knowledge that future citizens should possess.

From the end of the First World War until the April 12 coup in 1927, scouting spread across the coastal provinces. Prominent high schools adopted the organization and incorporated its program as part of their curricula. For reformist proponents, scouting embodied the latest American pragmatist education theories that privileged action in learning and the molding of children as social beings.[37] They also saw the movement as a device for nation-building, particularly in the face of attempts spearheaded by figures like Kemp to run scouting from Shanghai's International Settlement. The Nanjing-based Chinese Scouts Research Association (*Zhonghua tongzijun yanjiuhui*), initiated by organizers from Jiangsu in 1921, offered itself as the first contact point for scout troops across the fragmented country. Educators in Jiangsu also petitioned the provincial government, controlled by a Zhili clique warlord, to provide financial support for the 257 scout troops and their 7,237 participants through extra budget provisions for schools. In piquing the state's interest in scouting, the movement was portrayed as an international fraternity for full-fledged nations. Compared to the United States, where Congress passed a resolution identifying scouting as a national enterprise (*guojia shiye*), China did not even have a unified network for scouts organizations at the provincial level.[38] The state's failure to provide funding and an overall institutional structure for scouts from Tianjin in the north to Taishan in the south was, the argument went, a reminder of China's status as a semi-colonized and internally fragmented country unqualified to stand among the family of twentieth-century nations.

The alignment of scouting with the nationalist project in China echoed similar developments in colonial societies under the British. While Baden-Powell valued conformity to social order and contributed to the British Empire's civilizing and proselytizing missions, the youth movement he pioneered became a vehicle for nationalist agitations in Ireland,

[36] Tang Changyan, "Zhonghua Jiangsu Wuxi tongzijun zuzhifa dakewen [Q & A on the Organization of Scouts in Wuxi, Jiangsu]," *Jiaoyu yuekan*, no. 5 (1917): 42–53.
[37] Culp, *Articulating Citizenship*, 179–80.
[38] Tang, "Minguo shinian zhi tongzijun jiaoyu [Scouting in 1921]," *Xin jiaoyu*, no. 2 (1922): 236–40.

Palestine and India. In the 1910s, the British Raj refused to extend recognition to scouting for fear that Indian nationalists would turn it into a militant anticolonial movement. The lack of official sponsorship, however, did not prohibit nationalist activists and foreign missionaries from imitating the boy scouts in the metropole and launching similar undertakings for Indians.[39] In early twentieth-century China, the linking of scouting with nationalist mobilization was strongest in the GMD's base in Guangdong, where the movement was coordinated by the state. Robert Culp argues that the centralization of scouting was a new development during the Nanjing Decade (1927–37) that the GMD imposed on heretofore loosely federated troops in Shanghai, Jiangsu and Zhejiang.[40] While this might have been the case in the lower Yangzi region, the situation was rather different in the southern province. Authorities in Guangdong required all troops to register with a province-wide body run by American-educated Huang Xianzhao, a YMCA organizer who pioneered scouting in Guangzhou in 1915, and Cheng Zuyi of the Guangdong Higher Normal College. All scouts in the province wore the same uniform and operated under one organizational structure and students from different schools were sent to receive training as scout leaders. In the provincial capital, Mayor Sun Ke (1891–1973) placed scouting under the direction of the municipal education department in 1924 and began to formulate a unified curriculum. The practice was extended to girls and introduced to the school curriculum at the upper primary level and beyond.[41]

The hybridity inherent to scouting with hints of militarism, imperialism, reformism and nationalism allowed the newly reorganized GMD regime to build a disciplined mass organization on the foundation of an existing movement. A Leninist party was able to reach out to a Westernized, missionary school-educated urban elite committed not necessarily to Sun Yat-sen's political agenda but to training physically virile youngsters versed in technical skills and devoted to general social service. Furthermore, scouting's internationalist pretensions allowed the GMD to maintain

---

[39] Timothy H. Parsons, *Race, Resistance, and the Boy Scout Movement in British Colonial Africa* (Athens: Ohio University Press, 2004), 64–5.

[40] Culp, *Articulating Citizenship*, 180; Culp, "Zhongguo tongzijun – Nanjing shinian tongzijun shouce zhong de gongmin xunlian yu shehui yishi [Scouting for Chinese Boys: Civic Training and Social Consciousness in Nanjing Decade Boy Scout Handbooks]," *Xin shixue* 11, no. 4 (2000): 25.

[41] Chen Juequan, "Guangzhou tongzijun shilue [Brief History of Scouting in Guangzhou]," in *Guangdong wenshi ziliao*, ed. Zhongguo renmin zhengxie huiyi Guangdong sheng weiyuanhui wenshi ziliao yanjiu weiyuanhui, no. 73 (Guangzhou: Guangdong renmin chubanshe, 1993), 149–50. Li Pusheng, "Tongzijun zhi lueshi [Brief History of Scouting]," special edition on the scout carnival, *Guangzhou Minguo ribao*, May 23, 1925, 4.

a moderate image when dealing with foreign educators, who, as in the case of Shanghai, introduced the practice to Guangzhou and remained powerful organizers. The GMD and its affiliated institutions enjoyed a close working relationship with the American-funded Lingnan University. Lingnan scouts participated in province-wide activities while their American leaders were invited to train future scoutmasters at the party-run Guangdong University (the predecessor of Sun Yat-sen University that incorporated the Higher Normal College).[42] When an entourage of 125 scouts, scout leaders and photographers from Lingnan went camping outside Guangzhou in 1926, these "prominent Chinese citizens and students" enjoyed the protection of a seventy-five-strong contingent from the National Revolutionary Army.[43] Despite its increasingly fervent nationalism, the GMD's stance toward foreign scout organizers at this early stage was one of cautious co-optation rather than outright incorporation into party-controlled bodies.

The GMD's accommodating attitude did not mean that the party concurred with the values foreign scout organizers believed the movement should imbue in young boys and girls. While scouting as envisioned by Kemp belonged to an Anglo-American liberal tradition that valued the cultivation of individualistic citizenship and social activism that served no specific political causes, scout educators working under the GMD thought otherwise. Nationalism and anti-imperialism were the main motivations behind their efforts to promote the practice in institutions run by the party-state. Li Pusheng, an Aceh-born teacher who was among the first batch of scout leaders trained by Wang Xianzhao in 1917, cited Baden-Powell's military victories in South Africa and Japan's investment in building a young generation with strong physical prowess as his inspirations for scouting education in China. As the chief scout (*tongjun zhuren*) at the affiliated secondary and primary schools of Guangzhou's Higher Normal College, Li led boys in a citywide rally against British officers' brutal treatment of Shanghai textile workers on strike in May 1925. After the Guangzhou demonstration itself ended in bloodshed on June 23, at which a scout was killed by British troops along with some sixty protestors, Li decided that the GMD was the only force capable of freeing China from imperialist influence. Upon joining the GMD as a cadre at the

[42] "Canjia ben dahui tongzijun tuanshu renshu ji biaoyan zhonglei yilan [Number of Troops and Scouts, and the Nature of Their Performance at the Event]," special edition on scouting exhibition, 4; Li Pusheng to Guangdong University administrative meeting, October 17, 1925, Sun Yat-sen University Collection, 31–2–24, Guangdong Provincial Archives.

[43] *Newsletter for Americans*, no. 452, May 1926, reel 40, Lingnan University Collection, Guangdong Provincial Archives.

Youth Department, the radicalized activist suggested that the party
needed its own scouting apparatus.[44] In 1926, the Youth Department
submitted a plan to the party headquarters for the reorganization of
scouting as the Nationalist youth wing. Directly challenging the apolitical
claims Kemp and others made for scouting, the proposal accused the
organization of being a product of Anglo-American influence and a tool of
imperialist encroachment into China.[45] The GMD inaugurated the Party
Scouts (*dang tongzijun*) on May 5, 1926, shortly before it embarked on
a military expedition against the warlord regime in Beijing.

The Party Scouts constituted not so much an entirely new organization
as a reconfiguration of the existing scouting movement formed under
provincial and municipal aegis. Scout activists from Guangdong
University, including Li Pusheng, were charged with the formulation of
the new body's regulations and their implementation, while the university
president was to serve as the director-general (*zong ganshi*).[46] Aligning the
ideological import and operational infrastructure of scouting and the
party-state apparatus in Guangdong anticipated the GMD's approach
to the youth organization network after the April 12, 1927, coup.
Scouting methods were valorized due to their purported compatibility
with Sun Yat-sen's mass mobilization theory. The Youth Department's
proposal called on scout leaders to "penetrate deep down" (*shenqian*) into
the people's minds, just like how their British, American and Japanese
counterparts instilled support for the monarchy, bourgeois rule and
"Great Japanism" (*da Riben zhuyi*) in their respective young
citizenries.[47] They received training in military organization, learned to
master new media like cartoons and public speaking and were taught
GMD key policies through the angles of class analysis and mass
psychology.[48]

While the GMD claimed scouting for itself only in 1926, the party
made its imprint on scouting as part of its revolutionary praxis even before
the founding of the Party Scouts. Chinese Nationalist interest in curating
young people's everyday experiences with mass organizations was part of

[44] Li Pusheng, *Wo bushizi de muqin* [*My Illiterate Mother*] (Hong Kong: Dongnan yinwu chubanshe, 1956), 25–7.
[45] "Zhongyang qingnian bu tiyi chuangban Zhongguo Guomindang tongzijun an [Youth Department's Plan for the Establishment of the Nationalist Party Scouts]," 1926, *wubu*, 10738, Kuomintang Archives.
[46] Li, *Wo bushizi de muqin*, 27; GMD Youth Department to Guangdong University President, April 5, 1926, Sun Yat-sen University Collection, 31–2–24, Guangdong Provincial Archives.
[47] "Zhongyang qingnian bu tiyi chuangban Zhongguo Guomindang tongzijun an," 1926.
[48] Guangxi Party Branch Youth Department, "Report on Scout Organization," January 14, 1927, *wubu*, 11122, Kuomintang Archives; Liang Canwen, "Zhongguo Guomindang tongzijun jishi," *Zhongguo Guomindang tongzijun*, no. 2 (1926): 8.

an international trend. In Taiwan, for example, the Japanese colonial state took an increasing interest in managing local youth associations (*qingnian tuan/seinendan*) as the 1920s progressed. These scout-like groups promoted the Japanese language, organized hiking trips, held swimming classes and insulated young people from subversive ideas.[49] Despite scouting's controversial origins, the GMD found its infrastructure useful. It put together a Guangdong-wide scout carnival in 1925 to raise funds for a memorial hall dedicated to the recently deceased Sun Yat-sen. At the rally, Hu Hanmin, then provincial governor, led officials in inspecting some 1,500 scouts from thirty-four educational institutions. Zou Lu (1885–1954), the Guangdong University president who participated in early agitations against the United Front, censured Western imperialists for their militaristic (*jun guomin*) scouting education but exculpated Baden-Powell. The British lieutenant-general's military-inspired training methods were instead lauded for promoting order and beauty in schools and for imparting practical skills on adolescents with subjects like hiking, first aid and firefighting.[50] The imperialist pretensions that informed scouting were set aside in Li Pusheng's admiration for how Baden-Powell managed to deploy urban youths among the South African colonialist community in military tasks like transmitting messages, transporting supplies and gathering intelligence as if they were nothing more than enjoyable pastimes.[51] Scouting was a neutral social engineering template for China, as it was for advanced Western countries and Japan, to stop the "degradation of youths" (*shaonian de ehua*), perfect their personality and improve communal character.

Having separated scouting from its colonial history, GMD affiliates claimed the movement as their own. Anticipating developments in the Nanjing Decade, scout training in Guangdong was rebranded as a tool for putting into practice Sun's proclivity for guided action over political consciousness in working with the populace, a theory central to Dai Jitao's formulation of GMD vanguardism. The movement helped produce voluntaristic technocrats among the young generation. The emphasis on hands-on learning was touted as a natural extension of Sun's exhortation to his less intellectually inclined comrades to execute

---

[49] Guoli Guangdong daxue, *Guoli Guangdong daxue tongzijun niankan* (Guangzhou: n.p., 1925), 6. Chen Wensong, *Zhimin tongzhi yu "qingnian": Taiwan zongdufu de "qingnian" jiaohua zhengce* [*Colonial Rule and Youths: The Taiwan Governor-General Office's Youth Cultivation Policy*] (Taipei: Guoli Taiwan daxue chuban zhongxin, 2015), 173, 210.

[50] Zou Li, "Yanshuo ci [Speech]," *Guangzhou Minguo ribao*, May 23, 1925, 1.

[51] Li, "Tongzijun zhi lueshi." Li was referring to Baden-Powell's Mafeking Cadet Corps, a paramilitary group led by a thirteen-year-old during the Second Boer War (1899–1900). Considered highly effective in helping the small British force in its defense against Dutch settlers, the corps was one precursor to the scouting movement.

(*xing*) the revolution, even if they could not understand (*zhi*) it. Similarly, young children learned surveying techniques without understanding geometry; they knew how to identify directions by using a compass and observing stars, even if they were too young to make sense of physics and astronomy. Most significantly, scouts were constantly cheerful, putting on smiles as they received orders from superiors. The ability to appear joyful without appreciating the "philosophy of smiles" (*xiao zhi zhexue*) was touted as another instance of how actual practice took the pride of place in scouting.[52] Displaying happiness without being happy was thus the quotidian counterpart to mass enthusiasm for revolutionary action in the absence of conscious conviction in concrete revolutionary aims. Experiential learning, a core tenet of John Dewey's progressive education tradition to which scouting belonged, contributed to shaping a skilled, target-oriented citizenry whose social activism took the form of technocratic development rather than attacks on social injustices.

Politicization and Depoliticization

This depoliticization of political participation in the GMD's early experimentations with scouting, where insurrectionary activism against reigning power relations was replaced by orderly management of individual emotions, dispositions and morality, shaped the movement's direction after the April 12 coup in 1927. A cooperative, orderly and aesthetically pleasing community of efficient and authority-abiding scouts anticipated the conservative revolution's imaginary of a noncapitalist society begotten not by class struggle, but by state management. Of course, much had changed as the center of the GMD was shifted from Guangzhou to Nanjing. Activists like Li Pusheng remained in Guangzhou and were marginalized from the new order in the making.[53] With just over 8,000 party scouts divided into forty troops (*tuan*), the relocated Nationalist state did not believe the Guangdong-based youth movement provided a satisfactory foundation for a nationwide network.[54] Dai Jitao, who headed the GMD department responsible for training the masses, renewed the centralization drive. Yet the movement's modest size in the south was the least of party leaders' concerns. "In the past," Dai told his Guangdong comrades in 1931:

[52] Chen Bingquan, "Sun Zhongshan yu tongzijun [Sun Yat-sen and Scouting]," *Guangzhou Minguo ribao*, May 23, 1925, 2–3. In spite of its title, there is no evidence that Sun took an interest in scouting, much less was involved in its organization.
[53] Li, *Wo bushizi de muqin*, 27.
[54] Chen, "Guangzhou tongzijun shilue," 151. By March 31, 1930, just before the first national jamboree was held, 10,938 scouts and 116 troops were registered.

scouting was not initiated and run by the GMD but was a system imported from abroad, activists then were therefore not deeply tied to the party. If they were to work for us before scout training in various locales was given a unified form, they would not only fail to benefit the development of the movement but even jeopardize (*youwu yu*) party supervision of the scout enterprise ... The Central Executive's position on scouting organization in Guangdong is that our party must first control and unify things there. Only when this is achieved can we consider recruitment of personnel.[55]

The theorist overstated the degree to which scouting was free from state influence before 1927, but he articulated eloquently Nanjing's determination to take firm control over organizations that dealt with the masses and ensured their absolute loyalty to the post-coup regime. That the southern province was quickly slipping into the hands of warlord Chen Jitang (1890–1954), who held the reins of power in the former Nationalist base from 1929 to 1936, did not inspire confidence. In 1933, Dai accused scout leaders in Guangdong of the more serious crime of "Bolshevizing" (*chihua*) the movement.[56] A Nationalist-led scouting movement, loyal to the Republic and the Three People's Principles, was to be launched anew from the nation's new capital.

Like the GMD itself, therefore, streamlining of the youth organization targeted both Communist foes and those with Westernized or liberal-leaning backgrounds. Yet Dai's remark that activists long involved in imperialist institutions were disqualified from playing a central role in key party initiatives was more a statement of preference than a strictly enforced policy. One core scout functionary who worked to bring scouts across the country under Nanjing's fold was Zhang Zhongren (1898–1971), a graduate of the missionary-run Tianjin Anglo-Chinese School (*Xinxue xueyuan*). Zhang, who spearheaded his alma mater's scout troop in 1915 while working at the American consulate, was appointed a commander (*siling*) at the Scouts of the Chinese Nationalist Party (*Zhongguo Guomindang tongzijun*) in 1928 and played an active role in fine-tuning the Nationalist regime's centralizing imperative in disciplining youth activism. Commander Zhang and his unrelated fellow scout activist Zhang Xiaoliang (1905–82) served respectively on the planning and preparatory committees of the Scouts of China General Association (*Zhongguo tongzijun zonghui*). In fact, Zhang Zhongren was credited with proposing the general association to provide Chinese scouting with a national locus. The association was envisaged as a "sound, independent

---

[55] Dai Jitao, "Tongyi tongzijun zuzhi jiangci [Speech on Unifying Scouting Organization]," *DJTXSWC*, 808–9.
[56] Dai, "Wei xiugai tongzijun guilü gao tongzijun gongzuo renyuan shu [Letter to Scout Organizers on the Revision of Scout Laws]," *DJTXSWC*, 817.

and permanent central organization" modeled on the Boy Scouts of America.[57] Organizational reforms began in 1929, when Zhang Zhongren's central command (*siling bu*) was placed directly under the GMD Central Executive Committee instead of Dai's Training Department (although the latter continued to exert tight control over scouting in general). Another symbolic but no less significant change was to rebrand the Scouts of the Chinese Nationalist Party into the less partisan-sounding Scouts of China (*Zhongguo tongzijun*).

The results of these initiatives, which cumulated in the founding of the Scouts of China General Association in 1934, were ambiguous enough to allow for different interpretations. Zhang Zhongren saw the partial distancing of scouting from the GMD apparatus and his American-style organizational framework as salutary steps in a liberal direction. He heaped praise in a 1935 speech to future scout leaders on scouting bodies in Britain and particularly the United States for embodying the democratic principles that governed public life in the two countries, even as he was also enthusiastic about scouting in authoritarian Japan. Zhang touted the US Congress, which granted a charter to Boy Scouts of America in 1916, as a mechanism for citizens to push for change and progress without a revolution. While many GMD cadres saw scouts as future successors of the national revolution and envisioned thorough infusion of the Three People's Principles in the scout curriculum, Zhang argued that character (*pin'ge*) cultivation should hold pride of place.[58] As an admirer of the US political model, Zhang was more vigilant than Baden-Powell of Mussolini's Italy and fascist challenges to the liberal world order. Unlike the British military officer, who endorsed Opera Nazionale Balilla as a program that built character and body, Zhang accused the Fascist youth organization in a 1935 article of exhibiting a narrow nationalist vision. With its overt "political agenda and program," the Balilla was "a scouting-like concoction that was decidedly not scouting."[59] Governed by its own organizational apparatus instead of belonging to a department

---

[57] Zhang Xiaoliang, "Zhongguo tongzijun zonghui yundong xiaoshi [A Brief History of the Campaign for a Scouts of China General Association]," MS, April 1932, Zhang Xiaoliang Collection, National Pingtung University of Education Institutional Repository (hereafter cited as NPUE), http://140.127.82.166/handle/987654321/1677 (accessed August 10, 2012).

[58] Zhang Zhongren, "Ying-Mei he Riben tongzijun gaishuo [A Brief Introduction to Scouting in Britain, America and Japan]," in *Tongzijun wenxian* [*Documents on Scouting*] (Taipei: Zhonghua shuju, 1981), 247–55.

[59] Zhang Zhongren, "Yidali de Balila [Italy's Balilla]," in *Tongzijun wenxian*, 264–6. For Baden-Powell's flirtations with the Balilla and the Nazi Youth, see Rosenthal, *Character Factory*, 273–8.

of the GMD was for Zhang an indication that China's premier youth movement was approximating America's rather than Italy's.

Zhang's view that the Scouts of China was accorded relative independence from the GMD's ideological program left an imprint on the historiography. A recent Chinese-language study argues that the General Association's establishment signaled Nationalist retreat from prior heavy-handed politicization of scouting. Compared with copious appeals to the Three People's Principles, solidarity with peasants and workers and fidelity to the revolutionary party during much of the 1920s, the general regulations passed in September 1934 were less partisan and prized children's personal growth. Reorganization elevated the individual in favor of party ideology, encouraged more professionally produced training materials and returned the youth movement to its original mission of social service.[60] Robert Culp maintains that Nationalist leadership of scouting was characterized by "co-optation and indirect management rather than state monopoly and direct control."[61] Despite Nationalist efforts to establish centralized institutional control, everyday scout training still focused on imparting capabilities, hygienic habits and a competitive spirit conducive to individual creativity and independence. Scouting continued to promote a liberal model of citizenship that stood in contrast to the collectivist impulse that lent a fascistic vibe to some GMD cadres. Ultimately, scouting betrayed Nationalist China's pluralist approach to youth training that was distinct from the militaristic and homogenizing paradigm adopted in Germany, Italy and Japan.

Undoubtedly, the Scouts of China was not a goose-stepping, chest-thumping facsimile of Hitler Youth. Yet one must also realize that furthering individual character development was not antithetical to the conservative revolution. After all, spectacular public rallies, military parades and even blatant ideological indoctrination were not necessarily everyday norms under the most fascist of regimes. Indeed, the restructuring of scouts accompanied the GMD's post-purge shift from organizing mass activism to civilizing individual behaviors. As the locus of revolutionary building among the youthful masses moved from raucous demonstrations and endless debates to orderly classrooms and quiet study sessions, scouts were unsurprisingly no longer exhorted to side with oppressed classes. Yet, rather than withdrawing from scouting, the GMD was reexamining how best to immerse itself within existing communities, popular mores and social classes. At times, party cadres

---

[60] Sun Yuqin, *Minguo shiqi de tongzijun yanjiu* [*A Study on Scouting in the Republican Period*] (Beijing: Renmin chubanshe, 2013), 80–3.
[61] Culp, *Articulating Citizenship*, 180.

oscillated between their vanguardist identity and a strategy that called for less visible politicization of society. Dai, who would become the vice president of the General Association, headed a training department that opposed changes in nomenclature. As late as 1928, the department complained that the name "Scouts of China" failed to reflect the GMD's authority over the organization.[62] Even as central command was transferred out from the training department, Dai vowed that the party would continue to provide direction and ideological justification for scouting.[63]

The need to downplay the GMD's agitational function did, however, encourage a more hands-off attitude toward the scouts than potentially subversive bodies like student bodies. Whereas region-wide student unions were dismantled in favor of campus-confined self-governing associations isolated from one another, the GMD took a corporatist strategy in managing scouting. Functionaries within the scouting movement who had no prior connection with the national revolution were co-opted to serve the new cause, even if their ideological sensibilities were at some variance with the right-wing majority's. The penetration of overtly partisan groupings like Lixingshe into the organization was partial and took place in a low-profile manner.[64] This subtle approach helped the GMD project itself as a nonpartisan steward of the nation's youth. The regime's claim to political disinterestedness not only appealed to figures and organizations initially uneasy with the GMD but also rendered opponents of the party-state politically self-serving and even morally dubious. Among the first within the party to think seriously about the shape of mass politics under a consolidated Nationalist regime, Dai pledged in the lead-up to the April 12 coup that future youth movements would concentrate on improving academic attainments and cultivation of hearts and minds. Instead of treating teenagers as politicians' private soldiers, the conservative revolution aimed to revert young protesters to the humble, obedient receivers of canonical knowledge. Future struggle for national survival was to take place in "libraries, laboratories and workshops."[65] For educated youth, contributing to the new social order, not political factionalism, was the way forward.

---

[62] Zhongguo Guomindang zhongyang zhixing weiyuanhui xunlian bu, "Zhongguo tongzi-jun mingcheng ji zuzhi yuanze an [Proposal on Principles Governing the Naming and Organization of the Scouts of China]," July 31, 1928, *huiyi*, 3.3/47.10, Kuomintang Archives.

[63] Dai, "Tongyi tongzijun zuzhi jiangci," 808; Dai, "Tongzijun duiyu shehui guojia minzu shijie renlei yingfu de zeren jiangci [Speech on Scouting's Responsibility to Society, the Nation, the State and Human Race]," *DJTXSWC*, 814.

[64] Wakeman, *Spymaster*, 76–7.   [65] Dai, *Qingnian zhi lu*, 155.

Dai's dictum that the national revolution would no longer be launched from the street appealed to the habits of the Westernized bourgeoisie, to which Zhang Zhongren belonged, and to the aspirations of modestly educated white-collar "petit urbanites" who would by the 1930s make up 40 percent of Shanghai's population.[66] His revised *minsheng* program, with the two new additional categories of cultivation and leisure, had found a home in the middle-class civility that scouting promoted. Scout curriculum placed considerable emphasis on what Culp identifies as treaty-port ideals of hygiene and etiquette. Cub scouts (*you tongjun*), recruited from primary schools, were assessed in their ability to exemplify a modern, healthy, urban lifestyle that included practices such as keeping nails neat and short, taking regular baths, breathing with one's nose and avoiding used towels.[67] A 1930 article by Zhang Xiaoliang exhorted scouts to live a disciplined (*guilü*) life underpinned by twelve rules that included loyalty, fraternity, obedience, happiness and cleanliness.[68] While Zhang enlisted Confucius to support his argument, editors of *Scouts of China* provided a radically non-classicist illustration of composed, salutary lifestyle. A blue-and-white image on the cover of the in-house magazine showed an adolescent sound asleep in bed. In the background was a futurist-style montage comprising a school bag, the moon, a clock striking ten and the silhouette of a gigantic cogwheel. The implication was obvious: the discipline that scouts must internalize was one of a well-oiled industrial society, i.e., time management. Scouting groomed urban workers in a unified nation-state, not thinkers from an agrarian and loosely governed community.

To be sure, the association of scouting with premodern "chivalric heroism" (*qishi de yingxiong qigai*) and survival in the wilderness was not forgotten.[69] Yet Zhang Xiaoliang also acknowledged that a program that promised only rustic adventures could not be popular among parents. Urbanites were hardly excited by the prospect of sending their children out in the forest to brave the elements. While appealing to active and outdoor-loving children with a curriculum of camping, hiking, swimming, knot-tying and flag-signaling, scout leaders needed to persuade

---

[66] Hanchao Lu, *Beyond the Neon Lights: Everyday Shanghai in the Early Twentieth Century* (Berkeley: University of California Press, 2000), 63.

[67] Culp, *Articulating Citizenship*, 186; *Zhongguo tongzijun choubeichu gongzuo baogao* [*Report of the Preparatory Committee of the Scouts of China General Association*] (Nanjing: n.p., 1934), 93. Zhongguo Guomindang zhongyang zhixing weiyuanhui xunlian bu, *Tongzijun chuji kecheng* [*Elementary Scouting Curriculum*] (Nanjing: n.p., 1930), 245–52.

[68] Zhang Xiaoliang, "Guilü shijin [Some Observations on Discipline]," *Zhongguo tongzijun*, no. 18 (1931): 15–22.

[69] Xu Guanyu, "Jigei yiwei xiao pengyou de xin (yi) [Letter to a Child, I]," *Zhongguo tongzijun* 2, no. 2 (1936): 12.

skeptical parents that a training regime that traced its origins to the bush in southern Africa would produce "successful modern youths" in urban China.[70] Sensitivity to the tastes and social ideals of the upwardly mobile middle class defined the tenor of Chinese scouting. Exemplary scout members were billed as people who were not only multitalented but could afford to cultivate sophisticated and oftentimes expensive hobbies. Photographed in a neat scout uniform, a confident Zhu Heqin from Jiangsu played basketball, tennis and billiards, aside from contributing articles to *Scouts of China*. "From his face," readers were told of the seventeen-*sui* boy scout, "one sees an instinct for dramatic expressions, confirming a talent and interest in acting." Another contributor, a fifteen-*sui* deputy patrol (*xiaodui*) leader from Zhejiang, was "proficient in the arts" and enjoyed reading literary magazines in his free time.[71] The Scouts of China General Association's magazine treated young people to photography lessons. Those who did not have access to a camera could spend leisure time gathering mementos from everyday life. They could gather shells and plant specimens while camping or keep track of photographs, trademarks or advertisements for movies, spoken drama and exhibitions.[72] Girl scouts learned "feminine" labor like needlework. Scout programs socialized young people into gendered roles as consumers and homemakers in addition to being producers in a modern economy.

The activities Scouts of China promoted corresponded largely with its counterparts in countries not governed by party-states. Their emphasis on attainment of artistic and athletic skills by individual members complicates efforts to cast Nationalist China as concerned exclusively with regimentation and martial qualities, tendencies common among fascist regimes.[73] Nevertheless, scouting in China, like scouting in the British empire, had deep-seated affinity with elitism and conservatism. Despite its jealously guarded apolitical image, Baden-Powell's scouting was

---

[70] Zhang Xiaoliang, "Zenyang zhengqiu ertong laizuo tongzijun [How to Recruit Children into Scouting]," MS, October 1931, Zhang Xiaoliang Collection, NPUE, http://140.127 .82.166/handle/987654321/1680 (accessed August 10, 2012).

[71] "Jieshao ben kan tougao de xiao pengyou [Introducing Children Who Write for This Magazine]," *Zhongguo tongzijun*, no. 16 (1931): 46.

[72] Cao Yongfang, "Tongzijun sheying zhuanke jiangzuo [Special Lecture on Photography for Scouts]," *Zhongguo tongzijun* 2, no. 2 (1936): 14–16; Zhang Xiaoliang, "Ji'nian wu de baocun he souji [Preserving and Identifying Mementos]," *Zhongguo tongzijun* 2, no. 2 (1936): 4–6.

[73] Culp, for example, contrasts the GMD's pluralism with the totalitarian tendencies of Shôwa Japan, Fascist Italy and Nazi Germany (*Articulating Citizenship*, 206–7). Mabel Berezin argues, however, that reliance on violence petered out as Mussolini usurped state power and that Italian fascist sociocultural practices were not necessarily more repressive than nonfascist states in Europe and North America (*Making the Fascist Self*, 13–14).

a response to elite fears over decline in Britain's moral, physical and military qualities among the working masses of early twentieth-century industrial society. Not unlike Republican China, Edwardian Britain was beset by a deep sense of crisis: urbanization produced crime and weak bodies, labor unions threatened "natural" social hierarchy and the heretofore almighty empire was challenged by an ascendant Germany. To reinstall discipline and order, Baden-Powell proposed a "total ideology" that fully conditioned youths' values and emotional responses through carefully crafted games, rules and rituals. The urge to formulate an alternative to left-wing youth activism explained Baden-Powell's initial flirtations with the Ballila and the Hitler Youth.[74] Conservative revolutionaries in China appreciated the connection Baden-Powell made between political defiance, loose morals and declining strength of individuals and the body politic. In China as in Britain, scouting was a useful vessel for taming youths, both hormonally and socially. There was a lot in the very form of scout training that conformed with Nationalist sensibilities.

The analogous quality between scouting and the Nationalist vision explained the former's high transferability into the New Life Movement. Launched in 1934, the same year in which the Scouts of China General Association was founded, the New Life Movement traced its root to campaigns that targeted erstwhile Communist sympathizers after Nationalist forces wiped out the CCP-led Jiangxi Soviet in the rural hinterland. The movement was a revolutionary experiment that sought to eliminate waste, change habits, strengthen bodies, tame left-wing radicalism and prepare a nimble citizenry who took on production orders with relish and military-like determination. It intervened in the most mundane of everyday chores: the clothes one wore, the food prepared in family kitchens, the side of the street pedestrians walked on, spitting and urinating in public. In its exhortations for the populace to minimize consumption, uphold public civility, engage in household production and avoid foreign fashion items, the New Life Movement was a total mass movement that subsumed the more specific mandate of scouting. While the New Life Movement was not aimed at youths per se, it shared key features with scouting. In organizational form and personnel, both the New Life and scouting movements borrowed freely from Christianity and liberal, treaty-port civil bodies. They combined and oscillated between civic voluntarism and state imposition of social norms. Their goals, couched in protean nativist and moralist vocabularies, were those of twentieth-century anticommunism and what Maggie Clinton calls "the high

---

[74] Warren, "Citizens of the Empire," 238; Rosenthal, *Character Factory*, 10, 273–8.

modernism" of Taylorist civilization. Both promised to fix the quotidian, with a view to perfecting the national collective.[75] It was only natural that Chiang Kai-shek's 1934 "Outline of the New Life Movement" (*Xin shenghuo yundong gangyao*), a long list of proper behaviors that constituted a revolution in everyday culture, was duly reproduced in the commemorative publication marking the launch of the Scouts of China general association.[76] Scouts became foot soldiers of the New Life ideal, patrolling streets to make sure public spaces were hygienic and pedestrians wore clean, decent clothes.[77]

There was substantial "translingual" synergy between British scouting and the GMD's revolution of the everyday.[78] As vice president of the Scouts of China, Dai Jitao gave speeches to scout leaders and members interlaced with vocabularies of both traditions. Dai echoed Baden-Powell's warning against "snobbishness." Just as the 1908 Scouts Law exhorted the underclass not to resent the privileged, Dai derided his compatriots for being self-obsessed and envious of those who achieved fame and success. An edifying "new life" (*xin shengming*) for the future generation would see that contented young citizens went out of their way to help one another, no matter how far apart class distinctions set them from one another.[79] This cooperative spirit and meek acceptance of inequality fed into the GMD's core political agenda that was geared to diffuse left-wing influence in mass politics. The state's investment in scouting was intertwined with the ongoing military campaigns against Communists and predated the New Life Movement. Dai rehashed Hu Hanmin's case, casting insurrectionary politics as incurable moral lapse. As he explained in a 1932 speech to scouts in Hankou, a city close to a major Communist base on the border of Hubei province, "red

[75] Clinton, *Revolutionary Nativism*, 130; Lei, "Xiguan cheng siwei," 171–4; Liu, "Redefining the Moral and Legal Roles of the State in Everyday Life," 51–3; Ferlanti, "The New Life Movement in Jiangxi Province," 966–77.

[76] Zhongguo tongzijun zonghui choubeichu, *Zhongguo tongzijun choubeichu gongzuo baogao*, 113–23.

[77] Ji Diankai, "Wo suo zhidao de tongzijun [Scouting as I Know It]," Xinxiang shi jiaoqu wenshi ziliao, ed. Zhengxie Xinyang shi weiyuanhui wenshi ziliao weiyuanhui, no. 3 (Xinyang, Henan: Zhengxie Xinyang shi weiyuanhui wenshi ziliao weiyuanhui, 1994), 20; Culp, *Articulating Citizenship*, 195.

[78] For the concept of translingual practice, see Lydia H. Liu, *Translingual Practice: Literature, National Culture, and Translated Modernity – China, 1900–1937* (Stanford, CA: Stanford University Press, 1995), 26.

[79] Dai, "Tongyi gonggong mudi yu fangzhen shi tongzijun chenggong de yaojue jiangci [Unifying Social Goals and Targets Is Key to the Success of Scouting]," *DJTXSWC*, 828–9. The fourth law stated that "a scout must never be a SNOB. A snob is someone who looks down upon another because he is poorer, or who is poor and resents another because he is rich." For a full text of the 1908 Scout Law, see Rosenthal, *Character Factory*, 109–11.

bandits" (*chifei*) would not have existed had citizens duly benefited from scouting during their formative years. Dai said:

President Chiang of the Scouts of China, who is also the chairman of the Military Affairs Commission, visited Hankou recently. He had won a number of battles and purged many red bandits. We must press on to destroy red banditry from its roots. We should realize that these bandits are also Chinese; they are our compatriots and brothers. Why is it that they fail to seek self-improvement and instead make trouble? It is because they did not receive an education and never learned how to become truly human (*zuoren de daoli*). This is one sure indication of China's decay and gloom.[80]

Dai laid bare the GMD's political interest in the personality of young Chinese. Chiang Kai-shek's military prowess might be enough to suppress Communist strongholds, but it was scouting that could ultimately root out the communist threat. It was activities structuring the people's everyday life that could reform the self. Baden-Powell's doctrine of doing a good turn to somebody every day, translated pithily into Chinese as "a good deed a day" (*rixing yishan*), thus became Dai's potent weapon against Communist savagery and for the realization of the *minsheng* ideal.[81] English public school ethos, transplanted into civil war–ridden China, brought edification to a troubled generation and safeguarded the conservative revolution. Scouting, like the New Life Movement, located the source of progress on the individual, not social structure. It valued "one's own (*ziji*) knowledge, moral purpose and physical well-being," "one's own will" and "being answerable to oneself." Only through self-help could future citizens become "useful" to society. Otherwise, spoilt children would grow up becoming vermin (*duchong*).[82] If young men and women learned to pull themselves up by their bootstraps, they would stay away from idle lifestyles and movements that worked actively against Nationalist society.

National Jamborees: Convergence of Values

Petit-bourgeois outlook and focus on personal achievements appealed to the urban elite, who identified the solution to China's problems in the refinement of people's private life. At the same time, the scout program's origins in British empire-making left room for GMD cadres to project their own militaristic desires. This cohabitation of civic, cosmopolitan

---

[80] Dai, "Tongzijun duiyu shehui guojia minzu shijie renlei yingfu de zeren jiangci," 813.
[81] Ibid., 814.
[82] Dai, "Tongzijun xunlian zhi mude de jiangci [The Purposes of Scout Training]," *DJTXSWC*, 834–6.

and austere, martial ethos is vividly illustrated by events like the national jamborees, two of which were held in the capital, Nanjing, before the Nationalist retreat to Taiwan.[83] The 1930 and 1936 jamborees respectively brought 3,366 and some 11,000 boys and girls from across the nation to its ceremonial center, forging a sense of fraternity that transcended the cultural variations and political tensions that divided provinces.[84] They were rare occasions where young people interacted with fellow citizens from across the country and experienced Nationalist power in close proximity. The state's steely prowess was projected alongside the display of diverse talents by scout troops, and individual scouts' thirst for adventure and futuristic imagination. At the first jamboree, troops competed with one another on a list of eight skills that included first aid, communicating Chinese and English phrases in flag semaphore, cooking, setting up tents, building wooden bridges, transmitting spoken messages, tying knots and orientation after dark. Individual children had even more opportunities to test their achievements; the eleven competitions covered domestic knowledge like needlework and lighting a fire, outdoor activities such as cycling and treasure hunt and scouts rituals such as marching and wearing the uniform properly. Political fealty – knowledge of the Three People's Principle, GMD history and Sun Yat-sen's career – was another category among the competitive components of the 1930 camping assembly that rewarded adeptness and resourcefulness.

Indeed, identification with the Nationalist state was experienced in the jamboree as self-discovery. In June 1930, *Scouts of China* published an account penned by a participant in the jamboree held the previous spring. The article took the form of a personal diary over nine days, although the jamboree lasted only from April 18 to April 21. Readers learned details not only of the author's experience at the congregation in Nanjing but also his well-off urban background as the eldest son in a nuclear family who could afford to hire a nanny to take care of three young children. The reading public shared in the sixth grader's anticipation of travel, enjoyed the jokes his fellow scouts told one another and relived the activity-packed gathering. Young campers, readers were told, enjoyed wholesome meals of meat, green vegetable and rice. Dancing, singing and laughter filled the first evening of the jamboree. Children apparently

---

[83] The third jamboree was originally scheduled for October 1948 to coincide with National Day, but the contingencies of civil war delayed the event until 1956. It took place in the Taiwanese city of Kaohsiung ("Sanjie quanguo tongzijun dahui ding bennian shuangshi jie zai jing juxing [Third National Jamboree to Be Held on This Year's National Day in the Capital]," *Zhongguo tongzijun zonghui gongbao* 2: 12 [June 1948]: 12).

[84] Sun, *Minguo shiqi de tongzijun yanjiu*, 177–9.

had immense latitude roaming the capital – the diarist recounted buying fruits from stalls outside the campsite and failing to catch an afternoon movie at the newly built National Grand Theater (*Guomin da xiyuan*). Despite having the most advanced cinema, Nanjing underwhelmed the young cosmopolite. Streets in central Nanjing were lively but poorly paved and those around the campsite were much worse.

At the conclusion of the article, readers followed the sixth grader back home from the jamboree. "I felt," the author said as he went to sleep:

I was wandering into a beautiful metropolis. The architecture was perfect and unlike anything that I have seen in movies. Even more remarkable were the urbanites on the street: their spirit was courageous, their behaviors were as pure and clean as the clothes they wore, they all had smiles on their faces. Except for the cries of infants, there were no argumentative and fierce howls on the market. I have never been to a place like this and did not know what the city's name was. But I realized that it was my adorable Republic of China, for the street was filled with flags with the blue sky, the white sun and the red background.

It was in reverie that the intimate and personal meshed with the national and grandiose.

I did not have wings but I felt that I was flying. I was flying high until I leapt out of planet Earth and, with a pair of binoculars, saw a small Scouts of China badge sprouting from the ground. The badge grew until it shone upon the whole planet and when children from all corners of the world welcomed it with applause. [85]

These futuristic imaginaries were, as readers eventually learned with the diarist's younger brother, projections of the second national jamboree. The boy's growth as a scout and as a person was thus bound with the epic of the nation's modernization and pacification under Nationalist rule. The backwater that was the nation's capital would become an exemplar of urban modernity, its citizens contented and well behaved, Chinese scouts universally celebrated and the author literally a high flier.

But perhaps the *bildungsroman*-like diary was not that personal after all. The boy scout took on the pseudonym Kuohu or Parenthesis. While readers learned about his family circumstances and interest in movies, table tennis and the supplement of the Shanghai daily *Shenbao*, they were only told that the diarist hailed from a trading port called H and that his principal and scout leader were, respectively, G and B. Parenthesis could stand in for any ideal young citizen under the scout program: urbane, healthy, ambitious and relatively well-heeled. Given its authorship, the detailed exposé of the jamboree and its participants served as the

---

[85] Kuohu, "Yige tongzijun canjia quanguo zong jianyue ji da luying riji [The Diary of a Participant in the First National Review of Scouts and Jamboree]," *Zhongguo tongzijun*, no. 9 (1930): 45.

blueprint for a desirable lifestyle in which political dissent and unseemly urban pleasures played no part. That the jamboree appealed to a wider petit-bourgeois audience beyond the modest number of participants and their families was attested by its state-sponsored distribution in multiple media. Aside from reports in print, Scouts of China commissioned the renowned Mingxing Film Company, which was then releasing in installment its twenty-seven-hour-long *The Burning of the Red Lotus Temple* (*Huoshao hongliansi*, 1928), to capture on two rolls of film the review and scout camps. The movie was subsequently approved by the GMD Propaganda Department and screened across theaters in Shanghai and Nanjing. Texts, images and sound related to scouting joined commercial magazines and movies as cultural products that defined the habitus of the cosmopolitan middle class.

The second national jamboree reaffirmed the qualities shared by petit-bourgeois youths from across the vast and tenuously unified country. General Association official Zhang Xiaoliang, relishing his memory of the first national jamboree, enthused on the brotherhood and mutual cooperation of the transient young community despite differences in dialects, religions and customs. His guide for participants at the upcoming assembly, published in the General Association's magazine (also named *Scouts of China*), reiterated scout organizers' commitment to grooming self-reliant and resourceful citizens with distinct habits and tastes. Participants would learn to behave as privileged citizens who nonetheless strive for economic self-sufficiency and avoid conspicuous consumption. While realizing that the expensive trip would likely be paid for by middle-class parents or through pocket money, Zhang encouraged scouts to raise funds with their own labor. Urbanites could deliver newspapers or earn money by contributing to mass-circulating publications themselves; rural children could grow vegetables, farm fish or sell their own handicraft products. Those who eventually made their way to Nanjing were advised not to flaunt their wealth when bringing gifts for exchange with their peers. Instead of splurging on expensive souvenirs from confectionary stores and flashy department stores in the capital, campers should either prepare handmade mementos or purchase specialties from their hometowns with their own savings.[86]

Zhang exhorted participants not to repeat blunders that plagued the first jamboree. They were warned not to tamper with their scout uniforms and "force tailors in Nanjing to burn midnight oil" again.[87] In 1930, some

---

[86] Zhang Xiaoliang, "Canjia quanguo tongzijun da luying yingyou zhi zhunbei [Preparations for Participants at the National Jamboree]," MS, 1936, Zhang Xiaoliang Collection, NPUE, http://140.127.82.166/handle/987654321/1688 (accessed August 10, 2012).
[87] Ibid.

scouts found themselves having to remake their substandard outfits the day before the review.[88] At the campsite, located in the stunning Sun Yat-sen Mausoleum, young people would deftly deploy modern amenities to prepare food, communicate with their hometowns and make themselves warm and comfortable. They would have soap, threads and needles, stamps and letter pads, knives, basic medicine, a watch and a camera with extra film ready in their backpacks. They would tour and admire Nanjing's modernizing urban landscape in groups, making the most out of their hard-earned trip by doing prior research on tourist attractions and shopping venues in the capital.[89] Apart from dance or theatrical performances that drew on motifs from various provinces, the jamboree promoted a new nationwide class identity that traversed regional affiliations. It would avoid the embarrassing scene at the first jamboree that saw Troop 64 from Shanghai engaging scouts from the interior Hebei province in fistfights because of "misunderstanding in communication" (yuyan wuhui).[90]

The jamboree, like scouting in general, aimed to instill values and consumption patterns that united privileged Chinese urbanites with their counterparts from industrialized societies across the world. Cosmopolitanism, resourcefulness and good taste were valorized over sectarianism, provincialism and ideological confrontation. That does not mean, however, that martial expressions of nationalism were absent. With Japan's designs on China proper becoming increasingly obvious, observers counted on scouting to impress upon young people a "militaristic and patriotic (shangwu aiguo) spirit" so that scouts would be ready to serve as vanguards of mass militias or even patrol the trenches in combat situations.[91] Subservience to strictly delineated chains of demand, highly valued in the scout tradition, was no doubt helpful to a state fighting recurrent internal and international enemies. Jamborees reinforced scouts' military-style discipline in choreographed spectacles. At the first jamboree, the navy orchestra and its counterpart from the Nationalist government played the national song before Chiang Kai-shek

---

[88] Kuohu, "Yige tongzijun canjia quanguo zong jianyue ji da luying riji," 40; Zhongguo tongzijun silingbu, "Wei diyi ci quanguo zong jianyue ji da luying juxing hou gao Zhongguo tongzijun shu [Letter to the Scouts of China at the Conclusion of the First National Jamboree]," Zhongguo tongzijun, no. 11 (1930): 3.

[89] Zhang, "Canjia quanguo tongzijun da luying yingyou zhi zhunbei."

[90] Kuohu, "Yige tongzijun canjia quanguo zong jianyue ji da luying riji," 44; Zhongguo tongzijun silingbu, "Wei diyi ci quanguo zong jianyue ji da luying juxing hou gao Zhongguo tongzijun shu," 4.

[91] Cao Yongfang, "Xin shenghuo yundong yu tongzijun xunlian [New Life Movement and Scout Training]," Jiaoyuxue yuekan 3:4 (1936): 154; Li Shutang, "Tongzijun xunlian de yiyi jiqi shiming [The Meaning and Mission of Scout Training]," Changcheng jikan 1, no. 1 (1935): 47.

and Dai Jitao as Hu Hanmin reviewed the troops assembled. The closing ceremony of the jamboree was held at the successor of the Whampoa Military Academy, from which Chiang drew his most loyal followers.[92] In fact, children spent much of their time outside the campsite at the academy and experienced scouting as coterminous with the military.

The spatial symbolism invested in the jamboree was just as palpable in 1936. While scouts had merely visited the Sun Yat-sen Mausoleum six years before, the locus of nationalistic devotion and revolutionary ritual served as the campsite of the second national jamboree. The mausoleum, to which a cemetery for the National Revolutionary Army was added only a year prior, betrayed a seamless narrative of the GMD-led revolution since the Republic's founding in 1911. Its allusions to the Ming dynasty underscored the GMD's claim to inherit China's glorious traditions.[93] While the national shrine evoked the past, the rallying song sung by scouts alluded to its future. "We are young soldiers (*shaonian bing*) of the Three People's Principles!" the lyrics declared; "the blue sky is high and the white sun is bright," participants chanted in homage to the GMD colors beneath the monumental cream structure topped with dark blue tiles.[94] Review of scout troops was an elaborate affair. It was strategically held on National Day at the Central Stadium and, compared with the 1930 jamboree, the military played a more visible role. Boys and girls woke up on the morning of October 10 to tanks and sentries that dotted the Purple Mountain. At nine o'clock, Chiang Kai-shek, in his full regalia as head of the Military Affairs Commission (*Junshi weiyuanhui*), appeared with his deputy He Yingqin (1890–1987) and other officials to phalanxes of scouts in "Attention" position. The review was followed by an aerobatic performance in which smoke trails formed linked characters of *shi*, a symbol of the "Double Ten" National Day. Added to the political ritual was a nationalistic statement of China's sovereignty over Manchuria. To thunderous applause from the audience, which included foreign diplomats posted in Nanjing, entered a twenty-strong delegation from the four provinces that seceded after the Mukden Incident in 1931 to form the puppet state of Manchukuo. Not unlike Sun Yat-sen's burial at the same location seven years before, the ceremony helped the GMD

---

[92] Kuohu, "Yige tongzijun canjia quanguo zong jianyue ji da luying riji," 40–4.
[93] Henrietta Harrison, *The Making of the Republican Citizen: Political Ceremonies and Symbols in China, 1911–1929* (Oxford: Oxford University Press, 2000), 208–10; Rudolf G. Wagner, "Ritual, Architecture, Politics, and Publicity during the Republic: Enshrining Sun Yat-sen," in *Chinese Architecture and the Beaux-Arts*, eds. Jeffrey W. Cody, Nancy S. Steinhardt and Tony Atkin (Honolulu: University of Hawai'i Press, 2011), 263.
[94] Du Tingxiu, "Zhongguo tongzijun ge [Scouts of China Rally]," in *Zhongguo tongzijun choubeichu gongzuo baogao*, 176–7.

stake a symbolic claim on Manchuria and other regions that it failed to control.[95] While scouts admired the monumentality of the capital, they themselves were enlisted in a spectacle that highlighted the military preparedness and seamless unity between the Nationalist state and the citizenry.

Achievements and Limitations

The blend of militaristic state power and middle-class civility attested to the party-state's effort to project its mass politics as nonpartisan. The image of scouting as a path to personal refinement resonated with participants long after scouting was abolished following the Communist Revolution in 1949. A former scout, recalling a stint in the movement as a primary school pupil from 1933 to 1935, noted the increasing adulation for Chiang Kai-shek and the Three People's Principles. But he wondered, reminiscing on his training more than half a century later in mainland China, if there was something to be said for the effectiveness of scouting in imparting skills and moral refinement on children.[96] Others were less circumspect in praising how scouts broadened their horizons and afforded them experiences that the average youngster could have enjoyed only in their dreams, such as traveling beyond their hometown. Wei Ming, who joined the 240-strong delegation from Henan province to the 1936 jamboree as a twelve-year-old, reckoned that the experience increased his knowledge, opened his eyes to the wider world and reinforced his patriotism.[97] Another former scout, from the Wuchang-based school that hosted one of China's earliest scout troops, remembered being introduced to the "amazing world" of industrial modernity on a tour of the United States in 1935, and another, a hiking trip to Italy in 1937. Song Bailian, along with a delegation led by Yan Jialin, marveled at American factories and schools, slaughterhouses in Chicago and steel bridges in Los Angeles. He vividly recalled an incredible moment of

[95] Zou Jian, "Quanguo tongzijun di'er ci da jianyue [The Second National Scout Review]," *Xiandai qingnian* 5, no. 1 (1936): 8; Wei Ming, "Jiefang qian 'quanguo tongzijun di'er ci da jianyue da luying' qinli ji [Firsthand Account of the Second National Scout Review-cum-Jamboree before Liberation]," in *Luohe wenshi ziliao*, ed. Zhongguo renmin zhengzhi xieshang huiyi Luohe shi weiyuanhui wenshi ziliao yanjiu weiyuanhui, no. 1 (Luohe, Henan: Zhongguo renmin zhengzhi xieshang huiyi Luohe shi weiyuanhui wenshi ziliao yanjiu weiyuanhui, 1987): 146–7; Harrison, *Making of the Republican Citizen*, 233–4.

[96] Zhai Huaishi, "Zhongguo tongzijun 730 tuan jianjie [Brief Introduction of Scouts of China Troop 730]," in *Xinyang wenshi ziliao*, ed. Zhengxie Xinyang shi wenshi ziliao weiyuanhui, no. 6 (Xinyang, Henan: Zhengxie Xinyang shi wenshi ziliao weiyuanhui, 1992): 165.

[97] Wei, "Jiefang qian 'quanguo tongzijun di'er ci da jianyue da luying' qinli ji," 149.

internationalism when a pedestrian accosted him in New York upon seeing his Scouts of China badge, saying: "Hollo [sic] boy! This is a wonderful world, eh, you can do anything, if you want to, nobody will bother you."[98] Finally, the public identity of scouts – their distinct uniform and high spirits – was a novelty in itself.[99]

In all the excitement scouting generated through spectacles and travel opportunities, it was easy to forget that the mass movement was cultivated and jealously guarded by the GMD to serve specific political purposes, most noticeably to draw youths away from Communism. De Grazia observes that Mussolini's mass organizations appealed to young workers not by overt political indoctrination, let alone militarization, but by alluding to a better way of life distinct from that of either radical labor unionism or parochial local communities.[100] Likewise, in Nationalist China, while mass initiatives stressed Sunist orthodoxy, both scouting and the New Life movements appealed to urbanites by promising a more rewarding, salubrious form of existence. The fond memories many former participants shared testified to the extent to which scouting under the GMD served the function of building consent among a young populace by co-opting them in a glamorous and skill-focused mode of social activism that reaffirmed, rather than disturbed, class hierarchy and state power.

Yet the multiple agendas ascribed to scouting did render it susceptible to unorthodox appropriation. Underscoring this ideological ambiguity was the limitations of Nationalist political power. As an organization, scouting never made many inroads into the peasantry. Like the GMD itself, scouting was a mostly urban phenomenon. Plans for expansion into the impoverished rural hinterland, including such creative ideas as doing away with expensive uniforms and lowering the minimum number of members required to form a patrol from six to two, might have helped the movement spread inland.[101] However, increases in enrollment and extended geographical reach were no straightforward signs of strength. Youth associations proliferated in Japanese-ruled Taiwan through the

[98] Song Bailian, "Zhongguo tongzijun diandi [Tidbits of the Scouts of China]," in Wenshi ziliao cungao xuanbian, eds. Dang Dexin et al. (Beijing: Zhongguo wenshi chubanshe, 2002), 24: 648.
[99] Yang Jingsan and Chen Fu'an, "Tongzijun zuzhi zai Xixiang huodong de shishi jilue [Brief History of Scouting in Xixiang]," in Xixiang xian wenshi ziliao, ed. Zhongguo renmin zhengzhi xieshang huiyi Shaanxi sheng Xixiang xian weiyuanhui wenshi ziliao weiyuanhui, no. 6 (Xixiang: Zhongguo renmin zhengzhi xieshang huiyi Shaanxi sheng Xixiang xian weiyuanhui wenshi ziliao weiyuanhui, 1995): 116–17.
[100] De Grazia, Culture of Consent, 242–3.
[101] Cao, "Xin shenghuo yundong yu tongzijun xunlian," 8; Zhang Zhongren, "Xiangcun tongzijun [Village Scouts]," in Tongzijun xueshu jiangzuo [Academic Seminars on Scouting] (Taipei: Zhonghua shuju, 1978), 309.

late 1920s, but as concerned colonial officials realized, many local society bodies were haphazardly run and unready to adopt a centrally mandated program for civilizing (*jiaohua/kyôka*) native youths.[102] An enlarged youth movement also presented new problems. Like British colonial regimes in Africa, the Chinese state found it difficult to monopolize the iconic attire and rallies of scouting.[103] During the war of resistance against Japan, when the Nationalist state was struggling to exert power over its new southwestern base, scout leaders reported seeing individuals not registered with the GMD-led general association dressed in scout uniform.[104] In far-flung regions, even scout leaders overseen by the provincial education bureaus could be unreliable. A scout organizer in northwestern Xinjiang province apparently managed to smuggle Communist propaganda into nothing less than the county-run primary school. Jiang Lianchun remembered singing as a ten-year-old in 1937 a song called "Anti-imperialist Scouts Rally," humming lyrics like "we are soldiers of the New Democracy," alluding to the Communist plea for an interparty, interclass united front against Japan. It took another eight years before Jiang realized his scout leader's not-too-subtle subversion of GMD ideological indoctrination by changing the lyrics of the "Scouts of China Rally."[105] Even in Anhui province, where Chiang Kai-shek's authority was much more established, political resistance could find its way into tightly orchestrated youth rallies. The review of scouts at the local junior high school in Xuancheng county, held just months after the first national jamboree, was marred by the sudden appearance of banners like "Down with Chiang Kai-shek the new warlord!" and "Long live the Chinese Communist Party!" This embarrassing event, attended by Governor Chen Diaoyuan (1886–1943), led to confiscation of more anti-GMD materials from student dormitories.[106] Such developments confirmed Dai Jitao's worst fear – that mass, youth organizations could easily become breeding ground for political enemies.

In areas where scouting was more established, organizers found it hard to sustain enthusiasm among a movement growing in numbers. Despite

---

[102] Chen, *Zhimin tongzhi yu "qingnian,"* 211–13.
[103] Parsons, *Race, Resistance, and the Boy Scout Movement*, 13.
[104] Scouts of China General Association to Executive Yuan, April 5, 1942, Executive Yuan Collection, 2/3500, Second Historical Archives.
[105] Wang Renping, *Manasi wenshi ziliao yinyue zhuanji xubian* [*Second Installment of the Special Collection on Music of Manas County Literary and Historical Materials*] (Manas, Xinjiang: Zhongguo renmin zhengzhi xieshang huiyi Manasi xian weiyuanhui wenshi ziliao yanjiu weiyuanhui, 1995), 50–1.
[106] He Xianbi, "Danao 'tongzijun jianyue' [Sabotaging Review of Scouts]," *Xuancheng xian wenshi ziliao*, ed. Xuancheng xian zhengxie wenshi weiyuanhui, no. 3 (Xuancheng: Xuancheng xian zhengxie wenshi weiyuanhui, 1988), 7–8.

the very positive memory shared by some former scouts, responses from others were less effusive. After all, not many young people found their way to Nanjing, let alone New York or Rome. For most, scouting was a mundane part of school life. Making scouting mandatory ensured an exponential growth in membership; enrollment increased almost sixfold in seven years from 86,536 in 1934 to a staggering 507,839 in late 1941.[107] But increase in numbers did not guarantee earnest participation. Primary and junior high school pupils indulged in unworthy behaviors once they took their scout uniforms off and used every opportunity to excuse themselves from training activities or leave their troops altogether. Parents, meanwhile, were distrustful of scout leaders and the activities they designed.[108] In addition, the movement's school-based nature meant that it was difficult for scouts, even if they so wished, to continue participation once they graduated. Zhang Xiaoliang claimed that otherwise committed youngsters who entered senior high schools, where scouting was no longer compulsory, or joined the workforce often had to involuntarily end their involvement in the organization. He urged his colleagues to broaden Scouts of China's presence from schools to factories and retail shops. Just as teachers appreciated diligent and obedient students, employers would embrace the movement for molding "conscientious, improvement-seeking, hardship-bearing shopkeepers and workers."[109] Rapid growth in the number of scouts across the nation did not, in itself, strengthen the movement's influence in its constituents' way of life.

Aside from organizational weaknesses, ambiguity in goals and missions posed challenges for scouting. The movement's attention to petit-bourgeois aspirations allowed it to appeal to constituents outside the GMD. Yet tension between priorities also inspired intraparty contestation. Its missionary origins, military-like hierarchy and aesthetics continued to haunt scouting as activists like Zhang Xiaoliang edged the movement closer to the conservative revolutionary agenda of cultivating a voluntaristic, technically adept and politically reliable labor force without fully jettisoning its liberal or apolitical self-image. Dai Jitao acknowledged Zhang's concern in 1932 when he argued that *tongzijun* should not be taken literally to mean a military force (*jun*) staffed by adolescents.

[107] Zhongguo tongzijun zonghui choubeichu, *Zhongguo tongzijun choubeichu gongzuo baogao*, 113–23; Zhongguo tongzijun zonghui, *Sanshi nian de Zhongguo tongzijun* [*Thirty Years of the Scouts of China*] (Chongqing: n.p., 1941), 13–14.

[108] Zhang, "Zenyang zhengqiu ertong laizuo tongzijun."

[109] Zhang Xiaoliang, "Tongzijun de shengming [The Life of Scouting]," MS, December 1932, Zhang Xiaoliang Collection, NPUE, http://140.127.82.166/handle/987654321/1683 (accessed August 10, 2012).

Rather than only preparing future party-state functionaries, scouting had a broader mandate to groom young people into decent, capable and "squeaky clean individuals" (*gan'gan jingjing de ren*) so that they would become honest officials, valorous soldiers and contented (*anfen*) peasants or commit to any other role in society.[110]

But observations by senior Nationalists did not silence those who believed that the goal of producing a nimble and obedient workforce was not aligned closely enough with the party-state's. For some, the missionary background of scouting was an original sin that posed an unbridgeable gulf between scouting and the national revolution. Accusations flew that Yan Jialin, the Wuchang-based missionary, was exploiting a compulsory part of the schooling process to proselytize for Christianity.[111] The bourgeois internationalism of scouting, likewise, inspired suspicion. Its image as a "Westernized" (*xiyang hua*) and "patrician" (*guizu hua*) club lingered, as did doubts that the program promoted foreign or even Anglo-Saxon interests. Amidst new initiatives from rival party factions to cultivate pro-GMD activists among students after the Mukden Incident of 1931, scouting was admonished to first, firmly serve China's quest for "freedom and independence," and second, embrace military values in anticipation of war against Japan.[112] He Yingqin, Chiang's deputy in both the military and scout hierarchies, stressed in 1936 that moral and physical training of individuals helped enhance the entire nation's organization, productivity and self-defense in the face of a foreign enemy. Drawing from German philosopher Johann Fichte's prescriptions for nationalist resistance against French occupation, the general likened scouting to the nationalist philosopher's privileging of military training in schools for gearing up popular resolve against an invading force.[113] General He's association of Baden-Powell's brainchild with German romantic nationalism defied the liberal cosmopolitan image scout activities like Zhang Zhongren and Zhang Xiaoliang had painted for their program, and spoke to latent disagreements within the GMD on how to incorporate scouting into the conservative revolutionary project.

---

[110] Dai, "Duoshao ren kancuo le tongzijun [Countless People Had Misunderstood Scouting]," MS, 1932, Zhang Xiaoliang Collection, NPUE, http://140.127.82.166/han dle/987654321/1683 (accessed August 10, 2012).

[111] Dai, "Dui konggao Yan Jialin zhuren zhi pishi [Comment on Accusations against Yan Jialin]," in *DJTXSWC*, 833–4.

[112] Li, "Tongzijun xunlian de yiyi jiqi shiming," 47; Cao, "Xin shenghuo yundong yu tongzijun xunlian," 154–5; Huang, *Politics of Depoliticization*, 90.

[113] He Yingqin, "Tongzijun yingshen yu minzu fuxing" [The Spirit of Scouting and National Revival]," *Gongjiao xuexiao* 2, no. 25 (1936): 5.

With the outbreak of the Second Sino–Japanese War in 1937, the momentum swung decisively to the side of those who saw scouting as a means to prepare young activists for a vanguard role in a war that relied on total mobilization of civilians. Wartime service corps (*zhanshi fuwu tuan*), commissioned by the Scouts of China but mobilized outside the regular hierarchy of patrols and troops, sprung up in GMD-controlled provinces like Sichuan, Yunnan and Shaanxi. Similar initiatives emerged in more precarious locations like Zhejiang province and Shanghai. After the Battle of Shanghai of 1937, which resulted in the GMD's and the Scouts of China's retreat from the metropolis, the First Wartime Service Corps continued to operate out of the International Settlement. Its 2,027 members, aged between sixteen and thirty, accommodated refugees, serviced frontline troops, performed firefighting and first aid duties and wielded a sophisticated propaganda campaign that targeted not only a domestic audience but also expatriate communities and observers abroad. Young men and a smaller number of young women took on functions commonly ascribed to militias. They delivered warm clothes and food to soldiers, maintained public order and even gathered intelligence on the enemy. They deployed movie and radio to mobilize the populace in support of the nation's resistance and broadcast tips on surviving air raids and containing infectious diseases.[114] Appealing to the international clout of scouting, the Shanghai corps invited its foreign counterparts to join it in a "Junior League of Nations" and fight against "insensible militarists" and an "enemy of world culture."[115] They were public diplomats in a time when international support of the Chongqing-based GMD state was still lukewarm. They projected the increasingly militant organization as a cosmopolitan endeavor on a quest for peace and friendship with foreigners, not a nationalistic campaign against particular peoples. After all, as a commissioner (*weiyuan*) of the Shanghai wartime corps observed, scouts in both Britain and Germany were enlisted to play a part in "wartime work" (*zhanshi gongzuo*) during the Great War. This benign image received endorsements from scouts

[114] Zhao Bangheng et al., eds., *Kangzhan yu tongjun* [*The War of Resistance and Scouting*] (n.p., 1938), 103, 133, 153–5, 178; Hong Zhixin, "Huiyi canjia Zhongguo tongzijun zhanshi fuwu tuan de pianduan [Memories of My Participation in the Wartime Service Corps of the Scouts of China]," in *Jing'an wenshi*, ed. Zhongguo renmin zhengzhi xieshang huiyi Shanghai shi Jing'an qu weiyuanhui wenshi ziliao weiyuanhui, no. 7 (Shanghai: Zhongguo renmin zhengzhi xieshang huiyi Shanghai shi Jing'an qu weiyuanhui wenshi ziliao weiyuanhui, 1992), 30–3.
[115] "An Open Letter to the Scouts of the World," in *Kangzhan yu tongjun*, 30. The appeal, in English, also appeared in Chinese and French.

in Britain and India, not to mention the expatriate community in Shanghai.[116]

The Great War reference alluded unintentionally to the degree to which the GMD state counted upon civilians to run the war machine in China's first total war, to which our attention soon turns. In terms of membership, the various wartime services corps were pale shadows of the scouting movement now headquartered in Chongqing. But corps members were committed volunteers who more resembled militia members than schoolchildren, putting to high relief the militant streak inherent to scouting. Chapter 4 discusses the reconsolidation of the conservative revolution during China's extended resistance against Japanese encroachment. For now, it suffices to stress that wartime work performed by scouts involved tasks that fell well under the purview of the state. Wartime service corps in Yunnan swept up popular outrage against the invading army by recalling "atrocities committed by Japanese devils" in speeches, songs and drama. They urged the masses to join military service, subscribe to war bonds and help finance the cash-strapped National Revolutionary Army. More significantly, deliberate efforts were made to deploy scouts in intelligence-gathering operations. To identity Japanese infiltration into GMD-controlled areas, a select group of Yunnan service corps members listened to conversations in public areas, observed pedestrians' demeanor and belongings and surveilled travelers, refugees and "local ruffians and itinerant hooligans" (*dipi liumang*).[117] The call for young men and women to spy on their neighbors alarmed the Shanghai Municipal Council, the expatriate-staffed body that governed the embattled International Settlement until 1941. Scouts were arrested for interfering with the authority of the foreigner-run police force as the Shanghai wartime service corps, in turn, pleaded the enclave to afford its members greater room for maneuver.[118]

The *coup de grâce* that put to rest any illusions in the Scouts of China's professed political neutrality came in 1940, when the Three People's Principles Youth Corps overtook the movement. Founded in the spring of 1938, the Three People's Principle Youth Corps was envisioned by Chiang Kai-shek as a mass organization that appealed to politically minded young people disaffected by the intractable factional struggles

---

[116] Zheng Haozhang, "Tongzijun zhanshi fuwu tuan de yiyi he renwu [The Meaning and Mission of the Scouts Wartime Service Corps]," in *Kangzhan yu tongjun*, 40; "Tongzijun xiaoxi [Scouting News]," *Zhanshi tongzijun*, no. 28 (1938): 12.

[117] "Tongzijun xiaoxi," 13.

[118] Ni Jiaxi, "Cong jianku zhong fendou [Struggle amidst Hardship]," in *Kangzhan yu tongjun*, 86.

within the GMD.[119] It emerged amidst calls within the scouting community for a well-coordinated hierarchy of bodies modeled on the
Komsomol and Young Pioneers in the Soviet Union to rally young
citizens around the Three People's Principles.[120] At a meeting of the
Standing Committee of the GMD Central Executive Committee
on November 25, 1940, the Youth Corps was given the mandate to
work with all individuals under twenty-five. In other words, despite
objections from functionaries like Zhang Xiaoliang, scouting and the
larger youth movement were relegated under a parent organization on
which future generations of committed revolutionaries counted.[121] Three
years later, the entire Scouts of China General Association was subsumed
under the Youth Corps.[122] Until the Youth Corps was disbanded
in September 1947, scouts, like other youth activists, engaged in espionage and propaganda operations against the GMD's nemeses during the
war of resistance against Japan and subsequently the civil war against
Communism.

Scouting was symptomatic of a distinct GMD approach to mass politics that conflated everyday morality, physical strength and rejection of
left-wing ideology. Since the mid-1920s, youth had been romanticized in
Nationalist discourse as a fecund source of energy that could either renew
or derail the conservative revolution. Without proper outlets, young vigor
would be expended on sexual promiscuity and left-wing adventurism,
which, as Hu Hanmin argued, were two sides of the same coin.
Accordingly, scout training offered the urban middle class a means to self-
improvement, and that in itself was conducive to Nationalist rule.
Whether the quasi-military, missionary-originated program should take
on explicitly ideological themes was of secondary importance. Scouting
mediated GMD anticommunism, the conservative revolutionary agenda
of beautifying and rationalizing everyday life and individual needs. It was
an eloquent expression of what Dai defined as the ultimate meaning of the

---

[119] Wang, *Dangyuan, dangquan yu dangzheng*, 279.
[120] Xiong Feng, "Shaonian men zai Sulian [Youth in the Soviet Union]," *Zhanshi tongzijun*,
no. 39–41 (1939): 24–5.
[121] *Queding dang yu tuan zhi guanxi banfa* [*Guidelines on Distinguishing between the Party and
the Youth Corps*], November 25, 1940, Executive Yuan 2/10986, Second Archives;
Zhang Xiaoliang, "Zhongguo tongzijun zonghui ying lishu zhongyang zhi zuozheng ji
liyou [Facts and Reasons Supporting the Scouts of China General Association's
Subordination under the GMD Central Committee]," MS, September 10, 1941,
Zhang Xiaoliang Collection, NPUE, http://140.127.82.166/handle/987654321/1705
(accessed August 10, 2012).
[122] *Zhongguo tongzijun zonghui xingzheng shiyi gaili Sanmin zhuyi qingnian tuan zhuchi banli*
[*Transfer of the Administrative Matters of the Scouts of China General Association to the Three
People's Principles Youth Corps*], November 22, 1943, *huiyi* 5.3/219.5, Kuomintang
Archives.

Figure 3.1 Cover of *Scouts of China* special issue on discipline, 1931
(Courtesy of the Kuomintang Party History Institute)

minsheng principle and of the national revolution: providing "beautiful
and elegant enjoyment."[123] An individual's evolution into a properly
behaved, sexually composed being was a political process, although it
often took the guise of apolitical endeavors.

[123] Dai, *Sun Wen zhuyi zhi zhexue de jichu*, 11.

Figure 3.2 Girl scouts at a Nanjing high school performing needlework
(Courtesy of the General Association of the Scouts of China)

Thus, even as its mission changed to comply with wartime priorities, scout training continued to offer experience to which adolescents could relate at a personal level. Activities for preparing scouts to conduct intelligence gathering, for example, saw children tracing beans "enemy spies" left as markers, making their own markers with tree branches, bricks and wire to guide comrades to specific destinations and participating in remarkably realistic war games in which one group acted as the enemy army and the other played guerilla forces.[124] Such exercises were packaged as games that both answered the needs of a nation at war and the innate values of scout education – learning by doing, teamwork, obeying orders, acquiring new skills and having fun. This fusion of leisure management, moral cultivation and growing militancy in scouting enjoyed ever greater currency as the GMD's model of mass activism was leveraged to enlist the entire society, and not just youths from comfortable middle-class families, to fight a foreign enemy.

[124] Wu Yaolin, "Zhanshi huodong zhidao – (san) zhuisuo dizong [Wartime Activities Guide – (3) Tracking the Enemy]," *Zhanshi tongzijun*, no. 28 (1938): 4–6.

Figure 3.3 A scout from Nanjing Sanmin Junior High School in uniform: shorts, khaki shirt and group scarf and with the iconic campaign hat (Courtesy of the General Association of the Scouts of China)

Figure 3.4 Scouts of China expressing camaraderie with its US counterpart organization

4   State Comes First
Wartime Spiritual Revolution

China's extended resistance against Japanese invasion was the country's first total war. Nineteen thirty-seven, undoubtedly, did not mark the beginning of modern Chinese society's embroilment in military conflicts. Internecine conflicts had formed one salient experience of political life since Yuan Shikai's death in 1916, which resulted in destructive splits within the Beiyang army. Warlords governed different provinces, fought against one other, mobilized voluntary associations, built bureaucracies, made peace and fought against Nationalist revolutionaries. Meanwhile, revolutionaries were themselves responsible for producing "cultures of violence" that went hand in hand with the construction of the central government in Nanjing and the acrimonious strife between the GMD and the CCP.[1] In addition, as the previous chapter demonstrates, Nationalist cadres combined daily routine with martial symbolism, alertness and resourcefulness under its core mass mobilization strategy. The reality and anticipation of war were ingrained into the conservative revolution, as impetuses for personal development and as rallying points against class confrontations.

What was new to the resistance war was not a departure from these trends but their convergence and radicalization. It represented an extended moment, coinciding with but not confined to the eight years that saw the GMD fight together with the Communists, when the people, instead of just the military, were consciously called upon by the state to defend the country against foreign invasion.[2] Analyzing the

---

[1] For warlordism's wide-ranging impact on republican-era society and politics, see, among other examples, Edward A. McCord, "Warlords against Warlordism: The Politics of Anti-warlordism in Early Twentieth-Century China," *Modern Asian Studies* 30 (1996): 795–827, and Alfred H. Y. Lin, "Warlord, Social Welfare, and Philanthropy: The Case of Guangzhou under Chen Jitang, 1929–1936," *Modern China* 30 (2004): 151–98. For intersections between revolutionary and military violence under the GMD–CCP alliance, see Hans J. Van de Ven, *War and Nationalism in China* (London: RoutledgeCurzon, 2003), chap. 3.

[2] This is not the occasion to weigh in on the controversial move in the People's Republic to backdate the start of China's war with Japan from July 1937 to September 1931 in official

Sino–Japanese conflict under the total war paradigm highlights the inter-war origins of China's conservative revolution and the anticipation of a global showdown between nations that links as a coherent whole the years before full-scale conflict and after. Inasmuch as conflicts between nations further delegitimized those within them, total war, while posing tremendous challenges for the GMD regime, also opened opportunities for a revolution that prized interclass unity. Rana Mitter recently draws attention to the seemingly paradoxical significance of the resistance. On one hand, the conflict depleted China's modern industries and infra-structure on the coast, displaced eighty million inhabitants and caused at least fourteen million casualties. The advancing Japanese forces effectively robbed Chiang's government of its base in the lower Yangzi region, forcing it to abandon China's economic and political centers like Shanghai and Nanjing for the interior. On the other hand, the war left enduring but less tangible legacies such as enhanced state provision of welfare and improvements in health and hygiene. Prolonged resistance transformed gender roles and energized idealist youths. A society at war provided much potential for a mobilization program that demanded exclusive political loyalty and the active participation of the populace.[3] It is common knowledge that the CCP emerged as the beneficiary of this social convulsion. But subsequent Communist victory did not preclude the fact that total war was also a productive event for the conservative revolution.

It was not for no reason that Chiang Kai-shek foresaw as early as 1932 that out of a second world war could emerge a decolonized "new China" that stood shoulder to shoulder with other great powers.[4] A common external enemy lent urgency to the GMD's imperative to rally a fragmented nation around one single political center. In Chongqing, the GMD presided over a community of refugees who hailed from various

textbooks (Sian Cain, "China Rewrites History Books to Extend Sino–Japanese War by Six Years," *The Guardian*, January 13, 2017, www.theguardian.com/books/2017/jan/13/china-rewrites-history-books-to-extend-sino-japanese-war-by-six-years [accessed May 27, 2017]. Suffice it to say that periodizations are intellectual constructs that configure historical analyses rather than faithfully mirror facts. Incidentally, in Japan, the island nation's aggression against China has been commonly named the "15-Year War," starting with the Mukden Incident, since the late 1950s. The term, as Sandra Wilson observes, was not popular among the Chinese; one prominent exception was Mao Zedong, who believed that his country had become a Japanese colony in 1931 (Sandra Wilson, "Rethinking the 1930s and the '15-Year War' in Japan," *Japanese Studies* 21 [2001]: 155–64).

[3] Rana Mitter, *Forgotten Ally: China's World War II, 1937–1945* (Boston, MA: Houghton Mifflin Harcourt, 2013), 15–24. See also Diana Lary, *The Chinese People at War: Human Suffering and Social Transformation, 1927–1945* (New York: Cambridge University Press, 2010).

[4] Chiang, *Jiang Zhongzheng zongtong dang'an: shilüe gaoben*, 14:50.

Japanese-occupied regions. Total war expected citizens to contribute consistently to the resistance at work and at play. Individuals were to submit to authority, ready themselves for action and turn away from decadence and street politics. They were all to behave like scouts, seeing their personal welfare and service to society as inscribed into the nation's future. Insofar as it further delegitimized class politics and furthered micromanagement of citizens' lives, the resistance program represented a radicalization of the conservative revolution. The wartime slogan "nation-building through the war of resistance" (*kangzhan jianguo*) indicated that the party-state was not only struggling for basic survival but also harboring ambitions to perpetuate its ideological priorities beyond the immediate conflict against Japanese imperialism.

This chapter argues that China's first modern industrialized warfare – the Second Sino–Japanese War and the years leading up to it – accentuated the conservative revolution as social and cultural experience for the masses. Unlike previous conflicts in which combat was confined to frontline military forces, the entire society – its population, economy and culture – was mobilized to fight a common enemy. The nation became the sole object of devotion, pushing to the side class interests, liberal politics and some gender norms. The extent to which war mobilization led to actual policies is difficult to assess, but it certainly became a core element of Nationalist self-image as the people's vanguard. As Chiang told elite military officers, victory over both internal enemies and foreign invaders hinged on "the whole nation making a superhuman effort, putting all our heart and strength into the struggle." Chiang's assessment combined romantic celebration of the human *élan* and hardnosed assessment of China's military weakness. "We must," the Generalissimo declared almost poetically in 1934, "use every ounce of our mental and physical powers, we must be willing to pour out our life's blood in resisting the enemy's mechanical strength and in overcoming his superior material equipment."[5] Chiang's faith that the nation's spiritual strength would offset its material inadequacies was the impetus for the National Spiritual Mobilization Movement (*Guomin jingshen zong dongyuan yundong*), launched in 1939, two years after the Marco Polo Bridge Incident. The movement lent urgency and credence to the conservative revolution's vision of a cooperative national communion of puritan laborer-warriors. Despite the wide-ranging devastations the Nationalist modernization program sustained, prolonged resistance

---

[5] Chiang, "Resistance to Aggression and Renaissance of the Nation," *The Collected Wartime Messages of Generalissimo Chiang Kai-shek* (New York: John Day, 1946), 1:15.

reinforced the GMD's determination to recover the Chinese nation's immanent unity enervated by years of foreign control and internal conflicts. The wartime state attempted to materialize in the quotidian the heretofore abstract, state-directed national culture, thereby rendering the GMD's social engineering undertaking eminently comparable to the one the Shôwa fascist regime imposed on Japan and its empire.

"Emergency Period" and the Conservative Revolutionary Vision

Barely had the Nationalist state consolidated its power when the Japanese began a series of military offensives against the loosely- knit republic. Japanese encroachment into Manchuria and Shanghai in 1931 and 1932 provided occasions for re-articulations of the GMD's claim to ideological and political power over society. The party-state offered tutelage not only over the revolutionary subject as prescribed by Sun Yat-sen but also over a people in existential crisis. The concept of "emergency period" (*feichang shiqi*) gained wide currency after the Mukden and Shanghai incidents. This sense of intense crisis, colored by a palpable hint of anticipation over an end to the international system bequeathed by the Versailles Settlement, was not unique to Nationalist China but integral to the global ascendancy of the radical right. In Germany, former army general Erich Ludendorff (1865–1937), whose polemics such as *Total War* (*Der totale Krieg*, 1935) attracted quite a following in China, had contributed to a Weimar-era conservative revolutionary intellectual current since the early 1930s that took the Great War as only the prelude to another large-scale international confrontation. To prepare for an impending war, both the military and civilians had to be mobilized into one moral community. Like the postliberal regimes emerging in Italy and the Soviet Union, total mobilization was to become the norm, not an exception, in how the German state interacted with the populace. The 1931 Mukden Incident in China ushered in a "national emergency" (*hijôji*) in Japan, inspiring a "war fever" that swept across cultural, political and economic life and lasted through the 1930s and 1940s.[6] The heightened expectation of a showdown between nation-states suggests that there were significant continuities between the Second

---

[6] Roger Chickering, "Sore Loser: Ludendorff's Total War," in *The Shadows of Total War: Europe, East Asia, and the United States, 1919–1939*, eds. Roger Chickering and Stig Förster (Cambridge: Cambridge University Press, 2003), 171–3; Louise Young, *Japan's Total Empire: Manchuria and the Culture of Wartime of Imperialism* (Berkeley: University of California Press, 1998), 13.

Sino–Japanese War and the years leading to the eight-year conflict in the way the GMD state defined its sociopolitical agenda, if not military maneuvers.

While the Mukden Incident did not result in long-term, full-scale hostilities between China and Japan, the "emergency" it inspired in Chinese public discourse referred not to isolated skirmishes but to an ordeal that would continue for many months. A 1933 editorial in *Social News* (*Shehui xinwen*), a magazine managed by defectors from the CCP to the Nationalist camp, hailed a new era of formidable violence. "Our epoch, the 1930s, is one in which all struggles are sharpened to their extremity." While Japanese militarists "deployed the high-sounding term 'emergency period' to inflame the people's craze for invasion," it was China whose territory was annexed by a foreign power, whose "red bandits" were threatening the national government and whose economic and financial crises conspired to usher in extraordinarily difficult times for the republic. Taking their cue from the Fascist ascendance to power in Italy, the editors argued for the importance of "a political force that tied together the nation's life. That force must be a vital, violent one capable of smashing everything into pieces!"[7] Investment in the political center as a fearsome agent resisting imperialist expansion provided fresh impetus for the many measures the GMD instituted to tame internal opposition, including the 1931 Emergency Law on Crimes against the Republic. If national survival was at risk, demands such as widening political representation and respecting civil rights were luxuries that ran counter to the demands of the time.

"Emergency," like the conservative revolution as a whole, privileged nationalist commitments over communist and crumbling liberal capitalist values, domestic and international. Appeals to it were as much responses to immediate military threats from Japan as projections of a futural order. In economic management, Nationalist bureaucrats did not necessarily work against global norms emanating from New York or London; in response to the 1929 depression, they aligned the Chinese economy with international capital flow by adopting the gold standard in lieu of silver, effectively giving up autarkic control over the country's monetary system. In political sensibilities, however, GMD ideologists and intellectuals sympathetic to the state looked decidedly toward Berlin, and to a much lesser extent, toward Rome. If the organizational model the GMD emulated under Sun was the Bolsheviks', by the 1930s,

---

[7] "Feichang shiqi de feichang renwu [Extraordinary Tasks in Emergency Period]," *Shehui xinwen* 3:4 (1933): 50–1. See also Fanjun, "Zenyang yingfu zhege feichang shiqi [How to Handle This Emergency Period]," *Minzhong zhoukan* 5:8 (1933): 1–2.

Nationalist China's model party-state were European radical right parties as dictatorships were supposedly better prepared for international war.[8] Like conservative revolutionaries in the West, Chinese observers stressed that something akin to the Great War was soon to befall society in general. A 1933 editorial in the GMD-run daily *Shanghai Morning Post* (*Chenbao*) saw liberal norms of politics and economy giving way to total mobilization. Citing the Franco–Prussian War, in which some 400,000 civilians were called upon to fight alongside the French army as members of the Garde Mobile, the newspaper argued that the concept of battle line and protocols of traditional warfare had become obsolete in a full-scale clash of rival citizenries. "Strategically it would be permissible," the piece continued ominously, "to scorch the earth with fire and blast the enemies' bodies into pieces." China's coming showdown against Japan would immediately blanket the entire society under military goals, relegate private economic production and consumption under state *dirigisme*, and put full limits on civil liberties. American-educated historian Jiang Tingfu (1895–1965) told students at Tsinghua University that China in 1935 was like Europe on the eve of the Great War. As a student at Oberlin College, Jiang observed firsthand from Ohio youth enthusiasm during the war. Even before the United States declared war on Germany, military training was in place in many schools. By 1917, 90 percent of college students were either engaging in actual combat or contributing to home front defense. In Germany, mobilization for the nation blurred class boundaries. "Tasks handled by German university students," the Tsinghua professor remarked approvingly, "were no different from those of common youths." Across Europe, the skilled and the less educated, men fighting in the trenches and women "making coffee for soldiers," were bound together in "martial, sacrificial spirit." Willingness to take part in the nationalist cause without regard for personal power and wealth was a mentality that China must embrace in the emergency period.[9]

Emergency called not only for selfless devotion but for uniformity in political outlook. China's embroilment in an impending great war would lay to rest all commitments other than nationalist ones. In *The Way for Youth*, a 1928 volume, Dai Jitao cited the need for "national mobilization" (*guomin zong dongyuan*) to justify the anti-Communist purge. He exhorted the Chinese people to shake off the delusion of Marxism and

---

[8] Shiroyama, *China during the Great Depression*, 234–5; Kirby, *Germany and Republican China*, 155.

[9] "Suowei guomin zong dongyuan [The Meaning of National Mobilization]," editorial, *Chenbao*, October 16, 1933, 2; Jiang Tingfu, "Feichang shiqi zhi qiannian [Youths in the Emergency Period]," *Zhongyang ribao*, December 7, 1935, C3.

recognize communist internationalism for what it really was –
a universalist ideology that competed with Western imperialism for
control over Eastern nations. Tensions between these two expansionist
schemes and rivalries between nation-states would lead to a second world
war. "If we failed to make concrete efforts to enhance revolutionary
reconstruction and our capabilities," Dai warned, "no one could tell
how many innocent lives would be sacrificed when the Chinese people
and imperialists engaged in their final struggle ten years later."
The theoretician observed that Germany and other belligerents
accounted for only three million out of the twenty million casualties of
the Great War. The greatest numbers of deaths occurred in Russia, the
Balkans and the Middle East, where epidemics, hunger and minor religious strife wreaked havoc. Confucius had ostensibly taught that the state
should always prepare the common people for war. His wisdom appeared
all the more urgent in the twentieth century, when modern wars were
tussles between systems – scientific, economic and industrial. At stake
were not only artilleries, airplanes and tanks. Modernity meant "military
industries pitched against military industries, organizations against organizations" and "transport infrastructure against transport
infrastructure."[10]

With Japan's occupation of Manchuria, Dai's warning acquired fresh
urgency. As a group of former Communists interned in a government-run
reformatory argued in September 1931, "The Chinese nation was in
crisis; would there be any more class interests to talk of when the entire
nation was vanquished? If class interests were to be pursued, the nation's
independence and survival must first be safeguarded." War between
nations, these converts to the GMD told peers still fighting under the
Communist banner, would demand that working-class interests be put
aside. At the height of the Great War, instead of believing that workers
had no motherland, German and French socialists became "fervent patriots" (*jiduan de aiguo zhiyi zhe*). "Ah!" another political prisoner implored
CCP cadres, "discern the tide of our time – national loyalties trump over
all else!" The Mukden Incident was a stark reminder that nationalism
took primacy over proletarian solidarity and that young idealists must
disabuse themselves of empty internationalism. In a similar vein, students
at Nanchang No. 1 High School were told in 1936 to forget platitudes on
global peace and expect "the second great war to take shape in front of

---

[10] Dai, *Qingnian zhilu*, 252–60. The quotation attributed to Confucius, which Dai cited
with slight modifications, is from Book XIII of *Lunyu*. The English translation reads:
"To send the common people to war untrained is to throw them away" (D. C. Lau,
trans., *Confucius: the Analects*, 2nd edn. [Hong Kong: Chinese University Press,
1992], 131).

[their] eyes even before blood stains from the first one had yet to dry up."
Dismissing the liberal international order sustained by the League of Nations
as ineffectual, an article in the school magazine announced that "sanctions of
international conferences and treaties applied only to weak nations."
Germany's reemergence, Italian encroachment into Ethiopia and frequent
militarist-engineered coups in Japan conspired to usher in an emergency
period when China must prepare for a showdown between countries.[11]
It was not only repudiation of class war that rendered the global war,
anticipatory and actual, an integral feature of conservative revolutionaries. Preparations for the event were conducive to realizing post-purge
mass politics, by which all people participated in and contributed to
a community of hierarchal solidarity, cooperative labor, technical efficiency and stoic morality. Like scouting, but of much greater scale and
scope, prolonged military training leveraged personal ethics to counter
perceived malaises emanating from capitalist modernity such as individualism, consumerism and communism. *The Way for Youth* reckoned
that China had between five to ten years to get its act together before an
inevitable second world war broke out. To do their part for China,
citizens must stop protesting and "concretely and diligently prepare for
the war" in libraries, laboratories and workshops. Mass conscription, Dai
suggested, was to be introduced and military officers had to contribute to
the economic development of the regions to which they were posted.[12]
The corporatist vision attendant to war mobilization was to overcome the
defects of both communism and liberalism. Chiang Kai-shek's right-hand
man Chen Lifu argued in his 1933 book *Vitalism* (*Weisheng lun*) that
representative democracy was an outmoded form of political organization. For the mineralogist-turned-party theorist, congressional bickering
between Democrats and Republicans in the United States was
a gentrified form of tribalist warfare. If liberalism corroded social cohesion, communism was nothing other than institutionalized class warfare.
A cooperative order under the enlightened autocracy of a single-party
state was the apotheosis of human achievement.[13] Although *Vitalism* did

[11] "Zhejiang fanxingyuan quanti fangxing ren wei Rijun qinzhao Liao, Ji qigao Zhongguo
Gongchandang ren shu [Letter to Chinese Communists from All Inmates of the Zhejiang
Reformatory on the Japanese Military Occupation of Liaoning and Jilin]," *Zhejiang sheng
fanxingyuan yuekan*, no. 9 (1931): 165–8; Li Nannan, "Xinglai! Zhongguo de
Gongchandang ren [Wake Up, Communists in China!]," *Zhejiang sheng fanxingyuan
yuekan*, no. 9 (1931): 149–52; Guo Guanqun, "Feichang shiqi zhong qiannian yingyou
zhi zhunbei [Preparations for Youths during the Emergency Period]," *Yizhong xiaokan*,
3:3–4 (1935): 109–11.
[12] Dai, *Qingnian zhi lu*, 119, 154–5.
[13] Chen Lifu, *Weisheng lun (shang jun)* [*Vitalism*, Volume I] (Nanjing: Zhongyang zhengzhi
xuexiao, 1933), 69–71.

not address the "emergency period" directly, its prominence, along with Dai Jitao's *Philosophical Foundations of Sun Yat-senism*, as core text deployed in training programs catered to cadres and former Communists spoke to its influence as preparations for war gathered steam.[14] Chiang was fully on board with his subordinates with regards the certain prospect of war. As the future Generalissimo told military and police officers in April 1932, in the immediate aftermath of Japan's offensive against Shanghai, the nation must prepare for full-scale invasion by its eastern neighbor. He warned that China had entered a "time of unprecedented crisis" (*kongqian weixian qi*) and that the country had until 1936 to prepare before the entire world descended into violence.[15] The Chinese had to pull themselves up by their bootstraps; preparedness was not a prerogative exclusive to the military force that answered to the revolutionary party.

The coming war demanded inclusivity. Long-held social norms, such as gender roles, became moot. With the military taking on noncombatant roles and the citizenry's technical prowess and productivity invested with strategic urgency, the nation was enlisted in its fullness to fight a war that knew no geographical, temporal or social bounds. Women's participation in the patriotic cause, once reserved for elite men with formal military training, became imperative. "As long as one was a citizen (*guomin*)," Zhou Wenqu wrote in a Jiangsu-based magazine, "one would appreciate the responsibility to exert extra effort for the nation." Zhou emphasized the distinction between China's emergency period and that of Japan, from where the concept was supposed to originate. Whereas Japan's emergency resulted from aggression and a determination to follow Imperial Germany's lead in starting a global war, China's represented an extended ordeal of victimization. The uprising-ridden, disaster-battered, diplomatically embattled country had been under an "emergency period day in and day out" for the previous century. The latest threat from Japan, alongside Communist rebellion, was the most recent stumbling block frustrating China's revival. Despite China having more than its fair share of external and internal strife, the average Chinese person had no mastery over military skills. Zhou urged her female compatriots to

---

[14] Terry Bodenhorn, "Chen Lifu's Vitalism: A Guomindang Vision of Modernity Circa 1934," in *Defining Modernity: Guomindang Rhetoric of a New China, 1920–1970*, ed. Terry Bodenhorn (Ann Arbor: Center for Chinese Studies, University of Michigan, 2002), 91–122; Kikuchi Kazutaka, "Toshi-gata tokumu 'CC' kei no 'hankyô kô-Nichi' rosen ni tsuite – sono seisei kara kô-Nichi sensô niokeru igi to genkai [On the 'Anti-communist and Resist Japan' Line of the Urban-Based Espionage Organization, the CC Clique – Its Significance and Limitations from Inception to the Second Sino–Japanese War]," part 1, *Chikaki ni arite*, no. 35 (1999): 18.

[15] Chiang, *Jiang Zhongzheng zongtong dang'an*, 14:49.

familiarize themselves with tasks such as counterespionage, fire control, making and using masks, organizing rescue teams and driving vehicles. For "military victory depended not only on frontline forces and superior weapons but also backup support, knowledge and skills provided by people at home."[16] Men and women, troops and civilians must with no exception contribute to China's defense.

The emergency period exuded the illusion that socioeconomic hierarchies could be renegotiated under the mantra of broad participation. According to Harriet Zurndoffer, the Second Sino–Japanese War presented an opportunity for citizens joining the resistance, in particular urban women, to organize, become politically aware and claim a larger role in society.[17] Zhou posited that the nation must put in measures both to handle the present crisis and to consolidate its long-term foundation. She railed against those who sought to deprive (*boduo*) women of their responsibility to the nation. Women should have every opportunity to labor and serve, if not to fight and command. Zhou cited the research of American psychologist Helen Thompson Woolley, leaders such as Queen Victoria, Cixi and Wu Zetian and the important roles women played in the Soviet Union. She marshaled figures showing that differences in average height, weight, microvascular fluid and foot size between Chinese women and men were minimal. The argument was that the intelligence, ability and physical aptitude of Chinese women were comparable to their male counterparts'. Rural and working-class women had already engaged in industrial production at home and in factories. Women's groups across Jiangsu province had also taken part in social activism. They contributed to the promotion of revolutionary consciousness (*geming yishi*), undertook natural disaster relief work and fought for assassin Shi Jianqiao's release. Chinese women were not to be driven back to private quarters, as Hitler and Mussolini dictated for German and Italian women.[18]

Fascination with radical right nationalist movements in Europe, an article in the weekly women's supplement to GMD organ *Central Daily* warned, must not become "a pretext to place limits on women's liberation." Germany and Italy might have to remake female workers into mothers in order to reduce employment rates and increase birth rates,

---

[16] Zhou Wenqu, "Feichang shiqi Jiangsu funü yingfu zhi zeren [Responsibilities Jiangsu Women Should Bear in the Emergency Period], *Suheng*, no. 19 (December 1936): 15–18.
[17] Harriet Zurndoffer, "Wartime Refugee Relief in Chinese Cities and Women's Political Activism, 1937–1940," in *New Narratives of Urban Space in Republican Chinese Cities: Emerging Social, Legal and Governance Orders*, eds. Billy K. L. So and Madeleine Zelin (Leiden: Brill, 2013), 90–1.
[18] Zhou, "Feichang shiqi Jiangsu funü yingfu zhi zeren," 15–18.

but China's industrialization drive needed greater female participation in the economy, not less. Furthermore, China's demographical challenge was not that too few babies were born, but that too many of them did not have a chance to grow up due to high infant mortality rates. Instead of emulating fashionable policies from Europe, China should recognize the crucial role women played in maintaining production as men of various vocations went to fight during the Great War. "The key to managing this unprecedented national crisis was to train and guide women to take on professional lives (*zhiye shenghuo*)."[19] The best preparation for the emergency period, as the article's subtitle suggested in no uncertain terms, was to get women out from their families and working.

Calls for changes to gender norms did not, however, pose challenges to the conservative revolutionary vision. Arguments for increased female involvement in the public sphere were aligned with the imperative that all citizens, not just the military and political class, get ready for an inevitable resistance effort in a universal war. Modern industrial war democratized experiences of violence and labor, not means of production. Peasants were to join militia-like communities and acquire such skills as shooting, public speaking and fluency in military signals.[20] Yet these skills were supposed to empower the masses to thwart off foreign and domestic enemies, not question hierarchal relations. Indeed, wartime imperatives, by putting the onus of the nation's salvation on families, entrenched conservative gender norms that the emergency period was supposed to loosen up. For example, while Zhou Wenqu celebrated her compatriots' contribution to production and military endeavors, she continued to see motherhood as Chinese women's "unique virtue" (*dute de meide*). She warned "women of the new age" not to turn away from the responsibility of raising children, reminding them that the Chinese nation-state, like advanced countries such as France, the United States and the Soviet Union, had placed ever greater emphasis on future citizens' well-being. Zhou had little tolerance for ideological diversity, blaming Communists for sabotaging the women's movement in her home province of Jiangsu.[21] In addition, while women were encouraged to become politically aware, their new consciousness was put at the service of domestic duties. Mothers had a unique role in bringing up the nation's

[19] Miao Yuzheng, "Funü zhiye de biqie xuyao – guli funü zouchu jiating wei feichang shiqi de chunbei [The Urgent Necessity of Women's Participation in Labor – Encouraging Women to Leave Their Families as Preparation for the Emergency Period], *Zhongyang ribao*, May 13, 1936, C3.

[20] Xing Guangyi, "Feichang shiqi de minzhong jiaoyu [Mass Education during the Emergency Period]," *Zhongyang ribao*, November 28, 1935, C2.

[21] Zhou, "Feichang shiqi Jiangsu funü yingfu zhi zeren," 17–18.

young defenders. They must create patriotic households and "revolutionize" (*geming hua*) their children's minds. They would familiarize sons and daughters with the travails of revolutionary leaders, discuss with them how China had to concede its sovereignty and display a map showing when and how Chinese territories were annexed by foreign powers. All these tasks were added on top of ensuring that children ate healthily, dressed properly and developed sturdy bodies. Put simply, they were to bring the discipline of scout training into every home and family. The flip side of "natural" motherly duties was the image of idle, unskilled and decadent urban women.[22] What the emergency required of women was the shaping of the nation as one indivisible body in which they were to play an increasingly active but still auxiliary role. As a social category, women became docile, resourceful mothers to a struggling nation.

Shaping War Mobilization

Despite the significant role women were to play, elite men provided the most important intellectual and organizational labor to China's total war. These men, many of whom had agitated against cooperation with the Communists in the mid-1920s, were often organized in a Leninist mode and were familiar with the latest geopolitical trends in East Asia and Europe. The *Shanghai Morning Post*, for example, belonged to the CC Clique, a powerful pro-Chiang faction led by Chen Lifu and his elder brother Guofu (1892–1951). The clique presided over an empire of clandestine and open organizations that promoted European-style fascism, mirroring the organizational mode and ideological tenor of its more well-known intraparty rival, Lixingshe/the Blue Shirt Society.[23] It held appeal for the urban petit-bourgeoisie based in education institutions, the party bureaucracy and Nationalist labor unions. Among clique members were young cadres who had experienced firsthand the deepening social crises in the West as students at European and American universities. The faction accounted for 80 percent of lower-level state bureaucrats and for fifty members of the 180-strong GMD Central Executive Committee in 1936. During the war of resistance, clique members conducted espionage activities in Japanese-occupied territories, organized pro-China

[22] Xu Ruoping, "Feichang shiqi zhong muqin de zeren [Mothers' Responsibilities during the Emergency Period]," *Zhongyang ribao*, December 9, 1936, C3; Linxiang, "Feichang shiqi funü de zeren [Women's Responsibilities during the Emergency Period]," *Zhongyang ribao*, November 11, 1936, C3; Zhou, "Feichang shiqi Jiangsu funü yingfu zhi zeren," 19.
[23] Wakeman, *Spymaster*, 106–8; Kirby, *Germany and Republican China*, 162; Kikuchi Kazutaka, "Toshi-gata tokumu 'CC' kei no 'hankyô kô-Nichi' rosen ni tsuite," parts 1 and 2, *Chikaki ni arite*, no. 35 (1999): 10–12, 19; no. 36 (1999): 32–45.

activists in Japan and its colonies and even cooperated with the British intelligence service in Singapore, Burma and India.[24] While its internal workings were shrouded in secrecy, the clique certainly made public its views on politics and society.

Indeed, aside from oiling the security and public services, the faction placed a premium on propaganda, exerting an increasing influence over the party's ideological output. In Shanghai, it operated a network of film studios, magazines, publishers and newspapers. The *Shanghai Morning Post* was edited by Pan Gongzhan (1894–1975) and Tao Baichuan (1903–2002). During the resistance war, CC Clique members relocated inland and filled key party and state positions concerned with mass mobilization. Chen Lifu served as education minister from 1938 to 1944. Tao took charge of the two major party organs, the *Central Weekly* (*Zhongyang zhoukan*) in 1941 and the *Central Daily* (*Zhongyang ribao*) in 1942. As editor, he recruited celebrated liberal writers like Zhu Guangqian, on whom the next chapter focuses, and Liang Shiqiu to write for the party-run press. For his part, Pan headed the state's censorship board that policed print materials from 1943 to 1945.

The CC Clique's overall ideological tenor combined German-inspired celebration of the *völkisch* and Italian Futurist excitement in machine and industrial violence.[25] Such a mixture of the primitive and the avant-garde mirrored Dai's political thought. Rather than something to be dreaded, a global war was to be welcomed as mass violence had regenerative potential, centering collective faith in the revolutionary party and its doctrine. The GMD was adept in sanctioning isolated cases of homicide to energize the body politic; but war mobilization would, as expected by Nationalists in China following the interwar global trend, create a new type of subject and put an end to the old liberal order.[26] The *Shanghai Morning Post* identified the Nazi ascendance in 1933 as testament to Germany's refusal to remain an "economic colony" of Britain and France and operate under the Treaty of Versailles. Hitler's inexorable rise was, moreover, vindication of a dictatorial polity over representational democracy and proletarian internationalism. The militancy of Germany and Italy was a welcome expression of the resurgent ethnic spirit in nations emerging anew from the ashes of defeat.[27]

---

[24] Kikuchi, "Toshi-gata tokumu 'CC' kei no 'hankyô kô-Nichi' rosen ni tsuite," parts 1 and 2.

[25] Kirby, *Germany and Republican China*, 163; Clinton, *Revolutionary Nativism*, 43.

[26] Lean, *Public Passions*, 155–6; Alain Badiou, *The Century*, trans. Alberto Toscano (Cambridge: Polity, 2007), 32–7.

[27] "Zailun Xitela zhi zhizheng [More on Hitler's Hold on Power]," editorial, *Chenbao*, February 3, 1933, 2. See also "Xingdengbao lianren De zongtong [Hindenburg Reelected as German President]," editorial, *Chenbao*, April 12, 1932, 2, and "Xitela

By applauding Germany and Italy for challenging Wilsonian peace internationally and liberal democracy domestically, the *Shanghai Morning Post* celebrated war mobilization as signaling the advent of a futuristic social system that would please Chen Lifu.

The total war the *Shanghai Morning Post* envisioned, with its attendant promises of a postliberal future freed of communist strife, was given full expression in the National Spiritual Mobilization Campaign. Inaugurated two years after the Marco Polo Bridge Incident, China's spiritual mobilization campaign was the culmination of initiatives aimed at suppressing social strife and removing threats to political disunity. On March 12, 1939, the National Military Council announced the *Guiding Principles and Implementation Measures for National Spiritual Mobilization*. The document was first made public by Chiang Kai-shek at the Fifth Plenum of the Fifth GMD Central Executive Committee in January 1939.[28] It listed the "common purposes" of the conflict-ridden nation and the items that made up its "common morality and common conviction." Under the "supremacy of the state and the nation" (*guojia zhishang minzu zhishang*) principle, citizens were exhorted to "revolutionize" and "thoroughly improve" their collective consciousness, and maintain steadfast loyalty to the government and the Three People's Principles. The accompanying *Citizen Convention and Pledge (Guomin gongyue shici)*, which was to be read out loud at monthly meetings held in individual neighborhoods and workplaces, offered allegiance to Chiang Kai-shek himself.

Exclusive loyalty to the nation meant ideological uniformity. Political pluralism or, worse, organized opposition, were inherent threats, both unseemly testaments to human failures to work in hierarchal union that the conservative revolution was to overcome. In a thinly veiled reference to communism, *Guiding Principles* complained that public opinions were akin to messy branches of an otherwise strongly rooted tree. There was no place in a healthy "plant" for "political fantasizing" (*kongxiang lun*) that advocated allegiance to anything other than the nation. China's popular will would have to obey the Nationalist state's diktat. The document, thus, formalized views expressed in Nationalist papers during the "emergency period" in the early 1930s. What the nation needed was not rights and constitutional guarantees but "spiritual construction" (*jingshen jianshe*) based on Confucian philosophical traditions as revived by Sun Yat-sen and Chiang Kai-shek. Debates over civil rights were no better

zhizheng yihou [Since Hitler's Assumption of Government Power]," editorial, *Chenbao*, February 2, 1933, 2.
[28] Chiang Kai-shek to Zhu Jiahua, January 16, 1939, *yiban*, 130/90.2, Kuomintang Archives.

than "tired and hollow cries," student demonstrations urging the Nationalist state to resist Japan were useless in front of enemy planes and artillery and the failure of the political classes to leave their own views aside attested to the populace's inadequate organization and training. What China needed to pull itself from terminal decline was "steel-like organization" (*gang zhi tuanti*) – redirecting the people's energy from superfluous politicking to the noble goal of national defense.[29]

Even as Nationalists identified the national collective as their *raison d'être*, spiritual mobilization was highly individualist in practice, seeing personal habits and moral quality as determinants of national strength. The premium the wartime campaign put on everyday individual behaviors was in line with scouting and the New Life Movement, whereby aestheticizing everyday experiences replaced challenging unequal social relations as the national revolution's key task. While private businesses had to submit themselves under central command, the people's daily production and consumption routines were also called upon to serve the wartime economy. Outlining an expansive program that involved the entire cross-section of society from soldiers at the top to rural *baojia* communities at the grassroots, the document envisioned aims that ranged from getting people to get up early and eliminating wasteful consumption to unifying cultural production and uprooting corruption.[30] Echoing Dai Jitao's dictum in *The Way for Youths* that regulation of capital meant suppressing both capitalist control over the economy and personal desires, resistance against foreign invasion gave China a chance to not only recalibrate private and public ownership but also undo the decadent consumerism and disruptive working-class activism capitalism begot. In this sense, in addition to being a response to wartime needs, *Guiding Principles* affirmed anew the conservative revolutionary tenet: rally behind a new, cooperative nation in which hierarchical but harmonious relations replaced incessant political and economic strife.

Spiritual mobilization, like the New Life Movement, drew references from supposedly primordial Chinese values that predated even Confucius. But the crafters of the GMD's latest social engineering

---

[29] Zhang Mojun, "Guonan zhong zhi jingshen jianshe [Spiritual Construction during National Crisis]," *Chenbao*, October 1, 1933, 7. "Feichang shiqi de feichang renwu," 50; Peng Shouzu, "Feichang shidai xuesheng yingyou de zhunbei [Required Preparations for Students in the Emergency Period]," *Yizhong xiaokan*, 3:3–4 (1935): 113; Guo, "Feichang shiqi zhong qiannian yingyou zhi zhunbei," 110.

[30] "Guomin jingshen zong dongyuan gangling jiqi shishi banfa [Guiding Principles and Implementation Measures for National Spiritual Mobilization]," in *Zhonghua minguo zhongyao shiliao chubian – dui-Ri kangzhan shiqi*, vol. 4, *zhanshi jianshe*, ed. Qin Xiaoyi (Taipei: Zhongguo Guomindang zhongyang weiyuanhui dangshi weiyuanhui, 1988), no. 4: 580–601.

initiative did not shy away from the fact that their project was an exercise in twentieth-century patrilineal nationalism. *Guiding Principles* laid claim to loyalty (*zhong*) and filial piety (*xiao*), values integral to the reproduction of China's peasant society. Whereas the ancestral cult had long been part of imperial state ideology and local culture, Sun Yat-sen's revolutionary doctrine required that the modern nation-state, not just one's clan, be the recipient of patrimonial sentiments expressed by citizen-subjects. Furthermore, whereas filial piety in "primordial" (*guyou*) moral conventions were ritualistic – making sure that ancestors received offerings through generations – the nation was not just the apogee of one's ancestral lineage. Fidelity to the nation meant submission to institutionalized divisions of labor, laws and decrees, and the general strict discipline the state required.[31] Evoking the history of Han resistance against alien threats – including such "preemptive" expeditions as the subjection of Uyghurs, Tibetans and ethnic groups in the southwestern frontier under imperial Chinese suzerainty during the Han and Tang periods – Pan Gongzhan observed that a spirit of sacrifice had been the nation's best guarantor against foreign conquest.[32]

Yet the exemplary character of such heroic figures as the Southern Song general Yue Fei (1103–42) and Ming loyalist Koxinga (1624–62) was not good enough for a modern nation-state. For ancient heroes' indomitable courage in the face of invading enemies was derived from loyalty and fidelity to the ruling house only. A centrally directed campaign of mass mobilization was thus needed to collect these individual chivalric sentiments into popular militaristic devotion to the nation.[33] Chiang might have attributed absolute power to himself, but Nationalist ideologues styled him as a plebiscitary leader, not a dynastic ruler. The *l'état, c'est moi* principle of Louis XIV, Chen Lifu quipped in 1940, no longer held in a twentieth-century republic.[34] The Generalissimo was, to read Chen's analogy against its grain, a Louis Bonaparte, the "patriarchal benefactor of all classes."[35] The state was not an imposed power from which the masses were alienated but the highest embodiment of popular sovereignty. Rather than a machine to maintain social order, the state was

---

[31] Ibid., 586–7.
[32] Pan Gongzhan, "Guomin jingshen zong dongyuan yu zhongxiao de minzu daode [National Spiritual Mobilization and the National Morality of Loyalty and Fidelity]," *Zhongyang zhoukan* 1, no. 34 (1939): 4.
[33] Ibid.
[34] Chen, "Jingshen zong dongyuan de yiyi [The Significance of Spiritual Mobilization]," in *Zhonghua minguo zhongyao shiliao chubian – dui-Ri kangzhan shiqi*, vol. 4, *zhanshi jianshe*, no. 4: 650.
[35] Karl Marx, *The Eighteenth Brumaire of Louis Bonaparte* (New York: International Publishers, 1963), 133.

an idea, the "realization of our loyalty to the nation."[36] In a rhetorical move that spanned millennia, Chen warned that if China was to avoid the fate of the vanquished Ming court in the seventeenth century or occupied Czechoslovakia today, it needed to transform the spiritual certitude of such mythical figures as Yu the Great and Tang of Shang (circa 1675–1646 BCE) into a sentiment compelling the entire national collective into action. To drive home his plea for action, Chen the scientist added a new spin to Newton's second law of motion, which states that force is a function of mass and acceleration. A mass organization's prowess, Chen hypothesized, depended directly on the correlation between its size and its propensity to pursue unified purposes.[37] Eminently futuristic symbols, as much as traditionalist ones, were mobilized to conjure up the subliminal ideal of the nation.

The melding of war priorities and the state's enhanced role in social life with the nationalist investment in a homogenous people explained why the supposedly destructive war against Japan was paradoxically construed as a step toward national reconstruction. Spiritual mobilization was more than a short-term measure introduced under extraordinary circumstances. Chiang Kai-shek described the New Life Movement in July 1937 as a "spiritual revolution." Strong popular morale overcame China's material backwardness, helping it to out-compete Japan's technological sophistication. More importantly, however, overhauling people's habits and expectations was critical to "develop[ing] a vital and healthy social organism" for a "new nation."[38] Chiang's faith in the transformative potential of his compatriots' willpower was echoed by his wife. Speaking as director-general of the women's organization Wartime Child Welfare Protection Association, in 1941, Song Meiling compared the involvement of Chinese women in the War of Resistance to the extensive mobilization of American women during the Great War. China's ongoing total war, which Madame Chiang glossed as *quanneng zhanzheng*, offered an opportunity for female citizens to hone their "spiritual prowess" (*jingshen liliang*) and join the resistance efforts shoulder to shoulder with their male compatriots as producers and fighters. The emergence of a home front, shattering the sequestered domestic life of women into pieces, had advanced the feminist cause and added to China's credentials as a modern society.

While Song thought that wartime mobilization was a timely boost to her country's ongoing modernization process, others celebrated the

---

[36] Chen, "Jingshen zong dongyuan de yiyi," 650.   [37] Ibid., 647–54.
[38] Chiang, "Resistance to Aggression and Renaissance of the Nation," and "On National Reconstruction," *Collected Wartime Messages of Generalissimo Chiang Kai-shek*, 1:14, 30.

militarization of citizens' everyday life as critical to a future postwar order. Ru Chunpu, a Lixingshe member, argued that the common purposes as stated in the *Guiding Principles* – supremacy of the state and the nation, prioritization of the military and military victory (*junshi diyi shengli diyi*) and concentration of popular will and strength (*yizhi jizhong liliang jizhong*) – ought to be retained after the war. Commitment to national unity was not a matter of transient alliance between disparate forces and agendas but a timeless principle that enabled collective life. As international relations were based on states acting as the agents of their respective peoples or nations, any political ideology that posited transition to a world without nation-states would remain illegitimate after the war. In a world where even the Soviet Union was embracing nationalism, blind faith in internationalism could only result in capitulation to foreign invaders. Like Dai, Ru saw any alternative to the nation-state system as anathema to Sun Yat-sen's nationalist doctrine. Conflating communist internationalism with right-wing Pan-Asianism, Ru illustrated the danger of inadequate nationalist commitment by citing the currency Japan's Pan-Asianist ideology enjoyed among Chinese collaborationists, most notably the recently disgraced former premier Wang Jingwei. A formidable military force and a mobilized population must be constantly prepared to counter ideological heresies threatening the polity's coherence.[39] A permanent military-first policy might not have appealed to Chen Lifu since the CC Clique's influence was felt primarily within the civilian bureaucracy, but he did not object to drilling a militarist sense of discipline and honor in the wider populace. In fact, while military mobilization was expected to serve only the needs of war, Chen believed that spiritual mobilization should be pursued with determination beyond victory over Japan.[40] Normal life was decried as frivolous or primitive by most senior Nationalists, and its suspension by the war was therefore regarded as a blessing in disguise since it lent credence to the conservative revolutionary claim to the nation's future.

Ru and Chen's optimism for the auspicious birth of a Spartan and pliable national community was not totally misguided. At least in the initial years of the resistance war, the Communist challenge to Nationalist rule was placed, if grudgingly, on hold. One critical difference between the GMD state at total war and similar right-wing regimes in other countries was that the former had to reconcile with the CCP's stubborn presence. As a result of the Xi'an Incident in late 1936, Chiang was forced

---

[39] Ru Chunpu, "Chedi jiuzheng guanyu jingshen zong dongyuan gongtong mubiao de wujie [Fully Rectify Misconceptions concerning the Common Purposes of Spiritual General Mobilization]," *Zhongyang zhoukan* 1, nos. 39–40 (n.d.): 15–16.

[40] Chen, "Jingshen zong dongyuan de yiyi," 652.

into a common front with his internal nemesis against further intrusion by advancing Japanese militarists. The Second United Front, which technically lasted until 1946, was extremely volatile and filled with political intrigues and clashes between Nationalist forces and the Yan'an-based Communist movement. Yet the half-hearted coalition provided Chiang for the first time unquestioned legitimacy as the rightful successor of the national revolution. Even as frictions between the two parties began as early as 1938, the CCP had prized patriotism and national unity under Mao Zedong's New Democracy doctrine. Instead of calling for class warfare and an end to GMD rule, the Communists carried out electoral reforms along liberal democratic lines, rationalized the bureaucracy by adopting meritocratic principles and actively courted the local landed elite. Rather than Marxist–Leninism, Chinese Communists traced the ideological roots of their program to the Three People's Principles, claiming that they too were rightful successors of Sun Yat-sen's national revolution.[41]

The CCP's political flexibility and willingness to privilege the nationalist agenda defined its qualified support for general spiritual mobilization. An October 1940 list revealed that Communists Zhou Enlai (1898–1976) and Guo Moruo (1892–1978), as officials at the political department of the Military Affairs Commission, served as members of the spiritual mobilization campaign association planning committee. Their colleagues included such CC Clique stalwarts as Pan Gongzhan and activists from minor political parties like social democrat Zhang Junmai (Carsun Chang, 1886–1969). The list also included nonpartisan figures who were nonetheless sympathetic to the Nationalist cause such as Buddhist monk Taixu and India-based academic Tan Yunshan, whose careers are discussed in Chapter 6.[42] Before 1941, when armed conflicts between the Nationalist and Communist parties resumed, women activists, writers and artists from different parties and ideological backgrounds worked under the same umbrella organizations such as the Wartime Child Welfare Protection Association or the All-China Resistance Association of Writers and Artists.[43]

[41] Mark Selden, *China in Revolution: The Yenan Way Revisited* (Armonk, NY: M. E. Sharpe, 1995), 104–5, 125–31. For a dissenting view, see Chen Yongfa, *Zhongguo Gongchan geming qishi nian* [*Seventy Years of the Chinese Communist Revolution*], rev. edn. (Taipei: Lianjing chuban shiye gongsi, 2001), 346–67.

[42] "Guomin jingshen zong dongyuan hui sheji weiyuan yilan [List of Planning Committee Members at the National Spiritual Mobilization Association]," *Jingshen dongyuan*, no. 3 (1940): 183.

[43] Chang-tai Hung, *War and Popular Culture: Resistance in Modern China, 1937–1945* (Berkeley: University of California Press, 1994), 6; Zurndoffer, "Wartime Refugee Relief in Chinese Cities and Women's Political Activism," 79.

The Communists, reflecting their overall relationship with their senior partner, maintained a delicate distance from the GMD's monopoly on mass mobilization. They had to thread a thin line between challenging the Nationalist plea for exclusive devotion to the Leader and playing into the claim that Communists valued sectarian over national interests. One result of the CCP's precarious position within the body politic was a noticeable shift away from class politics. Chen Boda (1904–89), Mao Zedong's secretary, wrote in 1939 that with the laboring masses making up more than 90 percent of the Chinese nation, a government that claimed to uphold the supremacy of the state and the nation must not act against the interests of their agent, the Communist Party. Citing Chiang's speech at the launching ceremony of the spiritual mobilization campaign, Chen adeptly fused the Generalissimo's call for the creation of a new *zeitgeist* cleansed of old selfish habits and Lenin's faith in Third World nationalism, observing that China was set to emerge from the current crisis as an advanced civilization.[44] Yet, while asserting the politically advanced nature of the Chinese proletariat, the Communist theorist was adamant that class struggle had no place in a time when national survival was at stake. Echoing the GMD's definition of military resistance as a total war and its policy of prioritizing the military, Chen implored his compatriots to sacrifice their own political and economic interests and contribute to the nation's defense. Any action that heightened tensions among the people, including class warfare, was undesirable under the paramount goal of military victory. Instead of pushing for traditional communist policies, Yan'an undertook a social democratic reform program to ensure that workers were employed and peasants had land to till without jeopardizing the institution of private property. The Communists advocated national independence and promised greater civil and political liberties. At one point, Chen endorsed the coordinating role of a corporatist state, stating, as did many GMD cadres, that the vision of universal harmony (*datong*) sought an end to the anarchy of capitalist economics by rationalizing production under central planning.[45] In this way, the proletariat was denied its vanguard position in the defeat of capitalism and bourgeois rule.

Instead, the working class was subsumed under a homogenous "people," its political subjectivity bound to the nationalist agenda. The task was to make nationalism palatable to the oppressed and the marginalized,

---

[44] Chiang's speech, delivered in Chongqing on May Day 1939, was "Chujiu buxin gemian xixin [Abolish the Old, Establish the New and Reform]," in *Zhonghua minguo zhongyao shiliao chubian*, 4:610–15.

[45] Chen Boda, *Xin rensheng guan de chuangzao* [*The Making of a New Philosophy of Life*] (Shanghai: Chenguang shudian, 1939), 7–9, 21–2, 40–2.

not to replace it with another category of social analysis. "Supremacy of the state and the nation, as stated in the proposal for national spiritual mobilization," left-wing intellectual Zou Taofen (1895–1944) conceded, was "not be to questioned" (*wurong huaiyi*). Yet, prioritizing the nation-state did not mean the Chinese should subscribe to "the views of fascist countries." Zou associated Sunist nationalism with "global progressive thought" (*shijie de jinbu sichao*) and argued that independence was contingent on delivering succor to the downtrodden. The task Chinese nationalists confronted was to stand in solidarity with the 1.25 billion oppressed people around the world to dislodge their 250 million oppressors.[46] The scaling back of the Communists' core ideological appeals lent legitimacy to the Nationalist demand for absolute loyalty to the nation-state, even as neither party was willing to cede too much ground to its competitor. Indeed, just as the spiritual mobilization campaign entered its final stage of planning in early 1939, the GMD's Central Executive Committee had once again defined the CCP as an alien or heretical party (*yidang*) and adopted measures that restricted the latter's activities in areas controlled by Chongqing. Without naming the Communists, Pan Gongzhan warned that some people were sneakily "distorting the meaning of the [spiritual mobilization campaign] with theories other than the Three People's Principles."[47] While not advocating collaboration with the Japanese, class struggle and internationalism were nonetheless grave threats that spiritual mobilization must stamp out. It was all the more pugnacious that these ideas were couched in Sunist vocabulary, introducing again ambiguity into the state's core beliefs that the April 12 coup of 1927 was supposed to have banished.

Spiritual Mobilization in Action

Ingrained anticommunism and an assumed mandate to lead the entire nation toward victory over foreign invasion conditioned the GMD's centralized, commandeering approach to spiritual mobilization. Not unlike the New Life Movement, the wartime state sought to assert full command over the nation's human and material resources by restricting political expression, limiting conspicuous consumption and rationalizing

---

[46] Zou Taofen, "Jingshen dongyuan de zhengque renshi [Correct Understanding of Spiritual Mobilization]," *Quanmin kangzhan*, no. 85 (1939): unpaginated. Zou was citing the third lecture delivered by Sun on nationalism, in which the Chinese revolutionary credited Lenin for embracing the oppressed peoples of the world. See Sun, *Sanmin zhuyi*, 39.

[47] Pan, "Jingshen zong dongyuan shi kangzhan jianguo de yuandongli [Spiritual Mobilization Motivates Nation-Building through the War of Resistance]," *Zhongyang zhoukan* 1, no. 40 (1939): 4.

citizens' daily routines. Given the similarities between the spiritual mobilization campaign and the movement it incorporated, party officials took pains to rebuke views that the two campaigns were essentially the same. GMD propaganda chief Ye Chucang (1887–1946) explained at a seminar for intellectuals a few days after the *Guiding Principles* was proclaimed in March 1939 that wartime mobilization implied a different dynamic between state and society than the New Life Movement. National spiritual mobilization, he argued:

will be executed from the top down and, simultaneously, initiated by the people from the ground up. The movement is launched by the Nationalist government for the purpose of nation-building through the Resistance War and is inherently interventionist. The New Life Movement, on the other hand, was launched by a civil organization (*jituan*), namely the New Life Movement Promotion Association headed by Generalissimo Chiang. The New Life Movement is more exhortative than coercive, while spiritual mobilization will rely as much on exhortation as on coercion.[48]

The suggestion that the state played an auxiliary role in the New Life Movement was at best an understatement. The movement, which began in 1934 as a means to win over the rural population in the formerly Communist-controlled Jiangxi province, spread across the country thanks to aggressive promotion by provincial officials and the coordinated efforts of the police and the Scouts of China. Both civilian and military branches of the police were favored by the state over students to discipline the everyday because the latter, being more educated, were less reliable. Officers assumed the responsibility of patrolling citizens' behaviors in public spaces, acquiring powers not otherwise provided for under the law.[49] Ye's remark was illuminating nonetheless, for it indicated what the GMD had long identified as its core weakness in managing social movements, i.e., the failure to exert top-down control. Indeed, the tendency to favor party-state coordination over limited autonomy was obvious in how scouting was gradually incorporated into the Three People's Principles Youth Corps in 1940.

Wartime contingency presented the GMD the opportunity to reassert total command over the masses, even as measures introduced in the mid-1930s were carried forward to the National Spiritual Mobilization Movement. The preference for state coercion was well displayed in

---

[48] "Zhongyang xuanchuan bu zhaodai weihua jie taolun jingshen zong dongyuan jishi [Record of Cultural Sector Discussion on Spiritual Mobilization as Convened by the Central Executive Committee Propaganda Department]," *Zhongyang zhoukan* 1, no. 34 (1939): 22.

[49] Dirlik, "Ideological Foundations of the New Life Movement," 950–1; Liu, "Redefining the Moral and Legal Roles of the State in Everyday Life," 51.

Chiang's speech on the new year's day of 1940. "National spiritual mobilization," the Generalissimo observed, "should as a matter of course be a spontaneous movement." But had the nation, Chiang demanded of his audience, genuinely upheld the Three People's Principles as a faith that unified the people? Was everyone in society committed to national salvation? Had the common purposes as listed in the *Guiding Principles* pervaded the entire populace?[50] As long as the people's ideological allegiances and everyday commitments had yet to align with the GMD's military campaign, a mass movement of unprecedented scope and scale could not be led by anyone other than the state. Spiritual mobilization, commensurate with its ambiguous nomenclature, was envisioned as an umbrella movement branching out to include drives to ban frivolous entertainment, restrict import of luxury products, enhance productive capacity, strengthen internal propaganda, fight corruption, encourage donations to the country, eradicate media opinions hostile to the state and promote hygienic practices and physical training.[51]

In organizational terms, spiritual mobilization was coordinated by a body that derived its authority from the GMD's Supreme National Defense Council (*Guofang zuigao weiyuanhui*), a top party organ that operated from 1939 to 1947 with a view to concentrating military and government power in the party's hands. The appendix to the *Guiding Principles* provided for a National Spiritual Mobilization Association headed by Chiang. The new national body gathered together the premier, the GMD general secretary, the general secretary of the Supreme National Defense Council, the director general of the New Life Movement Association, the ministers of education and economic affairs, the chairman of the political department of the Military Affairs Commission and heads of the ruling party's organization, social affairs, propaganda, economics and education departments. At the subnational level, spiritual mobilization was to be conducted through a multitude of GMD-supervised organizations. Provincial associations led by local notables and current New Life Movement officials were to be set up within one month, with the party secretary, magistrate and high school principals of each county in attendance at their inaugural meetings.[52] Both state and

---

[50] Chiang, "Celi guoren nuli shixing guomin jingshen zong dongyuan – ershijiu nian yuandan guangbo jiangci [Encouraging Compatriots to Steadfastly Carry Out National Spiritual Mobilization – Speech Broadcast on New Year's Day 1940]," in *Sanda yundong*, ed. Sanmin zhuyi qingniantuan zhongyang tuanbu (n.p., 1942), 418–19.

[51] "Guomin jingshen zong dongyuan gangling jiqi shishi banfa," 595–7; "Guomin jingshen zong dongyuan gongzuo fenpei jihua [Plan for the Distribution of Duties Relating to National Spiritual Mobilization]," April 26, 1939, Nationalist Government Collection, 001000001614A, Academia Historica.

[52] "Guomin jingshen zong dongyuan gangling jiqi shishi banfa," 599–601.

party apparatuses assumed specific tasks in the larger scheme of spiritual mobilization. The interior ministry and the police were responsible for clamping down on improper entertainment; the economic affairs ministry took charge of resource saving, enhancement of production efficiency and promotion of national goods; the education ministry, working with the recently founded Three People's Principle Youth Corps, was to make sure that teachers and students formed the vanguard of mobilization.[53]

Party cadres, as custodians of the national revolution, were to take as much of a leading role in the movement as government and military officials.[54] The GMD social affairs department, for example, was tasked with rallying leaders from the various sectors and initiating "concrete campaigns" (*shiji yundong*). Even the overseas affairs department was enlisted to engage diasporic Chinese communities in supporting their Nationalist homeland.[55] The Chinese consulate in New York, along with the Chinese Consolidated Benevolent Association (*Zhonghua gongsuo*), held mass rallies in June 1939 where participants bowed to Sun Yat-sen's portrait and pledged support for the Nationalists' resistance war. Overseas GMD branches, like their domestic counterparts, held regular assemblies in Penang and Singapore.[56] As far as Brazil, where the right-wing regime under Getúlio Vargas professed neutrality vis-à-vis the Axis powers, spiritual mobilization activities reportedly took place underground in October 1939.[57] Domestically and abroad, through a combination of persuasion and raw coercion, the party-state would work to foster seamless synergy among communities and classes in creating a lifestyle befitting the total war ideals of political homogeneity and an altruistic, dynamic people.

Toward a New Wartime Culture

The heavy-handed execution of spiritual mobilization coupled with the fear that national cohesion would be perverted by degenerate popular habits defined the movement's emphasis on tackling everyday experiences such as physical culture, hygiene practices, consumption behaviors and vernacular artistic expressions. The determination to command not only institutions and enterprises but also the mundane but mercurial

[53] "Guomin jingshen zong dongyuan gongzuo fenpei jihua."
[54] "Guomin jingshen zong dongyuan gangling jiqi shishi banfa," 595–7.
[55] "Guomin jingshen zong dongyuan gongzuo fenpei jihua."
[56] "Dongyuan tongxun [Mobilization News]," *Jingshen dongyuan*, no. 4 (1941): 180.
[57] "Meiguo guomin jingshen zong dongyuan [National Spiritual Mobilization in the United States]," 1939–40, Foreign Affairs Ministry Collection, 020000002996A, Academia Historica.

habits of a war-stressed, diverse population put China in league with other societies working to rally their entire people behind grand military strategies. Apparently insignificant everyday matters from food and fashion to shopping and sports were, as Maureen Healy put it, "refracted" under the lens of total war and parachuted within the purview of public authority.[58] The *Guiding Principles* made the connection between national strength and everyday life succinctly thus: "Life is the root (*genben*) of spirit; if life lacks rationality, spirit lacks vitality and wholesomeness."[59] Meticulous attention to the quotidian was reminiscent of the importance Dai Jitao and Li Shizeng attached to the transformation of popular social life, rather than the simple usurpation of state power, as was the ultimate revolutionary goal back in the late 1920s. But there is a sense that anti-Japanese resistance, as a struggle against imperialist assault on human progress, mandated greater attention to the minutiae of personal routines. Spiritual mobilization meant sophisticated manipulation of the people's intellect and senses. Officers issued verbal commands, congregations responded enthusiastically or stayed silent in thought. Speeches, visual materials, drama and music appealed to the audiences' various faculties. People would attend evening talks so that otherwise idle time could be used to the fullest extent and the sober mood "stimulated and moved the spirit."[60]

Despite the conflicting military interests and putative ideological differences between Western-supported China and the Axis powers, there were striking parallels between these societies in the ways they carried out wartime mobilization. Rather than looking to the United States for models on how to engage the masses, Nationalist officials and intellectuals were more likely to turn to enemies like Germany and particularly Japan. GMD intellectuals cited Erich Ludendorff, a decorated Second Reich general who helped engineer Adolf Hitler's abortive 1923 coup against the Weimar Republic, as an important inspiration for the spiritual mobilization movement. Remarkably, Ludendorff's most famous work, *Der totale Krieg*, became familiar in China not through a Nationalist but through social democrat Zhang Junmai. Zhang's translation, titled *On War among Entire Nations* (*Quan minzu zhanzheng lun*), was reportedly so popular that first printing sold out in less than one month when it appeared in February 1937.[61] Zhang warned that the industrialization of

---

[58] Maureen Healy, *Vienna and the Fall of the Habsburg Empire: Total War and Everyday Life in World War I* (Cambridge: Cambridge University Press, 2004), 3.

[59] "Guomin jingshen zong dongyuan gangling jiqi shishi banfa," 588.

[60] Zhang Jinzuo, "Jingshen dongyuan lun [On Spiritual Mobilization]," *Zhongguo shehui* 4:4 (1938): 19.

[61] "Ludengdaofu zhu Quan minzu zhanzheng lun Zhang Junmai fanyi zaiban yidao Jing [Reprints of Zhang Junmai's Translation of Ludendorff's *Der totale Krieg* Arrive in the Capital]," *Zhongyang ribao*, April 24, 1937, B3.

warfare rendered his country vulnerable to foreign conquest because most industries were concentrated in Shanghai's foreign settlements. In one of the prefaces to the Chinese edition of *Der totale Krieg*, military strategist Jiang Baili (1882–1938) drove home the point that modern warfare was not a battle between militaries but a prolonged struggle between nations for their lives. While the translator cautioned that Ludendorff's animosity against Jews and Christians was "a bit remote from our country's situation," some Chinese readers found the supposed enervating effect on the nation's spiritual resources by alien ideologies very relevant indeed.[62] Jiang, a senior adviser of the Military Affairs Commission, lauded Italian Fascism for wrestling power from Catholic clergymen, Marxists and capitalists by remaking the nation-state into the custodian of both labor and capital. Instead of languishing under a cosmopolitan, oppressive ruling class, Italians contributed to a cooperative nation that was as harmonious as one's family.[63]

Fascism offered spiritual communion over materialist individualism under a strictly national framework. It offered the best defense, military and ideological, against forces from capitalism and communism to imperialism and transnational religious devotions. Bureaucrat Hu Menghua (1903–83), who led an earlier career as a literary critic, was impressed with Ludendorff's pronouncements on the military's supremacy in the body politic and the use of posters and radio broadcasts to encourage energetic participation. But he was inspired above all by the anti-Christian strategist's musings on deity and the German national psyche. Germans, as per Hu's reading of Ludendorff, were graced with a concrete sense of the divine that lent the nation a concrete basis for spiritual cohesion.[64] Ludendorff's God, moreover, was thoroughly German and cleansed of the foreignness and universalism in Christianity. Hu observed that like China through much of its history, religious and moral values in Germany did not constitute an abstract sphere of occult spirituality but pervaded the secular life of the people. They inspired healthy animosity against foreign enemies, bolstered popular concern for the nation's fragile existence and sustained a willed vigor and the emphasis of bodily strength among the population. Likewise, fascism, according to Jiang Baili, was a uniquely nationalist phenomenon.

---

[62] Zhang Junmai, trans., *Quan minzu zhanzheng lun* [*Der totale Krieg*] (Shanghai: Zhongguo guomin jingji yanjiusuo, 1937), x, xxvii.

[63] Jiang Baili, *Guofang lun* [*On National Defense*] (N.p., 1937?), 203–4.

[64] Ludendorff, ever scornful of politicians, eventually fell out with the Nazi movement in 1928 after Hitler rejected his doctrine of subjecting political processes to the control of the armed forces. In contrast, Nationalist China, run by the Generalissimo supported by his former cadets from the Whampoa Academy, was perhaps closer to the German general's ideal of a militarist society.

Mussolini's regime drew from ancient Rome and the "united front (*lianhe zhanxian*) between capital and labor revived Italy's glory."[65] China's revival, like Germany and Italy's, rested on the people embodying the country's primordial values in their quotidian morals, habits, thoughts and aspirations.

The identification of indomitable mass will as the only weapon that China could wield also explained why Nationalist leaders continued to hold their archenemy, Japan, in such high regard. To the party elite, many of whom had experienced the country firsthand as students, the Japanese people encapsulated the ideals of order, hierarchy and chivalry that seemed to forever elude poverty-stricken China. In mid-March 1940, impoverished urbanites, dissatisfied with the rocketing price of the grain, looted rice merchants and banks in the southwestern city of Chengdu.[66] Rather than attributing the incident to natural disasters or economic hardship, Chiang pointed his finger at China's weak nationalistic education in comparison with Japan's. During a banquet the Generalissimo hosted for educators in March 1940, Chiang opined that Japan had taken to heart ancient holistic ideals that put equal emphasis on moral rectitude, bodily strength and aesthetic creativity, thus producing citizens that were more virile than the Chinese. He called for an education experience that resonated with students' "everyday life" (*richang shenghuo*) and that cultivated a "benevolent concern for all things" (*ren'ai xiwu*), including animals and plants.[67] What Chiang characterized as Japan's creative adaptation of "Six Arts" (*liuyi*) education was in fact of much more recent vintage than the Confucianism from which it supposedly originated. Japan's focus on proper manners, calisthenics and martial arts in the schooling process was inseparable from the tenet that citizens, constituting the human resources of the state, had the responsibility to maintain good physical and mental health. Introduced in Japan and its colonies in earnest after the Mukden (1931) and Marco Polo Bridge (1937) Incidents, these more subtle strategies of home front

[65] Hu Menghua, "Guomin jingshen zong dongyuan de shiji yu shijian [National Spiritual Mobilization – Its Concreteness and Practice]," *Zhongyang zhoukan* 1, no. 34 (1939): 10–11; Jiang, *Guofang lun*, 182. For another example of Chinese intellectuals' interest in Ludendorff, see You Rulong, "Dangqian Zhongguo guomin jingshen zong dongyuan zhi lilun yu shijian [The Theory and Practice of National Spiritual Mobilization in Today's China]," *Dongfang zazhi* 37, no. 8 (1940): 37–44.
[66] The Chengdu rice riot quickly became another point of contention between the Nationalist and Communist parties, with each accusing the other of manipulating popular disaffection with inflation for political gains. See Chang Wenbin, "1940 nian Chengdu 'qiangmi' you minbian zhuanhua wei zhengzhi shijian de kaocha [An Analysis of the Politicization of the Popular Uprising 1940 Chengdu 'Rice Riot]," *Xi'nan minzu daxue xuebao – renwen sheke ban* 26, no. 10 (2005): 254–8.
[67] Chiang, *Jiang Zhongzheng zongtong dang'an: shilüe gaoben*, 43:293.

management were often the overlooked side of the *dirigist*, politically repressive turn of the Shôwa state.[68]

While Chiang was merely making an observation on Japan's strength, his party colleagues were more particular in their admiration for Japan's mobilization of its people's physical and spiritual capacities since the outbreak of the Sino–Japanese War. Ju Zheng (1876–1951), who headed the Nationalist government's judicial branch, suggested plainly that China should adopt Japan's extensive system of fitness tests and medical examinations to disqualify effete citizens from government employment, secondary and higher education and even marriages. Making the eugenicist connection between individual citizens' health and the nation's, Ju argued those who were deemed physically unfit or, worse, infected with venereal diseases, should be eliminated (*taotai*). He felt that wartime mobilization "would become no more than a scrap of paper" (*chengwei juwen*) if unfit party cadres, government officials and university and high school students were allowed to remain in their positions.[69] The Japanese-educated jurist was no doubt following with interest Tokyo's effort at stepping up its hygienic regime that, beginning from May 1938, brought together prefectural and municipal governments, the police and the newly established, army-initiated Ministry of Welfare. Through annual week-long campaigns of sports carnivals, public talks, film screenings and award programs, the state drove home the importance of regular exercises, nutrition, public morality and preventing tuberculosis and sexually transmitted diseases.

Personal health came to be touted as a patriotic duty, and those who suffered from illnesses and disabilities could be stripped of their citizenship rights. These public health campaigns constituted part of Japan's own National Spiritual Mobilization Movement (*kokumin seishin sôdôin undô*), which, launched in August 1937, shared the same set of Chinese characters in its nomenclature as the endeavor the GMD introduced two years later.[70] Citizens' bodies, more than anything else, were supposed to determine national strength. Despite its dramatic rise to dominance in

---

[68] Fujino Yutaka, *Kyôsei sareta kenkô – Nihon fashizumu shita no seimei to shintai* [*Forced Health – Life and Body under Japanese Fascism*] (Tokyo: Yoshikawa kôbunkan, 2000), 4–5; Jung Keun-sik, "Shokuminchi shihai, shintai kiritsu, kenkô [Colonial Rule, Body Discipline, Health]," in *Seikatsu no naka no shokuminchi shugi*, ed. Mizuno Naoki (Kyoto: Jinbun shoin, 2004), 70–4. Jung observes that while the Japanese colonial state began to take an interest in its Korean subjects as early as the 1920s, medical check-up was confined to female textile factory workers to ensure productivity. Korean males were not subjected to examination until 1938, when they became potential volunteers for the Japanese military.

[69] Ju Zheng to GMD Central Secretariat, January 20, 1939, *huiyi*, 5.2/23.7, Kuomintang Archives.

[70] Fujino, *Kyôsei sareta kenkô*, 25–6.

Asia, mastery of Western science, and the incredible body of knowledge its scholars produced over on China and India, Jiang Baili believed Japan's future was doomed. He supported this contrarian view by identifying a "malaise of progress" (*wenming bing*), namely the poor health of the Japanese populace. The percentage of Japanese men who failed to meet conscription requirements, Jiang observed in 1939, rose from twenty-five to forty-eight in the thirteen years since 1925. Students, in particular, were more likely to fall below the threshold than the general population. Urbanites were more likely than peasants in rural Shikoku or Hokkaido to suffer modernity's enervating effects.[71] While Chiang and Ju were clearly in awe of Tokyo's education and social engineering initiatives, Jiang captured the anxiety of Japanese bureaucrats over the people's physical state and its implications for a war that brought populations in close combat.

Across East Asia, aesthetic sensibilities, political organization and social mores were remolded under the total war paradigm. Chinese spiritual mobilization thus shared more than nomenclature with its Japanese counterpart. War between the two countries spurred both China and Japan, including the latter's colonies and puppet states, to step up transforming industries, marshaling social resources and mobilizing national identities.[72] More than control over enterprises and social organizations, a new regime of affective and visual experiences took shape. Military uniformity and clockwork efficiency now pervaded state management of human bodies and what used to be regarded as citizens' free time, particularly that of young people, who formed the backbone of the two warring nation-states. In Japanese colonies like Korea and Taiwan, spiritual mobilization entailed promoting mass calisthenics, hiking, youth corps and a strict work-and-rest regimen in schools and workplaces. Imperial subjects were expected to participate in anthem-singing and emperor-worshipping, speak only Japanese, accumulate savings and restrain from indulging in cosmetics, alcohol and even white rice.[73] Ju's proposal for a certification system to ensure that newlyweds and high school students were healthy was not adopted. Yet his conviction that the state needed to micromanage citizens' routines struck a chord with cadres

[71] Jiang, *Jiang Baili xiansheng wenxuan* [*Selected Works of Jiang Baili*] (N.p.: Guofang xuehui, n.d.), 21–2.

[72] Prasenjit Duara, *Sovereignty and Authenticity: Manchukuo and the East Asian Modern* (Lanham, MD: Rowman and Littlefield, 2003), 246–7.

[73] Jung, "Shokuminchi shihai, shintai kiritsu, kenkô," 75–89. For spiritual mobilization in Taiwan, see Kondô Masami, *Sôryokusen to Taiwan: Nihon shokuminchi hôkai no kenkyû* [*Total War and Taiwan: A Study on the Japanese Colony's Collapse*] (Tokyo: Tôsui Shobô, 1996), 145–89.

whose cult of productivity forged an indissoluble link between physical prowess, ideological conformity and singular devotion to the war cause.

These combined imperatives were well articulated at the National Spiritual Mobilization movement's launching ceremony, which took place in Chongqing on May Day evening. Party cadres, government officials, military officers, workers, peasants, merchants, youths and women participated in what the popular pictorial *Young Companion* (*Liangyou huabao*) described as an unprecedented torch parade (*kongqian zhi huoju da youxing*). Reported numbers of participants ranged from 3,000 to several hundred thousand.[74] Before the mass performance, President Lin Sen (1868–1943) urged workers to avoid labor disputes and understand the "true meaning" of May Day – cooperation between capitalists and workers in the common cause of furthering productivity. Chiang, set against the monumental spectacle of light, music and precise procession, lambasted the decadent, unruly aesthetics of dancing bodies. Referring specifically to the foreign concessions of Shanghai, Tianjin and Hankou, he urged young people to stop loitering around in cabaret halls and devote their energy to production.[75] Speech after speech delivered at mandated citizens' monthly assemblies (*guomin yuehui*) held across "free" China extolled the virtues of an austere, disciplined factory-floor lifestyle stripped of Western, consumerist indulgences.

At the June 1939 assembly for cadres from the GMD social affairs department, associate director Ma Chaojun (1886–1977) observed that China's average life expectancy had fallen from thirty-four to thirty-two years of age. He attributed this alarming development to how the people's vitality was being drained by unproductive entertainment like card games and mahjong. If every citizen was to rise up at six in the morning and labor for two extra hours instead, the benefit to the nation would be immeasurable. The flamboyant Ma then performed a few of his morning drills after offering his own spiritually rejuvenating routine for emulation: get up at 5:30 in the morning, down a cup of plain or salted water to cleanse the digestive system, and then empty one's bowel in the washroom.[76]

---

[74] "Jingshen zong dongyuan [National Spiritual Mobilization]," *Liangyou huabao*, no. 143 (1939): 4–5; "Jingshen zong dongyuan zuo shishi Jiang weiyuanzhang xiang quanguo guangbo [Spiritual Mobilization Launched Yesterday, Generalissimo Chiang Delivered Radio Address to Nation]," *Dagong bao* (Hong Kong), May 2, 1939, 3.

[75] "Jingshen zong dongyuan," *Dagong bao*, 3; Yin Ling, "Wo suo zhi de 'Guomin jingshen zong dongyuan' yundong [The 'National Spiritual Mobilization' Campaign That I Know]," *Hongyan chunqiu*, no. 99 (2006): 63. As a student attendee, Yin recalled that the scale and grandeur of the ceremony was rare for the then isolated and dull Chongqing.

[76] "Zhongyang shehui bu tuixing guomin jingshen zong dongyuan shishi baogao [Report by the Social Affairs Department on Its Implementation of National Spiritual Mobilization]," June 10, 1939, *tezhong*, 6/39.51, Kuomintang Archives.

Frivolous use of one's free time, especially when combined with habits associated with treaty-port cosmopolitanism, was now seen as a disease that literally threatened the nation's health and hence the resistance effort.

With the dislocation and inland migration of refugees from Japanese-occupied coastal regions, state officials found to their dismay that maligned urban indulgences were spreading to Chongqing. A woman who spent her high school years in the wartime capital was fascinated by how the city was transformed from a remote backwater in the early 1930s to a "cultured" place of ballroom dancing, revealing cheongsam and stylish pantyhose thanks to better transport connections, relocated universities and refugees who fled from the coast.[77] For cadres involved in spiritual mobilization, the arrival of consumer modernity was not a salutary development. Pan Gongzhan argued that consumerism did not make sense in an impoverished country that was aiming to transcend capitalism and save all the spiritual and material resources it could to fight the enemy. "Capitalist countries," he added, "which sometimes faced overproduction, encouraged both production and consumption. But once there was a war, all industries became militarized, and consumption was curtailed and conservation imposed." Pan cited *Zuozhuan*, stating that people's livelihood rested entirely on hard work. The imperative to conserve was not subject to debate when the nation's survival was on the line. "Some people thought that conservation was negative and that consumption helped stimulate production. Some further believed that even when those in trenches were bathing in blood, it did not hurt that the home front thrived in prosperity. But," Pan countered, "this idea was nothing more than a pretext for pursuing individual craving for material well-being."[78]

Zhang Qun (1889–1990), the Military Affairs Commission general secretary, complained in the official organ of the spiritual mobilization movement that "even though Chongqing had yet to sport amenities typical of modern urban life, it had already been infested with subpar urban habits like opium-smoking, gambling, non-observance of punctuality and hygienic prescriptions." He warned that if peasants in the vicinities were to adopt a similarly lax attitude toward time, they could

---

[77] Danke Li, *Echoes of Chongqing: Women in Wartime China* (Urbana: University of Illinois Press, 2010), 51–3.

[78] Pan, "Jingshen dongyuan yu wuzhi dongyuan de peihe [Coordination between Spiritual and Material Mobilization]," *Zhongyang dangwu gongbao* 21:2 (1940): 7–8. The *Zuozhuan* citation is from Book VII, Duke Xuan. James Legge's translation reads: "People's weal depends on diligence; with diligence there is no want" (*Chinese Classics*, vol. 5, *The Ch'un Ts'ew with the Tso Chuen*, 2nd edn. [Hong Kong: Hong Kong University Press, 1960], 318).

fail to heed nature's rhythm and miss farming seasons, putting into jeopardy the already strained food supply.[79] As a testament to the premium the state put on punctuality, a clock tower named the Spiritual Fortress (*Jingshen baolei*) was erected in March 1940 overlooking Chongqing's rapidly evolving urban space.[80] Citizens were told that "conservation" meant calibrating the use of not only material sources but also time, as labor time was simultaneously a source of value as realized in production and an immanent feature of the nation's collective strength.

The *Guiding Principles* committed the state to redressing China's debauched life of intoxicated reveries (*zuisheng mengsi*).[81] In the southern province of Guangdong, month-long "get-up-early" and punctuality movements were planned in 1940 alongside campaigns devoted to anticorruption, improving literacy, promoting hygienic habits, conserving scarce resources and planting trees.[82] Extravagant and bohemian indulgences like gambling, dancing, smoking, drinking and outlandish fashion (*qizhuang yifu*) became anathema and citizens were encouraged to take part, and then only in moderation, in healthy entertainment. Conspicuous consumption, including sleeping and getting up late, put to waste precious labor time and sapped the people's vigor and vitality. Young people, in particular, were warned not to spend too much time on social engagements, lest they became lethargic and forgot about work and study.[83] In Xichang, a multiethnic city in the frontier province of Xikang, officials went as far as to deploy a morning-call brigade in late June 1939 to make sure that residents maintained the optimal work-rest pattern.[84] Other places like the Guangxi province in the south put up placards outside eateries and theaters to inspire guilt among consumers and warn them away from hedonist pleasures. Printed on these placards were eye-catching slogans like "Those who arrive to dinners in limousines make an enslaved people!" and "Those who arrive to movies in limousines make an enslaved people!"[85] The efficacy of these harrowing messages in delivering the public from "intoxicated reveries" cannot be assessed,

[79] Zhang Qun, "Jingshen zong dongyuan shishi de shige zhuyi dian [Ten Important Items of Spiritual Mobilization]," *Jingshen dongyuan*, no. 1 (1940): 7.
[80] Yin, "Wo suo zhi de 'Guomin jingshen zong dongyuan' yundong," 63.
[81] "Guomin jingshen zong dongyuan gangling jiqi shishi banfa," 588.
[82] "Zhandi tongxun [News from the Battlefield]," *Jingshen dongyuan*, no. 1 (1940): 32.
[83] *Guomin shenghuo zhi di* [*Enemies of Citizens' Livelihood*] (N.p.: Neizheng bu and Guomin jingshen zong dongyuan hui, n.d.), 39; *Zhanshi jieyue* [*Wartime Conservation*] (N.p.: Guomin jingshen zong dongyuan hui, 1939), 16–18.
[84] "Biansheng tongxun [News from Frontier Provinces]," *Jingshen dongyuan*, no. 1 (1940): 50–84.
[85] "Dongyuan tongxun [Mobilization News]," *Jingshen dongyuan* 2, no. 1 (1941): 189–96.

but they eloquently expressed how the entangled web between rationaliza-
tion of everyday routines, the quest for economic productivity and
a nationalist reaction against cosmopolitan urban life was put into ever
sharper relief by total war mobilization.

Aside from threatening people into action, spiritual mobilization
included more positive measures with a view to encouraging citizens to
participate in reforms on the quotidian. In September 1939, the social
affairs ministry launched a series of contests that, if extensively held,
would at least create the appearance of an enthusiastic and healthy
citizenry. The contests, some of which were first held under the New
Life Movement, would involve citizens of varying education attainments
across the country. Urbanites worked to improve the general appearance
of their cities; peasants participated in the creation of a new rural lifestyle.
While students and the educated could submit their entries for essay
competitions on eradicating unsavory habits and promoting "proper"
entertainment, the illiterate could join sports competitions, maintain
cleanliness at home and follow instructions on getting rid of superstitious
customs at weddings and funerals. Activities were also designed specifically for public servants, merchants, students and educators.[86] By the
beginning of 1941, Guangdong, the eastern province of Zhejiang,
Chongqing and its neighboring provinces Hunan and Shaanxi had all
reported holding competitions in the social sectors and counties under
their jurisdiction with the support of the police and the New Life
Movement Association.[87]

Curiously, while senior GMD cadres often lambasted the consumerist
pleasures of petit-bourgeois youth epitomized by treaty-port cabaret
halls, their idea of wholesome leisure betrayed their own urban bourgeois
background. Cadres at the GMD social affairs department were treated
to hiking trips, traditional martial arts or *wushu* sessions and basketball
games.[88] Instead of indulging in sex, opium and dancing, citizens should
play sports, take up photography or join choirs and operatic groups.[89] Just
how a peasant in the impoverished rural hinterland could get regular hold
of an expensive camera did not appear as an issue for spiritual mobilization advocates. The obsession with the distinction between hygienic and
unhygienic practices, especially in domestic spaces, was likewise an

[86] "Guomin shenghuo gaijin jingsai kemu [Competition Items for the Improvement of
Citizens' Life]," Nationalist Government Collection, 001000004804A, Academia
Historica.
[87] "Dongyuan tongxun [Mobilization News]," *Jingshen dongyuan*, no. 2 (1940): 141–51;
"Dongyuan tongxun [Mobilization News]," *Jingshen dongyuan*, no. 3 (1940): 161–2;
"Dongyuan tongxun [Mobilization News]," *Jingshen dongyuan*, no. 4 (1941): 175.
[88] "Zhongyang shehui bu tuixing guomin jingshen zong dongyuan shishi baogao."
[89] *Guomin shenghuo zhi di*, unpaginated.

unmistakable class marker, traceable to the bourgeois fascination with colonial modernity in treaty ports like Tianjin in the early twentieth century.[90] Despite the movement's aspiration to being inclusive in its geographical and social reach, spiritual mobilization remained an undertaking centered on urban areas and the social elite. As a case in point, while civil servants, as well as teachers and students, were reminded that all monthly assemblies were compulsory, rural households could send just one representative to attend these meetings. In the impoverished Gansu province, officials conceded that assemblies were not regularly held in rural areas due to illiteracy, busy farming routines and a lack of qualified personnel.[91] China's chronic fragmentation, thanks to the country's disparate socioeconomic landscape and the GMD's limited sovereignty, meant that war mobilization was never going to be as "total" as intended.

The GMD attempted to attenuate the movement's regional and class biases by deploying both modern and traditional media forms, creating a diverse repertoire of wartime aesthetics that appealed to various cultural communities and social groups. Sitting in the interstices between popular pastime, modern propaganda and national culture, aesthetics formed a layer of everyday life that was eminently susceptible to unified production. Having been displaced from its traditional stronghold on the relatively prosperous east coast, the party-state was tasked with rallying behind a diverse population that included many poor peasants with little or no education and who could only speak their local dialects. Visual and oral media thus played a particularly crucial role in energizing a culturally disparate people for whom written words were much less familiar than vocal and operatic modes of expression. GMD cadres were remarkably flexible to choose from multiple artistic traditions in which they couched the spiritual mobilization message. A participant at the movement's Chongqing launch ceremony remembered singing the "Citizen Pledge Song," the score of which was adapted from a Christmas hymn.[92] While Chongqing-based officials were inspired by Western music, cadres in

---

[90] Ruth Rogaski, *Hygienic Modernity: Meanings of Health and Disease in Treaty-Port China* (Berkeley: University of California Press, 2004), 223.

[91] Judicial Yuan instruction no. 863, September 27, 1939, Ministry of Judicial Administration Collection 02200001263A, Academia Historica; "Dongyuan tongxun," *Jingshen dongyuan*, no. 4: 177–9.

[92] Yin, "Wo suo zhi de 'Guomin jingshen zong dongyuan' yundong," 63. Yin erroneously cited the song as the "National Spiritual Mobilization Pledge Song" (*Guomin jingshen zong dongyuan xuanshi ge*). The title was, however, published in 1940 as "Citizen Pledge Song" (*Guomin gongyue xuanshi ge*), referring to the document on which everyone was supposed to sign and read aloud at each monthly assembly (*Guomin jingshen zong dongyuan yaoyi* [*Principles of National Spiritual General Mobilization*] [N.p.: Zhongyang zhixing weiyuanhui xunlian weiyuanhui, 1940], app.).

Fujian province were busy rewriting a section of the *Guiding Principles* into local vernaculars and incorporating it into songs so that opera troupes of both traditional and modern varieties could perform them to different audiences in the province.[93] Zhejiang province reported a similar undertaking.[94] The national government had likewise taken an interest in transforming local cultural forms into vehicles for spiritual mobilization. An education ministry directive mandated that all state-run schools and universities establish singing and opera troupes with the purpose of educating the masses. Aided by four traveling drama education teams dispatched across the country, students were to devote their time out of classes to learning the art. The goal, the directive declared, was to create a drama education network that linked together campuses from different provinces.[95]

By 1941, the prestigious National Central University had registered five singing and drama troupes with at least twenty-eight members. The largest among them, Boxi Theatrical Troupe, claimed a membership of seventy-seven, not including instructors who otherwise taught music at the Chongqing-based university. It performed modern spoken drama to raise funds for the commission of the military glider Youth (*Qingnian*) and had plans to stage regular propaganda drama (*xuanchuan huaju*) sessions for the masses, traveling to counties outside Chongqing during the summer recess.[96] These troupes performed plays approved by the Central Commission for the Censorship of Books and Periodicals. Headed by Pan Gongzhan, the body kept a tight grip on even innocuous nationalistic propaganda plays produced by politically suspicious figures. For example, playwright Cao Yu's *Metamorphosis* (*Tuibian*), published in 1940, was purged of lurid colloquialisms and its protagonist Commissioner Liang was hailed as "an official refreshingly true to the Three People's Principles" instead of the original and less partisan "refreshingly true to China."[97] Such modifications were in line with Pan's dictum that anything that strayed from orthodox interpretations of the Three People's Principles was detrimental to the project of "nation-building through the war of resistance."

[93] "Guomin jingshen zong dongyuan shishi gaikuang [An Overview of the Implementation of National Spiritual Mobilization]," *Jingshen dongyuan*, no. 1 (1940): 13.
[94] "Dongyuan tongxun," *Jingshen dongyuan* 2, no. 1 (1941): 189–96.
[95] Education Ministry Order, December 22, 1940, Central University Collection 648/6094, Second Historical Archives.
[96] Central University survey forms for affiliated singing and drama troupes, 1941, Central University Collection 684/6092, Second Historical Archives.
[97] Education Ministry Order, October 9, 1943, Central University Collection, 648/6094, Second Historical Archives.

The result of these efforts was on display at the festivities associated with Chongqing's elevation to official alternate capital (*peidu*) status on October 1, 1940. Urbanites were treated to Sichuan, Beijing, Hubei and modern-style spoken dramas alongside Beijing-style crosstalk (*xiangsheng*), various forms of storytelling and magic shows. These performances were set against a spectacular light display and lantern parade crafted by the state-run production house, film studio and broadcaster, betraying the state's co-option of the urban fascination with electric lights and the industrialized nature of aesthetic experiences under a formidable propaganda machine.[98] The education ministry's drama initiative reflected the state's identification of students and teachers as the vanguard of the total war society. Teachers and students were expected to go beyond the classroom on Sundays and semester recesses and play a supervisory role in the implementation of spiritual mobilization. Students who joined the Three People's Principles Youth Corps were to serve as speakers at monthly assemblies. In rural areas, where educated cadres and officials were in short supply, students spending holiday in their hometowns were even asked to assist *baojia* heads in clamping down on "improper entertainment," "irrational habits" and "indulgences like gambling and smoking."[99] It was incumbent upon students, as the nation's future elite, to participate not only as consumers but also as producers of a centrally coordinated wartime culture that pervaded the people's working and leisure hours.

Mandating students to dedicate their school breaks to social mobilization was just one way of embedding the total war in citizens' leisure routine. While GMD's spiritual mobilization was intent on wrenching the populace from monotonous urban entertainment found in places like cabaret halls, it served to perpetuate rather than redress the vacuity and banality of citizens' everyday life under capitalism. The party operated its own culture industry and was adept in promoting what Theodor Adorno called "pseudo-activities" by affording an illusionary sense of leisure and satisfaction for nimble and subservient workers who needed to recreate their expended labor after many hours at work.[100] Children's games, like

---

[98] "Dongyuan tongxun," *Jingshen dongyuan*, no. 4: 181.

[99] "Quanguo qingnian shishi guomin jingshen zong dongyuan juti banfa [Implementation Measures of National Spiritual Mobilization Concerning Youths]," July 1939, Central University Collection, 684/2238, Second Historical Archives; "Gegi xuexiao ji shejiao jiguan tuijin guomin jingshen zong dongyuan ji xin shenghuo yundong gongzuo shishi gangyao [Principles on Schools and Education Institutions' Tasks in the Implementation of National Spiritual Mobilization and the New Life Movement]," April 17, 1942, Central University Collection, 684/2238, Second Historical Archives.

[100] Theodor Adorno, *The Culture Industry: Selected Essays on Mass Culture*, 2nd edn., ed. J. M. Bernstein (London: Routledge, 2001), 194–5.

camping and sports, were no longer idle play or even rebellious acts against the monotony of capitalist society but were tools that molded future workers and soldiers. The magazine *Young Soldiers* (*Shaonian bing*) was one fine example of how the nation's youngest citizens were not spared from total war mobilization. Launched in 1943, the Jiangxi-based publication was affiliated with the China Cultural Services Association (*Zhongguo wenhua fuwu she*), a CC Clique publishing house. It provided readers, mostly older primary school students in non-Japanese-occupied areas of the southern province, materials for leisure reading while socializing young citizens in the current state-led resistance objectives. The first three issues, distributed for free, offered illustrations, contributions by primary school students and introductions to historical and current events like Sun Yat-sen's revolutionary career and the recent signing of "friendship treaties" with Britain and the United States. Like any other party-run publication, it published speeches by major officials and followed closely the GMD's social initiatives. The editor duly admonished his young readers to maintain a disciplined and healthy work-and-rest schedule, adding that good health was the foundation of resilient spirit and the basic requirement for making future contributions to the nation.[101]

Distinct from publications that catered mainly to adults, however, *Young Soldiers* placed emphasis on contents that proffered amusement to its readers. It enjoined children to sing songs with perversely tongue-in-cheek lyrics like "Little precious ones (*xiao baobao*), stay healthy. Hop on your rocking horses, pick up your bamboo spears, charge ahead and heroically kill the devil Japanese!" Readers were urged to spend their time outside classes making "aerial bombers" with glass, nails, spindle and bamboo. Children playing in groups got a taste of military camaraderie in a game called "Recovering Lost Territories," whereby players divided themselves into teams, lined up and raced to "reclaim" flags marked with names of Japanese-occupied areas on the opposite side. Such conflation of amusement and military training reached its climax in an article that encouraged children in battle zones to trick Japanese soldiers by igniting matches in enclosed bottles through a convex lens, thereby producing a thunderous sound that resembled gunshots. After detailing the scientific principles behind the stun, the article ended with an enticing invitation: "Little friends, this small trick (*wanyir*) is really fun. Give it a try!"[102]

---

[101] Zeng Yizhi, "Jiankang diyi [Health First]," *Shaonian bing*, no. 3 (1943): 18.
[102] Wu Liping, "Erge xuanji [Some Children's Songs]," *Shaonian bing*, no. 1 (1943): 12; Deng Chongdi, "Hongzha ji [Aerial Bombers]," *Shaonian bing*, no. 1 (1943): 13–16; Xing Shuntian, "Shoufu shidi [Reclaiming Lost Territories]," *Shaonian bing*, no. 3

The chillingly nonchalant tone in which children were enticed to risk their lives playing "small tricks" indicated how total war pervaded the people's psyche, including the young generation's. The militarization of leisure in *Young Soldiers* underscored how, much more than just a series of army combats, total war was a highly mediated experience orchestrated under the GMD's monopoly. A sense that the entire Chinese people – from the very old to the very young, from urban workers to peasants – was bound by a common fate enveloped workplaces and domestic spaces alike as much through political propaganda, assembly speeches, alarming slogans as through laws and decrees. Wartime nationalism was moreover a mass aesthetics, a concrete way of life experienced through dramas, magazines, games, rallies, a hygienic lifestyle and the occasional bright lights that garnished embattled Chongqing. Spiritual mobilization aspired to create a people unified under the political and cultural authority of nationalist rather than class struggle, devotion to the conservative rather than the socialist revolution. As we have seen, under the imperative of survival, the CCP had no choice but to at least pledge symbolic loyalty to the now sacralized nationalist cause, downplaying its own ideological commitment to overthrowing capitalist social relations until after the establishment of the People's Republic.[103]

Limits and Persistence of Spiritual Mobilization

It is difficult to gauge how enthusiastic popular response was to the grand political and social experiment of "nation-building through the war of resistance." If we, however, were to take Chiang Kai-shek's own assessment as a cue, the state's call to overhaul everyday habits had been falling on deaf ears. Reflecting on the upcoming fifth anniversary of the National Spiritual Mobilization Movement, the Generalissimo observed in March 1944 that society was still lacking self-discipline, that overall morale was flagging day by day and that the nation as a whole, including party-state cadres and military officers, was ill-prepared for the most demanding stage of the war against Japan.[104] Chiang's complaint, particularly insofar

---

(1943): 47–8; Deng Chongdi, "Buyao huoyao de pao [A Gunpowder-Free Bomb]," *Shaonian bing*, no. 3 (1943): 50.

[103] Until 1955, the People's Republic implemented economic reforms akin to the Soviet New Economic Policy, putting the abolition of private ownership on hold in favor of modernizing production forces. Another inspiration for early Communist China, as economic historian Chris Bramall highlights, was the GMD's German-informed state capitalist strategy of devising five-year objectives and nationalizing major industries and infrastructure (*Chinese Economic Development* [New York: Routledge, 2009], 84–7).

[104] Executive Yuan Order, March 18, 1944, Ministry of Judicial Administration Collection, 02200000270A, Academia Historica.

as it concerned government officials, was not without precedent. As early as September 1939, there were signs that public servants were abusing their power by exempting their families and themselves from attending mandatory monthly assemblies.[105]

In response, the National Spiritual Mobilization Association started sending inspectors (*shicha yuan*) to various levels of government from early 1940. Inspectors made random visits to provinces and localities, having purview over matters from attendance at monthly assemblies and funding situations to subscription to the Citizens' Pledge and prevalence of various social campaigns. Inspectors were to specify clearly in an elaborate form how many people participated in assemblies in relation to the area's population. They were to avoid "abstract language" (*chouxiang yuqi*) and to collate figures on amounts raised in donation campaigns from people's savings and participants in literacy classes. They documented speeches, radio broadcasts, magazines, comics, slogans, pieces of music and slide presentations used in propaganda.[106] The effect of audit administration on the movement at local levels was insignificant, not least because the general sociopolitical situation remained unchanged. Local officials, in response to a nationwide review ordered by Chiang before the spiritual movement's fifth anniversary, blamed the stagnating rural economy and uneducated and uncouth (*wenhua shuizhun taidi*) citizens for the campaign's limitations.[107] The fact that three different divisions of the party-state had successively held the reins of the National Spiritual Mobilization Association – the Supreme National Defense Council in 1939, the GMD social affairs department in 1940 and the National Mobilization Conference in 1942 – in less than four years testified to the confusion the movement generated at the top.[108]

Indeed, even as the *Guiding Principles* and monthly assembly speakers promised draconian measures against wasteful consumption habits that could deplete the nation's material and human resources, officials were somewhat less resolute in bringing the state's coercive tendency to bear. In 1940, Xie Tianmin, the magistrate of Hechuan county in Sichuan

---

[105] Judicial Yuan Instruction no. 863, September 27, 1939, Ministry of Judicial Administration Collection, 02200001263A, Academia Historica.

[106] Judicial Yuan to Ministry of Judicial Administration, February 24, 1940, Ministry of Judicial Administration Collection, 02200000271A, Academia Historica.

[107] Shandong Provincial Government to Chiang Kai-shek, May 6, 1944, Nationalist Government Collection, 001000004769A, Academia Historica.

[108] Supreme National Defense Council Secretariat to GMD Central Secretariat, March 11, 1940, *huiyi*, 5.3/143.7, Kuomintang Archives; "Guomin jingshen zong dongyuan hui yewu guibing Guojia zong dongyuan huiyi jieban an [Plan to Subsume Tasks of the National Spiritual Mobilization Association under the National Mobilization Conference]," October 21, 1942, Ministry of Judicial Administration Collection 02200001263A, Academia Historica.

province, petitioned the Executive Yuan to ban the import of cigarettes and transform all domestic cigarette factories into enterprises that "benefitted the people's livelihood" and "supported the war of resistance."[109] The local chief stated that his county consumed more than 120,000 *yuan* worth of cigarettes each month. The central authorities, while acknowledging that banning cigarettes conformed to the wartime objective of resource saving, were surprisingly unimpressed by Xie's determination to stamp out this unhealthy indulgence. The brief written reply by a Chongqing bureaucrat, as attached to the petition, argued that the New Life Movement and the imperative to conserve resources had to be implemented patiently through persuasion and that Xie's heavy-handed measures could only result in confusion (*fenrao*).[110] More telling was the joint response drafted by four ministries in dismissal of the Henan provincial government's 1941 call to put a total ban on alcohol and tobacco consumption. Observing that drinking and smoking had long become common social customs, the finance, economic affairs, interior, and agriculture and forestry ministries reckoned that heavier taxes on these baleful products, particularly those imported from abroad, was more effective than an outright ban. "The people," the reply continued, "should be persuaded to practice thrift out of volition and not forced into doing so."[111] The ministries' relatively relaxed approach hinted that some GMD cadres did not share the urgency displayed in the *Guiding Principles*, which prioritized "complete redresses" (*chedi de gaizheng*) to an intoxicated, senseless lifestyle of dancing, sex, material consumption and private gains (*shengse huoli zhi zuisheng mengsi de shenghuo*).[112] At times, as the next chapter discusses, the strong moralizing bent of wartime mobilization operated more coherently at the discursive level, assimilating liberal intellectual scorn for mass culture.

Despite these inconsistencies, and Chiang's own admission of the movement's inadequacies, China's eventual victory had allowed spiritual general mobilization to be remembered as a successful undertaking rather than condemned as a fascist relic as in postwar Japan. Less than a decade after the end of the Second Sino–Japanese War, Taiwan-based GMD officials were calling for a new spiritual mobilization campaign against Soviet Russia and its Chinese ally instead of Japan. Commentators lauded

[109] Chongqing Garrison Command to Executive Yuan, January 1940, Executive Yuan Collection, 2(3)/3435, Second Historical Archives.

[110] Ibid.

[111] Ministries of Finance, Economic Affairs, Agriculture and Forestry, and the Interior to the Executive Yuan, Received on March 3, 1941, Executive Yuan Collection, 2(3)/3435, Second Historical Archives.

[112] "Guomin jingshen zong dongyuan gangling jiqi shishi banfa," 588.

Figure 4.1 Pictures of the National Spiritual Mobilization Campaign launching ceremonies on May 1, 1939. Events took place in Chongqing, Xi'an, Guangdong province and Hong Kong

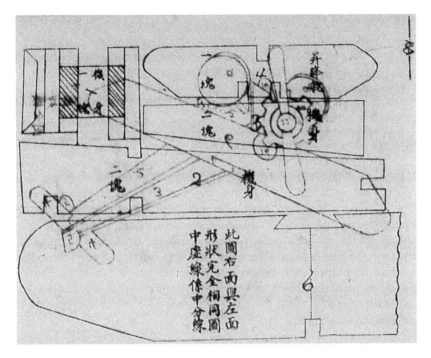

Figure 4.2 Children taught to make "aerial bombers"

spiritual mobilization as a viable military strategy, as well as an effective way to create an anticommunist, modern national culture. The total war social experiment became canonized as a climax of an unfinished quest to build a nationalist utopia of fraternal cooperation and austere efficiency. Just as Sun had fought against warlords in the 1920s by rallying ignorant masses behind the call for action, a doctrine well elaborated by Dai Jitao during party purification in 1927, Chiang had thwarted off Japanese invaders in the 1940s by elevating the spiritual coherence of the nation. It now rested upon the people in Taiwan to continue this anticommunist enterprise by harnessing the Chinese people's innate proclivity for loyalty, fidelity, clearly demarcated social hierarchy and mutual assistance.[113] The legacy of spiritual mobilization, and the conservative revolution the April 12 coup inaugurated in postwar "free" China, are the subject of the epilogue.

[113] Wang Guanqing, "Xinli jianshe, jingshen dongyuan yu Zhongguo geming [Psychological Reconstruction, Spiritual Mobilization and the Chinese Revolution]," *Guohun*, no. 130 (1956): 12–14.

5   Convergence
Liberal Sentimentalities and the Conservative Revolution

If conservative revolutionaries were ambivalent toward the masses, their relationship with the intelligentsia was equally fraught with tensions. The party's aversion to class war and high regard for urban petit-bourgeois culture appealed to Westernized educators and many sons and daughters of Nationalist China's privileged urbanites. Earning the trust of the intellectual elite who were the opinion leaders based in modernizing cities, was, however, another matter. By the time Chiang Kai-shek launched his attacks on Communists and labor unionists on April 12, 1927, the intellectual class that rose to the center stage in national life during the anti-traditionalist New Culture Movement had already been divided along fault lines that paralleled those in the political sphere. There was certainly little love lost between left-wing writers, Communist or otherwise, and the likes of Dai Jitao and Hu Hanmin. As for nonpartisan moderates, unlike the upwardly mobile petit-bourgeois, there also appeared to be little common ground between their aspirations and the GMD's. The party's intolerance for dissent alienated liberal intellectuals whose journalistic and literary work was self-conceitedly celebrated as the "Chinese Renaissance."[1] Yet liberals were not always at the GMD's throat. Instead, they wavered between conscious distancing and equivocal cooperation in their interactions with the Nationalist state. Some intellectuals reconciled themselves to delivering critiques within the system. Others resorted to quiet university campuses, particularly those operating from the deposed imperial capital of Beijing (renamed Beiping in 1928 by the victorious GMD state). Still

[1] Lin Yutang, *A History of the Press and Public Opinion in China* (Shanghai: Kelly and Walsh, 1936), 119. For literary strategies that consolidated the writer's role as the conveyor of enlightenment to the Chinese populace, see Liu, *Translingual Practice*, 73–6. More recently, historians have started to question the extent to which the New Culture elite could represent the mass public who usually patronized lowbrow cultural commodities (Lean, *Public Passion*, 74–6); Tang Xiaobing, *Xiandai Zhongguo de gonggong yulun – yi Da gongbao "Xingqi lunwen" yu* Shenbao *"Ziyou tan" weili* [*Public Opinion in Modern China – A Study Based on "Weekly Commentaries" of* l'Impartial *and "Free Talk" of* Shenbao] (Beijing: Shehui kexue wenxian chubanshe, 2012).

others, like the famed Hu Shi (1891–1962), managed to accomplish both: editing the vocal *Independent Critic* (*Duli pinglun*) while teaching at Peking University through the 1930s until taking up appointment as the Chinese ambassador to the United States in 1938.

Hu Shi's tense but at times close relationship with the Nationalist elite was not unique. Historian Jiang Tingfu (1895–1965), another founder of *Independent Critic*, mirrored Hu's career as a professor at Tsinghua University before joining the Nationalist government in 1935 and eventually becoming the Chinese ambassador to the Soviet Union. Both men remained nonpartisan, but did choose sides. Geologist Ding Wenjiang (V. K. Ting, 1887–1936), yet another collaborator of Hu, expressed liberal ideals of government in the 1920s before endorsing dictatorship in 1934. Ambivalence toward the conservative revolution was not just personal idiosyncrasy but ran deeper in the conflicting tendencies in what Edmund Fung calls the "differentiated category" of Chinese liberals.[2] There were elements in the Nationalist ideology and approach to governing the masses that struck a chord with liberal sentiments. These commonalities, accentuated in national crises, are seldom explored because cooperation between the intelligentsia and the Nationalist state was fleeting and haphazard. The curious case of aesthetician Zhu Guangqian (1897–1986) sheds light on these convergences at the ideological, instead of simply the practical, level. A liberal writer whose natural sympathies did not lay with a right-wing vanguard party nonetheless joined the GMD and wrote for party-run publications during the latter half of the eight-year war of resistance. Zhu's career grew out of a milieu that upheld the edifying function of cultural expression. For writers, artists and thinkers to perform their pedagogical role in society, they must be allowed unfettered access to the public and resist the state's restrictions on creative freedom. At the same time, intellectuals were even more anxious to keep at arm's length the multitude of their less accomplished fellow citizens, whom they feared and regarded with disdain. The regime might be repulsive, but it was the only possible guarantor of China's cultural and ethical order that transcended sectarian conflicts and mob violence.

Liberal endorsement was directed not so much to the mechanics of the conservative revolution but the body politic the Nationalist state

---

[2] Fung, *Intellectual Foundations of Chinese Modernity*, 134. Jerome Grieder begins his classic study on Hu Shi by stressing that his subject did not command a nonexistent liberal faction in China and that many men and women who inhabited Hu's end of the ideological spectrum held various views on social crises (*Hu Shih and the Chinese Renaissance: Liberalism in the Chinese Revolution, 1917–1937* [Cambridge, MA: Harvard University Press, 1970], xi–xii).

commanded. The apparently nonpartisan impulses driving support for the GMD allowed Zhu's reputation to remain unscathed from his collaboration. In fact, that he once championed the broad aims of the conservative revolution has not been seriously examined. In China, the British and French-educated academic remains to be seen as a public intellectual of impeccable idealism and wisdom. His many works on aesthetic theory and Continental philosophy introduced Immanuel Kant, Benedetto Croce and particularly Sigmund Freud to the Chinese academia. But it was Zhu's equally copious writings in the print media that consolidated the writer's acclaimed position as a purveyor of artistic refinement and moral accomplishment among the reading public. Compilations like *Twelve Letters to Youths* (*Gei qingnian de shi'er fengxin*) and *On Cultivation* (*Tan xiuyang*) were parsed through by generations of students for advice on negotiating the transition to adulthood in a society beset by unstable politics, external threats and widespread corruption. Yet the links between Zhu's cultural criticism and his political involvements have rarely been explored. Little attention has been paid to the very different contexts in which *Twelve Letters* and *On Cultivation* were written. Zhu's indictments against student involvement in oppositional politics are typically downplayed as peripheral to his illustrious academic career. In the People's Republic, where the aesthetician remained after the Communist Revolution in 1949, Zhu's transformation from a liberal-leaning idealist philosopher into an advocate of Marxian aesthetics overshadowed, if not completely offset, his involvement in Nationalist propaganda projects during the Second Sino–Japanese War. Unlike Hu Shi, who moved to Taiwan, Zhu Guangqian was not subject to sustained, campaign-style attacks in Communist China.

The manner in which a famed liberal New Culture intellectual was co-opted into the conservative revolution deserves closer scrutiny. At issue is the ways that Zhu's prolific output on aesthetics and cultivation during the Republican period can be considered anew by taking into account his short stint as a contributor to the party organ *Central Weekly* (*Zhongyang zhoukan*). It bears stressing that the purpose here is not to fill an unsavory lacuna in the biography of a celebrated intellectual figure. Instead, it is to interrogate the ideal of nonpartisanship by setting it against liberals' ambivalence toward the nation-state and the masses. Examining the tensions and unarticulated desires within Zhu's writings reveals intellectuals' preference for conservatism as Chinese society became increasingly radicalized over the course of the Republican period. The GMD's reluctance to share power with the general populace was compatible with elitist wariness over a political and cultural scene where the common people played an increasingly visible and vocal role,

influenced as they were by the forces of the market and radical ideologies. The dismissive view that most Chinese people, particularly young
people, had to be guided in their everyday deportment instead of treated
as fellow citizens was shared by both the party-state and intellectuals
who harbored no left-wing sympathies. Especially in times when
national unity was paramount, measures that claimed to tame destructive mob wrath and remold the masses into a productive force serving
common purposes found receptive minds among an otherwise skeptical
New Culture intelligentsia.

While the conservative revolution might have inspired much less
intellectual enthusiasm than the Communist movement, the GMD
managed to tap into the "Chinese Renaissance" for legitimacy.
Despite their self-fashioning as the voice of reason and transcendence,
intellectuals' disdain for mass society in both its capitalist consumerist
and left-wing insurrectionary forms often threw the otherwise nonaligned New Culture elite into the fold of the Nationalist state. Wielding
little political influence on their own, intellectuals like Zhu Guangqian
hedged the cultural visions they developed during the heady days of the
1920s on the regime that promised to put an end to the nihilistic
infighting between political camps and hedonistic habits among the
populace. As a liberal, Zhu's endorsement of GMD rule in the 1940s
echoed an earlier generation of anarchists who counterintuitively sided
with Chiang Kai-shek in the late 1920s against the Communists in a bid
to secure a stable political environment for nonviolent social change.[3]
Particularly in periods of emergency when China fought against
Japanese aggression, liberals, out of nationalism, often found themselves throwing their weight behind the political force most capable of
maintaining social order even if they remained disturbed by the state's
undemocratic and illiberal excesses. Lacking concrete investment in
the conservative revolution, however, liberal support for the GMD was
ephemeral. Zhu, like the majority of his peers, remained in mainland
China after the Communist Revolution in 1949.[4] Nevertheless, the fact
that the conservative revolution was able to attract liberal support at all
suggests that the GMD's vision of a cooperative, hierarchal fraternity
centered on the nation held wider social appeal.

---

[3] Zarrow, *Anarchism and Chinese Political Culture*, 197, 207.
[4] Another prominent liberal writer who stayed in Communist China was novelist Shen
  Congwen (1902–88). According to a list compiled by Max K. W. Huang, Zhu Guangqian
  and Shen Congwen were among the sixty-two Beiping-based intellectuals whom Chiang
  Kai-shek considered politically trustworthy and invited to Taiwan in 1948. However, only
  seven eventually accepted Chiang's invitation ("Jiang Jieshi yu He Lin [Chiang Kai-shek
  and He Lin]," *Zhongyang yanjiu yuan jindai shi yanjiu suo jikan*, no. 67 [2010]: 48–54).

Zhu Guangqian as a Liberal

Zhu Guangqian was born in 1897 in Tongcheng, Anhui. Like many who grew up at the turn of the twentieth century, Zhu was initially educated in the Confucian classics before joining Western-style institutions. Failing to make the trip to the capital for the Peking University (Beida) admission examination, he went to Hong Kong in 1918 to study education on Beiyang government sponsorship after finishing high school and spending two years at a normal college. Zhu might have missed out on the excitement following the Beijing-centered student movement in May 1919, but his career in the Republican period would become interwoven with the institutions and figures that contributed to the city's distinct milieu. Shortly after earning his bachelor's degree in 1922 from the University of Hong Kong, Zhu quit his teaching job and set up a high school and a publisher with up-and-coming writers like Feng Zikai (1898–1975), Xia Mianzun (1886–1946), Xia Yan (1900–95), Ye Shengtao (1894–1988) and Hu Yuzhi (1896–1986) in Shanghai. The Kaiming, or Enlightened, Publishing House gave Zhu the first taste of celebrity status in Shanghai's increasingly commodified print market. During his eight-year sojourn from 1925 to 1933 as a student in Britain and France, where he completed graduate work in English literature, philosophy and psychology, Zhu gained popularity among young readers for his columns in Kaiming-owned magazines *In General (Yiban)* and *High School Students (Zhongxue sheng)*. In 1929, a compilation of his magazine writings were published under *Twelve Letters for Youths (Gei qingnian de shi'er fengxin)*, which sold more than 50,000 copies by 1936.[5] The same publisher also brought to the market Zhu's academic treatises on psychoanalysis, Kantian philosophy and literary criticism, including a translation of Benedotto Croce's *Breviario di esticata (Essence of Aesthetic)*. After earning a master's and a doctoral degree at Edinburgh and Strasbourg universities, respectively, the admirer of Italy's most celebrated liberal philosopher in the twentieth century was recruited by Hu Shi to teach Western literature at Beida.

As a public intellectual, Zhu's long life was ridden with contradictions. Zhu earned popular acclaim and financed his graduate studies by being a savvy operator in Shanghai's exuberant print capitalism. But his critical and creative habitus was centered not in the bustling commercial city but in Beiping. Scrapped of its political preeminence and well-off bureaucratic community, the deposed imperial capital played host to

---

[5] Wen-hsin Yeh, *The Alienated Academy: Culture and Politics in Republican China, 1919–1937* (Cambridge, MA: Council on East Asian Studies, Harvard University, 1990), 270.

a distinct coterie of liberal-leaning intellectuals known paradoxically as
Jingpai or the "Capital School." For what it was worth, the Capital School
was not a school of thought defined by clearly articulated creeds; it existed
in opposition to *Haipai* or the "Shanghai School," which thrived on left-
wing politics and engagement with the crass commercialism for which the
vibrant treaty port was famous. The closely knit group of prominent
writers that operated around literary journals and shared similar aesthetic
dispositions did not have a common program. If anything, Zhu
Guangqian, Xia Mianzun and New Culture intellectuals such as Shen
Congwen (1902–88), Zhu Ziqing (1898–1948) and Zhou Zuoren
(1885–1967) detested ideological uniformity. The southern shift of political power after the Beiyang regime's demise rendered Beiping an ideal
sanctuary for those who saw themselves as constitutive of a third force
independent from both the GMD and the CCP along with writers and
publishers loyal to the two parties. Tucked away from the center of
authoritarian Nationalist power in Nanjing and the commercialism and
left-wing radicalism in Shanghai, Beiping provided Zhu and his friends
from the southern provinces an everyday milieu – classrooms, studios,
aligned publishers, salons, teahouses etc. – that underwrote the cultural, if
not political, integrity of the modern bourgeois individual.[6] Of course, the
former imperial capital was by no means isolated from the rest of the
country or the world. The city hosted nationally acclaimed journals such
as *Thread of Talk* (*Yusi*), *Contemporary Review* (*Xiandai pinglun*) and Hu
Shi's *Independent Critic*. Likewise, intellectual sojourners did not confine
their activities to Beiping. Xu Zhimo (1897–1931) and Liang Shiqiu
(1903–87), editors of *Contemporary Review*, also founded the Shanghai-
based *Crescent Moon* (*Xinyue*) together with Hu Shi and political scientist
Luo Longji (1896–1965).

   Liberalism in 1930s China was a disposition rather than a political
program. There were, to be sure, parties that advocated liberal values
such as constitutionalism and an end to one-party rule, the most prominent example being Zhang Junmai's Chinese National Socialist Party.
Yet most liberals shunned them and were more focused on resisting
ideological straitjackets demanded by mass parties of both the left and
the right. The prevailing sentiment among liberals was depoliticization.
Grieder draws attention to the liberal tendency to assert "the irrelevance,
or untimeliness, of 'politics'" and to affirm humble private pursuits over
student rallies, strikes and public campaigns. Yet, rather than

[6] Xudong Zhang, "The Politics of Aestheticization: Zhou Zuoren and the Crisis of the
Chinese New Culture (1927–1937)" (PhD diss., Duke University, 1995), 94–7;
Kuang Xinnian, *1928: Geming wenxue* [*1928: Revolutionary Literature*] (Jinan: Shandong
jiaoyu chubanshe, 1998), 243–4.

withdrawing from society, liberals touted individuals as the bearers of cultural values that in turn led to sound government. Social change was predicated on private endeavors free from the strictures of suffocating public authority.[7] Thus, as Grieder cites Hu Shi's mentor John Dewey, liberalism was a "habit of mind" rather than a set of policies. It was a lifestyle, one of "cosmopolites who felt more at home on the university campuses of China, and in her cities, than in the hinterland, sophisticated thinkers who addressed themselves not to the illiterate and the intellectually passive multitudes of the peasantry but to the literate, impressionable, and articulate students in the middle schools and universities."[8] Grieder's description belies, if unwittingly, that "liberal" in China was more a class than a doctrinal marker, denoting privileged intellectuals removed from the populace whom they found inadequate, immature and requiring guidance.

To be sure, the liberal temperament did compel Zhu to make political statements. On the eve of the Marco Polo Bridge Incident in 1937, as GMD ideologues were demanding ever more vehemently complete devotion to the party-state and its revolutionary doctrine, Zhu urged young people to avoid "following blindly a faction or a so-called 'leader.'" He called for a more active "thinking habit" and less concrete "thought," arguing that there are always multiple sides to each issue. Both left-wingers and right-wingers, however, tended to internalize propaganda "without having diligently worked through the facts and their logical connections."[9] Even in his writings for party-run publications during the Second Sino–Japanese War, Zhu was unafraid to express views apparently at odds with one-party rule. In 1942, he called for a greater participatory role for citizens in political decision-making at the local level. Democratic governance in villages or districts would lay the basis for a vibrant representative democracy at the national level.[10] He challenged the state not to impede freedom of speech. While curbs on free expression might be understandable during war mobilization, Zhu argued in a 1944 op-ed piece, alluding to a slogan of the National Spiritual Mobilization Campaign, that only when the "people had the opportunity to think collectively and discuss matters even-handedly" could the public

[7] James B. Grieder, "The Question of 'Politics' in the May Fourth Era," in *Reflections on the May Fourth Movement: A Symposium*, ed. Benjamin I. Schwartz (Cambridge, MA: East Asian Research Center, Harvard University, 1973), 95–101.
[8] Grieder, *Hu Shih and the Chinese Renaissance*, xi, 328.
[9] Zhu Guangqian, "Zhongguo sixiang de weiji [The Crisis of Chinese Thought]," in *Zhu Guangqian quanji* (hereafter cited as *ZGQQ*) (Hefei: Anhui jiaoyu chubanshe, 1993), 8: 517–18.
[10] Zhu, "Tan chuqun (xia) – chuqun de xunlian [On Civic-Mindedness III – The Cultivation of Civic-Mindedness]," in *ZGQQ*, 4:58.

spontaneously rally behind one common purpose (*yizhi jizhong*).[11]
Unlike mainstream GMD theoreticians, Zhu did not see ideological
diversity as a threat to national unity. Nor did he believe, as Dai Jitao
did, that the masses should submit themselves to the political elite
without thinking through the implications.

Yet Zhu's liberalism remained primarily concerned with private individuals. Integral to his vision was the idea that society's well-being came
down to its each and every member, unmediated by structures of power
and domination. The liberal position assumed the universality of the
urban bourgeois subject, emancipated from the shackles of ecclesiastical
and plutocratic power, fully realizing its potentials. Such celebration of
the "free human" (*ziyou ren*) sidestepped socioeconomic problems specific to China's semi-colonial predicaments.[12] Solutions to political problems rested on cultivating sound individuals. Zhu's advocacy of
representative democracy was, therefore, accompanied by the caveat
that "until they had received proper education in politics," the common
people should have less sway over the election system than the "well-
educated and trustworthy."[13] Character formation, moreover, was
likened to an aesthetic enterprise. According to Shu-mei Shih, *Jingpai*
writers predicated individuality on diverse, open-ended and noncommit-
tal expressions of creativity. Self-expression was unencumbered by
political ideologies such as nationalism.[14] While insistence on the autonomy of the artistic soul might serve as a defense against political strictures,
it also preempted overarching critiques of society. Instead of repressive
systems, China's many problems were blamed on citizens unable or
unwilling to pursue perfection.

Unlike determined and accomplished *Jingpai* writers, the bulk of
Chinese citizenry was, Zhu decried, allowing their creative power to
rust. Aesthetic gratification, Zhu posited in 1936, derived from "an
order and a form" that an artist endowed on an essay, a painting or
a sculpture. He criticized the common people (*xiao baixing*), particularly
youths, for shirking their duty as "artists" by faulting the government for

[11] Zhu, "Xianzheng cujin yu yanlun ziyou [Promotion of Constitutional Rule and Freedom of Speech]," in *ZGQQJ*, 9:172–3.
[12] Indeed, liberal intellectuals tended to describe their ideological belief as one that espoused "freedom" or "liberty" (*ziyou*) rather than the more partisan-sounding and controversial "liberalism" (*ziyou zhuyi*) (Zhang Qing, "*Duli pinglun* yu Zhongguo ziyou zhuyi de 'mingming' [*Independent Critic* and the 'Naming' of Chinese Liberalism]," *Wenren lunzheng: zhishi fenzi yu baokan*, ed. Li Jinquan [Guilin: Guangxi shifan daxue chubanshe, 2008], 95–125).
[13] Zhu, "Tan chuqun (xia) – chuqun de xunlian," 4:60.
[14] Shu-mei Shih, *The Lure of the Modern: Writing Modernism in Semicolonial China, 1917–1937* (Berkeley: University of California Press, 2001), 180–4, 187.

social chaos. If China were to become a democratic (*minzhi*) country like Britain, France or the United States, the people must first stop making demands on the state and worked actively to create social order. Unfortunately, the masses were too cowardly (*nuoruo*) to rein in their own excesses.[15] The liberal proposition that individuals should take charge of their own development inspired Zhu to indict his lower-class compatriots rather than to push for egalitarian social arrangements that would help "free" men and women realize their potential.

The ill-disciplined, morally weak masses was a theme to which Zhu regularly returned. As late as February 1948, Zhu remarked that "madness, impetuous hatred and cowardice" motivated antigovernment protests in urban centers.[16] Impeding the self-realization of the modern cosmopolitan individual was not only state tyranny but also the unruly beast that was mass society. As with the New Culture Movement in general, liberals in China saw themselves as agents of an ethical transformation of China by formulating new literary forms and interrogating familial authority and gender relations. The goal was to empower each and every Chinese person to reclaim authentic humanity from social conventions that numbed self-expression and disabled critical thinking. Individuals, freed from indigenous structures of power, were to then form the basis of a new social order.[17] The liberal discourse of individualism in this period had a collectivist bent, devised as it was with tradition, instead of the nation, as its prime enemy. It considered individual and nation as mutually complementary, going so far as to "invent *geren* [i.e., the individual] for the goals of liberation and national revolution."[18] Individual actions had direct bearing on and were ultimately responsible for the well-being of society. In the liberal vision, therefore, "men of goodwill and sincere purpose" were more urgently needed than drastic changes in how government and economic production operated.[19] Zhu inherited the New Culture obsession with reforming the moral constitution of the Chinese and he shared with conservative revolutionaries the belief that changing social habits and customs of the underclass was key to nation-building. Zhu placed his hope of collective rejuvenation on self-discipline and rigorous attachment to reason.[20] On the opposite side of open-

---

[15] Zhu, "Gei *Shenbao zhoukan* de qingnian duzhe (er) – zai hunluan zhong chuang zhixu [To Young Readers of the *Shenbao Weekly* (2) – The Search for Order Amidst Chaos]," in *ZGQQJ*, 8:440–1.

[16] Zhu, "Tan qunzhong peiyang qienuo yu xiongcan [On the Spread of Cowardice and Cruelty among the Masses]," in *ZGQQJ*, 9:357.

[17] Fung, *Intellectual Foundations of Chinese Modernity*, 133, 146; Grieder, *Hu Shih and the Chinese Renaissance*, 93–102.

[18] Liu, *Translingual Practice*, 91.

[19] Grieder, *Hu Shih and the Chinese Renaissance*, 334.   [20] Yeh, *Alienated Academy*, 273.

mindedness and nonpartisanship, qualities that *Jingpai* writers embodied, was plebian demagogy that pervaded street protests, picket lines, proletarian literature and the marketplace.

Zhu's liberalism was further complicated by his reluctant collaboration with the GMD as a regular contributor to the *Central Weekly* from 1942. His writings for the premier party mouthpiece formed the core of *On Cultivation* (*Tan xiuyang*) and parts of *On Literature* (*Tan wenxue*), published respectively by the Central Weekly Press and Kaiming in 1943 and 1946. Zhu's own 1980 reminiscences attributed his involvement in GMD propaganda work during the resistance war to a humble desire to keep his academic job amidst the ongoing struggle between rival political parties for support among liberal intellectuals. Zhu recalled how the GMD, knowing that he was courted by Marxist philosopher Zhou Yang (1908–89) to join the CCP in Yan'an:

marshaled old acquaintances like [Wuhan University president] Wang Xinggong and [dean of liberal arts] Chen Xiying of *Contemporary Review* (*Xiandai pinglun*) to take me to Wuhan and appoint me a professor at the foreign literatures department ... Established GMD practice dictated that faculty members who held senior administrative positions join the party. [As the registrar of Wuhan University,] I turned from being an opponent of the GMD to a close associate of the regime.

He further admitted that the two wartime essay collections *On Cultivation* and *On Literature* were works of him serving as Chiang Kai-shek's "hired scribbler" (*yuyong wenren*).[21] One might be inclined to take the confession of an intellectual who renounced his liberalism for communism after 1949 with a grain of salt. Curiously, however, Zhu had cited almost the same practical concerns forty-two years prior to defend his friend and *Jingpai* ally Zhou Zuoren's (1995–67) collaboration with the Japanese. In 1938, Zhou, who shared Zhu's fear that state overreach and mass politics could put intellectual freedom into jeopardy, appeared at the "Renewal of Chinese Culture" conference in Japanese-occupied Beiping. Zhu, having followed the Nationalists to Sichuan, dismissed accusations that his former Beida colleague was a traitor (*Hanjian*). Aside from regurgitating the liberal mantle that writers were above politics, he offered "the desire for comfort and dread of relocation" as explanations for Zhou's scandal.[22] Personal safety, not ideological motivation, was the primary pursuit for a writer under precarious

---

[21] Zhu, "Zuozhe zizhuan [Author's Autobiography]," in *ZGQQJ*, 1:vi.
[22] Zhu, "Zai lun Zhou Zuoren shijian [More on the Zhou Zuoren Incident]," in *ZGQQJ*, 9:11.

circumstances, whether it meant giving up resistance against an external enemy or joining hands with an unsavory regime.

Intellectual Complicity

Zhu's compromised nonpartisan position bespoke the tensions inherent to liberal cultural politics. There is no doubt some truth to his claim that intellectuals made decisions that were not entirely in harmony with their beliefs under extraordinary circumstances like warfare. It was not rare for erstwhile critics of the regime to join the GMD to secure a slightly more comfortable existence as the entire Nationalist political, social and cultural edifice was forced out by the Japanese from Beiping and other cities. At Southwestern Associated University, a wartime merger of North China's three premier institutions including Beida, as many as 40 percent of faculty members had joined the party. Most of them were recent recruits who joined the party for reasons other than political beliefs. Some wished to advance their careers, more than a few succumbed to peer pressure and others decided to acquire party membership out of nationalism.[23] War with Japan moved intellectuals from across the political spectrum to desire national unity and put aside their misgivings against the ruling party and its leader. Famed translator of English literature Liang Shiqiu, who had never joined the GMD, hailed the National Spiritual Mobilization Movement. Writing from Chongqing in March 1939, the self-proclaimed liberal agreed heartily with the "supremacy of the state and the nation" principle, arguing that individual freedom must give way in times of crisis. The government should by all means be broad and inclusive, but it must also tighten control over political life.[24] When the nation's survival was at stake, nationalist principles took precedence over liberal ones.

Yet nonpartisan intellectuals lent the GMD legitimacy not only by grudgingly accepting the party's stewardship; they also contributed ideological substance that resonated with conservative revolutionaries. Academics belonging to the Warring States Group (*Zhan'guo ce pai*), while not known for their liberal sympathies, were particularly enthusiastic in glorifying the total war. The group, led by scholars teaching at Southwestern Associated and other universities, published the short-lived journal *Warring States* (*Zhan'guo ce*) from 1940 to 1941.

---

[23] Wang Qisheng, *Geming yu fan geming: shehui wenhua shiye xia de minguo zhengzhi* [*Revolution and Counterrevolution: Republican Politics in Sociocultural Perspective*] (Beijing: Shehui kexue wenxian chubanshe, 2010), 237–47.
[24] Liang Shiqiu, "Yonghu Guomin jingshen zong dongyuan fa [In Support of the Decree on the National Spiritual Mobilization Movement]," *Zaisheng*, no. 18 (1939): 1–2.

The journal was succeeded by a supplement of the same name attached to the prestigious daily *L'Impartial* (*Da gongbao*). By reclaiming the classic account of the legendary Warring States period (475?–221 BCE), intellectuals idealized the martial qualities attributed to the peoples whose extended struggles ended with the formation of a unified civilization under the Qin state (221–206 BCE). The ideas championed by these Western-educated intellectuals mirrored closely those of German radical conservatives. Lei Haizong (1902–62), who earned a doctorate in European history from the University of Chicago, was deeply influenced by Oswald Spengler's proposition that culture steered the course of a nation's history. Civilizations were organic entities that underwent cycles of rise and decline. But whereas Spengler contended that Western civilization was destined for demise, as evinced by incessant warfare between European states, Lei argued that Chinese culture might well emerge from Japanese encroachment stronger by reclaiming the unique blend of martial and artistic accomplishments that blossomed during the Warring States period. Lin Tongji (1906–80), a Berkeley-educated political scientist, was likewise convinced that the decline of China's national character had to be arrested by resurrecting a total war consciousness that had been forgotten since the Qin empire had unified the country. Lei, Lin and other writers called on the Chinese people to join the Second Sino–Japanese War with heroic resolve and rescue China from its existential threat. The unique historical juncture of total war called for a strong central government and a firm leader. Yet, as recent scholars emphasize in contradiction to conventional leftist critique of the Warring States Group, the GMD and Chiang Kai-shek were not always considered up to task in providing inspiring leadership to the people.[25]

The case of German-educated writer Chen Quan (1903–69) illustrates the close but elusive relationship between nonpartisan intellectuals and the GMD. A playwright and literary critic, Chen hailed the Second Sino–Japanese War as an opportunity to resurrect the will to power among the Chinese people and to overcome the lethargy that had incapacitated the nation through the ages. Like many a CC Clique member, he admired the vigor and macho idealism of the German *volk* and longed for a hero to lead the nation through a baptism of fire.[26] Desiring a hero, Chen argued counterintuitively, was to forsake servitude. Slavish obedience was testament to the people's timidity and mediocrity, but hero worship was to free human will from these abject

[25] Michael R. Godley, "Politics from History: Lei Haizong and the *Zhanguo ce* Clique," *Papers on Far Eastern History*, no. 40 (1989): 96–105; Fung, *Intellectual Foundations of Chinese Modernity*, 120–4.
[26] Godley, "Politics from History," 105–6, 111.

qualities. If the people's will was to drive historical progress, then the hero was the one who garnered and commanded this mighty force. The larger-than-life figure was the "representative" (*daibiao*) and "prophet" (*xianzhi*) of the masses. He was someone who took the place of Jesus Christ: "If the masses lack a hero, they are no better than sheep without a shepherd. Even if they have the will to live, they may not necessarily stand the best chance to survive. They may stray into places that lack fine pasture. They may even find themselves surrounded by fierce wolves waiting to do harm."[27] It falls to the hero to ramp down material limitations with spiritual fortitude and make sure the flock conforms to the demands of different epochs. The allusion to Nietzsche's "God is dead" dictum was impossible to miss.

Chen, like many nationalistic intellectuals, bolstered the conservative revolution from outside, not within. Warring State members were no sycophants of the GMD; Lin Tongji, in particular, was scathing of official corruption and "bureaucratic capitalism."[28] At times, concededly, Chen wrote like a GMD theoretician. He extolled the singular, corporate (*jituan*) unity of the Chinese nation and argued that literature must complement nationalist politics, a view that superseded the outmoded May Fourth ideals of individualism and socialism. Literature must celebrate the nation's "primordial spirit" (*guyou jingshen*), facilitate "spiritual communion" (*jingshen hutong*) among each and every Chinese individual and gather loose thoughts into holistic consciousness. It must rechannel the masses from disparate individual and class considerations to "a central thought, a central personality, and a central political force."[29] At other times, however, Chen was much more ambiguous. His most successful play, *Wild Rose* (*Ye meigui*, 1941), presented a collaborator with the Japanese regime as an exemplar of iron will prepared to die for his ideals, however misguided they were. While the script also featured a spy who sacrificed her life for the nation, she was a *femme fatale* whose patriotic pronouncements sounded hackneyed and insincere.[30] Both figures were imperfect examples of the idealism that

---

[27] Chen Quan, "Lun yingxiong chongbai [On Hero Worship]," *Zhan'guo ce*, no. 4 (May 1940): 3.

[28] Fung, *Intellectual Foundations of Chinese Modernity*, 127.

[29] Chen, "Minzu wenxue yundong [Nationalist Literature Movement]," *Minzu wenxue* 1:1 (1943): 6–9; Chen, "Qinghua (lixiang zhuyi yu langman zhuyi) [Green Flower (Idealism and Romanticism)]," *Guofeng*, no. 12 (1943): 12.

[30] Godley, "Politics from History," 110. For an overview of *Wild Rose* and the controversy surrounding the play, see Ni Wei, *"Minzu" xiangxiang yu guojia tongzhi: 1928–1948 nian Nanjing zhengfu de wenyi zhengce ji wenxue yundong [National Imaginary and State Control: Literary Policies and Movements under the Nanjing Government, 1928–1948]* (Shanghai: Shanghai jiaoyu chubanshe, 2003), 278–81.

ought to propel the quest for truth, benevolence and beauty (*zhen, shan, mei*). The play's entertainment value undercut the uplifting function Chen ascribed to the human will.[31]

Chen Quan's experience is relevant for our discussion of Zhu Guangqian. The latter, though not identified as part of the Warring State Group, contributed to the *Zhanguo ce* magazine and shared with Chen a fascination with the heroic. Like Chen, Zhu was a writer whose endorsement for the Nationalists was marked by convergence, not confession. Indeed, Zhu's conversion to the GMD entailed little revision of his views on culture, society and politics. The only instance where Zhu discernibly toed the party line on the Communist Party was in an internal essay he wrote in November 1943 during a training seminar at the GMD party school, seven months after the university registrar was admitted as a Nationalist and member of the Three People's Principles Youth Corps. Zhu confessed he joined the party because he realized the need for focusing the nation's will and strength and that it was imperative on teachers to set an example for the younger generation. When the nation's survival was at stake, ideological diversity was not an option. "Those loyal to the nation," the professor exhorted, "should rally behind the Nationalist banner in the struggle for its defense." Zhu added that "unorthodox parties and factions (*yidang yipai*) had no reason to exist in society."[32] While Zhu did not specify what these unorthodox organizations were, cadres at the Central Training Corps (*Zhongyang xunlian tuan*) would understand that he meant the CCP. The derogatory term *yidang* was evoked, for one among multiple examples, in a classified April 1939 instruction circulated among local GMD branches. The instruction called on local party branches and government authorities to treat the "unorthodox party," formally an ally in Nationalist China's struggle against foreign Japan, as a grave threat to an unwieldy GMD establishment. It further urged local branches to organize students, workers, peasants and women under GMD-controlled mass organizations, with a view to undermining Communist dominance in civil society.[33] The unpublished essay was the closest among Zhu's expansive corpus to displaying the feigned passion in party orthodoxy one might

---

[31] Chen, "Qinghua," 11.
[32] The essay, filed on November 25, 1943, was written as a participant's submission to the twenty-eighth session of the Central Training Corps party affairs training program ("Zhu Guangqian," Military Affairs Commission Aides Office Collection, 129000029409A, Academia Historica).
[33] "Zhongguo Guomindang zhongzhihui mishuchu miding 'Fangzhi yidang huodong banfa' dian [The Secretariat of the Guomindang Central Executive Committee Drafts Classified Telegram 'Strategies to Counter the Dissenting Party's Activities']," in *Zhonghua minguo shi dang'an ziliao huibian*, vol. 5, no. 1, pt. 2, ed. Zhongguo di'er lishi dang'an guan (Nanjing: Jiangsu guji chubanshe, 1997), 21–4.

expect from a recent convert seeking to overcompensate for his erstwhile defiance.

Zhu's alignment with GMD positions was complicated by the fact that attacking communism and its manifestations in China was not uncommon in liberal discourse. Liberal critiques of the CCP, moreover, were informed by nationalist tenets with which GMD ideologues would have readily identified. For example, in his commentary on the Xi'an Incident, Hu Shi took a swipe at the Chinese Communists and questioned their nationalist credentials. In December 1936, warlord Zhang Xueliang took Chiang Kai-shek hostage to force the Generalissimo to cooperate with the Communists and fight the Japanese. For Hu, what Zhang committed was nothing less than high treason and the CCP's delight in Chiang's predicament proved that the party was more interested in toppling the government than fighting the Japanese. No patriot would weaken the Leader's (*lingxiu*) position. "Having been internationalists all along," Hu commented on Mao Zedong's offer to ally with the GMD against the Japanese, "the Communist Party could in no way suddenly become patriotic. Its recent call for a nationalist front was no more than a strategy hobbled together after failed armed rebellions." That the Communists' internationalism was an original sin for Hu, who was not by any means a zealous nationalist, testified to the ease with which Chinese liberals could side with the ruling party, undesirable as it otherwise was, in times of crisis. Liang Shiqiu, in the same article in which he hailed the National Spiritual Mobilization Movement, echoed GMD cadres' warning that parties that pledged cooperation with the government but acted otherwise would face decisive sanctions. Liang's disagreements with the Communists stemmed as much from liberal as nationalist principles. While he was uncomfortable with the CCP's disdain for private property and political pluralism, Liang confided in 1936 that he "was most dissatisfied" (*zui buman*) with its disdain for the national spirit.[34] Communism embodied something radically alien that predisposed many liberals to the national revolution as the GMD defined it.

Thus, even if Zhu was a "hired scribbler," he did not necessarily trade his soul in exchange for physical comfort. The liberal critic's collaboration with the GMD was less a radical break with than a logical outgrowth of his earlier career as an independent writer. In both guises, the aesthete explored the interstices between culture, morality and the individual, with a particular focus on the experience of growing up amidst China's

---

[34] Hu Shi, "Zhang Xueliang de pan'guo [Zhang Xueliang's Treason]," *Zhongyang zhoubao*, no. 447 (1936): 7–9; Liang, "Yonghu Guomin jingshen zong dongyuan fa," 1; Liang, "Wo wei shenme bu zancheng Gongchandang [The Reasons Why I Do Not Agree with the Communist Party]," *Yuzhou xunkan*, no. 501 (1936): 7–10.

tortuous modern transformation. Zhu was keen to downplay the changing political circumstances in which he operated by emphasizing continuity in his critical enterprise. He brought the rhetorical devices and commercial acumen tested in late 1920s to bear in the 1940s. The prologue of *On Cultivation* suggested that the 1943 publication was a sequel to *Twelve Letters to Youth*. Both combined a disarming aura of informality, flowing vernacular prose and self-help solutions to everyday concerns that were the formulae of the latter's popularity among urban young readers. *On Cultivation* marked an important improvement over the "letters," which the new GMD recruit dismissed self-deprecatingly as maudlin chats between imaginary friends. *Twelve Letters* was written by a puerile graduate student for even younger readers. The party-run *Central Weekly* was, moreover, not a profit-seeking venture, unlike the many commercially run publishers for which Zhu had refused to write.[35] No longer the lonely and emotionally immature young man that he was in the late 1920s, the literature professor found himself even better positioned to further the moral transformation that aesthetic experiences could deliver to ill-disciplined youths who indulged in frivolous pleasures, deviant sexual behaviors and mass politics.

Zhu's auto-critique disguised another dimension of continuity that traversed the two phases of his career: commercial savviness. Like most *Jingpai* intellectuals, Zhu embraced commercial publishing as a way to reach the urban reading public and maintain independence from the state. Yet high-minded writers were wary that they could be producing cultural commodities, not ideas that had real impact on society.[36] The transition from Kaiming to Central Weekly Press seemed to resolve this tension. Even as Zhu shunned publishing houses that operated under the commodity logic, he was obviously proud of his own mass market appeal. He complained with relish in *On Cultivation* how pirate copies of *Twelve Letters* appeared in Shanghai and Guangzhou. He recalled plagiarizers trying to earn a quick buck by imitating the popular book. A man who went by the dubious *nom de plume* Zhu Guangshan was singled out for mention.[37] In fact, the putative author of *Thirteen Letters to Youth* had caught the celebrity writer's attention back in 1936. Zhu Guangqian published a tongue-in-cheek "letter" to Zhu Guangshan in the Shanghai newspaper *Shenbao*, making the latter an object of ridicule.[38] By turning those

---

[35] Zhu, "Zixu [Prologue]," in *ZQGGJ*, 4:3–4.
[36] Timothy B. Weston, *The Power of Position: Beijing University, Intellectuals, and Chinese Political Culture, 1898–1929* (Berkeley: University of California Press, 2004), 245–7.
[37] Zhu, "Zixu."
[38] Zhu, "Zhu Guangqian gei Zhu Guangshan – wei *Gei qingnian de shisan feng xin*" (Zhu Guangqian to Zhu Guangshan – on *Thirteen Letters to Youths*), in *ZGQQJ*, 8:418–22.

who appropriated his fame on their heads, Zhu Guangqian displayed a shrewd talent for publicity, a skill he brought over from Beiping to Sichuan. *On Cultivation* was published with the Central Weekly Press as part of its book series. Its launch followed that of Tao Baichuan's political treatise *Three People's Principles and Communism* (*Sanmin zhuyi yu gongchan zhuyi*) and a translation of American war correspondent William L. Shirer's *Berlin Diary*. Advertisement for *On Cultivation* was rolled out months before the book was actually published.[39]

The prominence afforded to *On Cultivation* demonstrated that Zhu and the Central Weekly Press agreed that ruminations on life were as significant as ideological doctrines and reportage on war. Indeed, *On Cultivation* received privileged treatment in both marketing and distribution processes. Unlike the other two volumes in the series, Zhu's latest book was strategically pitched to its intended audience. In a clear allusion to *Twelve Letters*, Central Weekly Press ran an advertisement in May 1943 promising that the newest collection from Zhu "was the book that young friends would find most difficult to put down."[40] In addition, while the other publications were available only in one format, *On Cultivation* was launched in two versions with different paper stock, priced at fourteen and twenty-four *yuan* respectively. Less than four months later, the press released yet another version priced at thirty *yuan*. While the least expensive formats was printed on dark yellow and fragile paper, the deluxe edition used soft, pale yellow paper that facilitated easy reading. A new advertisement, which occupied one full page of the magazine *Lessons from the States* (*Guofeng*), urged eager readers to "act soon as copies were limited."[41] Zhu's hallmark facility with print capitalism contrasted with the stiff austerity of typical party propaganda.

Aestheticization of Life

Equally significant, however, was continuity in the contents of Zhu's "universally reputed" (*youkou jiebei*) writings.[42] In particular, Zhu remained invested in his analogy between aesthetic experience and everyday life. He was beholden to a pedagogical approach to young people's behaviors, which in turn grounded the man's supposedly non-existent politics. Aesthetic discourse, as Liu Kang argues, has had direct bearing on intellectuals' quest for national subjectivity since the late Qing. Notions of beauty were central to Liang Qichao's notion of free bourgeois

---

[39] "Tan xiuyang" (On Cultivation) (advertisement), *Guofeng*, no. 4 (Dec. 1942): 7.
[40] "Tan xiuyang" (On Cultivation) (advertisement), *Guofeng*, no. 13 (May 1943): 7.
[41] "Tan xiuyang" (On Cultivation) (advertisement), *Guofeng*, no. 19 (Aug. 1943): n.p.
[42] Ibid.

subject and desires for a new civilization that overcame dehumanizing massification under modern capitalism. They were intertwined with radical politics, giving rise to "a new culture and revolutionary subjectivity."[43] Ban Wang goes a step further by identifying Chinese aesthetic discourse, to which Zhu was a major contributor, as the "place at which politics is often rendered into an aesthetic experience." Intellectual ruminations mediated between state-building projects and the everyday, allowing the latter to operate through "sensation, perception, feeling, image, representation and myth."[44] Wang sees the ultimate expression of this aestheticized politics in the de-individualized, senseless and violent masses that was the Red Guards during the Cultural Revolution (1966–1976).[45] On the surface, Zhu's ideal young reader could not be more different than the shrill banality commonly attributed to youthful masses who dispensed with rationality and fell under the spell of a semi-deified political leader. Yet, both Zhu and Maoist mobilizers appreciated the everyday and the instinctive as the sites on which the populace internalized social relations and authority. Both called upon young people to rein in self-centered emotions and urges. But whereas Chinese youths in the late 1960s were invited to sublimate their desires and libidos into participation in politically- disruptive mass rebellion (albeit engineered by an authoritative figure), Zhu's liberal position placed hope on stoic command over intense personal anguish, distress and desires as key to maintaining the Republican political and social edifice.

Zhu observed youth activism with tremendous unease. His attitude on politics spilling on to the street was similar to other supposedly open-minded Beida academics like Hu Shi and Cai Yuanpei (1868–1940). In the mid-1920s, students, basking in post-May Fourth excitement, transformed Beida into a major site of the GMD–CCP alliance in Beiyang government-controlled North China. Hu Shi and those who craved gradual reforms were skeptical of the united front's radicalism. Oppositional politics involving large crowds troubled Cai Yuanpei, the well-respected Beida president. He struggled to reconcile his celebration of civic consciousness on the one hand and containment of what he considered disruptive politics on the other. After the April 12 *coup*, Cai worked actively with Dai Jitao in de-radicalizing students who might pose a threat to the Nationalist order.[46] Like Dai, mass activism of the

---

[43] Liu Kang, *Aesthetics and Marxism: Chinese Aesthetic Marxists and Their Western Contemporaries* (Durham, N.C.: Duke University Press, 2000), 17–18, 40–4.
[44] Wang, *Sublime Figure of History*, 7.   [45] Ibid., 200–2.
[46] Weston, *Power of Position*, 234; Lanza, *Behind the Gates*, 126–9; Huang, *Politics of Depoliticization*, 48–62; Zarrow, *Anarchism and Chinese Political Culture*, 204–6.

1920s left Hu Shi with longstanding skepticism of youthful immaturity, which he linked with political unreliability. It was because "their emotions were running high, patience wearing too thin, and understanding of facts lacking" that young people became sympathetic to Zhang Xueliang's treasonous designs against the state. Patriotic passion mixed with intellectual naivety led to dangerous politics.[47] Zhu inherited his senior Beida colleagues Cai and Hu's assessment that young people were ill-equipped for autonomous political actions. For him, student protesters were signs of social pathology, not civil society awakening. As educators, Zhu and other liberals were more likely to embrace discipline than celebrate freedom of assembly and of expression when their students were concerned.

Liberals and the GMD state were in agreement that the Chinese were citizens-in-training awaiting instructions from the enlightened. Where they disagreed was how tutelage was to be provided. Liang Shiqiu tasked intellectuals like himself, rather than party ideologues, to disabuse young people from misguided political thoughts like communism through persuasion. Fu Sinian, another liberal who taught at Beida among other institutions, had a high view of military training. The German-trained philologist, echoing Sun Yat-sen in *Independent Critic*, compared the Chinese people to a heap of loose sand, lacking discipline and beliefs shared by the entire nation. Chinese youths lacked the willpower to tame their own impulses, which led them to either romantic relationships or trendy political activism. These developments favored communism rather than nationalism. It rested on military training, on lessons on the GMD canons to impart to the young citizenry common purpose and tight discipline. Like many Nationalists agitating for total war, Fu welcomed the militarization of society for its edifying function. Japan's encroachment into north China provided a chance for citizens to concentrate their minds and fight for a nobler cause. Blurred distinctions between the military and the civilian were for the liberal academic not just contingency measures against foreign invasion but welcome developments turning impressionable youngsters into responsible citizens.[48] Suspicions over youth culture, the idea of a loftier cause that eluded most citizens and association of political unreliability with inadequate personal growth permeated liberal diagnoses of China's problems.

---

[47] Hu, "Zhang Xueliang de pan'guo," 8.

[48] Fu Sinian, "Jiaoyu bengkui de yuanyin [Reasons Why Education Collapsed]," *Duli pinglun*, no. 9 (1932): 2–6; Fu, "Zhongguo ren zuoren de jihui daole! [Here Comes the Chance for the Chinese People to Be Human]," *Duli pinglun*, no. 35 (1933): 6–8; Fu, "Zhongxue junxun ganyan [Ruminations on Military Training in Middle Schools]," *Gongjiao xuexiao* 1, no. 11 (1935): 7–9.

Zhu's critical career amply demonstrated how the intellectual elite acted as the agent of pacification against a restive population who lacked self-discipline and emotional stability. Edifying the masses through aesthetic experience defined Zhu's intervention in politics and the supposedly nonexistent ideological motivations for his collaboration with the Nationalist regime. GMD ideologues prized aesthetics as means to collect emotions, impart ideals and divert energies away from subversive politics. State-sponsored social movements discussed in the previous two chapters afforded ample sights and sounds through which the people expressed themselves in a controlled and, as far as conservative revolutionaries were concerned, constructive fashion. Rallies, parades and travels joined mass media – cinema, radio, newspapers and magazines – in reshaping mass activism into aesthetic experiences detached from autonomous political actions. GMD cadres' belief in the transformative potential of art and literature, as well as the motifs Nationalist publications incorporated, showed noticeable liberal influences.[49] The values Zhu wished to cultivate among the people were different from those of conservative revolutionaries; the liberal scholar was less keen on Confucian traditions and the Three People's Principles, for example. Yet, the idea that aesthetics could perform edifying functions and turn hearts and minds away from consumerism and disruptive politics appealed as much to Nationalists as to liberals. Just as state-supported initiatives like scouting and wartime mass campaigns insulated citizens from conspicuous consumption, Zhu's highly readable, bite-size essays promised the reading masses sober reason and good taste. Shunning pedantic language, *Twelve Letters to Youths* and the original columns that constituted it were conceived with high school students in mind. They presented the European-trained aesthetician as a personable companion who concluded every entry with the endearment "your friend Mengshi." He asked his imaginary reader if his prose was too long-winded, promising not to burden "you" (*ni*) with anything too onerous.[50] Yet affecting amicability did not mean that Zhu ever considered his readers equals. At the very moment he appeared to join the ranks of high school students, Zhu established distance between the accomplished graduate student and the adolescent reader. The "letters" were signed in Zhu's courtesy name (*zi*), an appellation that denoted adulthood and was traditionally used by others to refer to oneself in formal occasions.

If the subtleties of names were lost on the new generation, Zhu's paternalistic attitude toward student activism was barely disguised by

[49] Clinton, *Revolutionary Nativism*, 169–76.
[50] Zhu, "Tan dushu [On Reading]," in *ZGQQJ*, 2:10.

the intimate rhetoric. One entry, "On High School Students and Social Movements" (*Tan zhongxue sheng yu shehui yundong*), accused student activists of corruption, arrogance and hypocrisy, symptoms typically attributed to politicians in the republic. "How many ordinary students," Zhu angrily demanded,

are worthy of any revolutionary chatter? How many representatives to national student conferences squandered donations, gambled, or fiddled with prostitutes? Were there people who championed the sanctity of education only to band up with patrician politicians and disrupt the functioning of schools? How about those who penned vows of gratitude to the Japanese government or received Boxer Indemnity scholarships only then to call for the downfall of imperialism?[51]

The affable friend became a high priest of ethics, urging students to clean up their own moral mess before practicing revolution. While Zhu also criticized Nanjing's total ban on students' involvement in protests, the popular essayist shared the impatience of such GMD-friendly liberals as Cai Yuanpei and Hu Shi with radical youths who took their concern for society out from the classroom onto the street. For Zhu, the problem with social activists was that they harbored grandiose designs but were short on solutions for the common people. For him, concrete community work was always more important than theatrical politics. It was better, for example, to just humbly teach rather than to get organized and push for universal education. Opening a factory in the countryside, for example, was preferable to pushing for national goods. One could make small contributions but would do better to avoid all talk of revolution. His advice to readers? "Go to the people!"[52] Study hard, do good to society and don't disturb the peace.

Notwithstanding the half-hearted populism, Zhu's unease with radicalized students shared the same tenets as Dai Jitao's critique of student and labor politics discussed in Chapter 2. Immature students and workers were irrational, too gullible to see through deceptive rhetorical flourishes to find politicians' self-serving behaviors, and the demands they put forth were impractical and did not address the people's well-being in any case. Zhu's discomfort over mass participation in public affairs reflected *Jingpai* unease over print capitalism. While being a talented operator in China's burgeoning cultural industry, Zhu complained that the market endowed too much power on the populace. Having barely admonished his readers to "go to the people," Zhu bemoaned that philosophy and literature, once chased out of the ivory tower, could only lead to vulgarization (which he glossed as *suhua*). He dismissed British artist William

---

[51] Zhu, "Tan zhongxue sheng yu shehui yundong," in *ZGQQJ*, 1:21.   [52] Ibid., 1:18–21.

Morris and Russian writer Leo Tolstoy's call for the popularization of art as a recipe for turning intellectuals into profane objects of "market idols" (*shichang ouxiang*). He associated the marketization of culture with democracy, which was glossed in the Chinese phonetic transliteration as *demokelaxi*.[53] Zhu's unease over the marketplace was shared by Liang Shiqiu, who saw brisk business but little enlightenment in the publishing industry. Youths were attracted to Communist propaganda because left-wing writers dominated the market. In contrast, the GMD managed only to produce stale materials while scholars who could explain "sound theories" were unwilling to buck the trend. Public discourse became increasingly monopolized by Communist sympathizers as a result. Leaving impressionable young consumers to "absorb Communist propaganda on their own was extremely risky."[54]

Left to its own device, print capitalism banished moderation and good taste. Merchants of gaudy intellectual trends enticed consumers, while the few learned men and women languished in the shadows. Under the influence of demagogic scholars and social activists, Zhu feared, the people were set to become agents of terror. They were whipped by New Culture literary experimentations and Shanghai's Westernized high-street chic. They sleepwalked into following unscrupulous opportunists and formed a tyrannical mob that was bellicose and anti-intellectual. Consumer society was the latest incarnation of a transnational and trans-historical menace. It was an irrational and bloodthirsty mob that cheered on the papal persecution of Galileo Galilei in the seventeenth century and scorned European pacifists during the Great War. Common people, "shallow and obstreperous," coalesced in the marketplace, but modern China's intellectual elite was in no position to reverse their plebeian philistinism. Unlike Britain, China did not have the equivalents of Percy Shelley, Thomas Carlyle or Bertrand Russell who stood as "giants among the throng of dwarfs at the crossroad."[55] Liberal reason was squeezed between state authoritarianism and left-wing/consumerist mob rule.

The lack of towering intellectuals providing sound stewardship had dire consequences for China. The principle of natural selection dictated that an agent distinct from and superior to the normal type, i.e., the

---

[53] Zhu, "Tan shizi jietou [On the Crossroad]," in *ZGQQJ*, 1:22–3. When Zhu spoke of democracy as a political system in more positive terms, he rendered it in the character compound *minzhu* or *minzhi*.

[54] Liang, "Wo wei shenme bu zancheng Gongchandang," 7–9.

[55] Zhu, "Tan shizi jietou," 1:24. The opposition between proverbial crosswords and the ivory tower was frequently evoked in debates on the degree to which artists and art should contribute to the construction of a modern nation (Xiaobing Tang, *Origins of the Chinese Avant-garde: The Modern Woodcut Movement* [Berkeley: University of California Press, 2008], 35).

masses, preside over the struggle for survival. The future looked bleak for China in the current historical conjuncture. For "even in India," Zhu lamented,

a land under the domination of another country, they still have a Tagore and a Gandhi. The only things China has are pseudo-academics and pseudo-social activists. Every time those in authority make a tumult, their lesser compatriots chime in. Conservatives follow traditions blindly; radicals partake of fads blindly. Popular habits continue to degenerate and the venom of shallowness, stupidity and hypocrisy flows across society undeterred.

It was not clear whether Zhu saw his readers as giants or dwarfs. On one hand, Zhu rallied his "friends" to mobilize their youthful valor and "smash the idols."[56] On the other, his readers were precisely the consumers who subjected intellectual elites to the idolatry of the banal and fashionable. Bonnie McDougall identifies Zhu's conflicted attitude toward the masses as his core weakness. His strong desire for social change was incompatible with an elitist disdain for the young generation most inclined to it. This defeatist contradiction undercut the influence his popular works might have otherwise exerted among the educated youth.[57]

Defeatist or not, Zhu was in no doubt that the intellectual community must be protected from the *hoi polloi* if society was to remain sustainable. While Zhu often reserved the harshest comments for his compatriots in China, his fear of mob rule was shaped by firsthand experience of the dystopia that was Europe's consumer society. The Edinburgh-based graduate student, as he recounted in 1926, was horrified by the tawdry, commercialized entertainment of the British urban underclass – men and women indulging in alcohol in public, welfare beneficiaries skipping meals to pay for horrid thrillers and romances on cinema, young factory workers squandering Saturday afternoons filling dancehalls with the foul combination of sweat and cosmetics.[58] The inclusion in a country's political processes of unproductive, uneducated men and women who survived on handouts from the nascent welfare state was a terrifying prospect. He quoted in 1927 with approval Matthew Arnold's attack on the growing philistinism in modern Anglo-American societies, highlighting how the conservative cultural critic provided key insights for understanding the shallow plebeian tendencies in his own

---

[56] Zhu, "Tan shizi jietou," 1:25.
[57] Bonnie S. McDougall, "The View from the Leaning Tower: Zhu Guangqian on Aesthetics and Society in the Nineteen-Twenties and Thirties," in *Modern Chinese Literature and Its Social Context*, ed. Göran Malmqvist (Stockholm: Department of Oriental Studies, Stockholm University, 1975), 111.
[58] Zhu, "Lü Ying zatan [Fragments of My Sojourn in Britain]," in *ZGQQJ*, 8:184–5.

country.[59] Indeed, the author of *Culture and Anarchy* (1869) became an inspiration for a conservative humanist reaction in the 1920s against the iconoclasm, mass protests and increasingly radicalism unleashed by the May Fourth Movement in 1919. Zhu's embrace of culture – taken narrowly to mean humane values untainted by wealth and material obsessions – certainly evoked Arnold.[60] As a self-appointed guardian of culture, Zhu hedged his hope for an alternative social order on its proselytization and ability to transform rowdy protesters and philistine consumers into self-regulating and well-bred citizens. Both Arnold and Zhu, as we see later, would count upon the state to realize their vision of ideal citizenry.

Zhu shared with GMD ideologues the Arnoldian dichotomy that pitched humane values and good taste against unscrupulous protesters preoccupied by base desires. Western conservative cultural criticism reinforced lingering Confucian ideals that opposed masculine aesthetic enterprise to feminine sensuality and excesses. Traditionally, Confucian intellectuals prized gratification from art, poetry and music but shunned emotions and bodily pleasures, which were associated with worldly distractions.[61] Such aspirations to the stoic persisted into the twentieth century as a technology of the self. Aesthetics promoted studied moderation over disruptive passions, whether they meant indulging in sex and alcohol or turning up on the street as angry protesters. Aesthetic edification, thus, concerned the entire cross-section of public and private life. It was much more than reading Zhu's essays or, for that matter, any form of artistic production. Zhu called in his 1932 volume *On Beauty (Tan mei)* for the aestheticization of life (*rensheng de yishuhua*) as a strategy to replace the superficiality and thoughtlessness of ordinary people with the meticulousness of an artist. Seeing one's life as a piece of art was to resist the "mechanization of life" (*shengming de jixie hua*), the dumbing quality Henri Bergson attributed to the modern human.[62] Transferring the rigor of accomplished poets and essayists to how ordinary people went about their daily routine was to redress the mediocrity of industrial civilization in general and the Chinese people in particular.

---

[59] Zhu, "Ouzhou jindai san da piping xuezhe (er) – Anuode (Matthew Arnold) [Three Major Modern European Critical Scholars (II) – Matthew Arnold]," *ZGQQJ*, 8:216–24.

[60] Kuang Xinnian, *Xiandai wenxue yu xiandai xing* [*Modern Literature and Modernity*] (Shanghai: Yuandong chubanshe, 1998), 193; Raymond Williams, "A Hundred Years of Culture and Anarchy," in *Problems in Materialism and Culture: Selected Essays* (London: Verso, 1980), 5.

[61] Wang, *Sublime Figure of History*, 106–7.

[62] Zhu, "'Manman zou, xinshang a!' – rensheng de yishuhua ['Slow down and enjoy!' – The Aestheticization of Life], *ZGQQJ*, 2:92–3. Zhu was alluding to Bergson's *Le Rire: essai sur la signification du comique*, first published in 1900.

Zhu understood social life in strongly idealist, Nietzschean terms. Unlike Chen Quan, Zhu did not think that God was dead as such. But the two men agreed that the modern world had been unencumbered from old orthodoxies, fidelities and certainties. God, as Zhu saw it, created the world as a piece of art for no utilitarian purpose. Rather than residing in a modest Jewish carpenter, God was a spirit that transcended historical, bodily presence. He compelled humans to likewise relinquish attachment to their material existence and considerations, so as to partake in the creation and appreciation of the sublime universe. "Disinterested contemplation" (rendered by Zhu as *wusuowei erwei de wansuo*) allowed the severance of personal realization from the frustrations brought about by material society.[63]

Zhu's argument that aesthetics transcended worldly motives or interests was not one for moral agnosticism. Here he differed from the dictum of pure, amoral art as espoused by his spiritual mentor, Benedetto Croce. The Italian doyen of idealist philosopher, to which Zhu was often compared, conceived art as distinct from the search for virtues or true knowledge. Beauty (*mei*), as Zhu pithily summarized Croce, was not related to truth (*zhen*) and benevolence (*shan*).[64] While Zhu credited Croce for relieving literature of the traditional Confucian mandate to convey the truth (*wenyi zaidao*), he departed from the Italian by endowing art with an ennobling quality in regard to life.[65] Art was not to play a straightforward didactic role like realist works, but it could not stand outside morality. Moreover, whereas Croce consigned beauty neatly to its own independent realm populated by elite artists, Zhu injected into art a pseudo-egalitarian and totalistic quality. "A person's life history is his or her work … A person who masters living is an artist and his or her life a piece of art." He further compared one's lifetime venture to writing or painting, where an "artist's" everyday demeanors and major moral decisions were weaved together with technical adeptness to form one organic body (*youjiti*). Aesthetics infused even the most routine behaviors of every individual and the sublimely religious experience it delivered was available to anyone. The trick was to will a leisurely, playful twist to one's otherwise difficult, suffocating existence in twentieth-century China. Zhu's revelation for his poverty-stricken, war-ridden brethren was derived from a signpost he encountered while touring the Alps – "slow down and enjoy!"[66] If only the Chinese could "distance" themselves from

---

[63] Ibid., 2:94–6.
[64] Zhu, "Ouzhou jindai san da piping xuezhe (san) – Keluoqi (Benedetto Croce) [Three Major Modern European Critical Scholars (III) – Benedetto Croce]," in *ZGQQ*7, 8:235.
[65] McDougall, "View from the Leaning Tower," 107.
[66] Zhu, "'Manman zou, xinshang a!,'" 2:91–7.

"watching crowds of insignificant human beings rushing to catch an underground train or engaged in petty disputes with rascals and gamblers in a public tavern."[67] If only they could differentiate everyday "misfortunes and calamities" and the deliciously tragic. It was as if the country's many problems would be solved if the country's denizens would sublimate the brutalities of actual life into a richer and beautified being.

A theory of art that strode the middle ground between realism and idealism might have opened Zhu to persecution when Communists, who preferred ideological and formal certainties, took power after 1949.[68] But Zhu's derision of writing or even reading literature for "sympathy, justice or any other moral purpose" was formulated in the 1930s, when a very different revolution was taking its course.[69] It would be far more productive to compare Zhu's call for seeing art as a collective, moral pursuit that was ultimately apolitical with GMD theoreticians' formulation on beauty. Zhu saw the edifying functions of aesthetic pursuits free from political and economic concerns as having great social potential beyond individual character-building. Disinterested contemplation was the path to the Highest Good (*zhigao de shan*). In a society filled with calculations and mercenary hypocrites, art purified (*zhenghua*) the populace and relieved them from vulgar animal urges. China's quagmire was not "entirely a result of system or structure, but of putrefied hearts (*renxin taihuai*)."[70] Beauty washed clean perverted hearts and brought them toward the Highest Good. Politics, on the other hand, only targeted social structures. It was, more importantly, hijacked by "pseudo-academics and pseudo-social activists" who fanned the emotions of people who populated the maligned marketplace. Zhu's emphasis on aesthetic experience as ethical cultivation converged with similar ideas in *Vitalism*, the Central Political School textbook penned by Chen Lifu we encountered in the previous chapter. The CC Clique leader identified beauty as the apotheosis of human achievements where conflicts over material interests would be transcended.

Vitalism advocated leadership by the elite over the less well-endowed, both unburdened by self-interest. It presented a three-stage theory – veracity, benevolence and beauty – prognosticating the supersession of human rivalries over political and economic power by a utopia of "beauty" (*mei*). Betraying the inflection of Bergson, Chen Lifu saw life as constituted by anarchic elements (*shengyuan*) pulled against different

---

[67] Zhu, "Why Do We Take Pleasure in Tragedy?" *Guoli Beiping daxue xuebao wenli zhuankan*, no. 4 (1935): 134–5. This article was published in English.
[68] Shih, *Lure of the Modern*, 184–5.
[69] Zhu, "Why Do We Take Pleasure in Tragedy?" 140.
[70] Zhu, "Kaichang bai [Opening Remarks (for *On Beauty*)]," in *ZGQQJ*, 2:6.

directions by both good and evil forces. Through sincere devotion (*chen-gyi*) and purification of hearts and minds (*zhengxin*), humans learned to harness their desires and productive capacities for a glorious and beautiful existence.[71] In practical terms, the path to beauty dictated a period of "benevolence" (*shan*) when the less privileged in society put their material self-interests aside and submitted themselves willingly to the enlightened leadership of the well-endowed. Instead of being manipulated by crafty politicians, weaker citizens turned their backs on debilitating rivalries between political parties of both the liberal and revolutionary variants to contribute to one-party, interclass dictatorships like the GMD. A new form of social organization, i.e., national capitalism, ensured peace, efficiency and improved livelihood for the ignorant masses in lieu of political entitlement. This new order would usher in a realm of beauty whereby the well-being of all social elements was harmonized and valorized.[72] That beauty meant overcoming the fixation on material interests informed Zhu's as well as Chen Lifu's understanding of messy and confrontational mass politics as moral depravation.

Support for State-Led Aestheticization

China was hardly the only society that invested in moral edification as the missing link between idealist theories of aesthetics and political formation. Far from being the twentieth-century perversion of an innocent quest for refinement, aesthetics had been intertwined with state power since the European Enlightenment. In Victorian Britain, the liberal state saw itself as the ethical, as well as political, embodiment of the disparate and fragmented interests represented in the body politic. Culture provided the state the supposedly common and neutral bond of humanity as it confronted antagonistic social demands. In the second half of the nineteenth century, as the ascendant liberal hegemony in Britain was challenged by an emerging working class, figures as diverse as Matthew Arnold, Romantic poet Samuel Coleridge and liberal philosopher John Stuart Mill believed that the educational state apparatus needed to induct raucous and politicized citizens into the "common sense" and ethical judgments of a liberal capitalist society. The apparently universal and neutral experiences of aesthetics were counted upon to mold popular will so that it would serve the bourgeoisie and dissuade class-oriented analyses.[73]

---

[71] Chen, *Weisheng lun (shangjuan)*, 132–3.   [72] Ibid., 70–3.
[73] David Lloyd and Paul Thomas, *Culture and the State* (London: Routledge, 1998), 115–27, 145–7.

In Nationalist China, the convergence of state and humanist pursuits was at the core of the new regime's cultural policy. Since the earliest days of Chiang Kai-shek's regime, longtime aesthetic education advocate Cai Yuanpei and distinguished painter Lin Fengmian (1900–91) headed state agencies, led new art academies and promoted their agendas in government newspapers and state-sponsored exhibitions. For liberal humanists in the government, a new paradigm in art education and expression that emphasized social amelioration was to replace radical tendencies within the larger New Culture Movement that threatened to derail the fragile Nationalist order. However, before social edification could run its course, a reformist aesthetic vision had to wield the repressive state apparatus to suppress student dissenters, bring protesters off the streets and expel Communist sympathizers.[74] Zhu's participation in the wartime state in the 1940s followed on the heels of illustrious liberals who came to see the Nationalist state as the only hope, if an incredibly flawed one, for a social and cultural peace safeguarded from class struggle and mob rule.

From the GMD's perspective, securing the cooperation of a high-profile nonpartisan writer like Zhu was a way to show that the wartime state, even as it demanded unconditional loyalty from citizens, was an inclusive body that nurtured creative and academic freedom. Practicing censorship against left-wing writers and appealing to liberals were for the Chongqing-based regime complementary agendas.[75] Here again, China was not alone. The Fascist state in Italy adopted a dual strategy of discipline and patronage through the 1930s. Instead of asking authors to produce overtly propagandist works, the state took pains to support a variety of creative forms and to incorporate the latest debates on the relationship between art and social life. It worked to co-opt rather than suppress authors and critics who were not card-carrying supporters of the regime. The Fascist investment in art of a transformative function on popular behaviors was put in sync with intellectuals' collective desire to give voice to a new cultural order that replaced reactionary tendencies like individualism, middle-class banality and excessive foreign influences. A more subtle system of co-option, particularly compared to Stalinist Russia's heavy-handed approach, allowed Italian artists and critics who worked under Fascist patronage to claim fidelity to Croce's still influential dictum of artistic autonomy.[76]

---

[74] Tang, *Origins of the Chinese Avant-garde*, 30–40.

[75] "Zhongyang tushu zazhi shencha weiyuan hui sanshisan nian di er ji gongzuo jindu jiantao baogao biao [Central Commission for the Censorship of Books and Periodicals Progress Report for the Second Quarter of 1944]," Executive Yuan Collection, 2/6059, Second Historical Archives.

[76] Ruth Ben-Ghiat, *Fascist Modernities: Italy, 1922–1945* (Berkeley: University of California Press, 2001), 49–50.

A similar dynamic existed between Zhu and the Nationalist state. Aside from the offer of senior academic appointments, Nationalist leaders lured the aesthetician to continue his writing career with state-funded publications. Zhu was one of five scholars recruited in June 1941 to launch an academic journal exploring topics related to the Three People's Principles with funding from Chiang Kai-shek. Among the other editors of *Thoughts and Epochs* (*Sixiang yu shidai*) were philosopher He Lin (1902–92), who in turn was associated with the Warring States Group and supported hero worship. *Thoughts and Epochs* inspired mixed feelings among some non-partisan intellectuals who admired its high quality but dreaded the state's involvement in intellectual production.[77] A few months later, Zhu began writing for *Central Weekly* as a politically independent academic. His first article, "On Making Resolutions" (*Tan lizhi*), which appeared on New Year's Day in 1942, mimicked the form and substance of the "letters" that propelled the young writer to celebrity status in the late 1920s.

Zhu's subsequent installments in the party-state publication revisited themes that readers of *Twelve Letters to Youth* would find familiar. They discussed issues that occupied the everyday life of educated youths through generations, i.e., romantic love, sports, learning and reading, job hunting, searching for self-worth in society. The intertextual ties Zhu forged between his two personae lent credence to the critic's political impartiality, even as he was heaping praise on the "sagacious leader" Chiang Kai-shek and hailed the GMD's "nation-building through the war of resistance" program.[78] Zhu was aware that he was walking a tightrope between convincing state officials of his ideological reliability and sacrificing his reputation as a nonpartisan public intellectual. The preface to *On Cultivation* denied that the author's collaboration with *Central Weekly* had any political implications. The columns were "casual and idle talk" (*suibian xiantan*) that contained no systematic thought or agenda. They were the works of the same man who remained steadfast to such treasured sentiments as cool-headedness, sobriety, determination and approaching social affairs with a spirit of detachment.[79] In other words, Zhu's partnership with the GMD was the natural evolution of a stellar literary career.

[77] Huang, "Jiang Jieshi yu He Lin," 18; Sang Bing, "Kangzhan shiqi Guomindang cehua de xueren banbao [Scholar-Edited Periodicals as Initiated by the Guomindang during the Resistance War]," in *Wenren lunzheng*, 223–30.
[78] Zhu, "Yifan yuzhong xinchang de hua – gei xiandai Zhongguo qingnian [A Sincere Message for Contemporary Chinese Youths]," in *ZGQQJ*, 4:11.
[79] Zhu, "Zixu," 4:4–5.

To drive home his autonomy and nonpartisanship, Zhu was not afraid to occasionally criticize the wartime state in his *Central Weekly* articles. Potentially subversive views on the shape of the embattled republic were smuggled in through his continual intervention in the spiritual malaise that afflicted China's public culture. Like Lin Tongji, Zhu had little patience for official corruption. Civil servants, he asserted, behaved like local tyrants and evil gentry (*tuhao lieshen*) from a bygone autocratic era. They denied the public a role in local governance, impeding the evolution of Chinese people into mature contributors to communal life (*qunchu*). While accusing state bureaucrats of stifling popular deliberations, Zhu touted *baojia* as an ideal form of local government, despite the rural institution's notorious role in monitoring political expression and policing against dissent. He went as far as to compare the democratic potential of *baojia* to local councils in Britain.[80] The writer also made sure to embed his otherwise blunt critique of GMD authoritarianism in a wider discussion on the lack of civic-mindedness among the populace. A bad government, he suggested, was part of a social pathology that testified to China's difficult transition to modernity.[81] Thus, the object of Zhu's critique switched abruptly from repressive political arrangements to the spiritual crisis that tormented his compatriots. Specifically, Zhu identified at the crux of China's non-functioning polity a psychological perversion – a malaise attributed to students grappling with both the dislocation of war and conflicts on one hand, and deformed capitalist ethos and lingering feudal social structures on the other. Fathers seeing their children's university education as no more than an investment for handsome returns, chronic bureaucratic corruption and a dysfunctional schooling process compounded the inhospitable material circumstances under which refugees from the richer, more urbanized coastal regions found themselves in the hinterland. The results were such deleterious responses as apathy, despair, *ennui* and seeking comfort in careerist and materialist pursuits.[82] A cynical young generation indifferent to the world beyond its own narrow interests hardly boded well for a nation that counted on a voluntaristic citizenry for resistance and rebuilding efforts.

Zhu carried forward his formulation on aestheticization as urgently needed ethical training for the masses to his reading of the war against Japan. While he did not state explicitly that all Chinese were part of the

---

[80] Zhu, "Tan chuqun (xia) – chuqun de xunlian," in 4:58–61. For the *baojia* network as an anti-Communist measure, see "Zhongguo Guomindang zhongzhihui mishuchu miding 'Fangzhi yidang huodong banfa' dian," 23.

[81] Zhu, "Tan qingnian de xinli biantai [On the Psychological Perversion of Youths]," in *ZGQQJ*, 4:28.

[82] Ibid., 4:29–32.

resistance effort, victory over Japan was all but assumed to fall on the nation's collective willpower. It depended on all individuals to stoically sublimate their own misfortunes into concern for the greater good. Just as one must set aside sympathy for petty disasters to appreciate the other-worldliness of tragedy, the struggle against a powerful foreign enemy called upon the people to embrace a moral purpose much larger than insignificant individual selves. Echoing Chen Quan's use of biblical metaphors to illustrate collective human willpower, Zhu compared the Chinese people's struggle against Japan to Jesus' valiant rejection of Satan's temptations in the Judean desert. While Jesus was tempted to embrace worldly power and renounce his divinity, each and every Chinese individual was faced with the stark choice between painful resistance and making peace with the enemy for the sake of personal comfort. Infamous figures like Wang Jingwei who "sold the country off and turned their back on the party" (maiguo pandang) had no grand schemes. They simply traded in their will (yizhi li) for the easy path and became the devil's disciples.[83]

The critical importance Zhu attached to the human will meant that the common people must fend for themselves. Individuals must examine, reform and fortify their psychological and physical makeup, with guidance from the imperfect state if necessary. "Our life history was constantly a history of struggle between truth (li) and desire (yu), God and Satan."[84] Zhu wanted young Chinese to brave "the force of greatest resistance" and emulate the great Roman Empire in its toughness, severe discipline and adventurism.[85] Thus, even as Zhu saw the toll China's social crisis was taking on his students, going as far as blaming state repression of free speech and creative freedom as a factor contributing to a sense of hopelessness prevalent on university campuses, he laid the responsibility for redressing this predicament squarely on youths themselves.[86] Zhu called on young people to provide their own cure and salvation by changing the ways they thought, rather than being obsessed with the difficulties social hierarchies presented them. Solving psychological perversion, after all, required retuning the mind. Courage, a sense of responsibility and acceptance of difficult circumstances must substitute despair, purposelessness and passion-driven desires. Reiterating his suspicion of political activism in his earlier writings, Zhu deemed it more important for individual citizens to examine their own selves than to challenge sociopolitical arrangements. To rein in volatile

---

[83] Zhu, "Chao dikangli zuida de lujing zou [Follow the Path of Greatest Resistance]," in ZGQQJ, 4:22–3.
[84] Ibid.   [85] Ibid., 4:19–26.   [86] Zhu, "Tan qingnian de xinli biantai," 4:32–3.

and nihilistic thoughts, Zhu recommended the autosuggestion method popularized by French psychotherapist Emile Coué whereby young people would constantly occupy their minds with the idea that the situation was improving until they genuinely believed circumstances were getting better.[87] Nationalist China's structural problems that weighed down the ambitions of young people were therefore the greatest resistance that Zhu's readers had to overcome in their willed imagination before they could assume full subjectivity as modern social subjects.

Zhu's concern for the nation's spiritual prowess encompassed body and mind. The French psychotherapeutic techniques he identified as key to relieving the pathology of despair and apathy were equally effective in transforming unhealthy bodies. As physical and spiritual health were interrelated, sports complemented aesthetic pleasures in managing a discontented population. Zhu's prescription dovetailed with the GMD state's efforts in rationalizing daily routines – hygiene, leisure, entrenched customs, interpersonal interactions – that were integral to the National Spiritual Mobilization Movement. His diagnosis began with the uncontroversial observation that inadequate food and disregard for sports rendered adolescents into a pallid and emaciated lot, stunting growth and contributing to psychological agonies.[88] The social anomalies plaguing Chinese youths were the same as those that Zhu had recognized as pervading the working class in Edinburgh seventeen years before: consumerist indulgences and sexual licentiousness. Young men and women avidly consumed erotic romances and racy movies, took part in debaucheries like prostitution and succumbed to sexual urges by indulging in masturbation and homosexuality.[89] Even romantic love among university students was condemned as hedonism unworthy of a nation at war. The unleashing of libidinal desires through deleterious channels dealt a further blow to the collective social body. They filled the space vacated by productive employment and healthy recreational activities like art and sports that should have fully preoccupied (*longduan*) young people's creative energy.[90] Physical education not only helped maintain strong bodies but also instilled such values as "fair play" and "sportsmanship," as Zhu glossed in English, to counter dysfunctional social relationships among China's educated youth.[91] These British liberal ideals,

---

[87] Ibid., 4:33.   [88] Ibid., 4:29.
[89] Zhu, "Gei *Shenbao zhoukan* de qingnian duzhe (si) – youxi yu yule [For Young Readers of the *Shenbao Weekly* IV – On Games and Leisure]," in *ZGQQJ*, 8:452; Zhu, "Tan qingnian yu lian'ai jiehun [On Youths, Romance and Marriage]," in *ZGQQJ*, 4:115.
[90] Zhu, "Tan qingnian yu lian'ai jiehun," 4:115–16.
[91] Zhu, "Tan tiyu [On Sports]," in *ZGQQJ*, 4:134.

which also influenced GMD initiatives like scouting, were hailed as mitigating forces on antisocial behaviors.

Aside from sports, the literature professor prescribed aesthetic enjoyment as a way to turn the war-weary, overworked masses into a stoic, fit and devoted force loyal to the nation. Here, he gave a few suggestions of how aesthetic experience could be socially edifying and guide attention away from politics. Citing Sigmund Freud, Zhu asserted that modernity repressed human impulses and created complexes waiting to implode. Rather than interrogating the social relations that created psychoses, however, individuals would have to learn to catharsize or liberate (*jiefang*) frustrated desires through aesthetics, a realm free of violence, injustices and gaudy entertainments.[92] Enjoying the outdoors on a Sunday, common in Euro-American societies, helped one recuperate after a suffocating work routine. Zhu recounted staying with a rural family in France.

> The family head was an ordinary worker and earned just enough to make ends meet. He was careful with all expenses but when it came to holiday, he always spent the savings he earned with his hard work through the week on recreation. He was poor but life was comfortable. At night, his wife played the piano while the children sang along. They played games together; he might tell a story or a few jokes. The four or five of them led a convivial and happy life.[93]

The regulated rhythm of rural laborers was a far cry from the unhealthy, excitement-seeking urban lifestyle of the Edinburgh working class he had previously described. Without a healthy leisure culture, the Chinese endured prolonged backbreaking labor at the expense of the nation's long-term vitality.

A work–leisure routine added variety to the monotony of factory production and soothed workers' discontents. Playing music, enjoying the green pastures or reading fine literary works were not so much tickets to otherworldly grandeur as building blocks of a petty bourgeois lifestyle that China should import from industrialized Europe. Writing something like Johann Wolfgang von Goethe's loosely autographical *The Sorrows of Young Werther* (*Die Leiden des jungen Werthers*, 1774), a popular novel among young readers since the New Culture Movement, would make great therapeutic placebo against the emotional agonies created by wartime China's dystopian political modernity.[94] Leisure and art were easily available intervals of pleasure to keep workers contented, refuel expended labor power and, of course, diffuse discontents over real society and its

---

[92] Zhu, "Tan meigan jiaoyu [On Aesthetic Education]," in *ZGQQJ*, 4:147–8.
[93] Zhu, "Gei *henbao zhoukan* de qingnian duzhe (si)," 8:450.
[94] Zhu, "Tan meigan jiaoyu," 4:148.

injustices. Proper "liberation" of human impulses, far from softening the edges of an oppressive political order, served to further subsume individuals under the GMD-led spiritual mobilization project.

The laboring and self-contained nuclear family Zhu attributed to interwar France was a lifestyle with little potential in war-ridden China, where thousands of people were displaced, impoverished, orphaned or even killed. Self-administered psychotherapy alone was hardly enough to tame individual frustrations that threatened political stability. Eventually, it was up to the state to cultivate strong bodies and build salubrious families. Zhu endorsed the GMD's interest in eugenics as a strategy to revamp the strength of a population fighting a total war. Ideally, citizens would avoid marrying when they were too young, choose sturdy men or women over pretty faces when they were ready to get married and refrain from having too many children. But citizens' volition was not enough; the state should not hesitate to intervene if the people failed to oblige.[95] For unlike the contented family man from the French province, the Chinese people were more akin to the Edinburgh working class. Romantic writers fetishized free love and thought nothing else was more important. Leftists wanted to impose Soviet Communism and "saw love and marriage as a private matter totally separated from society and state, affording them absolute freedom and no discipline." While Zhu was certainly not suggesting that his compatriots should see sex as a taboo, maintenance of society demanded that it be grounded in heterosexual relationship that led to marriage and reproduction.[96] The state might be wrong to suppress the voice of deserving intellectuals, but it was right to highhandedly bring the benefits of family life to bear when selfish or misguided citizens failed to maintain social cohesion on their own initiative.

Desiring a Dictator

Disturbingly, but perhaps unsurprisingly, Zhu counted not only on the coercive state apparatus to maintain society's moral-cultural foundation. The GMD's political myth-making enterprise also appealed to him, who argued that a cult of personality might provide just the right ingredients

---

[95] Zhu, "Tan tiyu," 4:133.
[96] Zhu, "Tan xing'ai wenti [On Sex and Love]," in *ZGQQJ*, 4:111–12. The idea that the state should play an activist role in modern family planning gained popularity among New Culture intellectuals in the 1920s and became a core agenda of the Nationalist state with the enactment of the 1931 New Family Law. It is hard not to think that Zhu's criticism of romanticists and communists was intended simply to highlight the virtues of the regime for which he was working (Glosser, *Chinese Visions of Family and State*, 78–133).

for national cohesion. Despite its association with the formidable political dictatorships of Hitler and Stalin, personality cult should occupy a prominent place in democratic China. "The essence of politics," the new GMD recruit claimed in October 1942,

lies in fine organization, the building and maintenance of which necessarily rest on a leader. A political organization of which the leader can call the shots and convince others must be an enlightened one. There is no doubt that totalitarian countries need dictators (*ducai zhe*). Democratic countries, too, need dictators, no matter what name or title you want to call them.[97]

If the Hebrews needed their biblical heroes and modern educators worshiped Confucius and Plato, there is no reason why a political community should not pay homage to a dictator on whom order could rely. After all, religion, education and politics were all integral to culture (*wenhua*). Revisiting his earlier formulation on the entwinement of beauty and moral perfection, Zhu argued that pious devotion to a heroic leader was a quintessentially aesthetic gesture that lent "a sense of the sublime experience" (which he glossed for *chonggao xiongwei zhi gan*) to social life. Despite the inherent danger of superstition and emotionality, hero worship was commendable for it inspired awe, put individuals in communion with the social whole and lifted humans above their mundane existence. It helped overcome cynicism, selfishness and materialism in an individual.[98]

Zhu's apolitical impulse came full circle, but with one important twist. If the writer's aim before the war was to keep dirty politics out of art, the wartime *Central Weekly* contributor treated politics like sanctified art. The hero, in all his religious and superhumanly elements, was set apart in a near-divine position from the political party and class interests he represented. The dictator evoked the imagery (*yixiang*) of aesthetic perfection, affirming in flesh and blood the highest moral good.[99] He tamed the spiritually inadequate masses, beautified them and gave them a larger purpose. Zhu's lyrical paean to hero worship as sublimation of mass will evoked Chen Quan's argument that hero had liberatory potential. "Hero worship," Chen declared, "derived from sincere admiration without considerations of [one's own] advantages and costs. Slavish obedience derived from the lust for benefits and fear of punishment." Just as Zhu celebrated the sublime (*xiongwei*) as a grand masculine presence, Chen

---

[97] Zhu, "Tan yingxiong chongbai [On Hero Worship]," in *ZGQQ7*, 4:98–9.
[98] Ibid., 4:98.
[99] Ibid., 4:99. The charismatic leader's ability to dominate and recreate the people like an artist approached his work was a core theme in Italian Fascist theorization of state power (Simonetta Falasca-Zamponi, *Fascist Spectacle: The Aesthetics of Power in Mussolini's Italy* [Berkeley: University of California Press, 1997], 21–6).

suggested that heroes were mostly "strong and beautiful" (*zhuangmei*) instead of "quiet and beautiful" (*youmei*). Adoration of great, muscular beauty was a desire for transcendence: "We must forget our own self when we appreciate beauty. We must also forget our own self when we worship an hero. Otherwise, one's hero worship was impure and tainted by ulterior motives."[100] Just as in tragedy, a hero was the object of disinterested contemplation. The difference between *Hamlet* or the Theban plays and 1940s China is, of course, that the people were not mere onlookers but participants in the unfolding epic that took priority over their petty anguish, aspirations and demise. Both Chen and Zhu, it bears noting, stopped short of identifying Chiang Kai-shek as the people's hero. Yet, if the Leader was considered not up to the job, it was more the person who occupied the elevated position than Nationalist political culture that was in question.

About the liberalism of Zhu's intellectual hero Matthew Arnold, Raymond Williams had the following to say: "Excellence and human values on the one hand; discipline and where necessary repression on the other."[101] Just as Arnold maligned protestors congregating in London's Hyde Park as enemies of culture in 1866, Zhu remained hostile toward street politics through the late 1940s. At the conclusion of the resistance, Zhu returned to Beiping and resumed his teaching position at Beida. One of his students remembered the connoisseur of Western literature as a secluded scholar devoted to teaching, uninterested in political gatherings organized by US ambassador John Leighton Stuart (1876–1962) for liberal intellectuals. Yet the professor and his progressive students remained on opposite sides of the widening political divide.[102] Zhu railed against university students, workers and even cabaret dancers who took direct action against rocketing inflation, official corruption and the civil war between the GMD and the CCP in major cities. A frenzied mob, he wrote in a 1948 article tellingly titled "On the Spread of Cowardice and Cruelty among the Masses," was stirred up by delinquents who harbored ulterior motives under lofty principles like liberty, democracy and human rights. Unruly and excitable protesters in Beiping and Shanghai were compared to the bloodthirsty crowd who condemned great men like Socrates and Jesus to death or the Hindu fundamentalist who killed Mahatma Gandhi (1869–1948) in India.[103] Liberty and freedom were

---

[100] Chen, "Lun yingxiong chongbai," 6.
[101] Williams, "Hundred Years of Culture and Anarchy," 8.
[102] Luo Yijun, "Yi Zhu Guangqian xiansheng [Reminisces on Zhu Guangqian]," in *Qingchun de Beida: "Jingshen de meili" xubian*, ed. Zhao Weimin (Beijing: Beijing daxue chubanshe, 1998), 197–8.
[103] Zhu, "Tan qunzhong peiyang qienuo yu xiongcan," 9:354.

desirable as long as they remained in the hands of the cultured and the rowdy masses were kept at bay.

For reasons that remain obscure, Zhu chose not to accept the GMD's invitation to leave Beiping when the Communists took over the city in early 1949. Taking into account his vicissitudes dealing with the troubled Nationalists, it might well be that Zhu, like many liberal politicians by the end of 1948, had lost faith in Chiang's ability to restore peace and bring forth a stable, inclusive polity. It might also be because, as Zhu confided in literary scholar William Tay in the 1980s, that, like Zhou Zuoren in 1938, he did not want to leave Beiping and his family behind for a life of exile.[104] In the 1950s and through the 1960s, the idealist thinker came under attack by Communist intellectuals for his aesthetic theory and was made to repudiate Croce. Adopting a Marxian framework, Zhu modified but continued his search for an autonomous aesthetic subjectivity against the mechanical concept of beauty as an objective given. The persistent fixation on valor, muscular severity and the sublime in Zhu's aesthetic formulation arguably informed the excesses of Communist mass mobilization.[105]

Whatever influence he exerted on Maoist China and beyond, it was obvious that Zhu represented the converging cultural logic of elitist liberalism and the conservative revolution in the Republican period. The liberal wing of the New Culture elite took the cultural transformation of the Chinese people to heart, seeing it as the only way to bring fundamental changes to the nation. They hailed the creative will of individuals and shunned political orthodoxy, Nationalist or otherwise. Yet their fear of being overwhelmed by the masses trumped their desire to remain aloof of China's poisoned political scene. Much like conservative revolutionaries, liberal educators like Zhu Guangqian, Liang Shiqiu and Fu Sinian saw their role vis-à-vis the masses in pedagogical terms. The free-wheeling marketplace was open to manipulation by peddlers of unseemly entertainment and dangerous political ideas, for which young, ignorant consumers and activists invariably fell. Confronted with vulgar consumerism, permissive sexuality and destabilizing street protests, nonpartisan intellectuals desired a solid ethical order to sustain the autonomy and creative freedom of the elite aesthetic subject. That Chinese liberalism never found expression in an independent political bloc made intellectuals open to work with the lesser evil that was the

---

[104] Lutze, *China's Inevitable Revolution*, 8–12; Zheng Shusen [William Tay], *Jieyuan liangdi: Tai-Gang wentan suoyi* [*Attached to Two Lands: Reminiscences on the Literary Circles of Taiwan and Hong Kong*] (Taipei: Hongfan shudian, 2013), 135.

[105] Zhu, "Zuozhe zizhuan," 1:7; Liu, *Aesthetics and Marxism*, 122–33; Wang, *Sublime Figure of History*, 118, 157–9.

GMD. The only buffer between individual sanctity and mob tyranny was the Nationalist establishment, whose own relationship with the masses was equally strained. Liberal intellectuals differed substantially from conservative revolutionaries on the GMD's domination of state affairs and intolerance toward political dissent. Yet they were united in such tasks as redressing hedonism among urban-based young generation, arresting decline in society's moral standards and boosting the national body's virility.

Aesthetic creation in Zhu was simultaneously triumph of human will over material, social constraints and a tool for constraining mass revolt. Its practice and ideological impulses corresponded with those of state-sponsored scouting, itself a mixture of liberal and right-wing Nationalist concerns. It proffered liberation not by heeding popular demands but by asking individuals to diffuse their own discontent. Zhu's was a seemingly apolitical solution to the political and economic dilemmas of uneven capitalist development in China. To be sure, Zhu and other liberals were interested in building representative institutions and a public sphere through which citizens expressed views in an orderly and rational fashion. Yet the liberal elite and GMD vanguard shared the view that the nation's progress hinged not on spontaneous social activism, let alone revolutionary socialism, or even politics as such. For Zhu Guangqian and Fu Sinian as much as for Dai Jitao and Chen Lifu, the nation's revival rested on popular everyday norms and behaviors being transformed according to the highest aesthetic standards. Whether these ideals were couched in the *minsheng* principle or in British middle-class morality was not important.

The other ideal Chinese liberals and conservative revolutionaries could readily agree on was nationalism. As military conflicts with Japan escalated, nationalism became a common aspiration among Chinese politicians and intellectuals across the ideological spectrum. Yet liberal support for the Nationalist government went beyond shoring up national unity and toning down criticism against state excesses. The nationalism Hu Shi and Liang Shiqiu espoused during the war was openly partisan: accusing the CCP of undermining resistance against Japan or lacking nationalist commitments. Fu Sinian was almost excited that preparations for confrontation with Japan allowed lackadaisical Chinese youths to acquire military valor and discipline. Like proponents of total war, Fu deemed the transformation of atomized consumers and rebellious activists into nationalist warriors on the home front a salutary development. Zhu did not write much on war per se, but he argued that wartime aesthetic uplift had to be channeled through, among other things, the political establishment as personified by the Leader. The charismatic Leader ennobled and gave coherence to the people's feelings and sentiments, elevating them to a higher form of life whereby the banalities of consumerism, the craftiness of political agitators and the general baseness of the Chinese masses would be purged. As the custodian of this utopian order, the state linked aesthetic sublimation with moral perfection. Zhu's liberal claim on an individual's full creative autonomy over his or her own life was also laid for the state's stewardship of national well-being. A pastoral, nonpartisan image attributed to the GMD, in contradistinction to its manipulative, unscrupulous opponents, was the highest compliment liberals gave to the conservative revolution.

6 World Revolution
China, Pan-Asianism and India

In December 1940, Chiang Kai-shek received an encouraging letter from the frail Rabindranath Tagore (1861–1941). In the letter, the renowned Bengali poet reflected enthusiastically on Dai Jitao's recent visit to India. "I believe," Tagore declared, "that China has a special mission to fulfill in our Age." Long disillusioned with modern civilization as exemplified by Euro-America, Tagore touted Nationalist China for providing a potentially better alternative. The distinguished aesthete, both celebrated and pilloried for his skepticism of industrialization, told Chiang that:

> Your country can show us in different fields of national planning in industrial development, in agricultural progress and in the new building-up of civic existence in your great land how we can escape the danger of fatal cleavage between science and humanity that has proved the doom of the Western as well as the Eastern nations of our day.[1]

Tagore's laudatory assessment of the wartime Nationalist regime was most striking given how the author of *The Home and the World* (1916) was known for his humanist disdain for political mobilization, even one that involved such discipline and concessionary tendencies as Mohandas K. Gandhi's (1869–1948) *swadeshi* movement that advocated the boycott of British goods. Tagore, and key figures in the Indian National Congress (of whom the literary giant was sympathetic but not uncritically supportive), seemed oblivious to how violence was an integral part of GMD's ongoing mobilization of society, or that the party-state had always committed itself to building a modern industrial economy, even as factions differed vigorously on its composition.[2] On appearance, there was little in common between the Nationalist regime's anti-liberal conservative revolution and a political movement that, according to an

---

[1] Rabindranath Tagore to Chiang Kai-shek, December 10, 1940, Chiang Kai-shek Collection, 002000001294A, Academia Historica.
[2] See Zanasi, *Saving the Nation* for different priorities in economic development between the rival Chiang Kai-shek and Wang Jingwei camps.

authoritative account, was resolutely committed to nonviolence, parliamentary democracy and egalitarian social reforms.[3]

Affection for the GMD among followers of Indian leaders like Mohandas Gandhi and Jawaharlal Nehru (1889–1964) was as counterintuitive as Chinese liberal writers rallying behind the fiercely right-wing party. Yet the two nationalist parties were indeed allies, if half-hearted ones, during the Second Sino–Japanese War. China's courtship with the Indian National Congress, while no doubt part of wartime great power diplomacy, stemmed from the GMD's determination to leverage the nation in offsetting the economic, political and cultural problems attendant to the liberal capitalist order. Domestically, the national revolution was an exercise in interclass solidarity and moral cultivation, with a view to securing China's political independence and economic development. Internationally, the conservative revolution called for a common front with like-minded polities and movements abroad, appealing to an anti-Western fraternity between nationalist elites. Friendship with India, a society far from China's most obvious partner, stemmed from Pan-Asianism – an ideology that gained traction under the conservative revolution as an alternative form of anticolonial politics to Soviet internationalism.

This chapter reconstructs the international dimension of the conservative revolution, showing that the GMD's Pan-Asianist ideology appealed to Indian nationalists but failed to provide stable common ground to sustain an alliance. The convergence of senior GMD cadres and Indian nationalists within and without the Congress, like that between liberals and conservative revolutionaries within China, was fleeting but served to highlight features that informed Nationalist appeal for noncommunist reformers and activists despite its vanguardist, top-down approach to managing society. Aside from its nationalism and anticolonialism, other elements in the GMD's post-purge program resonated with intellectuals and activists abroad. The GMD's rejection of Soviet internationalism struck a chord with the Indian National Congress, which was suspicious of Indian Communists and the Comintern's intervention in India's nationalist movement. Chinese Nationalists' aversion to class war would have provoked little controversy among Congress activists. The primacy Chinese conservative revolutions afforded to moral rejuvenation and gentrifying mass behaviors was not, at least on the surface, incompatible with Gandhism. In fact, the GMD's identification of

<hr>

[3] Bipan Chandra, "The Indian National Movement: The Ideological Dimension," in Chandra et al., *India's Struggle for Independence* (New Delhi: Penguin Books, 1989), 518–28.

spiritual fecundity as key to a nation's vitality spoke to Gandhi's and Tagore's frustration with modernity. Western "materialism," perhaps even more than imperialism, was what Asia nationalisms – whether informed by the *minsheng* principle or by Gandhi's *swadeshi* ideal – had to overcome. Capitalist colonizers and Soviet Russia were, in this sense, part of the same industrial civilization. Like the conservative revolution as a whole, Nationalist Pan-Asianism looked forward to a futural domestic and global order whereby national spirit negated the adversarial relationships between individuals, classes and races.

The GMD's outreach to India, like scouting, tapped into civil society contributions, mobilizing figures whose agenda converged with rather than conformed to that of the conservative revolution. Interactions between the leading nationalist party in China and its Indian counterpart began as late as the 1920s, as Dai Jitao sought to rid the GMD of Soviet and communist influences. Throughout the 1930s and 1940s, Dai and educator-cum-government minister Zhu Jiahua (1893–1963) continued to promote collaboration between the Nationalist state and the Indian nationalist movement, culminating in Chiang Kai-shek's 1942 visit to the South Asian subcontinent. Senior Nationalist cadres capitalized on the institutional and cultural ties between the two societies, particularly those forged by India-based Buddhist scholar Tan Yunshan (1898–1983), who was on the faculty of Tagore's academy, Visva-Bharati. Tagore tasked Tan with creating an institute for sinological studies on his rural Bengal campus. The enterprise, named Cheena Bhavana, appealed to civilizational affinity, idealist commitment to world peace and romantic pleas for Pan-Asianist solidarity. By supporting and funding Cheena Bhavana, the GMD earned the goodwill of Tagore, whose literary output was internationally acclaimed. More importantly, the GMD was able to associate its anticommunist Pan-Asianism with the Nobel laureate's utopian and fiercely nonpartisan vision that Asian peoples' comraderies could overcome the mistrust, social dislocations and expansionist violence inherent to the Western industrial order.

Since the turn of the twentieth century, calls for concerted Asian action against European colonialism were tied to or in contention with Japan's empire-building project. For many Chinese and Indian activists, Japan was both an inspiration for and impediment to nationalist aspirations and solidarity among Asians. The GMD's partnership with the Congress partook in Pan-Asianist discourses that also lent theoretical credence to Japanese imperialism. Indeed, before becoming disillusioned with Japan's expansionist behaviors leading up to the Mukden and particularly the Marco Polo Bridge Incidents, many activists in China and India saw Japan as a more worthy ally in a common anticolonial enterprise.[4] Belief in an authentic, spiritual Asia's potential to overcome the dehumanizing effects of capitalism, Soviet communism and the machine age – all imposed by the West – informed not only GMD functionaries, Tan and Tagore but also right-wing Japanese intellectuals. Romantic and utopian, the desire for a revived Asia echoed Japanese philosophers' justification for their country's "war against all wars." Confrontations with Anglo-American power, these Japanese thinkers argued, would put an end to Western hegemony, allow the East to reclaim its spiritual essence and solve all malaises attendant to modernity.[5] As Japan and China became locked in military conflicts, the dream of a common Eastern resistance against imperialism gave rise to two rival Pan-Asianist projects, each wrestling for India's loyalty. Sharing many of its nemesis's ideological assumptions, the GMD's claim to leadership of a Pan-Asianist alliance against Japan demonstrated that China's conservative revolution harbored global ambitions. It added substance to what Chen Lifu in *Vitalism* and numerous contributors to magazines run by GMD factions argued: that the interwar global system, which privileged competition, liberal individualism and established Western powers, was untenable and demanded an alternative. Alliance between nationalist movements on the receiving end of this house of cards would create a better future. The irony is that Pan-Asianist solidarity between China and India was enabled by the former's participation in the liberal international order and eventually unraveled, thanks to differences between the two Asian nationalist parties on how to reconcile anticolonial aspirations with the persistence of postwar Western hegemony.

GMD Pan-Asianism and the Japan Dimension

Exchanges between nationalist activists from India and China began at the dawn of the twentieth century, when exiled anti-Qing revolutionaries collaborated with Indian anti-colonialists and Japanese socialists in 1907 to form the Asiatic Humanitarian Brotherhood (*Yazhou heqin hui* or, in Japanese, *Ashû washinkai*). For activists informed by new radical ideas

---

[4] Lu Yan, *Re-understanding Japan: Chinese Perspectives, 1895–1945* (Honolulu: Association for Asian Studies and University of Hawai'i Press, 2004), 250–4; Carolien Stolte, "'Enough of the Great Napoleons!': Raja Mahendra Pratap's Pan-Asian Projects (1929–1939)," *Modern Asian Studies* 46 (2012): 419–21.

[5] Tetsuo Najita and H. D. Harootunian, "Japan's Revolt against the West," in *Modern Japanese Thought*, ed. Bob Tadashi Wakabayashi (Cambridge: Cambridge University Press, 1998), 213. See also H. D. Harootunian, *Overcome by Modernity: History, Culture, and Community in Interwar Japan* (Princeton, NJ: Princeton University Press, 2000), 47–65.

such as feminism, anarchism and socialism, Asia was a platform for revolutionary experimentations and regional alliances based not on the commonality of culture and religion but on the struggle against modern imperialism. Unlike Continental Europe, Asia was refreshingly free of the strictly demarcated and heavily guarded boundaries of modern nation-states and open to revolutionary experimentation. At that stage, there was considerable ambiguity and indeterminacy in the ideological import of Pan-Asianism. Chinese revolutionaries and activities drew from Japanese Pan-Asianists, while disavowing the latter's assumption that the expansionist Meiji state, fresh from its military triumph over Russia in 1905, would lead the continent against the West and toward revival.[6] Indeed, according to Wang Hui, the twentieth century saw the rise of two conflicting Pan-Asianisms. There was a radical left tradition, to which revolutionaries like Vladimir I. Lenin and Sun Yat-sen belonged, which treated "Asia" as a set of dynamic political forces and an internationalist category centered on social revolutions and national liberation projects that were based in the region. Competing with this tendency were constructions of Asia based on culturalism, statism and theories of essentialized, monolithic civilizations. Of particular interest to Wang were Japanese Pan-Asianists like Miyazaki Toten and Kita Ikki who, as onetime participants in China's national revolution, eventually came to believe that the resurgence of Asia rested ultimately on the Japanese state's domination over the continent. What defined their transformation from supporters of China's independence into cheerleaders of Japanese expansionism, Wang argues, was their substitution of uncritical belief in notions such as "state" and "race" for concrete sociopolitical analysis.[7] Once political reason was banished by utopian investment in either the state or projection of cultural essence, Pan-Asianism ceased to have emancipatory potential and quickly degenerated into a guise for Japanese imperialism.

Wang's diagnosis of Pan-Asianism's deterioration in Japan from solidarity between political movements across the region into state-led military adventurism helps map out the development of Pan-Asianist thoughts in China as well. Under the May Fourth Movement after the Great War, Pan-Asianism, like party politics and the national revolution in general, was caught up in the dialectic between nationalism on one hand, and internationalism and participation in Comintern-sponsored activities on the other. Tensions inherent in the regionalist ideology were

---

[6] Rebecca E. Karl, *Staging the World: Chinese Nationalism at the Turn of the Twentieth Century* (Durham, NC: Duke University Press, 2002), 157–9, 169, 174.

[7] Wang Hui, "The Politics of Imagining Asia: A Genealogical Analysis," *Inter-Asia Cultural Studies* 8:1.

played out in the GMD. Under the united front policy, Nationalists contributed to Comintern-led anti-colonialism. With the Soviet Union hailed as a patron of the Chinese national revolution, the GMD formulated its international engagement around the Third International's agenda of supporting national liberation movements in Asia and the rest of the colonized world.[8] In February 1927, the GMD funded and sent the largest delegation to Brussels to attend the inaugural congress of the League against Imperialism, an international anticolonialist body influenced but by no means monopolized by the Soviet Union. In return, the association of communist, socialist and radical nationalist organizations from Asia, Africa, Latin America and Europe celebrated the GMD's recent triumph over foreign-supported warlords in the Northern Expedition. Asian nationalists, in particular, touted Nationalist China as an inspiration for their own struggles. Among these enthusiastic delegations from Asia was the Indian National Congress, headed by Nehru.[9] By aligning itself with movements facing active repression from colonial governments, the GMD inherited Tokyo-based anti-Qing revolutionaries' legacy of internationalist solidarity with weak nations in Asia and beyond.

Yet, just as many Nationalist cadres were wary of Communist class politics, they were not comfortable getting too close to the Comintern. This suspicion was due partly to Russia's history of imperialist intrusions and partly to the incompatibility between nationalism and a politics that supposedly questioned workers' loyalty to their country. For future conservative revolutionaries, the national revolution should aim for a strong nation-state, not to join insurrections against the interstate system. Rather than joining forces with foreign revolutionaries whose commitment to nationhood was less than absolute, GMD elders like Dai Jitao and Hu Hanmin contemplated an association of established and budding nation-states that regarded the West, both as a political and cultural bloc, as the common enemy. In early 1924, Dai and Hu submitted two separate proposals to Sun for a People's International (*Minzu guoji*). A hypothetical Chinese-led international would include Soviet Russia and colonized peoples such as Indians together in a struggle against the Western-dominated League of Nations.[10] The alliance, conceived to

---

[8] Consider, for example, Chiang's telegram to Stalin and Lenin on the ninth anniversary of the October Revolution, which wished for the furtherance of the common "revolutionary spirit" of China and Russia and the success of the "world revolution" (*shijie geming*). October 1926, Chiang Kai-shek Collection, 002000000002A, Academia Historica.

[9] Vijay Prashad, *The Darker Nations: A People's History of the Third World* (New York: New Press, 2007), 19–22; Hans Piazza, "The Anti-Imperialist League and the Chinese Revolution," in *Chinese Revolution in the 1920s*, 169.

[10] Mast, "Intellectual Biography of Tai Ch-t'ao," 228–37.

undercut Moscow's influence over East Asia, was one between equal nations, not parties with varying degree of attachment to the nation-state. As Dai emphasized in his 1925 *Philosophical Foundations of Sun Yat-senism*, universal harmony (*datong*) was premised on China's national revival and that of other oppressed (*yapo*) nations like India, Turkey, Persia and Korea. The theoretician, drawing attention to Sun's recent speech in Kobe, argued that his mentor was no chauvinistic Chinese nationalist or Pan-Asianist, for China's national independence would benefit weak peoples around the world. What Dai did not mention is that Sun's appeal for Asianist unity tapped into the Japanese state's increasing strength and its readiness to confront Western powers through military means. Sun's long-held openness to Japanese stewardship in Asia's fight against Western domination evinced a tension between the revolutionary's hardnosed realism and moral idealism.[11] Sun's desire for China to partner with strong states and sources of capital would continue to sit uncomfortably with the GMD's outreach to the Indian nationalist movement and its struggle against British colonial rule.

With the 1927 anticommunist purge, GMD's unease over participation in Comintern initiatives transformed into outright withdrawal. Rather than siding with colonized and semi-colonized nations across the world, Chiang Kai-shek's government focused primarily on cultivating solidarity with Asian nations fighting against Western domination in global affairs. As was the case with much of the conservative revolution, Dai Jitao played a pivotal role charting the course of the GMD's Asian regionalist engagements, most of which concerned Japan. Having represented the GMD in a goodwill mission to the island nation just before the April coup in early 1927, Dai witnessed firsthand the escalating belligerence toward China among military officers and politicians dissatisfied with the relatively moderate policy of the governing Minseitô. Yet, in his 1928 book *On Japan* (*Riben lun*), he still appealed to the Japanese political elite to ally with China and use their nation's formidable military power against the West, particularly Russia.[12] In March 1931, the party theoretician, along with associate Zhang Zhenzhi (1906–31), founded the New Asia Society. Located on the premises of the Examination Yuan, which Dai headed, the New Asia Society was the ruling party's front

---

[11] Craig Anthony Smith, "Constructing Chinese Asianism: Intellectual Writings on East Asian Regionalism (1896–1924)" (PhD diss., University of British Columbia, 2014), 254–77. A full translation of the famous Kobe speech can be found in Sun Yat-sen, *China and Japan: Natural Friends, Unnatural Enemies* (Shanghai: China United Press, 1941), 141–51. The title "Pan-Asianism" was added by the volume's editor, Tang Liangli, then vice minister of foreign affairs under the collaborationist Wang Jingwei regime.

[12] Lu, *Re-understanding Japan*, 154–62.

organization tasked with devising strategies in cultivating China's ties with "Eastern nations" and claiming control over frontier regions like Tibet, Manchuria, Mongolia and Xinjiang.[13] The main tenor of the New Asia Society's version of Pan-Asianism, reminiscent of the one outlined in Sun's Kobe address, was a stark dichotomy between East and West. But unlike Sun, who included Soviet Russia in the East's kingly way (*wang-dao*) in recognition of Lenin's support for anticolonial nationalist movements, Dai saw Russia in cultural essentialist terms as "Western" in its latent hostility toward China. As he observed in the society's in-house journal *New Asia* (*Xin Yaxiya*), "the world's fundamental trend" dictated that only "Eastern nations" (*Dongfang minzu*) would ever have amicable relationships with China. Attributing Qing China's immunity from full European colonization to Meiji Japan's rise, Dai urged his compatriots to win back the respect of Japan and other Asian nations by building a prosperous and culturally refined republic. "Once China became strong again, Japan would be our friend." To the contrary, "Russia would forever be China's foe."[14]

Thus, even as military conflicts between China and Japan escalated through the late 1920s and 1930s, Nationalists continued to hope that China and Japan would form the core of an anti-Western, anti-Soviet alliance. The GMD, inheriting Sun's adeptness in seeking support from multiple sources, tapped as much into Japanese politicians holding the reins of power as into marginal figures in the hope of realizing its Pan-Asianist goals. Most of these efforts led to naught, even if right-wing Japanese did share the GMD's animosity against the West and Russia. One illustrative example concerns right-wing Pan-Asianist Miyazaki Ryūsuke (1892–1971), in whom Nationalists invested much attention. The son of Miyazaki Tōten, the legendary supporter of Sun Yat-sen's anti-Qing revolution, Ryūsuke belonged to the Social Democratic Party (*Shakai minshū tō*, or Social People's Party), one of the many anticommunist "proletarian parties" permitted to operate in prewar Japan.[15]

---

[13] The society was never part of the GMD, but senior cadres staffed the executive committee and funded its activities. See Kubo Juntarō, "Zasshi *Shin Ajia* ronsetsu kiji mokuroku [Catalogue of Commentaries and Articles in the Journal *New Asia*]," *Kôbe daigaku shigaku nenpô*, no. 17 (2002): 82.

[14] Dai Jitao, "Zhong Ri E san minzu zhi guanxi [The Relationship between China, Japan, and Russia]," *Xin Yaxiya* 1, no. 2 (1930): 9–10.

[15] Founded in December 1926, the Social Democratic Party, aligned with a right-wing labor union, was one of the major working-class political parties along with the centrist Labor-Farmer Party that participated in national elections during the Taishô period. Parties with stronger left-wing tendencies, including the Japanese Communist Party, were suppressed. The two sanctioned parties merged to form the Social Masses Party in 1932, lending "proletarian" support to the military campaign against China in 1937. In 1940, the Social Masses Party joined the mass organization Imperial Rule Assistance

Common anticommunism and unease with capitalist excesses endeared Miyazaki and his fledging party to Nanjing, although both eventually made peace with Japanese continental adventurism. In May 1927, Chiang Kai-shek, Dai Jitao and Hu Hanmin welcomed Miyazaki to Nanjing with much fanfare, evoking Sun's appeal for Pan-Asianist unity in Kobe. The visitor delivered a speech castigating "capitalist imperialists" in Japan for supporting warlords against whom the GMD was still fighting. He expressed his party's admiration for the Three People's Principle, and enthused that the Social Democratic and Nationalist parties would mobilize the masses of Japan and China and liberate the weaker nations of the world. He added that while world revolution was commendable, a communist-inspired one was to be avoided at all costs.[16]

In the 1930s, however, Miyazaki's desire for Sino–Japanese solidarity against Western colonialism increasingly hinged upon the Japanese state's continental adventurism. Indeed, alignment of Japanese Pan-Asianism with Tokyo's military "liberation" of Asia from Western colonial rule became increasingly obvious. Yet the GMD continued to see Miyazaki as a potential ally sympathetic to China's agenda. The Nationalist leadership was seemingly unnerved when Miyazaki urged in 1933 that Chiang relieve American-educated finance minister T. V. Soong (Song Ziwen, 1891–1971) of his post, in case Japan came to the view that China was drawing its economy too close to those of the dreaded Great Britain and the United States.[17] In a 1935 letter addressed to Chiang, Miyazaki even suggested that Japan's continental adventurism was only to thwart Anglo-American imperialism and Soviet expansion, and urged China to cooperate with the Japanese military.[18] As late as the summer of 1937, after the Marco Polo Bridge Incident, Chiang was still ready to receive Miyazaki to China as the personal envoy of Prime Minister Konoe Fumimaro. Konoe "wanted cooperation, not [Chinese] territories," the military attaché at the Chinese embassy in Tokyo advised.[19] Discussions between the two former comrades-in-arm never took place, as Miyazaki was arrested by Japanese military police under suspicious circumstances

Association as part of Konoe Fumimaro's fascist new order (Andrew Gordon, *Labor and Imperial Democracy in Prewar Japan* [Berkeley: University of California Press, 1991], 200, 328–9).
[16] Miyazaki Ryûsuke, "Gongqi Longjie zai Nanjing zhi yanjiang [Miyazaki Ryûsuke's Speech in Nanjing]," in *Ya Dong zhi dong*, ed. Chen Yiyi (n.p., 1927), 52–7.
[17] General Materials for 1933, Chiang Kai-shek Collection, 002000001492A, Academia Historica.
[18] Miyazaki Ryûsuke to Chiang Kai-shek, July 17, 1935, Chiang Kai-shek Collection, 002000001884A, Academia Historica.
[19] Zhang Hongchun to Chiang Kai-shek, July 25, 1937, Chiang Kai-shek Collection, 002000001669A, Academia Historica.

as he was about to leave for China. It would be impossible to tell if the course of history would have changed if Miyazaki managed to return to Nanjing ten years after he first visited the Chinese capital. What is obvious is that shared aversion to communism and investment in Asia's revival was not enough to bring peace between China and Japan. To the contrary, when it was no longer identified with popular anticolonial movements, Pan-Asianism became hijacked by raw state power and fed into Japan's own imperialist ambitions.

Tagore's Apolitical Asianism and Chinese Politics

Compared to Sino–Japanese interactions, Nationalist China's dealings with India, drawing also on reaction against the dominance of Western civilization, yielded more amicable results. The convergence of Pan-Asianism, conservative revolutionary ideals and general intellectual interrogation of industrial modernity was equally, if not more, palpable in how Chinese and Indian writers and activists understood the relationship between their two nations. The significance attributed to an Asia centered on Sino–Indian amity was beyond politics proper or mere independence from colonial rule. It entailed the revival of a humane order sustained by religious pilgrims and wisdom sharing rather than geopolitical and economic interests. Together, China and India would not create a new sociopolitical system but rather reintroduce a supple morality and spirituality displaced by Western capitalism. Such investment of hope in Sino–Indian amity emerged in the late 1910s among nonpartisan intellectuals as a countercurrent against the radical mass politics of which the GMD was a part. Yet Dai Jitao's reinterpretation of Sun Yat-sen's Pan-Asianism as a spiritual revolt against Western civilization opened the door for such grand visions of selfless transnational fraternity to be incorporated by the conservative revolution. This confluence of depoliticized intellectual trends and the GMD's anti-Soviet, anticolonial program was akin to how Zhu Guangqian's writings on aesthetics lent credence to the party-state's wartime mobilization efforts. In both cases, nonpartisan musings on morality and spirituality fed into the conservative revolution's emphasis on edifying citizens' behaviors and thoughts over empowering them materially.

Chinese intellectual fascination with India formed a part of a global reaction, into which conservative revolutionaries tapped, against modernity that became in vogue after the Great War. The orgy of violence unleashed by what in China was known as the "European War" (*Ouzhan*) disabused many New Culture intellectuals of their admiration for liberal capitalism and Western technological prowess. Some of these disillusioned activists, including GMD cadres, became attracted to communism and other forms of socialism. Those unnerved by the increasing radicalism of their country's campuses, publishing houses and literary salons looked not to Russia but came to celebrate the epiphany of a new Asia-centric civilization. Luminaries like social reformer Liang Qichao (1873–1929), publisher Du Yaquan (1873–1933) and philosopher Liang Shuming (1893–1988) hailed Eastern spirituality as an antidote to various modern malaises. They echoed conservative critics of the Enlightenment in the West like Oswald Spengler and Irving Babbitt in the hope for a "humanistic" future free from the strictures of industrial society, violence of political rivalries and bastardization of high culture. In Asia, the most eloquent advocate of Eastern spirituality was Rabindranath Tagore, who once cited Spengler approvingly as he denounced the West's pursuit for material wealth as a "modern form of barbarism" and offered Asia's "spirit of generous co-operation" as humanity's best hope against "mechanized high speed life."[20] In Tagore, Chinese cultural conservatives found a celebrated Indian thinker who could lend support to their investment in Eastern culture.

The convergence of Chinese and Indian advocacy for Asian spirituality was thus initially a meeting of intellectual minds that had no direct bearing on state or party politics. In 1923, Liang Qichao invited Tagore to China for a lecture tour. Grandiose in vision and short on particulars, neither the host nor the guest intended to use their highly publicized speeches to intervene in specific events. Liang's welcoming address posited that Tagore personified India, a country with which the Chinese, more than people from any other country, felt affinity. While Europeans and Americans' adoration for the Nobel laureate was superficial hero worshipping, most Chinese held deep affection for Tagore as a representative of a country that was China's brother. "Before most of the civilised races became active," Liang spoke as though he embodied his country, "we two brothers had already begun to study the great problems which concern the whole of mankind. We had already accomplished much in the interests of humanity." The rekindled exchange of people and ideas between China and India reaffirmed the two nations' role as beacons of civilization besieged by shallow Euro-Americans, reminiscent of the way China had to hold on to its noble philosophical traditions despite being surrounded by uncivilized frontier peoples in the past.[21]

---

[20] "Unity of Asia: A Symposium," *India and the World: Monthly Organ of Internationalism and Cultural Federation* 1, no. 7 (1932): 149–50.
[21] Liang Qichao, "The Kinship between Chinese & Indian Culture," in *Talks in China*, Tagore (Calcutta: Arunoday Art Press, n.d.), 2–3.

The world-historical significance Liang attached to Tagore's China tour appealed to some Chinese young intellectuals. One of them was twenty-six-year-old Tan Yunshan, who would become the GMD's most important contact in the Indian nationalist community in the 1930s. A lay Buddhist who spent his earlier career as a teacher and journalist with the Malayan Chinese community, Tan was not in China during Tagore's visit but retrospectively hailed it for having "awakened the dormant conscience of the Chinese nation" in his 1942 eulogy of the poet.[22] The "awakening" to which Tan referred was diametrically opposed to the political mobilization by disciplined mass parties that formed the core of the "awakening" enterprise in the 1920s.[23] Awakening for Tan entailed striving not to achieve sociopolitical trans-formation but to escape being "intoxicated and doped by the modern splendours and glories of [the] materialistic [W]est."[24] Tagore's appeal was spiritual, an invitation to turn away from Western-style bickering over material resources and embrace the humanity hidden inside Eastern cultures. As Tagore argued repeatedly in Hangzhou and Beijing, Asia-wide awakening meant refashioning the ways in which societies interacted, basing relationships not on geopolitical calculations or eco-nomic interests but on "the fruit of love and peace and friendship."[25] Addressing his young Chinese audience as a self-appointed representative of the vast continent, the celebrated poet announced that Asians would not follow the West, which was "becoming demoralized through being the exploiter, through tasting the fruits of exploitation." Once Asians rediscovered their "own birthright" and "undying worth" from their own traditions, Tagore prophesied in an apocalyptic tone, all of humanity would be saved.[26]

Despite what Liang and Tan might have wished, Tagore's paean to Eastern spirituality quickly became embroiled in China's polarized poli-tical landscape as national revolution gathered steam under Sun's united front with the Communists. Tagore's association with Liang Qichao and admiration for conservative critics of Enlightenment modernity in Europe did not go unnoticed by left-wing critics in China and elsewhere. Detractors like Chinese Communist theoretician Qu Qiubai echoed Hungarian Marxist philosopher Georg Lukács in criticizing Tagore's aversion to mass mobilization. The Bengali poet's romantic idealization of spiritual traditions meant withdrawal from confronting modern power

---

[22] Tan Yunshan, "Rabindranath, the Gurudeva," in *Professor Tan Yun-shan and Cultural Relations between India and China*, ed. V. G. Nair (Madras: Indo-Asian Publication, 1958), 15.

[23] Fitzgerald, *Awakening China*, 330–2.   [24] Tan, "Rabindranath, the Gurudeva," 15.

[25] Tagore, *Talks in China* (Calcutta: Arunoday Art Press, n.d.), 42.   [26] Ibid., 44.

relations, be it imperialism or the exploitation of labor.[27] In fact, fears that Tagore's elitist cosmopolitanism could result in dubious political judgments were not completely ungrounded. Tagore's espousal of Asian civilization and fascination with an aestheticized Japan untainted by industrial modernity meant that he was not always forthcoming in condemning the militaristic tendencies of the Japanese state. Indeed, while Tagore loathed the violence of modern political mobilization and military conflicts, he seemed concerned more with the means by which violence was perpetrated than with violence itself. In the midst of the Russo–Japanese War (1904–5), he congratulated Japanese soldiers for refusing to be "mere cogs in the wheel" and repudiating Western mechanized warfare through their willingness to sacrifice for their emperor.[28] Even in his renowned 1938 debate with Japanese modernist poet Yone Noguchi (1875–1947) on Japan's full-scale invasion of China, Tagore's categorical denunciation of Japanese aggression was juxtaposed with the striking lament that "the land of Bushido, of great Art and traditions of noble heroism" was being conquered by the "scientific savagery" of modern mechanical warfare.[29]

Tagore's devotion to pan-Asian spirituality was thus not immune to appropriation by nationalist politics. If Japan's nationalism reconciled with Western-style material prowess by expanding to the continent, Nationalist China seemed to have long made a salutary return to the country's cultural essence. The party, freed of Communist influence, saw itself as a vanguard of Eastern culture, of which China's was a preeminent part. Conservative revolutionaries were as much trenchant critics of capitalist culture, although not of capitalist social relations, as Chinese cultural conservatives and adherents of Tagore and Gandhi. As Dai asserted in *Philosophical Foundations of Sun Yat-senism*, the conservative revolution's canonical text, Sun's Pan-Asianism not only aimed to secure China and its neighbors' independence but represented a "declaration of war against the fundamentals of European culture." The GMD sought to steer an economy anchored on capital accumulation, yet it promised to bring about a form of aesthetics, morality and

[27] Qu Qiubai, "Taige'er de guojia guan yu Dongfang [Tagore's Views on the Nation-State and the East]," in *Qu Qiubai wenji: zhengzhi lilun bian* (Beijing: Renmin wenxue chubansbe, 1988), 2:511–19; Georg Lukács, "Tagore's Gandhi Novel," *Marxists Internet Archive*, www.marxists.org/archive/lukacs/works/1922/tagore.htm (accessed September 23, 2012).

[28] Tagore, *Swadeshi Samaj*, cited in Rustom Bharucha, *Another Asia: Rabindranath Tagore and Okakura Tenshin* (New Delhi: Oxford University Press, 2006), 58.

[29] Rabindranath Tagore to Yone Noguchi, September 1, 1938, *In the Footsteps of Xuanzang: Tan Yun-shan and India*, ed. Tan Chung (New Delhi: Gyan Publishing House and Indira Gandhi National Centre for the Arts, 1999), 209–10.

everyday habits untainted by capitalist modernity. The *minsheng* doctrine, Dai asserted, rejected capitalism and class struggle, the latter stemming from a "European understanding of history centered on material problems (*wuzhi wenti*)."[30] The GMD's elevation of national spirit over "materialist" capitalism and communism thus dovetailed with Tagore's diagnosis of the modern malaise. Disillusioned with Japan, whose technologically advanced weapon was symptomatic of the standardized, mass anonymity inherent to capitalist modernity, the poet turned his attention to China. Since the "the land of Bushido" no longer exuded spiritual chivalry, Chiang Kai-shek's "unconquerable" China became the East's new hope.[31] Tagore's sweeping civilizational outlook gave short shrift to the violent anticommunism that conditioned the conservative revolution's espousal of spirituality. What began as Tagore's apolitical, intellectual enterprise questioning Western-style mass politics ended up lending credibility to a Leninist regime that promised to bring industrial modernity to China.

A Twentieth-Century Xuanzang

Aside from the prestige Tagore enjoyed on his own virtue, the writer-cum-educator's extensive ties with the Indian National Congress, centered on the college Visva-Bharati, provided the GMD a platform to sustain its Asianist project as Sino–Japanese relations continued to deteriorate. If Dai's New Asia Society mostly served as a think tank on all aspects of life in Asia and on China's frontier, the Sino–Indian Cultural Society, founded in 1933, had a more specific mandate of fostering relationship between the GMD and the Congress in a time when civil society was the only arena in which interactions between the two nationalist movements could be carried on without further provoking the ire of the British colonial authority. One key figure in the Sino–Indian Cultural Society and the GMD's dealings with India at large was Tan Yunshan, the Tagore enthusiast. A Hunan native, Tan went to the First Provincial Normal College, at which he made friends with Mao Zedong and other prominent Communist revolutionaries. After graduation in 1924, Tan traveled to British Malaya and spent three years there as an educator and publisher. He founded Malaya's first Chinese-language literary supplement *Star Light* (*Xingguang*), attached to the Singapore-based daily *Lat Pau* (*Lebao*). The magazine had a strong reformist bent. Contributors promoted new ideas, attacked old customs and pushed for a modern

---

[30] Dai, *Sun Wen zhuyi zhi zhexue de jichu*, 27–9.
[31] Tagore to Yone Noguchi, September 1, 1938, 210.

written vernacular. They berated attachment to native-place associations among the diaspora, calling instead for a unified Chinese identity and an end to schools and hospitals that served descendants who hailed from particular counties or provinces. Yet Tan was equally scathing of Chinese people who blindly followed new trends, particularly consumerist fads from Europe.[32] Like many of his compatriots after the Great War, Tan did not see the West as providing the solutions to the cultural and social debauchery that plagued Chinese societies.

In temperament, Tan belonged to the conservative wing of the New Culture Movement. Like *Jingpai* writer Zhu Guangqian, who was one year his junior, Tan had little interest in mass movements and party politics. For him, a nation's transformation hinged on an individual's moral perfection, not the socioeconomic structures that mediated human relationships. While Zhu turned to aesthetics, Tan became interested in Buddhism and the spirituality of Indian thinkers. The Malaya-based sojourner was not in China when Tagore visited in 1924, but the two men eventually met in Singapore three years later, when the latter persuaded Tan to join Visva-Bharati as a Chinese studies professor. Located in the quiet Bengali town of Santiniketan, Visva-Bharati was no ordinary academic institution. The college, funded by his Nobel prize proceeds, was Tagore's most concrete challenge to Western materialism. Its rustic environment and lack of a formal curriculum served as antidotes to the elitist and bureaucratized educational model the British introduced to modern colonial cities. In the two decades since his relocation to Santiniketan in 1928, Tan worked successfully to bridge the Pan-Asianisms of Tagore and the GMD, mediating between the Chinese nationalist movement and its Indian counterpart. In spite of his prominent role in Chinese diplomacy, the devout Buddhist actively fashioned himself as a modern-day pilgrim contributing to Sino–Indian "cultural intercourse" who had "nothing to do with any kind of politics," even as he was urging Indian nationalists in 1942 to wholeheartedly join the Allies' war effort against Japan.[33]

Much like many nonpartisan intellectuals back home, Tan's relationship with the GMD was ambiguous. He saw the GMD as the custodian of order, seeing aspects of the conservative revolution as means to edify Communist delinquents and the population at large. Being physically absent from China for most of his life, and lacking interest in

---

[32] Fang Xiu, *Notes on the History of Malaysian Chinese New Literature, 1920–1942*, trans. Angus W. MacDonald (Tokyo: Centre for East Asian Cultural Studies, 1977), 29–31, 72–3; Tan, "Bianyu zahua – qianzu yu gaogen xie [Miscellaneous Talk – Foot-Binding and High-Heeled Shoes]," *Lebao*, November 13, 1925, 20.

[33] Tan, "An Appeal to Conscience," in *In the Footstep of Xuanzang*, 172.

revolutionary politics, Tan retained an impressionistic view of the ideological and armed battles raging in his native country. Yet unfamiliarity did not deter the Visva-Bharati academic from expressing views on developments in China. Tan suggested to students and academics at Andhra University in 1938, for example, that captive Communist insurgents from Jiangxi were "very generously treated by the national government," that GMD authority was "well established all over the country" and that the government enjoyed "the allegiance of the entire Chinese nation." His depiction of the Communist movement resembled those of Dai, Chiang and other conservative revolutionaries. The GMD wielded a "big mop to sweep the undesirable communists out" because the latter were forming their own clique within the national revolution. Locked in the interior, Communists "carried on their quixotic class war in which massacre of the dissentient was the only principle of action." The New Life Movement was hailed as a salutary revision of the overly radical New Culture Movement, a campaign to balance "Chinese philosophy and ethics as the foundation of Chinese culture" with "Western scientific spirit."[34] As in Zhu Guangqian's case, Tan lent his support for the GMD from the outside because he counted on the state to turn the tide against social revolution.

Tan's contributions to the GMD's Pan-Asianist project drew on the Tagorean celebration of Eastern civilization against a predatory West, a position that was out of place among neither nonpartisan intellectuals nor conservative revolutionaries. In 1930, Tan joined a delegation of Nationalist state representatives on a mission to Lhasa. Fresh from the victory of the Northern Expedition, Nanjing was anxious to assert sovereign claim over the financially impoverished but independently governed Tibet.[35] The dramatic trip saw Tan play for the first time the role of unofficial diplomat as Nanjing's envoy, Xie Guoliang, unexpectedly died from illness before setting foot on Tibetan territory. Aside from delivering Chiang Kai-shek's messages to the thirteenth Dalai Lama, Tan helped deliver a letter from the Tibetan leader to Gandhi on his return journey. After returning to Nanjing through British India, Tan wrote a letter to the Dalai Lama urging his government to rally behind the Nationalist state and support a union between Tibet and China. Demonstrating a shrewd understanding of the geopolitics of imperialism, Tan argued further in an open letter to the theocrat, published in *New Asia*, that offers of independence and autonomy by imperialist powers were just precursors to

[34] Tan, *Modern Chinese History: Political, Economic and Social* (Madras: n.p., 1938), 32, 69.
[35] Hsiao-ting Lin, *Tibet and Nationalist China's Frontier: Intrigues and Ethnopolitics, 1928–49* (Vancouver: University of British Columbia Press, 2006), 51–71.

outright colonization, citing as examples Korea, Vietnam, Bhutan and Sikkim. He urged Lhasa to accept autonomy under Chinese sovereignty. After all, the spirit of human salvation (*jiushi jingshen*) in Buddhist thought – Tan alluded to Sun's Pan-Asianism – was in sync with the Three People's Principles.[36] Tan might have been a diplomat by accident, but it was obvious he took the interests of the Nanjing-based regime seriously.

Despite his facility in the international dimension of the *minsheng* program, Tan held jealously onto his apolitical persona. Like liberals at home, Tan's ability to lend support to the conservative revolution from the periphery attested to the compatibility between elements of China's non-partisan intellectual ideals and GMD political ideology. The fact that the peripatetic scholar had never been a member of the Nationalist government until 1948, when he was appointed Nanjing's cultural representative in India, allowed the idealistic academic to project his travels between India and China through heavily contested Tibet as instances of civilizational dialogue.[37] Fashioning himself as a pilgrim, Tan mixed religious solemnity and ethnographic curiosities in an account of his remarkable trip, focusing on his extended journey conveying the Dalai Lama's message to Gandhi. Published by the New Asia Society, and adorned with calligraphies of key GMD officials including Dai Jitao, Yu Youren (1879–1964) and Zhang Ji (1882–1947), *India Travelogue* (*Yindu zhouyou ji*) portrayed the author's increasingly active role in India as a pilgrimage and pure-minded quest for spiritual truth and revival of historical ties, reminding readers repeatedly of the fabled Tang Buddhist pilgrim Xuanzang (circa 602–64).[38] Tan's highly symbolic tour, which took place from March to May 1931, retraced the religious interactions between India and China by visiting Buddhist structures along the Ganges, including a structure reputedly commissioned by the eleventh-century Song emperor Renzong.[39] He quenched his thirst with simple brown sugar syrup served by a local monk in the rustic pilgrimage site of Kushinagar, declaring its superiority to the fancy tea and coffee consumed by well-heeled urbanites.[40]

---

[36] Tan, "Zhi Dalai Lama shu [Letter to the Dalai Lama]," *Xin Yaxiya* 3, no. 5 (1932): 136–9.

[37] The position of cultural representative (*wenjiao zhuanyuan*) was placed under the Ministry of Education rather than the Ministry of Foreign Affairs, probably out of the consideration that a formal diplomatic appointment would have compromised Tan's apolitical identity. See Zhu Jiahua to Maulana Azad, January 27, 1948, Zhu Jiahua Collection, 301–01-18–020, IMH Archives.

[38] Tan, *Yindu zhouyou ji* [*Travelogue to India*] (Nanjing: Xin Yaxiya xuehui, 1933), 1, 45.

[39] Ibid., 41–2.   [40] Ibid., 80.

The travelogue, while structured as a journey of spiritual discovery, did not disguise the intricate ties between religious or cultural exchanges and the politics of Asian nationalisms. Instead, the author actively sought to seek commonalities between the nationalist movements of China and India. In Calcutta, Tan toured testaments to British imperial might like the Imperial Library, the Indian Museum and the Victoria Memorial. He ruminated how Queen Victoria's ascension to the Indian throne in 1876 was a humiliating episode in the history of a glorious civilization that no self-respecting Indian would forget and lamented how China suffered a similar fate under Western imperialism with the cessation of Hong Kong.[41] Tan's visit to Gandhi, undoubtedly the climax of the trip, entailed discussion over the Congress's tortuous negotiation with London over India's political status and a common pledge to revive the spiritual bonds between the two Asian nations.[42] Like many of those captivated by Gandhi's formidable charisma, Tan saw the Indian nationalist as a philosopher king leading a struggle for not only Indian or Asian, but also universal salvation. He called on the Mahatma in an outfit consisting of a Gandhi cap and *khadi* or Indian homespun cloth, a telling symbol of devotion to an independent Indian nation.[43] Tan characterized the non-cooperation movement, the nonviolence doctrine and the civil disobedience movement as embodiments of sincerity (*cheng*), compassion (*ai*) and harmony (*he*), respectively.[44] Drawing on Sun Yat-sen's eight traditional virtues (*ba de*), a key ideological component of GMD conservative revolutionaries and their vision for a rejuvenated citizenry, in conceptualizing Gandhi's anticolonial program, Tan ensured that cultural ties between India and China assumed critical contemporary relevance.[45]

The immediate effect of the convergence of Chinese and Indian nationalisms as the alternative core of Pan-Asianism at Japan's expense was a boost to Tan's academic activities in India. Tasked by Tagore to raise funds for a Chinese studies institute that was eventually named Cheena Bhavana (Chinese Hall, *Zhongguo xueyuan*), Tan expressed in *India Travelogue* his disappointment that promised donations from Singaporean Chinese entrepreneur Aw Boon Haw (1882–1954) were not to materialize.[46] Disappointments with the Southeast Asian

---

[41] Ibid., 22.   [42] Ibid., 138.

[43] For the cultural politics of homespun cloth, see Lisa Trivedi, *Clothing Gandhi's Nation: Homespun and Modern India* (Bloomington: Indiana University Press, 2007), 72–80.

[44] Tan, *Yindu zhouyou ji*, 145–6.

[45] The "eight virtues" were in fact eight Chinese characters that conveyed four core concepts: filial piety (*zhongxiao*), benevolence (*ren'ai*), honor (*xinyi*) and peace (*heping*).

[46] Tan, *Yindu zhouyou ji*, 30.

Chinese diaspora, however, soon gave way to success in the homeland. After returning to China from Tibet and India in September 1931, Tan overcame his initial reluctance deriving from "the self-respecting character of a Chinese scholar," took advantage of his connections with the political, religious and academic establishments of Nationalist society and transformed himself into an effective fundraiser. Responses from such luminaries as Academia Sinica president Cai Yuanpei, Buddhist leader and philosopher Taixu (1890–1947) and Dai Jitao were "unexpectedly favourable."[47] A result of Tan's efforts was the initiation of the Sino–Indian Cultural Society, with one chapter in Nanjing in 1933 and another at Visva-Bharati in 1934. With honorary presidents who included nationalist leaders of no less stature than Gandhi, Nehru, Chiang and his wife, Song Meiling, the India chapter immediately worked toward the inauguration of Cheena Bhavana.[48]

Both the Sino–Indian Cultural Society and Cheena Bhavana were infused with the Asian spiritual idealism as conceived by Tagore and Tan, even as the two institutions were, from their conception, deeply embedded in the political machineries of organized nationalisms in both countries.[49] Parallel to the nationalist communion at home, China's relations with India were sustained by fraternal sentiments. Tagore's 1937 speech marking the opening of Cheena Bhavana amounted to nothing less than a proposal for an alternative world order to the capitalist system of competing nation-states. The poet told the assembled audience – of which the young Indira Nehru (1917–84), then a student at Visva-Bharati, was a member representing her ailing father – that Sino–Indian relations would not be beset by conflicting interests because the Indians, as a colonized people, did not have a state. India's lack, however, would prove to be an advantage since "not know[ing] how to help you or injure you materially," Tagore and his compatriots could be nothing other than "your guests, your hosts, your brothers and your friends." He categorically condemned capitalist globalization and its attendant system of nation-states, decrying that "in a world so closely knit by railways, steamships and air lines," a "wrong kind of nearness"

---

[47] Tan, *Twenty Years of the Visva-Bharati Cheena Bhavana 1937–1957* (Santiniketan: Sino–Indian Cultural Society of India, 1957), 18–19.

[48] Tan, *Twenty Years of the Visva-Bharati Cheena Bhavana*, 19; Tan, *The Visva-Bharati Cheena-Bhavana and the Sino–Indian Cultural Society* (Chongqing and Santiniketan: The Sino–Indian Cultural Society, 1944), 18.

[49] At the basic financial level, the day-to-day operation of Cheena Bhavana was funded primarily by donations from the GMD and its senior cadres, either through the Sino–Indian Cultural Society or the Nationalist regime itself, until Visva-Bharati became a "central university" under the Republic of India. Donations from private individuals were not significant (Tan, *Twenty Years of the Visva-Bharati Cheena Bhavana*, 49–50).

brought about a "terrorised world" of blunder, oppression and invasion at the expense of "peaceful races."[50] He hailed Cheena Bhavana as the first step toward revitalizing India and China's "exchange of gifts" between "noble friends" and as an antidote to the alienation and violence of industrial modernity. "The moral force which has given quality to our civilization" – cooperation and love, mutual trust and mutual aid – would empower humans to "assimilate" twentieth-century scientific advances. Otherwise, Tagore warned in apocalyptic terms, science would "dominate and enslave them."[51] As a manifestation of the increasingly close relationship between India and China, energized not least by Japan's full-scale continental invasion, Cheena Bhavana was for Tagore a realization of his vision of a cosmopolitan utopia that would overcome the violent divisions in modern mass politics engendered by rival nation-states and political movements. The sinological institute was the first step toward a politics of fellow feeling that consciously detached itself from the everyday social processes of a conflict-ridden world.

Asianist Utopia and Wartime Diplomacy

As a concrete testament to the coming together of the GMD's anticommunist Pan-Asianism and India's anticolonial movement, Cheena Bhavana soon became less an epiphany of universal harmony and disinterested friendship than a platform for wartime diplomacy. The Second Sino–Japanese War broke out just three months after the inauguration of the school, which now hosted the Sino–Indian Cultural Society in India. Tagore compared Japan's "murderous attack" on China to Fascist Italy's invasion of Ethiopia in 1935, recognizing, if belatedly, that the "land of Bushido" had capitulated to the temptations of imperialist grandeur.[52] Braving the volatile situation in coastal China, Tan traveled to Nanjing, working to bridge ties between the GMD and the Congress. At the same time, Tan kept Cheena Bhavana's research and teaching programs away from current affairs and focused instead on cultural and religious synergy between China and India. The two countries' high cultures, including languages, literatures, history, religions and philosophical innovations all fell under the institute's purview. In particular, Buddhism formed "the nucleus of all such studies."[53] One highlight of Cheena Bhavana's publication program was the "restoration" into Indian languages of lost

---

[50] Tagore, "China and India," in *Twenty Years of the Visva-Bharati Cheena Bhavana*, 42.
[51] Ibid., 41–3.
[52] Tagore to Noguchi, September 1, 1938, in *In the Footsteps of Xuanzang*, 209–10.
[53] The General Rules of Visva-Bharati Cheena-Bhavana, article 2 (1937), cited in Tan, *Twenty Years of the Visva-Bharati Cheena-Bhavana*, 20.

Sanskrit works translated into Chinese or Tibetan since the seventh century.[54] Aside from scholars of Indian, Chinese and Tibetan Buddhism, faculty members had expertise in the languages, philosophy and art of the three cultures. Compared to classical studies and religion, modern topics received much less attention. Except for one specialist who worked on modern Chinese literature, nobody at Cheena Bhavana wrote anything substantial on modern topics. The only scholar who wrote regularly on modern China and its relations with India was Tan Yunshan himself.[55] The day-to-day functioning of Cheena Bhavana conformed to Tan's determination to retrace the trail blazed by Xuanzang.

Historical religious exchanges underscored desires for brotherly solidarity between China and India in a time when a rival Pan-Asianism backed by the Japanese army was rampaging the continent. Unlike the violent and self-interested nature of Japan's offer to liberate Asia from colonialism, cooperation between the Chinese and Indian nationalist parties was supposed to be altruistic, peaceful and morally superior. This relationship exemplified Dai's argument, distancing Sun's Pan-Asianism from proletarian internationalism, that world peace hinged not on economic or political arrangements but on China's benevolent national spirit writ large.[56] Tan played a hands-on role in furthering this cardinal relationship. The Sino–Indian Cultural Society arranged Nehru's visit to China in August 1939. Just months later, senior Buddhist monk Taixu led a delegation to India. The religious leader, who inducted Tan to the faith in the early 1920s and enjoyed close ties with the GMD, shared views on strengthening wartime Sino–Indian cooperation with Congress president Subhas Chandra Bose (1897–1945) and Nehru. Nehru, despite being a moderate socialist and admirer of the Soviet Union, reportedly endorsed Taixu's critique of Western civilization. The deepening military crisis, Taixu argued, was a result of the unfettered valorization of the material dimension of human existence. A union of China and India (*Zhong Yin liangguo lianhe*), with their strengths in furthering harmonious human relationships and cultivating pure minds, would steer the world away from the fundamental flaw of Western civilization.[57]

In late 1940, it was Dai Jitao's turn to visit India, becoming the first and only senior Nationalist official to have met with the regime's unlikely

[54] The Rules Regarding Studies in Cheena-Bhavana (1937), cited in Tan, *Twenty Years of the Visva-Bharati Cheena-Bhavana*, 20.
[55] Tan, *Twenty Years of the Visva-Bharati Cheena-Bhavana*, 56–69.
[56] Dai, *Sun Wen zhuyi zhi zhexue de jichu*, 29.
[57] Yin Shun, *Taixu fashi nianpu* [*Chronological Biography of Master Taixu*] (Beijing: Zongjiao wenhua chubanshe, 1995), 251–2.

admirer, Tagore. Accompanied throughout his trip by Tan, Chiang Kai-shek's trusted theoretician was advertised by the Congress as a "distinguished Buddhist scholar" on "a cultural goodwill mission."[58] Not unlike Tan's tour of India almost a decade before, Dai traveled "to see the historical places of the Buddhist faith."[59] Behind the scenes, however, it was obvious to those in positions of authority that Dai represented the embattled GMD state. Chiang wrote to Gandhi and told him in no uncertain terms that Dai was a "representative of the Nationalist Party" on a mission to persuade Indian nationalists to join China in "frustrating the chief aggressor [Japan] and protecting Asian civilization." British Secretary of State for India and Burma Leo Amery advised Dai to meet with representatives of the Muslim community and the princely states, reminding Guo Taiqi (1888–1952), the Chinese ambassador to Britain, that "Indian sympathy for China was not confined to the Congress."[60]

The self-appointed custodian of Asian civilization was welcome by his Congress hosts with grand statements. At Swaraj Bhavan, the residence of the Nehrus in Allahabad, Dai heard: "We are familiar with the exploitation that results from the contact of our country with another. But our ancient relations [with China] have always been of a peaceful and brotherly nature." Alluding to GMD elder's Buddhist pilgrim persona, the Congress's speech hailed India as the historic birthplace of the faith. It assured the Chinese guest that while most Indians were Hindus, not Buddhists, their Hinduism incorporated the principles of the pan-Asian religion.[61] Reciprocating Dai's professed admiration for the nonviolence movement, Congress officials introduced the visitor as "one who preaches the same doctrine of the supremacy of the law of love" as Gandhi.[62] The fact that the GMD routinely deployed terroristic tactics against political opponents did not seem to have registered among Dai's Indian hosts. Bringing the doctrine of love to bear in a world suffering from the worst excesses of the capitalist nation-state system, the speech concluded by calling on India and China to "establish in the east a bloc of free nations and thus bring about a new order, based upon equity . . . and human brotherlyness [sic]."[63]

[58] Belkrishna Keskar to Amaranatha Jha, Vice-Chancellor of Allahabad University, November 18, 1940, A.I.C.C. Collection, G-40/312, NMML.
[59] Jivatram Kripalani to Congress Provincial Committees, October 28, 1940, A.I.C.C. Collection, G-40/2075, NMML.
[60] Chiang, Jiang Zhongzheng zongtong dang'an, 44:451–2, 514.
[61] Indian National Congress Speech Welcoming Dai Jitao, December 3, 1940, A.I.C.C. Collection, G-40/1940, NMML.
[62] Ibid.   [63] Ibid.

Tenuous Alliance

India–China amity anticipated a different new order under which moral and philosophical outlooks rather than economic and political interests guided human interactions. This position found a ready audience among anticommunist nationalists in both countries. Some members of the Indian National Congress, in deference to Hindu religious traditions, would have little difficulty appreciating the GMD's valorization of national spirit and culture. Like conservative revolutionaries in China, conservative Indian nationalists were as much against European imperialism and consumerist decadence as "Western" and "materialist" class war. Gandhi himself was reluctant to confront the caste system and deeply skeptical of political organizing initiated by the untouchables.[64] Chinese conservative revolutionaries' social engineering experiments, which prized authority-abiding producers, appealed to some Indian activists. Vadilal L. Mehta, a prominent industrialist who participated actively in Gandhi's rural reconstruction program, enthused that the strategy of compulsion deployed in the New Life Movement yielded better results than the decentralized voluntarism that was supposed to fuse India's rural economy.[65] A Pan-Asianist alliance between the Chinese and Indian national movements was not far-fetched.

Yet the fraternity between GMD and Congress was anchored on unstable ground. Nehru, who led the Congress movement's left wing, shared much more the GMD's anti-imperialism than its brand of anticommunist Pan-Asianism. In the mid-1920s, reflective of their participation in the League against Imperialism conference, the two parties were bound together by the common aspiration toward national liberation. They signed a joint declaration that would have committed the parties to the exchange of intelligence, personnel and information offices.[66] After the April 12 purge in 1927, there was a split within the Congress on how to understand the anticommunist coup that now defined the newly established Nationalist government in Nanjing. Nehru complained in a 1929 letter to Song Qingling, the left-leaning widow of Sun Yat-sen, that many of his colleagues believed the party-state delivered China from the shackles of imperialism. "A resolution congratulating China was passed by the National Congress," he added, "although some of us pointed out

---

[64] Vijay Prashad, *Untouchable Freedom: A Social History of a Dalit Community* (New Delhi: Oxford University Press, 2000), chap. 5, particularly 117, 120–1.

[65] V. L. Mehta, "Comparative Studies in Rural Economic Conditions," *Harijan* 4, no. 9 (April 1936): 71.

[66] Piazza, "Anti-Imperialist League and the Chinese Revolution," 170.

the true facts and opposed the resolution."[67] Only when the Second Sino–Japanese War began did Nehru overcome his initial distrust of the GMD and argue in 1938 that Nationalist China was an ally in the fight against global fascism of which Japan was a part.[68] In August 1939, Nehru visited Chongqing and held talks with Chiang Kai-shek, whom the former now saw as the personification of "the unity of China and her determination to free herself."[69] The nationalist leaders of the two societies agreed to enhance cooperation between the GMD and the Congress. Evoking the Brussels resolution, the two organizations promised again to send representatives to each other's annual meeting, share information and develop a "common outlook and policy" on foreign affairs.[70] Given the sensitive nature of a political relationship between China's governing party and an Indian movement whose ultimate goal was the demise of the British Raj, the Sino–Indian Cultural Society was identified as a front organization by which agendas formulated by the two parties could be relayed through seemingly benign religious, academic and educational exchanges.[71] There should be no doubt that the "religious" visits of Taixu and Dai to India were highly politicized contacts conceived and actively planned between senior figures of the two nationalist movements.

The renewed alliance between the GMD and Congress was shaky even at its conception. Not all members of the Congress were willing to support Britain's war efforts against Japan, especially when the colonizers, under Winston Churchill, showed no signs that they were willing to grant India any form of independence. Some Indian nationalists were unsurprisingly receptive to, or at least not actively opposed to, Japan's version of Pan-Asianism, to which Tagore and Dai were once attracted. Former Congress president Subhas Chandra Bose's abrupt switch in 1941 to allying with Japan and mobilization of militant Indians attracted to Japan's call for an anti-imperialist Asian alliance was no doubt the most scandalous case of Indian nationalism's vicissitudes vis-à-vis Japanese imperialism. But even Gandhi, who was hardly a Pan-Asianist, expressed as late as April 1942 that he was willing to negotiate with the Japanese empire as long as it would bring about immediate independence to India. Gandhi, who rallied behind him the more conservative and antisocialist

[67] Jawaharlal Nehru to Mme. Sun Yat-sen, January 16, 1929, A.I.C.C. Collection, F.D. 1 (ii)/1929, NMML.
[68] Jawaharlal Nehru, "Why India Supports China," in *Selected Works of Jawaharlal Nehru* (New Delhi: Orient Longman, 1972–82), 9:210.
[69] Nehru, "Diary of a Journey," in *Selected Works of Jawaharlal Nehru*, 10:85.
[70] "A Note on the Development of Contact between China and India," August 29, 1939, *tezhong*, 13/1.14, KMT Archives.
[71] Chen Lifu and Zhu Jiahua to Chiang Kai-shek, October 6, 1939, *tezhong*, 13/1.2, KMT Archives.

wing of his party, was under pressure from industrialists who feared destruction of their properties during fighting between Allied forces and the Japanese.[72]

The conciliatory attitude segments of the Congress adopted toward Japan alarmed Tan Yunshan, forcing him to steer beyond his jealously guided role of apolitical interlocutor. Disclaiming in September 1942 that he was no more than a "simple Chinese Buddhist scholar," Tan nonetheless proceeded to caution his "Indian brethren" against Japan's pretense to anti-imperialism and support for Indian independence. He even found it necessary to refute Gandhi, whose nonviolence policy and spiritualism he admired, and the Congress's argument that shifting from languishing under British imperialism to living within the Japanese sphere of influence amounted to nothing more than a "change of Master." Faced with the military prowess of a German-backed Japan, Tan adopted an internationalist position in urging India to support the Allies in order to save the world and India's aspiration for independence from being "trampled under Hitler's iron heel."[73] Tan's rare deviation from his primary concern in "cultural intercourse and co-operation" was a tacit acknowledgment that Pan-Asianism – with its inherent contradictions, ambiguities and mysticism – was no stable basis for a nationalist movement busy revising its strategies amidst the rapidly changing contours of global military and ideological conflicts.

Gandhi's eventual assurance to Chiang that all the Congress's decisions would "lead to the strengthening of India's and China's defence" in June 1942 was, in spite of the well wishes of Tagore, Tan and their associates, a result less of Pan-Asianist conviviality than a marriage of political calculations.[74] In February 1942, when Chiang Kai-shek, now the Supreme Allied Commander in China, spent two days in Santineketan with his wife while on an official visit to India, he reaffirmed Cheena Bhavana as a symbol of revived Sino–Indian amity. The Generalissimo told Gandhi that "colored peoples (*youse renzhong*) ought to find their own way towards liberation." Now that Japan had forfeited its responsibility to lead Asia and joined the ranks of imperialist oppressors, the liberation of humankind rested with the combined forces of China and India, whose relationship through the past 2,000 years was

---

[72] Johannes H. Voigt, "Co-operation or Confrontation?: War and Congress Politics, 1939–42," in *Congress and the Raj: Facets of the Indian Struggle, 1917–47*, ed. D. A. Low, 2nd edn. (New Delhi: Oxford University Press, 2004), 366–7.

[73] Tan, "An Appeal to Conscience," 217–20.

[74] Mahatma Gandhi to Chiang Kai-shek, June 14, 1942, *Across the Himalayan Gap: An Indian Quest for Understanding China*, ed. Tan Chung (New Delhi: Indira Gandhi National Centre for the Arts, 1998), 41.

one of cultural and economic fusion and never of conquests and wars.[75] The Congress's response to active participation in the Allied war efforts as a renewed expression of India's historical camaraderie with China was equivocal at best, insisting instead that India's support was contingent on Britain's promise of independence. "I would not think," Gandhi told Chiang, "that Japanese soldiers were more evil than the British."[76] Nehru explained to Chiang on another occasion that the Congress's active participation would be seen as collaboration with the British colonizers and undermine the party's legitimacy in Bengal, Subhas Bose's home province and support base. As for the increasingly impatient Generalissimo's proposal that China and India should fight shoulder to shoulder (*bingjian zuozhan*) for national liberation, Nehru offered this less than subtle rebuttal:

Before the war, Japan had sent people to be in touch with me, offering money and weapons in support of India's revolution ... [Yet the Congress declined the offer because] whenever foreigners came about to support our independence, we invariably got vanquished in the end.[77]

Neither Gandhi nor his successor, whose sympathies for Chongqing were obvious, were prepared to contemplate an alliance with their fellow Asians once practical political agendas of the two sides diverged. Tagore's vision for a relationship of pure compassion and spiritual generosity between two societies free from the distractions of nation-state-building and embroilment in "Western" diplomacy proved ephemeral.

Ultimately, the Congress's professed solidarity with China was a result of Chongqing's hard-headed calibrations of its own interests in relation to India's nationalist goals. Anti-imperialist and sympathetic to the colonized Chiang might have been, Lu Fang-shang observes, the GMD leader was neither willing nor able to challenge imperialist power. In fact, Chiang walked a tightrope between being an anti-imperialist agitator among his fellow Asians and partaking in an international order dominated by the West.[78] China's response to the Congress-initiated Quit India Movement attests to the Nationalists' delicate balancing act. On August 8, 1942, the Congress passed a resolution calling for non-violent mass struggle against the British. The decision to demand an

---

[75] Transcript of Chiang Kai-shek's discussion with Mahatma Gandhi, New Delhi, February 18, 1942, Chiang Kai-shek Collection, 002000000375A, Academia Historica.

[76] Ibid.

[77] Transcript of Chiang Kai-shek's discussion with Jawaharlal Nehru, Calcutta, February 20, 1942, Chiang Kai-shek Collection 002000000375A, Academia Historica.

[78] Lu Fang-shang, "Jiang Jieshi – yiwei tanxing guoji zhuyi zhe: yi 1942 nian fang Yin weili de taolun [Chiang Kai-shek, a Flexible Internationalist: On His 1942 Visit to India]," *Guoli zhengzhi daxue lishi xuebao*, no. 37 (2012): 121–46.

immediate end to British colonialism was informed in part by Gandhi's assessment that Japan, having already reached the Indo–Burmese border, would soon prevail over the Allies. The colonial regime reacted swiftly and angrily to what it portrayed as a pro-Axis act, imprisoning the entire Congress leadership, including Gandhi and Nehru, on August 9. Popular protests followed suit across India, prompting Chinese fear over a sudden collapse of colonial rule. Chiang conveyed to the British ambassador to China that the Nationalist regime had no business in telling Britain how to run its empire, but the Chinese leader suggested nonetheless that the arrest of Congress leaders was premature. By no means a paragon of political tolerance himself, Chiang mused that if China were to adopt the same hardline stance toward India, the latter "might feel beleaguered and threw itself to Japan's embrace."[79] The last thing the GMD wanted was an Indian declaration of independence with Japan waiting at the doorstep to fill the power vacuum. Grandiose proclamations of world-wide salvation gave way to unsentimental realism and military strategizing.

The Limits of Pan-Asianism

The limits of Pan-Asianist fellow feeling were put to sharper relief by the stark social and ideological choices that nation-states and political movements worldwide had to make after 1945 as the thinly veiled rifts between the wartime allies resurfaced. The GMD's Pan-Asianism, as an extension of its conservative revolution, stemmed from the party's rejec-tion of the Comintern and distancing from subversive political move-ments. For Dai, Tan and even Tagore, the struggle for national and Asianist subjectivity was fundamentally an aesthetic process of over-coming servitude to communism and capitalism, products of the mate-rialist West. Modern imperialism, and the capitalist modernity with which it was entwined, was understood as an expression of nihilism and moral depravity tied to the Euro-American culture of excessive material wealth and industrial standardization. While Nehru did not shy away from culturalist rhetoric, his idea of Asian solidarity was clearly conditioned by his analysis of the political and social conjuncture that produced inter-imperialist rivalries and eventually the Second World War. When Nehru wrote in the US-based journal *Fortune* in 1942 that Asia and Africa would play a critical role in determining the outcome of the Second World War, he meant nations that were subjected under the

---

[79] Transcript of Chiang Kai-shek's discussion with Horace James Seymour, August 12, 1942, Chiang Kai-shek Collection, 002000000376A, Academia Historica.

forces of imperialism and fascism.[80] Nehru's notion of Asia – which he often mentioned alongside Africa, Spain and Soviet Russia – was thus not a cultural or spiritual entity pitched against the West's debased civilization but a coalition of colonized and semi-colonized peoples fighting to free themselves from the politico-economic savagery of imperialism. The imprint of his involvement in Comintern anti-colonialism, an experience that the GMD would rather forget, is obvious. Indeed, the Soviet experiment, like nationalist movements elsewhere, was for Nehru a laudable attempt to put an end to the hegemony of "finance-imperialism."[81] Nehru's "Asia" was a call for social changes that, for colonized peoples, was inseparable from the quest for national independence.

The clash between Nehru's incipient Third Worldism and the GMD's Pan-Asianist diplomacy was brought to bear in the quiet unraveling of the uneasy alliance between China and independent India in the few years leading up to the Cold War. In 1947 Tan played the unofficial diplomat again as a member of China's delegation to the Asian Relations Conference. The conference, held in the heady days shortly before the creation of an independent Indian state in 1947, was envisioned by Nehru as a forum to assert Asia's independence from European and American interests. Asian countries, he declared, must "have their own policies in world affairs" and an independent "political, social and economic struc-ture." The prime minister designate asserted again Asia's affinity with Africa as fellow colonized peoples fighting for national independence.[82] As a sovereign Asian nation-state, India was to have no part in helping the capitalist West in its suppression of communist and other radical nation-alist movements in Southeast Asia, which Nehru saw not as malicious expansion of the Soviet empire but as legitimate nationalist struggles.[83] These strategies were to form the core of a nonaligned movement that Nehru pioneered in order to project India as the true champion of a decolonizing Asia.[84]

Nehru's radical tone alarmed the GMD, whose Pan-Asianist affinities with India were strained by its involvement in the US-led international system. Even during the Pacific War, the GMD had concluded that its interests were best served by being aligned with Washington. Just months

[80] Nehru, "India's Day of Reckoning," in *The Oxford India Nehru* (New Delhi: Oxford University Press, 2007), 501.
[81] Nehru, "India in the World," in *Oxford India Nehru*, 479–85.
[82] Nehru, "A United Asia," in *Oxford India Nehru*, 512–13.
[83] Nehru, "Basic Principles," in *Oxford India Nehru*, 520.
[84] Mark Mazower, *No Enchanted Palace: The End of Empire and the Ideological Origins of the United Nations* (Princeton, NJ: Princeton University Press, 2009), 167–80.

after China managed to persuade the United States and Britain to replace the infamous "unequal treaties" with new treaties in 1943, Chiang told one of his negotiators that "not only would we not dread U.S. hegemony (*chengba*) over East Asia in the next thirty years, we only feared that the U.S. would refrain from seeking such hegemony."[85] Nanjing was also frustrated that Tibet, over whose sovereignty Dai and Tan engaged in claiming, was invited to send a delegation to the Asian Relations Conference. In an article written for the GMD headquarters, Dai argued that while Nationalist China could not afford to simply turn down Nehru's invitation, it should send a delegation of academics and avoid commenting on anything of substance like international relations because "China's position was different" to India as far as Europe and the United States were concerned.[86] These individuals, comprised of Tan and figures associated with Dai through the New Asia Society, the Sino–Indian Cultural Society or the Examination Yuan, were sent as a subtle snub to Nehru's plea for Third World solidarity. When Tan suggested – apparently doing nothing more than echoing the Sino–Indian Cultural Society – that an All Asia Cultural Association should be set up to promote Asian culture and world peace, he was lampooning "our fashionable socialist friends," to which Nehru probably belonged, and their vision of social change.[87] Tan did suggest in another article written not for the conference but for a magazine that an "Asia Union," with the multiethnic British outpost Singapore as its capital, be formed. But that Asia Union, as part of the Great World Union (*datong*), would be bound by nothing but amity, mutual help and self-sacrifice to offset the self-interest that energized imperialism, including that of Soviet Russia.[88] Tan was quick to assure that his musing on a post-national order was not intended to upset the status quo or "existing powers and interests."[89] The apparently ambitious proposal for global and Asian unity, which under another set of circumstances played a pioneering role in mediating between the two nationalist movements of China and India, marked the parting of ways between the GMD's staunch anticommunism and Nehruvian India's left nationalism in the emerging Cold War order.

As part of Visva-Bharati, Cheena Bhavana, along with the India chapter of the Sino–Indian Cultural Society, survived the financial fallout of the

---

[85] Chiang, *Aiji chugao* [*Preliminary Draft of the Record of Compassion*], April 16, 1943, vol. 3, Chiang Kai-shek Collection, 002060200018006, Academia Historica.

[86] Dai, "Dui Yindu Nehelu faqi zhaoji fan-Ya huiyi zhi ganxiang [Thoughts on Nehru's Convening of the Asia Relations Conference]," in *DJTXSWC*, 386–7.

[87] Tan, *Inter-Asian Cultural Co-operation and Union of Asia* (Santiniketan: The Sino–Indian Cultural Society in India, 1949), 6–9.

[88] Ibid., 14–19.   [89] Ibid., 18.

GMD's demise in mainland China. The China chapter, however, was liquidated and its assets, including the funds raised in 1943 in support of India's famine relief efforts, were transferred to Visva-Bharati.[90] By the early 1950s, the once wartime allies descended into full-blown Cold War rhetoric. Zhu Jiahua, a former chair of the Sino–Indian Cultural Society in China who in 1942 pleaded with Gandhi for India to work together with China to realize Asia's renaissance (*fuxing*), now lambasted Nehru for his compromising attitude toward Mao Zedong and appeasement of Soviet Russia.[91] At about the same time, the principal of Cheena Bhavana made a remarkable shift of allegiance from the GMD to the People's Republic. In 1956, Tan visited Communist China with his daughter on Zhou Enlai's invitation and was feted in Beijing by Mao Zedong. One year after, Tan welcomed the Communist premier to Cheena Bhavana and received a one-off donation from Beijing.[92] The symbolic donation, which afforded a veneer of continuity in Sino–Indian relations, could not hide the fact that the school was no longer the front organization for important and clandestine interactions between a China under Japanese imperialist assault and an India still searching for its own nation-state. It also marked the fact that the Pan-Asianist idealism that Tagore and Tan represented was no longer compatible with the internationalist agendas of either independent India or Maoist China.

It was unsurprising that the romantic longing for a unified Asia based on moral and cultural values was no blueprint for effective political action. The Pan-Asianism that brought the GMD, Tan and Indian nationalists together was based on lofty ideals and common enemies – the West in all its myriad guises – but few concrete goals. Like how the conservative revolution appealed to nonpartisan reformers, visions of national vitality, moral certitude and social harmony were proffered to an elite wary of challenges to hierarchy, order and good sense. Tan emphasized numerous times that he cared about nothing but culture, even when he made interventions in political developments. This seemingly contradictory claim suggested not that Tan – or, for that matter, Zhu Guangqian's apparently apolitical support for Chiang – was disingenuous but that his involvement in state affairs and vision of Asia was not tainted by concern for particular nations or social groups. In other words, Tan's Asia entailed an aesthetical unity – in the Kantian sense of a complete disregard of interest – that had little or no bearing on social

[90] Tan, *Twenty Years of the Visva-Bharati Cheena-Bhavana*, 50.
[91] Zhu Jiahua to Mahatma Gandhi, July 31, 1942; *Zhonghua ribao* (China Daily News, Taipei), November 22, 1951, Zhu Jiahua Collection, 301–01-18–033, IMH Archives.
[92] Tan, *Twenty Years of the Visva-Bharati Cheena-Bhavana*, 50.

relations and power structures.[93] The substitution of cultural imagination for the contest of socioeconomic interests through political action explained why Pan-Asianists and liberals in China and abroad could endorse the GMD without agreeing fully with its ideological platform or behaviors in government. In fact, the Nationalists, as soon as they assumed state power in 1927 and more so when it was fighting Japan, were keen to present their program as beyond the political fray compared with their domestic and foreign rivals. They claimed to transcend Communist class warfare and any sectarian interests that drove mass protestors and the expansionist greed that characterized Soviet internationalism and Japanese nationalism.

The pitfalls of this disinterested aesthetics were succinctly revealed by philosopher Karatani Kojin in his analysis of the ambiguous relationship between many Japanese intellectuals and the Shôwa state's expansionism during the Pacific War. Reading wartime figures like Yasuda Yojûrô and Nishida Kitarô, whose intellectual genealogy could be traced to the great Pan-Asianist Okakura Tenshin, Karatani observes how romantic disinterestedness negated the need to tackle social contradictions as they were deemed to have been sublated a priori in one's consciousness. This procedure allowed Yasuda, Nishida and others to jettison concrete political programs and simply entrust their desires for a conflict-free human order to the state and its objectives. Japan's Greater Asia Co-prosperity Sphere was hence idealized and celebrated as having transcended both the capitalist nation-state and Soviet internationalism.[94]

Tan and Tagore, to be sure, had no illusions about Japan's continental ambitions. Yet their call for Asia's spiritual unity and disdain for any consideration of interest resulted in a politics that dovetailed nicely with the GMD's conservative revolution of everyday aesthetics as the party actively oppressed any "materialist" challenge to the social-political hierarchy. Prasenjit Duara observes that regimes of authenticity and idealizations of cultural essences such as Pan-Asianism were expressions of alternative conceptions of time, history and collective identity that coexisted with and challenged the abstract and linear time of capitalist modernity. Yet it is precisely their posture of transcendent existence vis-à-vis capitalist modernity that prevented them from actively engaging with the contradictions of capitalist modernity.[95] Refusing to adopt a politics that confronted social relations and material exploitation

---

[93] Terry Eagleton, *Ideology of the Aesthetic* (Oxford: Basil Blackwell, 1990), 97–8.
[94] Karatani Kojin, "Overcoming Modernity," in *Contemporary Japanese Thought*, ed. Richard Calichman (New York: Columbia University Press, 2005), 106–14.
[95] Prasenjit Duara, *Sovereignty and Authenticity: Manchukuo and the East Asian Modern* (Lanham, MD: Rowman and Littlefield, 2003), 26–8.

Figure 6.1 Tan Yunshan in Gandhian cap and *khadi*, 1931

underpinned by capitalism, Pan-Asianist ideologies, whether they originated from India, China or Japan, were volatile and resulted either in
religious withdrawal from the concrete injustices of the world or in co-
option by the reactionary politics of Nationalist China and Shôwa Japan.
Reading Tagore's paean to Chiang Kai-shek cited in the beginning of this
chapter and Tan's pledge that his proposal of Asia Union would accom-
modate US-dominated geopolitical configurations, one cannot help but
feel the hollowness in their denunciation of modern imperialist violence.

Figure 6.2 Tan Yunshan welcoming Song Meiling and Chiang Kai-shek to Cheena Bhavana, 1942

Figure 6.3 Tan Yunshan welcoming Zhou Enlai to Cheena Bhavana, 1957

For the GMD, the key contradiction dooming China's Pan-Asianism was the party-state's increasing inability to balance its sympathy for anti-imperialist movements and involvement in the international system that, in many ways, continued interwar arrangements. Since the Pearl Harbor attack, Nationalist China had become a part of the very order, led by the United States and Britain, that many conservative revolutionaries believed to be manifestly unjust, unaccountable to nationalist aspirations and an object to overcome in a global total war. Domestically, Nationalists could retain its revolutionary identity by putting the economy and social relations aside and applying mass mobilization on culture, habits and everyday aesthetics. The conservative revolution, after all, was designed to leave economic development to gradual, expert management while making the nation a realm of beauty and harmony to which the masses were enjoined to contribute by reforming their own lives. With ending Western domination as its main feature, however, it was much harder to reconcile Pan-Asianism with an Anglo-American world order, especially when Nehru's nonalignment posture offered India as a more compelling example of an independent Asian nation-state for other societies undergoing decolonization. As the Nationalist regime submitted itself fully to the US imperium during the Cold War, the conservative revolution survived in a diminished form, focused on social mobilization but reducing its universal ambitions from pursuing *datong* to overthrowing communism.

Epilogue

The Nationalist Party, as of the time of writing, is still an active political force. Driven out of power by Chinese Communist forces in 1949, Chiang Kai-shek's government decamped to Taiwan, onto which it held, thanks to US military protection. In many ways, the conservative revolution – adoration of national traditions, reform of everyday habits and sentiments, mass mobilization with a view to consolidating social order – enjoyed a new lease on life in the former Japanese colony. Anticommunism, which begot the conservative revolution in the 1920s, remained the party's main mission. With the Soviet Union and its alleged Chinese puppets taking Japan's place as existential threats, the GMD extended the total war well into the 1950s, whereby the island's population was enjoined to contribute to an all-frontal struggle against Communists governing from Beijing or operating under cover in Taiwan. Yet it was obvious that elements of the conservative revolution were never to be recovered. First, the promise to bring about a non-Western-dominated global order was abandoned as participation in the US-led global crusade against communism became imperative. Concomitantly, the ambition to overcome capitalist competition and dehumanization gave way to the far more conventional goal of building a managerial, welfarist society.

The most obvious continuity between GMD rule in 1950s Taiwan and that in Republican China was anticommunism. As in the time when the Nationalists governed the mainland, citizens were told that a wholesome, harmonious national community was an unattainable dream without purging malcontents who preached equality in class and gender relations. State-controlled media pedaled a Manichean worldview dividing innocent people loyal to the GMD from wicked operatives loyal to Beijing or Moscow.

Newspapers and novels tapped into charges of promiscuity and thuggery that had been attributed to Communists since the April 12 coup in 1927. Chinese Communist apparatchiks allegedly relished gory torture rituals and sadistic domination of women or garnered their own sexual appeal to curry favor from male cadres. Much like how citizens were supposed to identify potential Japanese infiltrators living in their midst during the resistance war, Nationalist authorities required that Taiwanese society be on guard against an internal enemy constantly lurking beneath everyday normalcy. Fear that Communists had penetrated schools and national and local assemblies, the military and even the security service compelled neighbors and colleagues to spy on one another. Since even the most exemplary Nationalist citizens could be "bandits" in disguise, one's clothes, words, public comportment and financial situation must come under scrutiny.[1] The same mélange of sexual licentiousness, inhuman cruelty and organizational sleekness formed the omnipresent Communist threat to a state that confronted not only a rising military power in Beijing but also a wary exile community from mainland China and a disaffected local population in Taiwan.

The conservative revolution's ideological underpinnings were rehashed. In *Basic Treatise on Anti-Communism and Resistance against Russia* (*Fan'gong kangE jiben lun*), Chiang reiterated the same themes that characterized an earlier movement born out of fear over internation-alist class struggle and disdain for liberal capitalism. Party reform (*gaizao*) from 1950 to 1952 sidelined the CC Clique to make way for figures not associated with factions active on the mainland, particularly Chen Cheng (1897–1965) and Chiang Ching-kuo (1910–88). Dai Jitao, the doyen of Sun's revolutionary thought, reportedly killed himself in February 1949 out of desperation over the impending Communist victory. The conservative revolutionaries who provided the initial theoretical ammunition against the Communists were displaced. Yet Chiang inher-ited the theoretical enterprise of Dai and Chen Lifu. He alluded to Chen's *Vitalism* in refuting historical materialism, postulating that all matters were constellations of dynamic elements. Since humans were not static material beings, a valid intervention into historical evolution must be a holistic project based on the *minsheng* principle rather than privileging material needs and launching class-based economic struggles.[2]

[1] Zeng Xunhui [Tseng Hsun-hui], "Shuxie 'yiji': wuling niandai baise kongbu shiqi 'feidie' zhi xiangzheng fenxi [Writing the 'Other': The Construction of 'Bandit Spies' under White Terror in the 1950s]," *Danjiang renwen shehui xuekan*, no. 5 (2000): 135–47; Zhang Shiying, "Suzhu kongju: 1950 niandai chuqi Taiwan zhengzhi manhua de fengge [Appealing to Fear: Political Cartoon in Early 1950s Taiwan]," in *Liang'an fenzhi: xueshu jianzhi, tuxiang xuanchuan yu zuqun zhengzhi (1945–2000)*, ed. Yu Minling (Taipei: Institute of Modern History, Academia Sinica, 2012), 139–200.

[2] Chiang Kai-shek, *Fan'gong kangE jiben lun* (Taipei: Zhongyang wenwu gongyingshe, 1955; Taipei: Zhongguo Guomindang zhongyang weiyuan hui dangshi wenyuan hui, 1984), chap. 5 (page citations are to the reprint edition).

To highlight aesthetic uplift in the revolutionary enterprise, Chiang also codified Dai Jitao's idealist interpretation of Sun Yat-sen's *minsheng* principle, asserting that morality and people's intelligence were just as important as regulating capital and rationalizing landownership in realizing social utopia. Two "supplementary" chapters to *The Three People's Principles* committed the GMD to a socialism distinct from the Communists': promising equality without "pauperiz[ing] the rich" and a range of everyday benefits from music, films and instruction in Chinese boxing and dancing to urban parks, public cemeteries and mass education.[3] With their occasional nods to the Confucian scholar-gentry ideals and strident anticommunism, the 1953 additions to the Sunist canon re-brandished the nation as an ameliorative agent on poverty, uneven development and confusing social changes attendant to capitalism.

The party's class politics was rearticulated, again in order to differentiate between the movement Sun found and its nemesis now governing from Beijing. The party's national revolution (*minzu geming*) and "peaceful reform of economy and society" were juxtaposed against Communist class struggle and armed usurpation of the state. Land reform, pioneered by Taiwan governor Chen Cheng (1897–1965) in the spring of 1949, distributed land the state acquired from the Japan colonizers and landlords to peasants without revolutionary violence. This exercise, which encountered great resistance from the Taiwanese landlords and their mainland counterparts who fled to the island with Chiang, was the GMD's answer to the mobilization of the peasantry in mainland China and the general attraction communism held for the people of Taiwan.[4] As part of the party's reform from 1950 to 1952, the GMD defined clearly that its constituents included youths, intellectuals, peasants, workers and "ordinary producers" (*yiban shengchan zhe*). The corporatist vision that underlined this characterization was the same core ideal of conservative revolutionaries carried over from the earliest agitations against Chinese Communists.

Total war mobilization, just as former Lixingshe affiliate Ru Chunpu anticipated, became the norm as the Nationalists presided over a permanent state of emergency under the anti-Communist, anti-Soviet banner. Civil liberties enshrined in the 1947 constitution were replaced by repressive "temporary articles" (*linshi tiaokuan*) that lasted forty-three

---

[3] Sun, *San Min Chu I*, 213–329.
[4] Liu Jinqing, *Taiwan zhanhou jinji fenxi* [*Taiwan Postwar Economic Analysis*], revised edn. (Taipei: Renjian chubanshe, 2012), 83–9; Wan-wen Chu, "Taiwan jingji qiji de Zhongguo beijing: chaoke fenduan tizhi jingji shi de mangdian [The China Factor in Taiwan's Economic Miracle]," *Taiwan shehui yanjiu jikan*, no. 74 (2009): 60–2.

years, during which the president enjoyed increasing power. Everyday culture and social relationships came to be shaped by actual and imaginary existential threats: Communist armed forces from across the Taiwan Strait and an even murkier communist threat at home. The vocabulary of military campaigns – strategy (*zhanlüe*), tactic (*zhanshu*), front (*zhanxian*) – guided the party-state's engagement with the populace.

Cadres and the masses were to treat duties in normal times (*pingshi de gongzuo*) no differently than duties in wartime (*zhanshi de gongzuo*).[5] The new total mobilization campaign entreated citizens to be foot soldiers in the struggle to ensure the nation's survival. Hygienic practices and military training in schools gained renewed currency along with a robustly enforced household registration system to ensure the strength and political reliability of the state's "human resources" (*renli*).[6]

The GMD's unique take on vanguardism continued to be relevant. The masses were not to be passive onlookers but active contributors to the struggle against Mao Zedong and Zhu De. Cadres were told that the National Spiritual Mobilization and New Life Movements were mighty weapons against communism and had contemporary relevance.[7] On February 1, 1952, Chiang Kai-shek inaugurated the Anti-Communism and Resist Russia Mobilization Movement (*Fan'gong kangE zong dongyuan yundong*). The movement followed on the heels of the GMD's reorganization plan launched in 1950 that streamlined the leadership, eliminated factions and integrated the party hierarchy with state institutions and mass organizations. Modeling on the wartime campaign, party cadres attempted once again to ramp up popular enthusiasm for a life-and-death conflict with an external enemy that hinged not only on military might but also on cultural consciousness and lifestyle. In a pronouncement that would not have been out of place in 1940s China, Chiang demanded that military, economic and political reforms be broadened into a program that aimed for an overhaul of sociocultural life. Punning on the character *dong*, cadres were reminded that mobilization (*dongyuan*) must not only be an imposition by state and party institutions but also spontaneous actions (*dong*) individuals took to reshape everyday life. Only by transforming social mores could revolutionary

---

[5] Chiang, "Chongjian geming jiben zuzhi, cejin fan'gong geming yundong de minyun fangzhen [Our party's Directions in Rebuilding Fundamental Revolutionary Organizations and Launching a Revolution of Counter-attack through Popular Movement]," *Xian zongtong Jiang gong sixiang yanlun zongji*, 25:371.

[6] Chiang, "Sishi niandu xingzheng gongzuo de jiangping ji sishiyi niandu shizheng zhongxin de zhishi [Commentary on the Work of the Government in 1951 and Instructions on Core Policy Implementation in 1952]," *Xian zongtong Jiang gong sixiang yanlun zongji*, 24:289.

[7] Chiang, "Weishei er zhan weihe er zhan [Whom Do We Fight For and Why]," *Xian zongtong Jiang gong sixiang yanlun zongji*, 24:99–100.

cadres hope to rally the masses behind in defeating Communism. If a party "could not even mobilize a few hundred or a thousand people a day," Chiang asked, "it is no wonder that others do not see us as a nation-state, let alone a modern one." Like Dai Jitao more than twenty years before, Chiang insisted that the GMD, in rejecting communism, must not throw the baby out with the bathwater by turning against mass politics.[8]

Citizens were pigeonholed into mass organizations based on occupation, age and gender, ensuring that the working class did not develop autonomous political agency. Students joined the China Anti-Communist Youth Corps (*Zhongguo qingnian fan'gong jiuguo tuan*), headed by Chiang Kai-shek's son Ching-kuo. Hailed as the vanguard of the nation, young people were challenged to relive moments of revolutionary triumph, particularly the Northern Expedition and the resistance against Japan, and herald the GMD's glorious return to power on the mainland. They were to learn revolutionary discipline, submit themselves to productive labor and anticipate a reign of cooperation and service. As in scouting, a propensity to battle (*zhandou xing*) was not professionalism confined to the military but part and parcel of cultural remaking to detoxify society from the human lust, material desires and class animosity unleashed by communism. In fact, Chiang stated clearly that scouting was the adolescent equivalent of military training.[9] The anti-Communist and anti-Soviet movement was genuinely total in two senses: first, it aspired to transformation in society's military, political, economic and cultural constitution; second, under the leadership of GMD revolutionary cadres, the entire populace was to *live* the revolution, whether it meant joining a sanctioned union or women's association, informing against a neighbor or submitting individual freedom to collective dictates.

The movement's multimedia presence ensured that the resurrected conservative revolution made an impact on the popular psyche, connecting with consumers of both high culture and more popular varieties. Rituals carried over from Chongqing, such as monthly ceremonies of lectures, meetings and pledges, encouraged a scripted form of grassroots

[8] Chiang, "Sishi niandu xingzheng gongzuo de jiangping ji sishiyi niandu shizheng zhongxin de zhishi," 24:289; Chiang, "Chongjian geming jiben zuzhi, cejin fan'gong geming yundong de minyun fangzhen," 25:366.
[9] Chiang, "Sishi niandu xingzheng gongzuo de jiangping ji sishiyi niandu shizheng zhongxin de zhishi," 24:286–9; Chiang, "Zhongguo qingnian fan Gong jiuguo tuan chengli dahui jiangci [Speech at the Inauguration Ceremony of the China Anti-Communist Youth Corps]," *Xian zongtong Jiang gong sixiang yanlun zongji*, 25:173–6; *Fan'gong KangE zong dongyuan yundong gangling* [*Guiding Principles of the Anti-Communist and Resist Russia Mobilization Movement*], in *Zhonghuo minguo zhengzhi fazhan shi*, eds. Qin Xiaoyi et al. (Taipei: Jindai Zhongguo chubanshe, 1985), 4:1640–2; Sun, *Sanmin zhuyi*, 45.

political expression in factories, schools and rural communities. Another state-sponsored mode of cultural production, one that combined propaganda and entertainment, included film, literature and art. Examples of this aesthetic paradigm in popular music provided contrast and variety to the liturgy and catechism at mobilization monthly assemblies (*dongyuan yuehui*). Mass-circulating songs like "Mao the Mongrel Put People in Jeopardy" (*Mao zazhong hairen zhen buqing*) and "The Communist Party Has No Conscience" (*Gongchandang wu tianliang*) tapped into vernacular anticommunist discourse in their graphic and brash language. Mao "treated young people like cannon fodder" and his military adventurism "left corpses piling up like a mountain."[10] Others capitalized on the emotional distress of mainland émigrés wrenched from their homeland. Taking the form of a folk ballad, "Selling Dumplings" (*Mai jiaozi*) told the sentimental encounter between a seventeen-year-old girl making ends meet by selling the iconic northern Chinese staple and a customer who also hailed from Manchuria. In stylized northeastern Mandarin, the dumpling seller told her compatriot that she missed her class struggle–ravaged hometown. The poignant sentimentality of two exiles stranded on an unfamiliar subtropical island then gave way abruptly to combative hatred:

FEMALE SINGER: When will Communist bandits in my hometown all die out so that we can return to the Northeast (*dongbei*) and spend a peaceful spring festival?
MALE SINGER: Be patient, young girl!
TOGETHER: Let's come together, reconquer the mainland, and return home in triumph![11]

Appeal to northerners' homesickness was balanced by the trumpeting of ambivalent enthusiasm for the new, albeit temporary, Nationalist base. "The Great Alishan" (*Weiwei Alishan*) called upon loyal Nationalists to regroup on the Pacific Ocean–facing mountain range in Taiwan and look forward to the day when they would cross over the ocean to southern China, reoccupy the Yangzi in triumph and camp around the Yellow River.[12] Still others alluded directly to the historical precedent of anti-Communist total mobilization. Chen Lifu's lyrics for "Spiritual Mobilization" (*Jingshen dongyuan*) hailed the supremacy of the state and the nation, called for the prioritization of the military and pressed for the concentration of will and power.[13] Finally, some songs

---

[10] Li Liquan and Cheng Qiheng, *Fan'gong kangE gequ yibai shou* [*A Hundred Anti-Communist and Resist Russia Songs*], 2nd edn. (Taichung: Taiwan sheng xinwen chu, 1953), 24, 34.
[11] Ibid., 122.   [12] Ibid., 91.   [13] Ibid., 85.

exhibited the familiar tendency to imbue violence with pleasure. In "Recapture the Mainland Rhapsody" (*Fan'gong dalu kuangwu qu*), excitement flowed from vows like "Charge, good men!," "Capture Mao Zedong live!" and "Work with the armed forces, defeat Stalin, and target your artillery at Moscow!"[14] Like drama performances, movie screenings and mass gatherings aimed at mobilizing the populace against Japan a decade ago, the diverse tropes and registers anti-Communist songs employed attested to a total war paradigm catering to a GMD loyalist community with diverse linguistic backgrounds, an ambivalent relationship with its adopted society and a deep nostalgia for a land to which many would never return.

Despite joining the US-led capitalist camp, the GMD retained its suspicion, common among interwar right-wing regimes, of the liberal order. In Western countries, President Chiang complained, democracy empowered the people at the expense of the government. In a country faced with grave foreign threats like China, democracy must empower the people and the state alike. One area in which the state's command manifested itself was in its commitment to guided capitalism. The GMD vowed to resume a modernization program that curbed monopoly capital (*longduan ziben*) in favor of state-owned enterprises, redistributed landownership to tillers and developed consumers' cooperatives to eliminate predatory mercantile interests. Finally, the world-historical significance of China's conservative revolution was reaffirmed. The GMD was keen to remind Chinese nationalists of its Pan-Asianist credentials, justifying Taipei's cooperation with former Euro-American colonizers as a contribution to Asia's collective security and world peace. Identifying the Soviet Union as the latest installment of the czarist empire trampling over China's independence and freedom, Chiang presented his subordination under the Western capitalist camp as a strategy to recover China's and Asia's political independence from Communist imperialism.[15] With not a shred of irony, the nationalist goals envisioned as responses to the semicolonization of China were now underwritten by the country's submission to the American imperium.

The conservative revolution's core ambitions, however, were diminished if not demolished. The GMD's nationalism and anticipation of a postcapitalist global community based on Asian spirituality were compromised by Taipei's subservient role under the US informal empire. The tension between its anticolonial Asianism and participation in the Western-led international system began during the Pacific War. Yet total political and economic dependence on the United States and the

---

[14] Ibid., 20.   [15] Chiang, *Fan'gong kangE jiben lun*, 54, 59–70.

anticommunist "liberal democratic" (*ziyou minzhu*) camp it led was new. Through the 1950s, it was Communist China that developed close relationships with newly decolonized Asian countries, particularly India. Sun Yat-sen's *minsheng* principle, which Dai Jitao and Chen Lifu touted as prophetic insights that overcame capitalist and communist competition and materialism, became under Chen Cheng a more modest state-led developmentalist undertaking inspired by the policies of the British Labour Party. The GMD's industrialization program was carried out under powerful American advisers stationed at almost every branch of Nationalist government and industry, not to mention being fueled by financial aid from Washington. Presidents Truman and Eisenhower's military Keynesianism conspired with Chiang's state capitalism to create an economy that thwarted the spread of communism on one hand and departed from the US obsession with free flow of capital and goods on the other.[16] The price the GMD paid for regime survival was the conservative revolution's *raison d'être* – the nation's political and economic independence and its ability to reform capitalism.

As I was wrapping up this study, the interwar radical right made a major comeback in the public consciousness. Since the unexpected ascendency of the Mussolini-citing Donald Trump in 2016, historians and laypeople alike have wondered aloud in popular media outlets if the politics of 1930s Germany and Italy presaged the style and substance of the forty-fifth US president. Commentators juggled with different terms to describe the anti-liberal populist: authoritarian, reactionary, demagogic and, most controversially, fascist. They might disagree on how to characterize the real estate magnate-turned-politician, but features once thought to have been relegated to the fringes of Euro-American societies – radical nationalism, permanent state of emergency, dirigisme, challenging the liberal international order – suddenly became mainstream again in the second decade of the twentieth-first century. The point, as a prominent expert on Nazi Germany remarked, was not so much to pin down definitely Trump's nature as to leverage our knowledge of twentieth-century Europe to comprehend the drama unfolding at the very heart of the "free world."[17]

---

[16] Nick Cullather, "'Fuel for the Good Dragon': The United States and Industrial Policy in Taiwan, 1950–1965," in *Empire and Revolution: The United States and the Third World since 1945*, eds. Peter Hahn and Mary Ann Heiss (Columbus: Ohio State University Press, 2001), 246–50; Chu, "Taiwan jingji qiji de Zhongguo beijing," 57.

[17] Jane Caplan, "Trump and Fascism: A View from the Past," *History Workshop Online*, www.historyworkshop.org.uk/trump-and-fascism-a-view-from-the-past/ (accessed July 15, 2017).

This book makes the case that trends prevalent in the interwar world are critical to understanding the Nationalist project and Chinese revolutionary history. It acknowledges that the GMD insisted on its revolutionary credentials but complicates this claim by showing that its social goals were conservative. Single-minded devotion to the nation, social hierarchy, production and inter-class cooperation undergirded a state managed by professional mass mobilizers. The backdrop to this agenda, as theoreticians like Dai Jitao, Hu Hanmin, Li Shizeng and Chen Lifu reckoned, was a heightened sense of both danger and optimism. The Chinese nation, long encroached upon by a myriad of imperialist powers, faced an existential crisis. The liberal international order, shaken by the Great War, was challenged by German and Italian nationalist aspirations. Japanese militarists were baring their teeth and, despite unease on the part of Western powers, making advances onto China. The "independence" of Manchukuo went ahead despite nonrecognition by the League of Nations. A world war between nation-states was inevitable and the state must prepare the citizenry for this eventuality. With the Republic's survival on the line, class struggle and communism were at best frivolities of urban intellectuals deracinated from their native culture if not acts of treason at Soviet imperialist behest. At the same time, however, the anticipated demise of the post-Versailles peace presented ample opportunities for nation-building. Human competition for material interests – whether under the guise of capitalism, class struggle or imperialism – proved unsustainable. Replacing it was a cooperative realm, inspired by Eastern cultural traditions and crystallized in Sun's *minsheng* doctrine, in which each nation's social pecking order was revered by a contented, hardworking populace. The GMD's mass organizations provided channels for citizens to express themselves, contribute to and partake in the comraderies of nationhood. China's solidarity with India evinced a shift of humanity's ethical might to Asia, and the two countries' emergence as nation-states ended colonial domination. The nation was to fully realize its potential as a custodian of production and an object of reverence. The vanguard party, staffed by prophets versed in the Three People's Principles, would lead the people and deliver them from the horror of capitalist imperialism, class warfare and senseless economic competition.

Aside from the liberal international order, the GMD, perhaps even more so than radical right movements abroad, structured its politics around reactions to global communism and the Chinese Communist experiment. Antagonistic class politics, tolerated if not endorsed under the united front Sun forged, was seen as a symptom of youth impertinence, a threat to economic development and a menace sapping the nation's vitality. The conservative revolution did not put the genie of mass politics back into the bottle but attempted to divert it from challenging socioeconomic arrangements. It aimed to energize but not empower the masses. It enjoined the people to take part in mass events but denied them political agency. It promised to revamp social life but kept social revolution at bay. The purge of April 1927, carried out mostly by the Green Gang, did not leverage mass zeal against Chinese Communists and trade unionists. It was not a March on Rome; the GMD radical right's usurpation of state power was not driven by populist angst against the establishment. Yet conservative revolutionaries were keen to stress their organic relationship with the people. GMD cadres were not to sit comfortably behind desks and allocate resources; they were to get their hands dirty rallying the multitude. Scouting and total war mobilization represented alternatives to Communist class politics. Their goal was to disabuse the people of "materialist" fantasies and provide aesthetic, spiritual uplift, which took center stage in Dai Jitao's extension of Sun's *minsheng* doctrine. GMD mass politics disarmed the populace by reasserting discipline and hierarchy. The people were instructed to sync their lifestyle with the needs of twentieth-century production and warfare. Rallies, drama troupes, film screenings and excursions provided spectacles for individuals to partake in in collective anguish and joy.

These superficial but at times emotionally intense experiences temporarily abstracted individuals from the production relations that mediated their everyday existence and directed sentiments toward the national community. The purpose was to impress social power on individuals' pieties, impulses and routines. This emphasis on the aesthetic, rather than structural, dimension of social life was also apparent in the GMD's attempt to forge an alternative to communist internationalism. Pan-Asianist courtship with Japan and India appealed to an anticolonialism, the main aim of which was to restore the fraternal elegance and sentimental harmony of human relationships. Class struggle was dismissed as a manifestation of "materialism," the same obsession with interest and instrumentalization of human interactions that propelled capitalism.

Although conservative revolutionaries were keenly aware of developments abroad and cited them as sources of inspiration, particularly Germany and Japan where the radical right was in ascendance, the GMD calibrated its ideology and practice in response to China's domestic circumstances. The *minsheng* program, touted as a return to Sun Yat-sen's original intentions, was deployed to justify the severance of ties with Chinese Communists but was vague enough to allow the GMD to earn consent from segments of civil society. This book has shown that the GMD enjoyed success co-opting liberals. The party-state tapped into scouting's emphasis on individual resourcefulness and Zhu Guangqian's psychological approach to alleviating social discontent. The GMD offered liberal educators and writers maintenance of order and cloistered, elevated existence vis-à-vis the rest of the populace. By contrast, Communists, many of them young and prone to violence, offered endless social strife. That Chinese Communists were seen as doing Soviet Russia's bidding was a further affront to liberals' patriotic sensibilities when the nation faced increasingly grave threats. More crucially, political structures aside, there was little to differentiate conservative revolutionaries from liberals on how the general citizenry should be managed. Both camps treasured hierarchal order and were deeply suspicious of class warfare. Liberals from Zhang Xiaoliang and Zhang Zhongren to Fu Sinian and Zhu Guangqian saw their role in relation to increasingly radical youths as a pastoral one. The Chinese masses were treated as citizens under training whose political agency had yet to be molded by an elite. It was not surprising that many liberals only withdrew consent from the GMD in the late 1940s, when conservative revolutionaries supplied neither social order nor nationalist credentials. Throughout this study, I point out areas – mass organizations, fascination with total war mobilization, promise to forge a third way between communism and capitalism, anticipation of the international system's demise – in which the GMD shared similarities with European and Japanese fascisms. These parallels were results not of China's adaptations of foreign models but of the GMD's responses to prevailing historical forces in the interwar global conjuncture.

   If conservative revolution sounds like a contradiction in terms, it is because there was genuine confusion at the heart of the GMD's project. The *minsheng* enterprise, with universal harmony as its ultimate goal, implied revolutionary transcendence of capitalist modernity. Yet the party was conservative in its maintenance of existing power relations. It promised to confront colonialism and Western epistemological dominance, but joined the US-led international order and eventually depended on it for survival. Cadres ministered to the *hoi polloi* to sustain the party's revolutionary, vanguardist identity; mass organizations featured prominently in the GMD's revolutionary strategy.

   Conservative revolutionaries, however, agreed with liberals that social vitality depended not on what structural changes the collective could bring but on how each and every individual disciplined their mind and body. It bears stressing that these apparent contradictions, by themselves, did not doom GMD rule but instead afforded the party room to maneuver vis-à-vis figures of other persuasions. Consistency was not the Nationalists' forte, yet they form the longest-surviving political party in the Chinese-speaking world. If there is anything to draw from China's conservative revolution in order to contemplate the scandal of a billionaire occupying the most powerful political office in the world by positioning himself as an antiestablishment firebrand, it is perhaps this.

Glossary of Selected Romanized Terms

A

ai	愛
anfen	安分
Aw Boon Haw	胡文虎

B

bade	八德
Bai Chongxi	白崇禧
baojia	保甲
Beida	北大
Beiping	北平
Beiyang	北洋
bing	病
bingjian zuozhan	並肩作戰
bo'ai	博愛
boduo	剝奪
Boxi	柏溪劇社

C

Cai Hesen	蔡和森
Cai Yuanpei	蔡元培
Cao Yu	曹禺
chedi chengqing	徹底澄清
chedi de gaizheng	徹底地改正
Chen Boda	陳伯達
Chen Cheng	陳誠
Chen Diaoyuan	陳調元
Chen Duxiu	陳獨秀

Chen Guofu	陳果夫
Chen Jiongming	陳炯明
Chen Jitang	陳濟棠
Chen Lifu	陳立夫
Chen Quan	陳銓
Chen Xiying	陳西瀅
Chenbao	晨報
cheng	誠
Cheng Zuyi	程祖彝
chengba	稱霸
Chengdu	成都
chengwei juwen	成為具文
chengyi	誠意
chi	恥
Chiang Ching-kuo	蔣經國
Chiang Kai-shek	蔣介石
chifei	赤匪
chihua	赤化
chongdong	衝動
chonggao xiongwei zhi gan	崇高雄偉之感
chouxiang yuqi	抽象語氣
Cixi	慈禧

D

Da gongbao	大公報
Da Riben zhuyi	大日本主義
dadao	打倒
Dai Jitao	戴季陶
daibiao	代表
danchun	單純
datong	大同
Daxue yuan	大學院
demokelaxi	德謨克拉西
diao bangzi	吊膀子
diketuiduo	狄克推多
Ding Wenjiang	丁文江
dipi liumang	地痞流氓
dong	動
Dongbei	東北
Dongfang minzu	東方民族

dongyuan yuehui	動員月會
douzheng	鬥爭
Du Yaquan	杜亞泉
Du Yuesheng	杜月笙
ducai zhe	獨裁者
duchong	蠹蟲
Duli pinglun	獨立評論
duzhan	獨佔

E

erxi	兒戲

F

Fan'gong dalu kuangwu qu	反攻大陸狂舞曲
Fan'gong kangE jiben lun	反共抗俄基本論
Fan'gong kangE zong dongyuan yundong	反共抗俄總動員運動
fandong fenzi	反動分子
fanmen	煩悶
feichang shiqi	非常時期
Feng Zikai	豐子愷
fenqi cuoza	分歧錯雜
fenrao	紛擾
fenzhi hezuo	分治合作
Fu Sinian	傅斯年
fuxing	復興

G

gan'gan jingjing de ren	乾乾淨淨的人
gang zhi tuanti	鋼之團體
gaohuang	膏肓
Gei qingnian de shi'er feng xin	給青年的十二封信
geming hua	革命化
Geming jun qi, geming dang xiao	革命軍起，革命黨消
geming yishi	革命意識
genben	根本
gesi qishi	各司其事
Gongchandang wu tianliang	共產黨無天良

gongde	公的
gongting geming	宮廷革命
gongtong shenghuo	共同生活
gongzuo	工作
Gu Jiegang	顧頡剛
guilü	規律
guizu hua	貴族化
Guo Moruo	郭沫若
Guo Taiqi	郭泰祺
guocui	國粹
Guofang zuigao weiyuanhui	國防最高委員會
Guofeng	國風
guojia	國家
guojia shiye	國家事業
guojia zhishang, minzu zhishang	國家至上，民族至上
Guomin da xiyuan	國民大戲院
guomin geming	國民革命
Guomin geming yu Zhongguo	
Guomindang	國民革命與中國國民黨
Guomin gongyue shici	國民公約誓詞
Guomin jingshen zong dongyuan yundong	國民精神總動員運動
guomin xing	國民性
Guomin yuehui	國民月會
guomin zong dongyuan	國民總動員
Guomindang	國民黨
guyou chuantong	固有傳統
guyou jingshen	固有精神

H

Haipai	海派
Han Yu	韓愈
hanjian	漢奸
he	和
He Lin	賀麟
He Yingqin	何應欽
Hechuan	合川
Hu Hanmin	胡漢民
Hu Menghua	胡夢華
Hu Shi	胡適
Hu Yuzhi	胡愈之

Huang Xianzhao	黃憲昭
Huang Xing	黃興
Huoshao hongliansi	火燒紅蓮寺

J

Jiang Lianchun	蔣廉淳
Jiang Tingfu	蔣廷黻
Jianguo dagang	建國大綱
jianshe de gongzuo	建設的工作
jianshe qilai	建設起來
jianshi de shenghuo jichu	堅實的生活基礎
jiaofei	剿匪
jiaohua/kyôka	教化
jiaoyu	教育
Jiaoyu zazhi	教育雜誌
jiduan de aiguo zhuyi zhe	極端的愛國主義者
jiefang	解放
jieji xing	階級性
jiezhi yuwang	節制慾望
jinchan tuoke	金蟬脫殼
jindai wenming	近代文明
Jingpai	京派
jingshen baolei	精神堡壘
jingshen dongyuan	精神動員
jingshen hutong	精神互通
jingshen jianshe	精神建設
jingshen liliang	精神力量
jisheng	寄生
jiushi jingshen	救世精神
Ju Zheng	居正
juewu	覺悟
jun guomin	軍國民
junguo zhuyi	軍國主義
junshi diyi, shengli diyi	軍事第一，勝利第一
Junshi weiyuanhui	軍事委員會

K

Kaiming	開明書店
kangzhan jianguo	抗戰建國

Kita Ikki	北 一輝
kongqian weixian qi	空前危險期
kongqian zhi huoju da youxing	空前之火炬大遊行
kongxiang lun	空想論
Konoe Fumimaro	近衛 文麿
Koxinga	鄭成功
Kuohu	括弧

L

le	樂
Lebao	叻報
Lei Haizong	雷海宗
li	禮
Li Pusheng	李樸生
Li Qifan	李啟藩
Li Shizeng	李石曾
lian	廉
Liang Qichao	梁啟超
Liang Shiqiu	梁實秋
Liang Shuming	梁漱溟
Liangyou huabao	良友畫報
lianhe zhanxian	聯合戰線
Lin Fengmian	林風眠
Lin Sen	林森
Lin Tongji	林同濟
lingxiu	領袖
linshi tiaokuan	臨時條款
liuyi	六藝
Lixingshe	力行社
longduan ziben	壟斷資本
Lu Xun	魯迅
lubu dang	盧布黨
lunchang	倫常
Luo Longji	羅隆基

M

Ma Chaojun	馬超俊
Mai jiaozi	賣餃子
maiguo pandang	賣國叛黨

mamu	麻木
Mao zazhong hairen zhen buqing	毛雜種害人真不輕
Mao Zedong	毛澤東
mei	美
Minbao	民報
minggen	命根
Minguo ribao	民國日報
Minseitô	民政党
minsheng zhuyi	民生主義
minzhi	民治
minzhong	民眾
minzhu zhuyi de jituan zhidu	民主主義的集團制度
minzu geming	民族革命
Minzu guoji	民族國際
Miyazaki Ryûsuke	宮崎 龍介
Miyazaki Toten	宮崎 滔天

N

ni	你
Nishida Kitarô	西田 幾多郎
nuoruo	懦弱

O

Okakura Tenshin	岡倉 天心
Ouzhan	歐戰

P

paita	排他
Pan Gongzhan	潘公展
peidu	陪都
pin'ge	品格
pingshi de gongzuo	平時的工作
Pu pai geming	普派革命

Q

qingdang	清黨
qingnian tuan/seinendan	青年團
Qingnian zhi lu	青年之路
qishi de yingxiong qigai	騎士的英雄氣概
qizhuang yifu	奇裝異服
Qu Jingbai	瞿景白
Qu Qiubai	瞿秋白
Quan minzu zhanzheng lun	全民族戰爭論
quanmin geming	全民革命
quanneng zhanzheng	全能戰爭
quanti	全體
quke	軀殼
qunchu	群處
qunzhong yundong	群眾運動

R

ren	仁
ren'ai heping	仁愛和平
renli	人力
rensheng de yishuhua	人生的藝術化
renxin taihuai	人心太壞
Riben lun	日本論
richang shenghuo	日常生活
rixing yishan	日行一善
Ru Chunpu	茹春浦

S

Sanmin zhuyi yu gongchan zhuyi	三民主義與共產主義
seqing kuang	色情狂
Shakai minshû tô	社会民主党
shan	善
shangren	商人
shangwu aiguo	尚武愛國
Shaonian bing	少年兵
shaonian de ehua	少年的惡化
Shaonian yiyong tuan	少年義勇團
Shehui xinwen	社會新聞

shehui zhuyi	社會主義
Shen Congwen	沈從文
Shen Zemin	沈澤民
Shenbao	申報
sheng de chongdong	生的衝動
shengcun de yuwang	生存的慾望
shengji	生機
shengming de jixie hua	生命的機械化
shengse huoli zhi zuisheng mengsi de shenghuo	聲色貨利之醉生夢死的生活
shengyu	生育
shengyuan	生元
shenqian	深潛
shi	十
shi	食
Shi Huangdi	始皇帝
Shi Jianqiao	施劍翹
shicha yuan	視察員
shichang ouxiang	市場偶像
shiji liyi	實際利益
shiji yundong	實際運動
shijie de jinbu sichao	世界的進步思潮
Shiyong	世鏞
side	私的
siling bu	司令部
siren xingwei	私人行為
Sixiang yu shidai	思想與時代
Song Bailian	宋百廉
Song Emperor Renzong	宋仁宗
Song Jiaoren	宋教仁
Song Meiling	宋美齡
Song Qingling	宋慶齡
Song Ziwen	宋子文
songsi	送死
suhua	俗化
suibian xiantan	隨便閒談
Sun Ke	孫科
Sun Wen zhuyi zhi zhexue de jichu	孫文主義之哲學的基礎
Sun Yat-sen	孫逸仙

T

Taixu	太虛
Tan Guofu	譚國輔
Tan lizhi	談立志
Tan mei	談美
Tan wenxue	談文學
Tan xiuyang	談修養
Tan Yunshan	譚雲山
Tan zhongxue sheng yu shehui yundong	談中學生與社會運動
Tang of Shang	商湯
Tao Baichuan	陶百川
taotai	淘汰
tianxia	天下
tianxing	天性
tongjun zhuren	童軍主任
tongyi sixiang	統一思想
tongzijun	童子軍
tuhao lieshen	土豪劣紳
tuibian	蛻變

W

Wang Jingwei	汪精衛
Wang Xinggong	王星拱
wangdao	王道
wanyir	玩意兒
Wei Ming	魏明
Weisheng lun	唯生論
Weiwei Alishan	巍巍阿里山
weixian de qunzhong xinli	危險的群眾心理
weiyuan	委員
wenhua	文化
wenhua shuizhun taidi	文化水準太低
wenming bing	文明病
wenyi zaidao	文以載道
woxin changdan	臥薪嘗膽
Wu Zetian	武則天
Wu Zhihui	吳稚暉
wurong huaiyi	無容懷疑
wushu	武術
wusuowei erwei de wansuo	無所為而為的玩索

wuzhi de jianshe	物質的建設
wuzhi wenti	物質問題

X

Xia Mianzun	夏丏尊
Xia Xi	夏曦
Xia Yan	夏衍
Xiandai pinglun	現代評論
xiangsheng	相聲
xiangyue	鄉約
xianzhi	先知
xiao	孝
xiao baixing	小百姓
xiao baobao	小寶寶
xiao zhi zhexue	笑之哲學
xiaoci	孝慈
xiaodui	小隊
xiaoxian wenxue	消閒文學
Xie Tianmin	謝天民
Xikang	西康
Xin qingnian	新青年
Xin shenghuo yundong gangyao	新生活運動綱要
xin shengming	新生命
Xin Yaxiya	新亞細亞
xinfeng	信奉
xing	行
xingfu de diwei	幸福的地位
Xingguang	星光
Xingshi	性史
xingshi zhuyi	形式主義
xinyang	信仰
xinyi	信義
xiongwei	雄偉
xitong	系統
xiyang hua	西洋化
Xu Zhimo	徐志摩
xuanchuan huaju	宣傳話劇
Xuanzang	玄奘
xueqi weiding	血氣未定

Y

Yan Jialin	嚴家麟
yangsheng	養生
yangyu	養育
yanku	嚴酷
Yanxi yu pingmin	演戲與平民
yapo	壓迫
Yasuda Yojûrô	保田 與重郎
Yazhou heqin hui/Ashû washinkai	亞洲和親會
Ye Chucang	葉楚傖
Ye meigui	野玫瑰
Ye Shengtao	葉聖陶
yi	衣
Yiban	一般
yiban shengchan zhe	一般生產者
yidang	異黨
yidang yipai	異黨異派
yidang zhiguo	以黨治國
Yindu zhouyou ji	印度周遊記
yingchou	應酬
yixiang	意象
yizhi jizhong, liliang jizhong	意志集中，力量集中
yizhi li	意志力
Yone Noguchi	野口 米次郎
you tongjun	幼童軍
you'ai	友愛
youjiti	有機體
youkou jiebei	有口皆碑
youmei	優美
youmei gaoshang de xiangle	優美高尚地的享樂
youqing bing	右傾病
youse renzhong	有色人種
youwu yu	有誤於
youzhi de lao guomin	幼稚的老國民
yu	育
Yu the Great	大禹
Yuan Shikai	袁世凱
Yue Fei	岳飛
yufang	預防

Yusi	語絲
yuyan wuhui	語言誤會
yuyong wenren	御用文人

Z

zhandouxing	戰鬥性
Zhang Ji	張繼
Zhang Jingsheng	張競生
Zhang Junmai	張君勱
Zhang Qinqiu	張琴秋
Zhang Qun	張群
Zhang Taiyan	章太炎
Zhang Xiaoliang	張效良
Zhang Xueliang	張學良
Zhang Zhenzhi	張振之
Zhang Zhongren	張忠仁
Zhang Zuolin	張作霖
Zhanguo ce	戰國策
zhanlüe	戰略
zhanshi fuwu tuan	戰時服務團
zhanshi gongzuo	戰時工作
zhanshu	戰術
zhanxian	戰線
zhen, shan, mei	真，善，美
zhengdang	政黨
zhengge de geming zhuyi	整個的革命主義
zhengke	政客
zhengxin	正心
zhi	知
zhigao de shan	至高的善
zhiye shenghuo	職業生活
zhong	忠
zhong le fengmo	中了瘋魔
Zhong Yin liangguo lianhe	中印兩國聯合
Zhongguo Guomindang tongzijun	中國國民黨童子軍
Zhongguo minzu de jingshen	中國民族的精神
Zhongguo qingnian fan'gong jiuguo tuan	中國青年反共救國團
Zhongguo tongzijun	中國童子軍
Zhongguo wei	中國味
Zhongguo wenhua fuwu she	中國文化服務社

Zhongguo xueyuan	中國學院
Zhonghua gongsuo	中華公所
Zhonghua tongzijun yanjiuhui	中華童子軍研究會
Zhongxue sheng	中學生
Zhongyang ban yuekan	中央半月刊
Zhongyang ribao	中央日報
Zhongyang xunlian tuan	中央訓練團
Zhongyang zhoukan	中央周刊
Zhou Enlai	周恩來
Zhou Wenqu	周文蘘
Zhou Yang	周揚
Zhou Zuoren	周作人
zhu	住
Zhu Guangqian	朱光潛
Zhu Guangshan	朱光潸
Zhu Hanjie	朱漢傑
Zhu Heqin	朱鶴琴
Zhu Jiahua	朱家驊
Zhu Ziqing	朱自清
zhuangmei	壯美
zhuanheng	專橫
zhuanzhi zhengti	專制政體
zhuyi	主義
zi	字
ziben jia	資本家
zixin li	自信力
ziyou minzhu	自由民主
ziyou ren	自由人
zizhi hui	自治會
zong ganshi	總幹事
zongyu	縱慾
Zou Lu	鄒魯
Zou Taofen	鄒韜奮
zui buman	最不滿
zuisheng mengsi	醉生夢死
zuoren de daoli	做人的道理
Zuozhuan	左傳

Bibliography

Public Archives and Manuscript Collections

Academia Historica, Taipei
Guangdong Provincial Archives, Guangzhou
Institute of Modern History Archives (IMH), Academia Sinica, Taipei
Kuomintang Party History Institute (Kuomintang Archives), Taipei
National Pingtung University of Educational Institutional Repository (NPUE), Pingtung City, Taiwan. Zhang Xiaoliang Papers. r.nptu.edu.tw/handle/987654321/1086
Nehru Memorial Museum and Library Archives (NMML), New Delhi
Second Historical Archives of China, Nanjing

Newspapers

Chenbao [*Shanghai Morning Post*], April 12, 1932–October 16, 1936
Dagong bao [*Ta Kung Pao*] (Hong Kong), May 2, 1939
Guangzhou Minguo ribao [*Guangzhou Republican Daily*], May 23, 1925
Lebao [*Lat Pau*] (Singapore), November 13, 1925
Zhongyang ribao [*Central Daily*], November 28, 1935–May 14, 1939

Published Sources (Books, Collections, Articles, Pamphlets)

Adorno, Theodor. *The Culture Industry: Selected Essays on Mass Culture.* 2nd edn. Edited by Jay M. Bernstein. London: Routledge, 2001.
Alitto, Guy S. *The Last Confucian: Liang Shu-ming and the Chinese Dilemma of Modernity.* 2nd edn. Berkeley: University of California Press, 1986.
Althusser, Louis and Étienne Balibar. *Reading Capital.* Translated by Ben Brewster. London: Verso, 1979.
Anderson, Perry. *Lineages of the Absolutist State.* London: New Left Books, 1974.

Antliff, Mark. "Classical Violence: Thierry Maulnier, French Fascist Aesthetics and the 1937 Paris World's Fair." *Modernism/modernity* 15 (2008): 45–62.

Arrighi, Giovanni. *The Long Twentieth Century: Money, Power, and the Origins of Our Times*. London: Verso, 1994.

Badiou, Alain. *The Century*. Translated by Alberto Toscano. Cambridge: Polity, 2007.

Badiou, Alain and Jean-Claude Milner. *Controversies: A Dialogue on the Politics and Philosophy of Our Times*. Cambridge: Polity, 2014.

Bauman, Zygmunt. *Modernity and the Holocaust*. Ithaca, NY: Cornell University Press, 1989.

Ben-Ghiat, Ruth. *Fascist Modernities: Italy, 1922–1945*. Berkeley: University of California Press, 2001.

Bezerin, Mabel. *Making the Fascist Self: The Political Culture of Interwar Italy*. Ithaca, NY: Cornell University Press, 1997.

"Biansheng tongxun [News from Frontier Provinces]." *Jingshen dongyuan*, no. 1 (1940): 50–84.

Bodenhorn, Terry. "Chen Lifu's Vitalism: A Guomindang Vision of Modernity circa 1934." In *Defining Modernity: Guomindang Rhetoric of a New China, 1920–1970*, ed. Terry Bodenhorn, 91–122. Ann Arbor: Center for Chinese Studies, University of Michigan, 2002.

Bramall, Chris. *Chinese Economic Development*. London: Routledge, 2009.

Burke, James. *My Father in China*. New York: Farrar and Rinehart, 1942.

Cao Yongfang. "Tongzijun sheying zhuanke jiangzuo [Special Lecture on Photography for Scouts]." *Zhongguo tongzijun* 2, no. 2 (1936): 14–16.

"Xin shenghuo yundong yu tongzijun xunlian [New Life Movement and Scout Training]." *Jiaoyuxue yuekan* 3, no. 4 (1936): 146–56.

Caplan, Jane. "Trump and Fascism. A View from the Past." *History Workshop Online*. www.historyworkshop.org.uk/trump-and-fascism-a-view-from-the-past/.

Chandra, Bipan. "The Indian National Movement: The Ideological Dimension." In *India's Struggle for Independence*, eds. Bipan Chandra, Mridula Mukherjee, Aditya Mukherjee, Sucheta Mahajan and K. N. Panikkar, 518–28. New Delhi: Penguin Books, 1989.

Chang, Maria Hsia. *The Chinese Blue Shirt Society: Fascism and Developmental Nationalism*. Berkeley: Institute of East Asian Studies, University of California, 1985.

Chang Wenbin. "1940 nian Chengdu 'qiangmi' you minbian zhuanhua wei zhengzhi shijian de kaocha [An Analysis of the Politicization of the Popular Uprising 1940 Chengdu 'Rice Riot']." *Xi'nan minzu daxue xuebao – renwen sheke ban* 26, no. 10 (2005): 254–8.

Chatterjee, Partha. *The Nation and Its Fragments: Colonial and Postcolonial Histories*. Princeton, NJ: Princeton University Press, 1993.

Chen Boda. *Xin rensheng guan de chuangzao [The Making of a New Philosophy of Life]*. Shanghai: Chenguang shudian, 1939.

Chen Duxiu. "Gei Dai Jitao de yifeng xin [A Letter to Dai Jitao]." *Xiangdao zhoubao*, no. 129 (1925): 4–8.

"Guomindang youpai zhi guoqu xianzai ji jianglai [The Past, Present and Future of the Guomindang Right]." *Xiangdao*, no. 148 (1926): 2–3.

Chen, Jianhua. "Chinese 'Revolution' in the Syntax of World Revolution." In *Tokens of Exchange: The Problem of Translation in Global Circulations*, ed. Lydia H. Liu, 355–74. Durham, NC: Duke University Press, 1999.

Chen Juequan. "Guangzhou tongzijun shilue [Brief History of Scouting in Guangzhou]." In *Guangdong wenshi ziliao*, ed. Zhongguo renmin zhengxie huiyi Guangdong sheng weiyuanhui wenshi ziliao yanjiu weiyuanhui, no. 73: 148–55. Guangzhou: Guangdong renmin chubanshe, 1993.

Chen, Leslie H. *Chen Jiongming and the Federalist Movement: Regional Leadership and Nation Building in Early Republican China*. Ann Arbor: Center for Chinese Studies, University of Michigan, 2000.

Chen Lifu. "Jingshen zong dongyuan de yiyi [The Significance of Spiritual General Mobilization]." In *Zhonghua minguo zhongyao shiliao chubian – dui-Ri kangzhan shiqi*. Vol. 4, *zhanshi jianshe*, ed. Qin Xiaoyi, no. 4: 647–54. Taipei: Zhongguo Guomindang zhongyang weiyuanhui dangshi weiyuan-hui, 1988.

The Storm Clouds Clear over China: The Memoir of Ch'en Li-fu, 1900–1993. Stanford, CA: Hoover Institute Press, 1994.

Weisheng lun (shang juan) [*Vitalism, Volume I*]. Nanjing: Zhongyang zhengzhi xuexiao, 1933.

Chen Quan. "Lun yingxiong congbai [On Hero Worship]." *Zhan'guo ce*, no. 4 (May 1940): 1–10.

"Minzu wenxue yundong [Nationalist Literature Movement]." *Minzu wenxue* 1, no. 1 (Jul. 1943): 6–9.

"Qinghua (lixiang zhuyi yu langman zhuyi) [Green Flower (Idealism and Romanticism)]." *Guofeng*, no. 12 (1943): 10–12.

Chen Wensong. *Zhimin tongzhi yu "qingnian": Taiwan zongdufu de "qingnian" jiaohua zhengce* [*Colonial Rule and Youths: The Taiwan Governor-General Office's Youth Cultivation Policy*]. Taipei: Guoli Taiwan daxue chuban zhong-xin, 2015.

Chen Yongfa. *Zhongguo gongchan geming qishi nian* [Seventy Years of the Chinese Communist Revolution]. Rev. edn. Taipei: Lianjing chuban shiye gongsi, 2001.

Chiang Kai-shek. "Celi guoren nuli shixing guomin jingshen zong dongyuan – ershijiu nian yuandan guangbo jiangci [Encouraging Compatriots to Steadfastly Carry Out National Spiritual General Mobilization – Speech Broadcast on New Year's Day 1940]." In *Sanda yundong*, ed. Sanmin zhuyi qingniantuan zhongyang tuanbu. N.p., 1942.

"Chujiu buxin gemian xixin [Abolish the Old, Establish the New and Reform]." In *Zhonghua minguo zhongyao shiliao chubian – dui-Ri kangzhan shiqi*. Vol. 4, *zhanshi jianshe*, ed. Qin Xiaoyi, no. 4: 610–15. Taipei: Zhongguo Guomindang zhongyang weiyuanhui dangshi weiyuanhui, 1988.

Collected Wartime Messages of Generalissimo Chiang Kai-shek. Vol. 1. New York: John Day, 1946.

Fan'gong kangE jiben lun [*Basic Treatise on Anti-Communism and Resistance against Russia*]. Taipei: Zhongyang wenwu gongyingshe, 1955; Taipei:

Zhongguo Guomindang zhongyang weiyuan hui dangshi wenyuan hui, 1984.

Jiang Zhongzheng zongtong dang'an: shilüe gaoben [*Chiang Kai-shek Collections: The Chronological Events*]. 82 vols. Xindian, Taipei County: Academia Historica, 2003–13.

Xian zongtong Jiang gong sixiang yanlun zongji [*Complete Collection of Chiang Kai-shek's Thoughts and Talks*]. 40 vols. Taipei: Zhongguo Guomindang zhongyang weiyuanhui dangshi weiyuanhui, 1984.

Chickering, Roger. "Sore Loser: Ludendorff's Total War." In *The Shadows of Total War: Europe, East Asia, and the United States, 1919–1939*, eds. Roger Chickering and Stig Förster, 151–78. Cambridge: Cambridge University Press, 2003.

Chu, Wan-wen. "Taiwan jingji qiji de Zhongguo beijing: chaoke fenduan tizhi jingji shi de mangdian [The China Factor in Taiwan's Economic Miracle]." *Taiwan shehui yanjiu jikan*, no. 74 (2009): 49–93.

Clinton, Maggie. *Revolutionary Nativism: Fascism and Culture in China, 1925–1937*. Durham, NC: Duke University Press, forthcoming.

Coble, Parks M., Jr. *The Shanghai Capitalists and the Nationalist Government, 1927–1937*. Cambridge, MA: Council on East Asian Studies, Harvard University, 1980.

Cullather, Nick. "'Fuel for the Good Dragon': The United States and Industrial Policy in Taiwan, 1950–1965." In *Empire and Revolution: The United States and the Third World since 1945*, eds. Peter Hahn and Mary Ann Heiss, 242–68. Columbus: Ohio State University Press, 2001.

Culp, Robert. *Articulating Citizenship: Civic Education and Student Politics in Southeastern China, 1912–1940*. Cambridge, MA: Harvard University Asia Center, 2007.

[Gao Yihan]. "Zhongguo tongzijun – Nanjing shinian tongzijun shouce zhong de gongmin xunlian yu shehui yishi [Scouting for Chinese Boys: Civic Training and Social Consciousness in Nanjing Decade Boy Scout Handbooks]." *Xin shixue* 11, no. 4 (2000): 25.

Dai Jitao. *Dai Jitao xiansheng wencun* [*Collected Works of Dai Jitao*]. 4 vols. Taipei: Zhongguo Guomindang zhongyang weiyuanhui, 1959.

Dai Jitao zuijin yanlun [*Dai Jitao's Latest Remarks*] 2nd edn. N.p.: Shangwu yinshuguan, 1928.

Guomin geming yu Zhongguo Guomindang [*China's National Revolution and the Guomindang*]. 1925. Reprint, n.p., 1928.

"Jiu lunli de benghuai yu xin lunli de jianshe [The Collapse of Old Ethics and the Development of the New]," Parts 1 and 2. *Xingqi pinglun*, no. 20 (1919): 1–2; no. 25 (1919): 1–2.

Qingnian zhi lu [*The Way for Youth*]. Shanghai: Minzhi shuju, 1928.

Sun Wen zhuyi zhi zhexue de jichu [*Philosophical Foundations of Sun Yat-senism*]. 1925. Reprint, Taipei: Zhongyang gaizao weiyuan hui wenwu gongying chu, 1951.

"Yanxi yu pingmin [Drama and the Common People]." In *Zhongguo Guomindang gaizu jinian Minguo ribao tekan*, 51–56. Guangzhou: Guangzhou Minguo ribao she, 1924.

"Zhong Ri E san minzu zhi guanxi [The Relationship between China, Japan, and Russia]." *Xin Yaxiya* 1, no. 2 (1930): 9–10.

Zhongguo duli yundong de jidian [*The Basis of China's Independence Movement*]. Guangzhou: Minzhi shuju, 1925.

Dai Jitao and Hu Hanmin, trans. *Ziben lun jieshuo* [*The Economic Doctrines of Karl Marx*]. Shanghai: Minzhi shuju, 1927.

De Grazia, Victoria. *The Culture of Consent: Mass Organization of Culture in Fascist Italy*. New York: Cambridge University Press, 1981.

Deng Chongdi. "Buyao huoyao de pao [A Gunpowder-Free Bomb]." *Shaonian bing*, no. 3 (1943): 50.

"Hongzha ji [Aerial Bombers]." *Shaonian bing*, no. 1 (1943): 13–16.

Dirlik, Arif. *Anarchism in the Chinese Revolution*. Berkeley: University of California Press, 1991.

"The Ideological Foundations of the New Life Movement: A Study in Counterrevolution." *Journal of Asian Studies* 34 (1975): 945–80.

"Mass Movements and the Left Kuomintang." *Modern China* 1 (1975): 46–74.

The Origins of Chinese Communism. New York: Oxford University Press, 1989.

"The Predicament of Marxist Revolutionary Consciousness: Mao Zedong, Antonio Gramsci and the Reformulation of Marxist Revolutionary Theory." *Modern China* 9 (1983): 182–211.

"Dongyuan tongxun [Mobilization News]." *Jingshen dongyuan*, no. 2 (1940): 141–51.

"Dongyuan tongxun [Mobilization News]." *Jingshen dongyuan*, no. 3 (1940): 161–6.

"Dongyuan tongxun [Mobilization News]." *Jingshen dongyuan*, no. 4 (1941): 173–82.

"Dongyuan tongxun [Mobilization News]." *Jingshen dongyuan* 2, no. 1 (1941): 189–96.

Duara, Prasenjit. *Culture, Power, and the State: Rural North China, 1900–1942*. Stanford, CA: Stanford University Press, 1988.

Sovereignty and Authenticity: Manchukuo and the East Asian Modern. Lanham, MD: Rowman and Littlefield, 2003.

Eagleton, Terry. *The Ideology of the Aesthetic*. Oxford: Basil Blackwell, 1990.

Eastman, Lloyd E. *The Abortive Revolution: China under Nationalist Rule, 1927–1937*. Cambridge, MA: Harvard University Press, 1974.

Falasca-Zamponi, Simonetta. *Fascist Spectacle: The Aesthetics of Power in Mussolini's Italy*. Berkeley: University of California Press, 1997.

Fang Xiu. *Notes on the History of Malaysian Chinese New Literature, 1920–1942*. Translated by Angus W. MacDonald. Tokyo: Centre for East Asian Cultural Studies, 1977.

Fanjun. "Zenyang yingfu zhege feichang shiqi [How to Handle This Emergency Period]." *Minzhong zhoukan* 5, no. 8 (1933): 1–2.

Fatica, Michele. "The Beginning and the End of the Idyllic Relations between Mussolini's Italy and Chiang Kai-shek's China (1930–1937)." In *Italy's Encounters with Modern China: Imperial Dreams, Strategic Ambitions*, eds. Maurizio Marinelli and Giovanni B Andornino, 89–115. New York: Palgrave Macmillan, 2014.

"Feichang shiqi de feichang renwu [Extraordinary Tasks in Emergency Period]." *Shehui xinwen* 3, no. 4 (1933): 50–1.

Ferlanti, Frederica. "City-Building, New Life and the 'Making of Citizen' in 1930s Nanchang." In *New Narratives of Urban Space in Republican Chinese Cities: Emerging Social, Legal and Governance Orders*, eds. Billy K. L. So and Madeleine Zelin, 45–64. Leiden: Brill, 2013.

"The New Life Movement at War: Wartime Mobilisation and State Control in Chongqing and Chengdu, 1938–1942." *European Journal of East Asian Studies*, no. 11 (2012): 187–212.

"The New Life Movement in Jiangxi Province, 1934–1938." *Modern Asian Studies*, no. 44 (2010): 961–1000.

Fewsmith, Joseph. *Party, State, and Local Elites in Republican China: Merchant Organizations and Politics in Shanghai*. Honolulu: University of Hawaii Press, 1985.

Finchelstein, Federico. *Transatlantic Fascism: Ideology, Violence, and the Sacred in Argentina and Italy, 1919–1945*. Durham, NC: Duke University Press, 2010.

Fitzgerald, John. *Awakening China: Politics, Culture, and Class in the Nationalist Revolution*. Stanford, CA: Stanford University Press, 1996.

Fu Sinian. "Jiaoyu bengkui de yuanyin [Reasons Why Education Collapsed]." *Duli pinglun*, no. 9 (1932): 2–6.

"Zhongguo ren zuoren de jihui daole! [Here Comes the Chance for the Chinese People to Be Human]." *Duli pinglun*, no. 35 (1933): 6–8.

"Zhongxue junxun ganyan [Ruminations on Military Training in Middle Schools]." *Gongjiao xuexiao* 1, no. 11 (1935): 7–9.

Fujino, Yutaka. *Kyōsei sareta kenkō – Nihon fashizumu shita no seimei to shintai [Forced Health – Life and Body under Japanese Fascism]*. Tokyo: Yoshikawa kōbunkan, 2000.

Fung, Edmund S. K. *The Intellectual Foundations of Chinese Modernity: Cultural and Political Thought in the Republican Era*. New York: Cambridge University Press, 2010.

Gandhi, Mahatma. Letter to Chiang Kai-shek. 14 June 1942. In *Across the Himalayan Gap: An Indian Quest for Understanding China*, ed. Tan Chung, 40–1. New Delhi: Indira Gandhi National Centre for the Arts, 1998.

Glosser, Susan. *Chinese Visions of Family and State, 1915–1953*. Berkeley: University of California Press, 2003.

Godley, Michael R. "Politics from History: Lei Haizong and the Zhanguo ce Clique." *Papers on Far Eastern History*, no. 40 (1989): 95–122.

Gordon, Andrew. *Labor and Imperial Democracy in Prewar Japan*. Berkeley: University of California Press, 1991.

Gramsci, Antonio. *The Gramsci Reader: Selected Writings 1916–1935*. Edited by David Forgacs. New York: New York University Press, 2000.

Selections from the Prison Notebooks. Translated by Quintin Hoare and Geoffrey Nowell Smith. New York: International Publishers, 1971.

Gregor, A. James. *The Faces of Janus: Marxism and Fascism in the Twentieth Century*. New Haven, CT: Yale University Press, 2000.

A Place in the Sun: Marxism and Fascism in China's Long Revolution. Boulder, CO: Westview Press, 2000.

Grieder, Jerome B. *Hu Shih and the Chinese Renaissance: Liberalism in the Chinese Revolution, 1917–1937.* Cambridge, MA: Harvard University Press, 1970.

"The Question of 'Politics' in the May Fourth Era." In *Reflections on the May Fourth Movement: A Symposium,* ed. Benjamin I. Schwartz, 95–101. Cambridge, MA: East Asian Research Center, Harvard University, 1973.

Griffin, Roger. *The Nature of Fascism.* New York: St. Martin's Press, 1991.

Guo Guanqun. "Feichang shiqi zhong qingnian yingyou zhi zhunbei [Preparations for Youths during the Emergency Period," *Yizhong xiaokan,* 3, nos. 3–4 (1935): 109–11.

Guoli Guangdong daxue. *Guoli Guangdong daxue tongzijun niankan.* Guangzhou, 1925.

"Guomin jingshen zong dongyuan gangling jiqi shishi banfa [Guiding Principles and Implementation Measures of National Spiritual General Mobilization]." In *Zhonghua minguo zhongyao shiliao chubian – dui-Ri kangzhan shiqi.* Vol. 4, *zhanshi jianshe,* ed. Qin Xiaoyi, no. 4: 580–601. Taipei: Zhongguo Guomindang zhongyang weiyuanhui dangshi weiyuanhui, 1988.

"Guomin jingshen zong dongyuan hui sheji weiyuan yilan [List of Planning Committee Members at the National Spiritual General Mobilization Association]." *Jingshen dongyuan,* no. 3 (1940): 183.

"Guomin jingshen zong dongyuan shishi gaikuang [An Overview of the Implementation of National Spiritual General Mobilization]." *Jingshen dongyuan,* no. 1 (1940): 13.

Guomin jingshen zong dongyuan yaoyi [Principles of National Spiritual General Mobilization]. N.p.: Zhongyang zhixing weiyuanhui xunlian weiyuanhui, 1940.

Guomin shenghuo zhi di [Enemies of Citizens' Livelihood]. N.p.: Neizheng bu and Guomin jingshen zong dongyuan hui, n.d.

Harootunian, Harry D. *Overcome by Modernity: History, Culture, and Community in Interwar Japan.* Princeton, NJ: Princeton University Press, 2000.

Harrison, Henrietta. *The Making of the Republican Citizen: Political Ceremonies and Symbols in China, 1911–1929.* Oxford: Oxford University Press, 2000.

He Xianbi. "Danao 'tongzijun jianyue' [Sabotaging Review of Scouts]." In *Xuancheng xian wenshi ziliao,* ed. Xuancheng xian zhengxie wenshi weiyuanhui, no. 3, 7–8. Xuancheng: Xuancheng xian zhengxie wenshi weiyuanhui, 1988.

He Yingqin. "Tongzijun jingshen yu minzu fuxing [The Spirit of Scouting and National Revival]." *Gongjiao xuexiao* 2, no. 25 (1936): 4–5.

Healy, Maureen. *Vienna and the Fall of the Habsburg Empire: Total War and Everyday Life in World War I.* Cambridge: Cambridge University Press, 2004.

Hofmann, Reto. *The Fascist Effect: Japan and Italy, 1915–1952.* Ithaca, NY: Cornell University Press, 2015.

Hon, Tze-ki. *Revolution as Restoration: Guocui xuebao and China's Path to Modernity, 1905-1911*. Leiden: Brill, 2013.

Hong Zhixin. "Huiyi canjia Zhongguo tongzijun zhanshi fuwu tuan de pianduan [Memories of My Participation in the Wartime Service Corps of the Scouts of China]." In *Jing'an wenshi*, ed. Zhongguo renmin zhengzhi xieshang huiyi Shanghai shi Jing'an qu weiyuanhui wenshi ziliao weiyuanhui, no. 7: 30–3. Shanghai: Zhongguo renmin zhengzhi xieshang huiyi Shanghai shi Jing'an qu weiyuanhui wenshi ziliao weiyuanhui, 1992.

Hoston, Germaine A. "Marxism and National Socialism in Taishô Japan: The Thought of Takabatake Motoyuki." *Journal of Asian Studies* 44 (1984): 43–64.

Hu Menghua. "Guomin jingshen zong dongyuan de shiji yu shijian [National Spiritual General Mobilization – Its Concreteness and Practice]." *Zhongyang zhoukan* 1, no. 34 (1939): 9–13.

Hu Shi. "Zhang Xueliang de pan'guo [Zhang Xueliang's Treason]." *Zhongyang zhoubao*, no. 447 (1936): 7–9.

Huang Jianli. *The Politics of Depoliticization in Republican China: Guomindang Policy towards Student Political Activism*. Bern: Peter Lang, 1996.

Huang Kewu [Max K. W. Huang]. "Jiang Jieshi yu He Lin [Chiang Kai-shek and He Lin]." *Zhongyang yanjiu yuan jindai shi yanjiu suo jikan*, no. 67 (2010): 17–58.

Hung, Chang-tai. *War and Popular Culture: Resistance in Modern China, 1937–1945*. Berkeley: University of California Press, 1994.

Ji Diankai. "Wo suo zhidao de tongzijun [Scouting as I Know It]." *Xinxiang shi jiaoqu wenshi ziliao*, ed. Zhengxie Xinyang shi weiyuanhui wenshi ziliao weiyuanhui, no. 3: 14–20. Xinyang, Henan: Zhengxie Xinyang shi weiyuanhui wenshi ziliao weiyuanhui, 1994.

Jiang Baili. *Guofang lun* [*On National Defense*]. N.p., [1937?].

Jiang Baili xiansheng wenxuan [*Selected Works of Jiang Baili*]. N.p.: Guofang xuehui, n.d.

"Jieshao ben kan tougao de xiao pengyou [Introducing Children Who Write for This Magazine]." *Zhongguo tongzijun*, no. 16 (1931): 46.

"Jingshen zong dongyuan" [National Spiritual Mobilization]. *Liangyou huabao*, no. 143 (1939): 4–5.

Jung Keun-sik. "Shokuminchi shihai, shintai kiritsu, kenkô [Colonial Rule, Body Discipline, Health]." In *Seikatsu no naka no shokuminchi shugi*, ed. Mizuno Naoki, 59–102. Kyoto: Jinbun shoin, 2004.

Karatani Kojin. *History and Repetition*. New York: Columbia University Press, 2012.

"Overcoming Modernity." In *Contemporary Japanese Thought*, ed. Richard Calichman, 101–18. New York: Columbia University Press, 2005.

The Structure of World History: From Modes of Production to Modes of Exchange. Translated by Michael K. Bourdaghs. Durham, NC: Duke University Press, 2014.

Karl, Rebecca E. "Journalism, Social Value and a Philosophy of the Everyday in 1920s China." *Positions: East Asia Cultures Critique* 16, no. 3 (2008): 539–67.

Staging the World: Chinese Nationalism at the Turn of the Twentieth Century.
Durham, NC: Duke University Press, 2002.

Kemp, G. S. K. "Boy Scouts Association of China." *Xin Qingnian* 2, no. 5 (1917): 1–2.

Kikuchi Kazutaka. "Toshi-gata tokumu 'CC' kei no 'hankyô kô-Nichi' rosen ni tsuite (jô) – sono seisei kara kô-Nichi sensô niokeru igi to genkai [On the 'Anti-communist and Resist Japan' Line of the Urban-Based Espionage Organization, the CC Clique – Its Significance and Limitations from Inception to the Second Sino–Japanese War]." Parts 1 and 2. *Chikaki ni arite*, no. 35 (1999): 2–22; no. 36 (1999): 26–47.

Kirby, William C. *Germany and Republican China.* Stanford, CA: Stanford University Press, 1984.

Kondô Masami. *Sôryokusen to Taiwan: Nihon shokuminchi hôkai no kenkyû [Total War and Taiwan: A Study on the Japanese Colony's Collapse].* Tokyo: Tôsui Shobô, 1996.

Kuang Xinnian. *1928: Geming wenxue [1928: Revolutionary Literature].* Jinan: Shandong jiaoyu chubanshe, 1998.

Xiandai wenxue yu xiandai xing [Modern Literature and Modernity]. Shanghai: Yuandong chubanshe, 1998.

Kubo Juntarô. "Zasshi *Shin Ajia* ronsetsu kiji mokuroku [Catalogue of Commentaries and Articles in the Journal *New Asia*]." *Kôbe daigaku shigaku nenpô*, no. 17 (2002): 80–124.

Kuhn, Philip A. *Origins of the Modern Chinese State.* Stanford, CA: Stanford University Press, 2002.

Kuohu. "Yige tongzijun canjia quanguo zong jianyue ji da luying riji [The Diary of a Participant in the First National Review of Scouts and Jamboree]." *Zhongguo tongzijun*, no. 9 (1930): 34–47.

Laclau, Ernesto. *Politics and Ideology in Marxist Theory: Capitalism, Fascism, Populism.* London: NLB, 1977.

Lam, Tong. *A Passion for Facts: Social Surveys and the Construction of the Chinese Nation-State, 1900–1949.* Berkeley: University of California Press, 2011.

Landa, Ishay. *The Apprentice's Sorcerer: Liberal Tradition and Fascism.* Leiden: Brill, 2010.

Lang Xingshi, ed. *Geming yu fan geming [Revolution and Counterrevolution].* Shanghai: Minzhi shuju, 1928.

Lanza, Fabio. *Behind the Gates: Inventing Students in Beijing.* New York: Columbia University Press, 2010.

Lary, Diana. *The Chinese People at War: Human Suffering and Social Transformation, 1927–1945.* New York: Cambridge University Press, 2010.

Lau, D. C., trans. *Confucius: The Analects.* 2nd edn. Hong Kong: Chinese University Press, 1992.

Lean, Eugenia. *Public Passions: The Trial of Shi Jianqiao and the Rise of Popular Sympathy in Republican China.* Berkeley: University of California Press, 2007.

Lee, Chiu-chun. "From Liberal to Nationalist: Tai Chi-t'ao's Pursuit of a New World Order." PhD diss., University of Chicago, 1993.

Legge, James, trans. *Chinese Classics*. Vol. 5, *The Ch'un Ts'ew with the Tso Chuen*. 2nd edn. Hong Kong: Hong Kong University Press, 1960.

Lei, Sean Hsiang-lin [Lei Xianglin]. "Xiguan cheng siwei: Xin shenghuo yundong yu fei jiehe yufang zhong de lunli, jiating yu shenti [Habituating the Four Virtues: Ethics, Family and the Body in Anti-tuberculosis Campaigns and the New Life Movement]." *Jindai shi yanjiusuo jikan*, no. 74 (2011): 133–77.

Levenson, Joseph R. *Confucian China and Its Modern Fate: A Trilogy*. Berkeley: University of California Press, 1968.

Li, Danke. *Echoes of Chongqing: Women in Wartime China*. Urbana: University of Illinois Press, 2010.

Li Hsiao-t'i. "Making a Name and a Culture for the Masses in Modern China." *Positions: East Asia Cultures Critique* 9 (2001): 29–68.

Li, Lincoln. *Student Nationalism in China, 1924–1949*. Albany: State University of New York Press, 1994.

Li Liquan and Cheng Qiheng, eds. *Fan'gong kangE gequ yibai shou* [*A Hundred Anti-Communist and Resist Russia Songs*]. 2nd edn. Taichung: Taiwan sheng xinwen chu, 1953.

Li Pusheng. *Wo bushizi de muqin* [*My Illiterate Mother*]. Hong Kong: Dongnan yinwu chubanshe, 1956.

Li Shutang. "Tongzijun xunlian de yiyi jiqi shiming [The Meaning and Mission of Scout Training]." *Changcheng jikan* 1, no. 1 (1935): 47.

Liang Canwen, "Zhongguo Guomindang tongzijun jishi," *Zhongguo Guomindang tongzijun*, no. 2 (1926): 8.

Liang Qichao. "The Kinship between Chinese & Indian Culture." In *Talks in China, by Rabindranath Tagore*. Calcutta: Arunoday Art Press, n.d.

Liang Shiqiu. "Wo wei shenme bu zancheng Gongchandang [The Reasons Why I Do Not Agree with the Communist Party]." *Yuzhou xunkan*, no. 501 (1936): 7–10.

"Yonghu guomin jingshen zong dongyuan fa [In Support of the Decree on the National Spiritual Mobilization Movement]." *Zaisheng*, no. 18 (1939): 1–2.

Lin, Alfred H. Y. "Warlord, Social Welfare, and Philanthropy: The Case of Guangzhou under Chen Jitang, 1929–1936," *Modern China* 30 (2004): 151–98.

Lin, Hsiao-ting. *Tibet and Nationalist China's Frontier: Intrigues and Ethnopolitics, 1928–49*. Vancouver: University of British Columbia Press, 2006.

Lin, Yutang. *A History of the Press and Public Opinion in China*. Shanghai: Kelly and Walsh, 1936.

Liu Jihui [Joyce C. H. Liu]. *Xin de bianyi: xiandaixing de jingshen xingshi* [*Perverted Heart: The Psychic Forms of Modernity*]. Taipei: Maitian chuban, 2004.

Liu Jinqing. *Taiwan zhanhou jingji fenxi* [*Taiwan Postwar Economic Analysis*]. Revised edn. Taipei: Renjian chubanshe, 2012.

Liu Kang. *Aesthetics and Marxism: Chinese Aesthetic Marxists and Their Western Contemporaries*. Durham, NC: Duke University Press, 2000.

Liu, Lydia H. *Translingual Practice: Literature, National Culture, and Translated Modernity – China, 1900–1937*. Stanford, CA: Stanford University Press, 1995.

Liu, Wennan. "Redefining the Moral and Legal Roles of the State in Everyday Life: The New Life Movement in China in the Mid-1930s." *Cross-Currents: East Asian History and Culture Review*, no. 7 (2013): 30–59.

Liu Zhipan. "Mosike Zhongshan daxue shouhua zhi jishi [A Veritable Record of Bestialization at Moscow Sun Yat-sen University]." *Anhui jiaoyu xingzheng zhoukan* 2, no. 9 (1929): 5–6.

Lloyd, David and Paul Thomas. *Culture and the State*. London: Routledge, 1998.

Lu Fang-shang. *Cong xuesheng yundong dao yundong xuesheng: minguo ba nian zhi shiba nian* [*From Student Movements to Mobilizing Students in China, 1919–1929*]. Taipei: Institute of Modern History, Academia Sinica, 1994.

"Jiang Jieshi – yiwei tanxing guoji zhuyi zhe: yi 1942 nian fang Yin weili de taolun [Chiang Kai-shek, a Flexible Internationalist: On His 1942 Visit to India]." *Guoli zhengzhi daxue lishi xuebao*, no. 37 (2012): 121–46.

Lu, Hanchao. *Beyond the Neon Lights: Everyday Shanghai in the Early Twentieth Century*. Berkeley: University of California Press, 2000.

Lu Yan. *Re-understanding Japan: Chinese Perspectives, 1895–1945*. Honolulu: Association for Asian Studies and University of Hawai'i Press, 2004.

Lukács, Georg. "Tagore's Gandhi Novel." *Marxists Internet Archive*. www .marxists.org/archive/lukacs/works/1922/tagore.htm.

Luo Yijun. "Yi Zhu Guangqian xiansheng [Reminisces on Zhu Guangqian]." In *Qingchun de Beida: "Jingshen de meili" xubian*, ed. Zhao Weimin, 197–8. Beijing: Beijing daxue chubanshe, 1998.

Lutze, Thomas D. *China's Inevitable Revolution: Rethinking America's Loss to the Communists*. New York: Palgrave Macmillan, 2007.

Marx, Karl. *The Eighteenth Brumaire of Louis Bonaparte*. New York: International Publishers, 1963.

Marx, Karl and Frederick Engels. "On the Polish Question." In *Collected Works*, vol. 6, 545–52. London: Lawrence & Wishart, 1976.

Mast, Herman William, III. "An Intellectual Biography of Tai Chi-t'ao from 1891 to 1928." PhD diss., University of Illinois, 1970.

Mazower, Mark. *No Enchanted Palace: The End of Empire and the Ideological Origins of the United Nations*. Princeton, NJ: Princeton University Press, 2009.

McCord, Edward A. "Warlords against Warlordism: The Politics of Anti-warlordism in Early Twentieth-Century China," *Modern Asian Studies* 30 (1996): 795–827.

McDougall, Bonnie S. "The View from the Leaning Tower: Zhu Guangqian on Aesthetics and Society in the Nineteen-Twenties and Thirties." In *Modern Chinese Literature and Its Social Context*, ed. Göran Malmqvist, 76–122. Stockholm: Department of Oriental Studies, Stockholm University, 1975.

Mehta, V. L. "Comparative Studies in Rural Economic Conditions." *Harijan* 4, no. 9 (1936): 71.

Mitter, Rana. *Forgotten Ally: China's World War II, 1937–1945*. Boston, MA: Houghton Mifflin Harcourt, 2013.

Miyazaki Ryûsuke. "Gongqi Longjie zai Nanjing zhi yanjiang [Miyazaki Ryûsuke's Speech in Nanjing]." In *Ya Dong zhi dong*, ed. Chen Yiyi, 52–57. N.p., 1927.

Mizoguchi Yuzo. *Zhongguo de chongji* [*China's Impact*]. Translated by Wang Ruigen. Beijing: Shenghuo, dushu, xinzhi sanlian shudian, 2011.

Morris, Andrew D. *Marrow of the Nation: A History of Sport and Physical Culture in Republican China*. Berkeley: University of California Press, 2004.

Mosse, George L. *The Fascist Revolution: Toward a General Theory of Fascism*. New York: Howard Fertig, 1999.

Najita, Tetsuo and H. D. Harootunian. "Japan's Revolt against the West." In *Modern Japanese Thought*, ed. Bob Tadashi Wakabayashi, 207–72. Cambridge: Cambridge University Press, 1998.

Nehru, Jawaharlal. *The Oxford India Nehru*. New Delhi: Oxford University Press, 2007.

Selected Works of Jawaharlal Nehru. 15 vols. New Delhi: Orient Longman, 1972–82.

Neocleous, Mark. *Fascism*. Minneapolis: University of Minnesota Press, 1997.

Imagining the State. Maidenhead, England: Open University Press, 2003.

Ni Jiaxi. "Cong jianku zhong fendou [Struggle amidst Hardship]." In *Kangzhan yu tongjun*, 85–6.

Ni Wei. *"Minzu" xiangxiang yu guojia tongzhi: 1928–1948 nian Nanjing zhengfu de wenyi zhengce ji wenxue yundong* [*National Imaginary and State Control: Literary Policies and Movements under the Nanjing Government, 1928–1948*]. Shanghai: Shanghai jiaoyu chubanshe, 2003.

Osborne, Peter. *The Politics of Time: Modernity and Avant-garde*. London: Verso, 1995.

Pan Gongzhan. "Guomin jingshen zong dongyuan yu zhongxiao de minzu daode [National Spiritual General Mobilization and the National Morality of Loyalty and Fidelity]." *Zhongyang zhoukan* 1, no. 34 (1939a): 3–4.

"Jingshen dongyuan yu wuzhi dongyuan de peihe [Coordination between Spiritual and Material Mobilization]." *Zhongyang dangwu gongbao* 21, no. 2 (1940): 7–8, 14.

"Jingshen zong dongyuan shi kangzhan jianguo de yuandongli [Spiritual Mobilization Motivates Nation-Building through the War of Resistance]." *Zhongyang zhoukan* 1, no. 40 (1939b): 3–4.

Parsons, Timothy H. *Race, Resistance, and the Boy Scout Movement in British Colonial Africa*. Athens: Ohio University Press, 2004.

Peng Shouzu, "Feichang shidai xuesheng yingyou de zhunbei [Required Preparations for Students in the Emergency Period]." *Yizhong xiaokan* 3, nos. 3–4 (1935): 111–13.

Piazza, Hans. "The Anti-Imperialist League and the Chinese Revolution." In *The Chinese Revolution in the 1920s*, eds. Mechthild Leutner et al., 166–76. London: RoutledgeCurzon, 2002.

Polanyi, Karl. *The Great Transformation: The Political and Economic Origins of Our Time*. 2nd paperback edn. Boston, MA: Beacon Press, 2001.

Prashad, Vijay. *The Darker Nations: A People's History of the Third World*. New York: New Press, 2007.

Untouchable Freedom: A Social History of a Dalit Community. New Delhi: Oxford University Press, 2000.

Proctor, Tammy M. "'A Separate Path': Scouting and Guiding in Interwar South Africa." *Comparative Studies in Society and History* 42 (2000): 605–31.

Qin Xiaoyi et al. *Zhongguo minguo zhengzhi fazhan shi.* Vol. 4. Taipei: Jindai Zhongguo chubanshe, 1985.

Qu Qiubai. *Qu Qiubai wenji: zhengzhi lilun bian.* Beijing: Renmin wenxue chubansbe, 1985–96.

Robin, Corey. *The Reactionary Mind: Conservatism from Edmund Burke to Sarah Palin.* New York: Oxford University Press, 2011.

Rogaski, Ruth. *Hygienic Modernity: Meanings of Health and Disease in Treaty-Port China.* Berkeley: University of California Press, 2004.

Rosenthal, Michael. *The Character Factory: Baden-Powell and the Origins of the Boy Scout Movement.* New York: Pantheon Books, 1986.

Ross, Kristin. *May '68 and Its Afterlives.* Chicago: University of Chicago Press, 2002.

Ru Chunpu. "Chedi jiuzheng guanyu jingshen zong dongyuan gongtong mubiao de wujie [Fully Rectify Misconceptions concerning the Common Purposes of Spiritual General Mobilization]." *Zhongyang zhoukan* 1, nos. 39–40 (n.d.): 13–16.

Sang Bing. "Kangzhan shiqi Guomindang cehua de xueren banbao [Scholar-Edited Periodicals as Initiated by the Guomindang during the Resistance War]." In *Wenren lunzheng: zhishi fenzi yu baokan,* ed. Li Jinquan, 210–30. Guilin: Guangxi shifan daxue chubanshe, 2008.

"Sanjie quanguo tongzijun dahui ding bennian shuangshi jie zai jing juxing [Third National Jamboree to Be Held on This Year's National Day in the Capital]." *Zhongguo tongzijun zonghui gongbao* 2, no. 12 (1948): 12.

Sartori, Andrew. *Bengal in Global Concept History: Culturalism in the Age of Capital.* Chicago: University of Chicago Press, 2008.

Schivelbusch, Wolfgang. *Three New Deals: Reflections on Roosevelt's America, Mussolini's Italy, and Hitler's Germany, 1933–1939.* Translated by Jefferson Chase. New York: Metropolitan Books, 2006.

Schwartz, Benjamin I. "Notes on Conservatism in General and in China in Particular." In *The Limits of Change: Essays on Conservative Alternatives in Republican China,* ed. Charlotte Furth, 3–22. Cambridge, MA: Harvard University Press, 1976.

Selden, Mark. *China in Revolution: The Yenan Way Revisited.* Armonk, NY: M. E. Sharpe, 1995.

Shapiro, Hugh. "The Puzzle of Spermatorrhea in Republican China." *Positions: East Asia Cultures Critique* 6 (1998): 551–96.

Shen Lumin. "Wo suo zhidao de Shanghai tongzijun [Scouting in Shanghai According to My Knowledge]." *In Shanghai wenshi ziliao cungao huibian,* ed. Shanghai shi zhengxie wenshi ziliao weiyuanhui. Vol. 11. Shanghai: Shanghai guji chubanshe, 2001.

Shih, Shu-mei. *The Lure of the Modern: Writing Modernism in Semicolonial China, 1917–1937.* Berkeley: University of California Press, 2001.

Shiroyama, Tomoko. *China during the Great Depression: Market, State, and the World Economy, 1929–1937*. Cambridge, MA: Harvard University Asia Center, 2008.

Silver, Beverly J. and Eric Slater. "The Social Origins of World Hegemonies." In *Chaos and Governance in the Modern World System*, eds. Giovanni Arrighi and Beverly J. Silver, 151–216. Minneapolis: University of Minnesota Press, 1999.

Smith, Craig Anthony. "Constructing Chinese Asianism: Intellectual Writings on East Asian Regionalism (1896–1924)." PhD diss., University of British Columbia, 2014.

So, Wai-chor. *The Kuomintang Left in the National Revolution, 1924–1931*. Hong Kong: Oxford University Press, 1991.

Song Bailian. "Zhongguo tongzijun diandi [Tidbits of the Scouts of China]." In *Wenshi ziliao cungao xuanbian*, eds. Dang Dexin et al. Vol. 24: 647–49. Beijing: Zhongguo wenshi chubanshe, 2002.

Song, Mingwei. *Young China: National Rejuvenation and the Bildungsroman, 1900–1959*. Cambridge, MA: Harvard University Asia Center, 2015.

Song Qingling. *The Struggle for New China*. Peking: Foreign Languages Press, 1953.

Spengler, Oswald. *Preußentum und Sozialismus [Prussiandom and Socialism]*. In *Politische schriften*, 83–5. Cited in Roger Woods, *The Conservative Revolution in the Weimar Republic*, 66. New York: St. Martin's Press, 1996.

Sternhell, Zeev. *The Birth of Fascist Ideology: From Cultural Rebellion to Political Revolution*. Princeton, NJ: Princeton University Press, 1994.

Stolte, Carolien. "'Enough of the Great Napoleons!': Raja Mahendra Pratap's Pan-Asian projects (1929–1939)." *Modern Asian Studies* 46 (2012): 403–23.

Strand, David. *An Unfinished Republic: Leading by Word and Deed in Republican China*. Berkeley: University of California Press, 2011.

Sun Yat-sen. *San Min Chu I: The Three Principles of the People*. Translated by Frank W. Price. Taipei: China Publishing Company, n.d.

Sanmin zhuyi [Three People's Principles]. Taipei: Zhengzhong shuju, 1954.

Sun Wen xuanji. [Selected Works of Sun Yat-sen]. 3 vols. Guangzhou: Guangdong renmin chubanshe, 2006.

Sun Yuqin. *Minguo shiqi de tongzijun yanjiu [A Study on Scouting in the Republican Period]*. Beijing: Renmin chubanshe, 2013.

Tagore, Rabindranath. "China and India." In *Twenty Years of the Visva-Bharati Cheena Bhavana, by Tan Yunshan*, 41–5. Santiniketan: Sino–Indian Cultural Society of India, 1957.

Letter to Yone Noguchi, September 1, 1938. In *In the Footsteps of Xuanzang: Tan Yun-shan and India*, ed. Tan Chung, 209–10. New Delhi: Gyan Publishing House and Indira Gandhi National Centre for the Arts, 1999.

Swadeshi Samaj. Cited in Rustom Bharucha, *Another Asia: Rabindranath Tagore and Okakura Tenshin*, 58. New Delhi: Oxford University Press, 2006.

"Unity of Asia: A Symposium." *India and the World: Monthly Organ of Internationalism and Cultural Federation* 1, no. 7 (1932): 146–50.

Takeuchi Yoshimi. "Tai Kitô no 'Nihon ron'." In *Riben lun*, trans. Ichikawa Hiroshi. Tokyo: Shakai shisôsha, 1972.

Tan Yunshan. "An Appeal to Conscience." In *In the Footsteps of Xuanzang: Tan Yun-shan and India*, ed. Tan Chung, 172. New Delhi: Gyan Publishing House and Indira Gandhi National Centre for the Arts, 1999.

Inter-Asian Cultural Co-operation and Union of Asia. Santiniketan: Sino–Indian Cultural Society in India, 1949.

Modern Chinese History: Political, Economic and Social. Madras: n.p., 1938.

"Rabindranath, the Gurudeva." In *Professor Tan Yun-shan and Cultural Relations between India and China*, ed. V. G. Nair, 1–3. Madras: Indo-Asian Publication, 1958.

Twenty Years of the Visva-Bharati Cheena Bhavana 1937–1957. Santiniketan: Sino–Indian Cultural Society of India, 1957.

The Visva-Bharati Cheena-Bhavana and the Sino–Indian Cultural Society. Chungking and Santiniketan: Sino–Cultural Society, 1944.

Yindu zhouyou ji [*Travelogue to India*]. Nanjing: Xin Yaxiya xuehui, 1933.

"Zhi Dalai Lama shu [Letter to the Dalai Lama]." *Xin Yaxiya* 3, no. 5 (1932): 136–9.

Tang Changyan. "Minguo shinian zhi tongzijun jiaoyu [Scouting in 1921]." *Xin jiaoyu*, no. 2 (1922): 236–40.

"Zhonghua Jiangsu Wuxi tongzijun zuzhifa dakewen [Q & A on the Organization of Scouts in Wuxi, Jiangsu]." *Jiaoyu yuekan*, no. 5 (1917): 39–60.

Tang, Xiaobing. *Origins of the Chinese Avant-garde: The Modern Woodcut Movement*. Berkeley: University of California Press, 2008.

Tang Xiaobing. *Xiandai Zhongguo de gonggong yulun – yi Da gongbao "Xingqi lunwen" yu Shenbao "Ziyou tan" weili* [*Public Opinion in Modern China – A Study Based on "Weekly Commentaries" of l'Impartial and "Free Talk" of Shenbao*]. Beijing: Shehui kexue wenxian chubanshe, 2012.

Tansman, Alan. "Introduction to the Culture of Japanese Fascism." In *The Culture of Japanese Fascism*, ed. Alan Tansman, 1–28. Durham, NC: Duke University Press, 2009.

Tao Baichuan, ed. *Jiang zhuxi de shenghuo he shenghuo guan* [*Chairman Chiang's Daily Life and His Outlook on Daily Life*]. Chongqing: Zhongzhou chubanshe, 1944.

Taylor, Jay. *The Generalissimo: Chiang Kai-shek and the Struggle for Modern China*. Cambridge, MA: Belknap Press, 2009.

Tianmin. "Meiguo shaonian yiyong tuan [Scouting in the United States]." *Jiaoyu zazhi* 8, no. 5 (1916): 39–43.

"Tongzijun xiaoxi [Scouting News]." *Zhanshi tongzijun* no. 28 (1938): 12–13.

Trivedi, Lisa. *Clothing Gandhi's Nation: Homespun and Modern India*. Bloomington: Indiana University Press, 2007.

Tsin, Michael. *Nation, Governance and Modernity in China: Canton, 1900–1927*. Stanford, CA: Stanford University Press, 1999.

Van de Ven, Hans J. *War and Nationalism in China*. London: RoutledgeCurzon, 2003.

Voigt, Johannes H. "Co-operation or Confrontation?: War and Congress Politics, 1939–42." In *Congress and the Raj: Facets of the Indian Struggle, 1917–47*, ed. D. A. Low. 2nd edn., 349–74. New Delhi: Oxford University Press, 2004.

Wagner, Rudolf G. "Ritual, Architecture, Politics, and Publicity during the Republic: Enshrining Sun Yat-sen." In *Chinese Architecture and the Beaux-Arts*, eds. Jeffrey W. Cody, Nancy S. Steinhardt and Tony Atkin, 223–78. Honolulu: University of Hawaii Press, 2011.

Wakeman, Frederic, Jr. "A Revisionist View of the Nanjing Decade: Confucian Fascism." *China Quarterly*, no. 150 (1997): 395–432.

  Spymaster: Dai Li and the Chinese Secret Service. Berkeley: University of California Press, 2003.

Wang, Ban. *The Sublime Figure of History: Aesthetics and Politics in Twentieth-Century China*. Stanford, CA: Stanford University Press, 1997.

Wang Guanqing. "Xinli jianshe, jingshen dongyuan yu Zhongguo geming [Psychological Reconstruction, Spiritual Mobilization and the Chinese Revolution]." *Guohun*, no. 130 (1956): 12–14.

Wang Hui. *The End of the Revolution: China and the Limits of Modernity*. London: Verso, 2009.

  "The Politics of Imagining Asia: A Genealogical Analysis." *Inter-Asia Cultural Studies* 8 (2007): 1–33.

Wang Qisheng. *Dangyuan, dangquan yu dangzheng: 1924–1949 nian Zhongguo Guomindang de zuzhi xingtai [Party Cadres, Power and Conflict: The Guomindang's Organizational Patterns, 1924–1949]*. Shanghai: Shanghai shudian chubanshe, 2003.

  Geming yu fan geming: shehui wenhua shiye xia de minguo zhengzhi [Revolution and Counterrevolution: Republican Politics in Sociocultural Perspective]. Beijing: Shehui kexue wenxian chubanshe, 2010.

Wang Renping. *Manasi wenshi ziliao yinyue zhuanji xubian [Second Installment of the Special Collection on Music of Manas County Literary and Historical Materials]*. Manas, Xinjiang: Zhongguo renmin zhengzhi xieshang huiyi Manasi xian weiyuanhui wenshi ziliao yanjiu weiyuanhui, 1995.

Wang Youqian. "Wo suo zhidao de tongzijun [The Scouts of China According to My Knowledge]." In *Zhenjiang wenshi ziliao*, ed. Zhongguo renmin zhengzhi xieshang huiyi Jiangsu sheng Zhenjiang shi weiyuanhui wenshi ziliao yanjiu weiyuanhui, no. 25: 169–86. Zhenjiang: Jiangsu sheng Zhenjiang shi zhengxie, 1993.

Warren, Allen. "Citizens of the Empire: Baden-Powell, Scouts and Guides and an Imperial Ideal." In *Imperialism and Popular Culture*, ed. John M. Mackenzie, 232–54. Manchester: Manchester University Press, 1986.

Wei Ming. "Jiefang qian 'quanguo tongzijun di'er ci da jianyue da luying' qinli ji [Firsthand Account of the Second National Scout Review-cum-Jamboree before Liberation]." In *Luohe wenshi ziliao*, ed. Zhongguo renmin zhengzhi xieshang huiyi Luohe shi weiyuanhui wenshi ziliao yanjiu weiyuanhui, no. 1: 146–9. Luohe, Henan: Zhongguo renmin zhengzhi xieshang huiyi Luohe shi weiyuanhui wenshi ziliao yanjiu weiyuanhui, 1987.

Weston, Timothy B. *The Power of Position: Beijing University, Intellectuals, and Chinese Political Culture, 1898–1929*. Berkeley: University of California Press, 2004.

Williams, Raymond. *Problems in Materialism and Culture: Selected Essays*. London: Verso, 1980.

Wilson, Sandra. "Rethinking the 1930s and the '15-Year War' in Japan." *Japanese Studies* 21 (2001): 155–64.

Woodley, Daniel. *Fascism and Political Theory: Critical Perspectives on Fascist Ideology*. London: Routledge, 2010.

Woods, Roger. *The Conservative Revolution in the Weimar Republic*. New York: St. Martin's Press, 1996.

Wu Liping. "Erge xuanji [Some Children's Songs]." *Shaonian bing*, no. 1 (1943): 12.

Wu Weimin. "Zhang Qinqiu yu Shen Zemin – feiqu jianwen [Zhang Qinqiu and Shen Zemin – Eyewitness Accounts from Bandit Areas]." In *Hubei fanxing yuan tekan*, ed. Hubei fanxing yuan, miscellaneous section, 9–10. Wuchang, 1935.

Wu Yaolin. "Zhanshi huodong zhidao – (san) zhuisuo dizong [Wartime Activities Guide – (3) Tracking the Enemy]." *Zhanshi tongzijun*, no. 28 (1938): 4–6.

Xiao, Tie. "In the Name of the Masses: Conceptualizations and Representations of the Crowd in Early Twentieth-Century China." PhD diss., University of Chicago, 2011.

Xing Shuntian. "Shoufu shidi [Reclaiming Lost Territories]." *Shaonian bing*, no. 3 (1943): 47–8.

Xiong Feng. "Shaonian men zai Sulian [Youth in the Soviet Union]." *Zhanshi tongzijun*, nos. 39–41 (1939): 24–5.

Xisan. "Tongzijun zhi taolun [A Dialogue on Scouting]." *Jiaoyu zazhi* 8, no. 5 (1916): 9–13.

Xu Guanyu. "Jigei yiwei xiao pengyou de xin (yi) [Letter to a Child, I]." *Zhongguo tongzijun*, 2, no. 2 (1936): 12.

Yang Jingsan and Fu'an Chen. "Tongzijun zuzhi zai Xixiang huodong de shishi jilue [Brief History of Scouting in Xixiang]." In *Xixiang xian wenshi ziliao*, ed. Zhongguo renmin zhengzhi xieshang huiyi Shaanxi sheng Xixiang xian weiyuanhui wenshi ziliao weiyuanhui, no. 6: 109–21. Xixiang: Zhongguo renmin zhengzhi xieshang huiyi Shaanxi sheng Xixiang xian weiyuanhui wenshi ziliao weiyuanhui 1995.

Yang Kuisong. *Guomindang de "lian Gong" yu "fan Gong" [Kuomintang: Unity with Communists and anti-Communism]*. Beijing: Shehui kexue wenxian chubanshe, 2008.

Yeh, Wen-hsin. *The Alienated Academy: Culture and Politics in Republican China, 1919–1937*. Cambridge, MA: Council on East Asian Studies, Harvard University, 1990.

Yen, Hsiao-pei. "Body Politics, Modernity, and National Salvation: The Modern Girl and the New Life Movement." *Asian Studies Review*, no. 29 (2005): 165–86.

Yin Ling. "Wo suo zhi de 'guomin jingshen zong dongyuan' yundong [The 'National Spiritual Mobilization' Campaign That I Know]." *Hongyan chunqiu*, no. 99 (2006): 62–64.

Yin Shun. *Taixu fashi nianpu* [*Chronological Biography of Master Taixu*]. Beijing: Zongjiao wenhua chubanshe, 1995.

You Rulong. "Dangqian Zhongguo guomin jingshen zong dongyuan zhi lilun yu shijian [The Theory and Practice of National Spiritual General Mobilization in Today's China]." *Dongfang zazhi* 37, no. 8 (1940): 37–44.

Young, Louise. *Japan's Total Empire: Manchuria and the Culture of Wartime Imperialism.* Berkeley: University of California Press, 1998.

Yu, Miin-ling. "A Reassessment of Chiang Kaishek and the Policy of Alliance with the Soviet Union, 1923–1927." In *The Chinese Revolution in the 1920s*, eds. Mechthild Leutner et al., 98–124. New York: RoutledgeCurzon, 2002.

Zanasi, Margherita. *Saving the Nation: Economic Modernity in Republican China.* Chicago: University of Chicago Press, 2006.

Zarrow, Peter. *After Empire: The Conceptual Transformation of the Chinese State, 1885–1924.* Stanford, CA: Stanford University Press, 2012.

Anarchism and Chinese Political Culture. New York: Columbia University Press, 1990.

Zeng Xunhui [Tseng Hsun-hui]. "Shuxie 'yiji': wuling niandai baise kongbu shiqi 'feidie' zhi xiangzheng fenxi [Writing the 'Other': The Construction of 'Bandit Spies' under White Terror in the 1950s]." *Danjiang renwen shehui xuekan*, no. 5 (2000): 125–60.

Zeng Yizhi. "Jiankang diyi [Health First]," *Shaonian bing*, no. 3 (1943): 18.

Zhai Huaishi. "Zhongguo tongzijun 730 tuan jianjie [Brief Introduction of Scouts of China Troop 730]." *In Xinyang wenshi ziliao*, ed. Zhengxie Xinyang shi wenshi ziliao weiyuanhui, no. 6: 161–5. Xinyang, Henan: Zhengxie Xinyang shi wenshi ziliao weiyuanhui, 1992.

"Zhandi tongxun [News from the Battlefield]." *Jingshen dongyuan*, no. 1 (1940): 16–49.

Zhang Jinzuo. "Jingshen dongyuan lun [On Spiritual Mobilization]." *Zhongguo shehui* 4, no. 4 (1938): 19.

Zhang Junmai, trans. *Quan minzu zhanzheng lun* [*Der totale Krieg*]. Shanghai: Zhongguo guomin jingji yanjiusuo, 1937.

Zhang Qing. "*Duli pinglun* yu Zhongguo ziyou zhuyi de 'mingming' [*Independent Review* and the 'Naming' of Chinese Liberalism]." In *Wenren lunzheng: zhishi fenzi yu baokan*, ed. Li Jinquan, 95–125. Guilin: Guangxi shifan daxue chubanshe, 2008.

Zhang Qun. "Jingshen zong dongyuan shishi de shige zhuyi dian [Ten Important Items of Spiritual General Mobilization]." *Jingshen dongyuan*, no. 1 (1940): 5–9.

Zhang Shiying. "Suzhu kongju: 1950 niandai chuqi Taiwan zhengzhi manhua de fengge [Appealing to Fear: Political Cartoon in Early 1950s Taiwan]." In *Liang'an fenzhi: xueshu jianzhi, tuxiang xuanchuan yu zuqun zhengzhi (1945–2000)*, ed. Yu Minling, 139–200. Taipei: Institute of Modern History, Academia Sinica, 2012.

Zhang Xiaoliang. "Guilü shijin [Some Observations on Discipline]." *Zhongguo tongzijun*, no. 18 (1931): 15–22.

"Ji'nian wu de baocun he souji [Preserving and Identifying Mementos]." *Zhongguo tongzijun* 2, no. 2 (1936): 4–6.

Zhang, Xudong. "The Politics of Aestheticization: Zhou Zuoren and the Crisis of the Chinese New Culture (1927–1937)." PhD diss., Duke University, 1995.

Zhang Zhongren. *Tongzijun wenxian.* Taipei: Zhonghua shuju, 1981.

"Xiangcun tongzijun [Village Scouts]." In *Tongzijun xueshu jiangzuo.* Taipei: Zhonghua shuju, 1978.

Zhanshi jieyue [Wartime Conservation]. N.p.: Guomin jingshen zong dongyuan hui, 1939.

Zhao Bangheng et al., eds., *Kangzhan yu tongjun [The War of Resistance and Scouting].* N.p., 1938.

Zheng Shusen [William Tay]. *Jieyuan liangdi: Tai-Gang wentan suoyi [Attached to Two Lands: Reminiscences on the Literary Circles of Taiwan and Hong Kong].* Taipei: Hongfan shudian, 2013.

Zhongguo di'er lishi dang'an guan. *Zhongguo Guomindang diyi, di'er ci quanguo daibiao dahui huiyi shiliao [Historical Materials on the First and Second National Congresses of the Guomindang].* [Nanjing?]: Jiangsu guji chubanshe, 1986.

Zhongguo Guomindang zhongyang zhixing weiyuanhui xunlian bu. *Tongzijun chuji kecheng [Elementary Scouting Curriculum].* Nanjing: n.p., 1930.

"Zhongguo Guomindang zhongzhihui mishuchu miding 'fangzhi yidang huo-dong banfa' dian [The Secretariat of the Guomindang Central Executive Committee Drafts Classified Telegram 'Strategies to Counter the Dissenting Party's Activities']." In *Zhonghua minguo shi dang'an ziliao huibian.* Vol. 5, no. 1, pt. 2, ed. Zhongguo di'er lishi dang'an guan, 21–4. Nanjing: Jiangsu guji chubanshe, 1997.

Zhongguo tongzijun silingbu. "Wei diyi ci quanguo zong jianyue ji da luying juxing hou gao Zhongguo tongzijun shu [Letter to the Scouts of China at the Conclusion of the First National Jamboree]. *Zhongguo tongzijun,* no. 11 (1930): 2–12.

Zhongguo tongzijun zonghui. *Sanshi nian de Zhongguo tongzijun [Thirty Years of the Scouts of China].* Chongqing: n.p., 1941.

Zhongguo tongzijun zonghui choubeichu. *Zhongguo tongzijun choubeichu gongzuo baogao [Report of the Preparatory Committee of the Scouts of China General Association].* Nanjing: n.p., 1934.

"Zhongyang xuanchuan bu zhaodai weihua jie taolun jingshen zong dongyuan jishi [Record of Cultural Sector Discussion on Spiritual General Mobilization as Convened by the Central Executive Committee Propaganda Department]." *Zhongyang zhoukan* 1, no. 34 (1939): 19–22.

Zhou Wenqu. "Feichang shiqi Jiangsu funü yingfu zhi zeren [Responsibilities Jiangsu Women Should Bear in the Emergency Period]." *Suheng,* no. 19 (Dec. 1936): 15–19.

Zhu Guangqian. "Why do we take pleasure in tragedy?" *Guoli Beiping daxue xuebao wenli zhuankan* 1: 4 (1935): 131–57.

Zhu Guangqian quanji [Complete Works of Zhu Guangqian]. 20 vols. Hefei: Anhui jiaoyu chubanshe, 1987–1992.

Žižek, Slavoj. *In Defense of Lost Causes.* London: Verso, 2009.

The Sublime Object of Ideology. London: Verso, 1989.

Welcome to the Desert of the Real!: Five Essays on September 11 and Related Dates. London: Verso, 2002.

Zou Jian. "Quanguo tongzijun di'er ci da jianyue [The Second National Scout Review]." *Xiandai qingnian* 5, no. 1 (1936): 4–8.

Zuo Taofen. "Jingshen dongyuan de zhengque renshi [Correct Understanding of Spiritual Mobilization]." *Quanmin kangzhan*, no. 85 (Mar. 1939): unpaginated.

Zurndoffer, Harriet. "Wartime Refugee Relief in Chinese Cities and Women's Political Activism, 1937–1940." In *New Narratives of Urban Space in Republican Chinese Cities: Emerging Social, Legal and Governance Orders*, eds. Billy K. L. So and Madeleine Zelin, 65–91. Leiden: Brill, 2013.

Index

Adorno, Theodor, 149–50
aesthetics and politics, 13–17, 171, 172–82,
    225, *See also* liberalism, *minsheng*
    principle
    aesthetic perfection, 189–91
    autonomous aesthetic subjectivity, 191
    Britain, 182
    disinterested aesthetics, 224–6
    diversion from social revolution,
      14–16, 67
    edifying functions, 42, 174–6, 178–82,
      187, 192–4
    new social norms and values, 60,
      142, 143
    revolution of aesthetics, 43–50
    spiritual mobilization, 127–9, 142, 143,
      147–8, 149, 151
    state leadership of, 182–9
    Zhu Guangqian on, 157–8
agrarian economy, 44
Alitto, Guy, 9
All Asia Cultural Association, 223
Amery, Leo, 215–16
anarchism, 52–4
    affinity with GMD, 51–2, 158
    Dai Jitao on, 52–4
    in April 1927 coup, 35
    Li Shizeng and, 34, 51–2
    mass emotions and, 56 n. 89
    Three People's Principles and, 51
    United Front and, 49–51
Anderson, Benedict, 47
Anderson, Perry, 31
anticolonialism, 18, 196, 197, 201, 206–7,
    222, 238, *See also* anti-imperialism
    League against Imperialism, 199
    opposition to a Euro-American
      modernity, 196–9
    Pan-Asianism, 200, 202–3
    Tan Yunshan's travels and, 211–12
anticommunism, 237–8, *See also* April 1927
    coup, Chinese Communist Party

anarchism and, 52
Anti-Communism and Resist Russia
    Mobilization Movement, 232–3
continuity in Taiwan, 229–35
cultural expression and, 14–15, 60–1
Dai Jitao on, 37–9, 64
Indian response to, 217
Japan and, 202
language used about 1927 coup, 57–9
liberal attacks, 169–71
moves towards, 35–6
nationalist activism, 66
spiritual mobilization and, 134
youth targeted, 62, 67
anti-imperialism, 198, 218–19, *See also*
    nationalism
Dai Jitao on, 38–40
Dai on, 11
hollowness of, 225, 227f
part of international system, 226
spiritual significance, 16
apoliticization. *See* depoliticization of
    political participation
April 1927 coup, 26–7, 35, *See also*
    anticommunism, party purification
as counterrevolution, 26
birth to the conservative revolution,
    26–7, 31
Bolshevik model continued after, 33
GMD careers inseparable from, 2–3
language used about, 57–9
relations with India and, 217
Arendt, Hannah, 50
Arnold, Matthew, 178–9, 182, 191
Arrighi, Giovanni, 6
art and literature, 174–8
    aesthetics and, 180–1, 183, 188
    fascist investment in, 183–5
    patronage of authors, 183–5
    politics and, 190
    popularization of, 177 n. 55, 178 n. 57
    transformative potential of, 174–6, 180

275

moral improvement, 74–5, *See also*
aesthetics and politics, New Life
Movement, spiritual mobilization
Dai Jitao on, 44–7
GMD and liberal agreement on, 192
India and China commonalities, 196
moral activism, 77, 164, 171, 175–6
moral edification, 182, 185, 196
national ethics, 46–7
politics collapsed with lifestyle, 15–18
Sino-Indian amity and, 203–6
socialist ethics, 44–6, 47–9
state shaping of norms, 46–7
Tan Yunshan on, 208
Mukden Incident (1931), 101, 114
n. 2, 117
Mussolini, Benito, 6–8, *See also* Fascist Italy

Nanjing-based government, 87, *See also*
Nationalist government
nation building, 46–7, 59, *See also* spiritual
mobilization
as priority during war, 120
industrial modernity, 62–3
national identity (*guomin xing*), 48
national jamborees. *See* jamborees
national psyche. *See* aesthetics and politics
national revolution (guomin geming). *See*
also vanguardism
capitalism's role in, 63–4, 66–7
Chiang Kai-shek as leader of, 26
communists and, 132, 199–201
conservative socioeconomic goals,
3–4, 64–6
cultures of violence, 114
decoupling from social revolution,
27–8, 31–2
enjoyment or moral uplift in, 42
goal of, 65, 67
inertia and nihilism to suppress, 61
launched by Sun Yat-sen, 2–3
mass activism and, 68
meaning of *geming*, 29, 39
nature of political struggle, 32
Pan-Asianism and, 199
rightward shift of, 35
workers and peasants in, 63–4
national revolution (*minzu geming*)
(Taiwan), 231
national spirit. *See* spiritual mobilization
National Spiritual Mobilization Movement
(*Guomin jingshen zong dongyuan
yundong*), 116–17, 127, 134, 135,
151–3, 162, 166, 169, 187
Chiang and, 136, 151–2

Citizen Pledge Song, 147 n. 92, 147, 151
inspectors, 151–3
Japan, 141
launching ceremony, 143 n. 75, 143,
147, 194
national unity, 28, 130–2
intellectual complicity and, 166,
167–71
nationalism, 18–20, *See also* India,
liberalism, Three People's Principles
basis of fascist mobilization, 6
conservative consensus in, 207
Donald Trump, 236–7, 239
GMD brand of, 8–10
India and China commonalities, 195–7,
212–14, 215–16, 217–21
opposition to class struggle, 6–10
Tan Yunshan's travels and, 211–12
traditional culture as central to, 9–11
Nationalist government. *See also*
Confucianism, democratic centralism,
fascist tendencies, Taiwan
administrative role, 18–19
anticommunism as focus of, 2–4, 26
China as part of international system,
226
cultural policy, 182, 210, 211 n. 37
Dai Jitao on bureaucracy, 59–60
for the people as a whole, 37
India and, 195, 215–16, 217–21
international counterparts, 3–5
interwar period, 236–8
liberals and, 156–8, 192
management of society, 17
modernization program, 116
move to Nanjing, 26, 87
party-state alignment, 54
policy on CCP, 28
product of national revolution, 2–4
scouting and, 82–3, 84–6, 94, 96–8,
100–2, 103, 105, 106, 107, 109
spiritual mobilization, 127–9,
140 n. 65
state governed by, 33
Nationalist Party. *See* Guomindang
Nationalist Revolution (Dai), 55–6
Nationalist vision. *See* anticolonialism,
anticommunism, Guomindang,
liberalism
nation-state. *See also* fascist tendencies,
state
as target of loyalty, 128–31, 200
formation of, 7–9, 28–31
Rabindranath Tagore and, 213–14
supremacy of, 3, 8, 133–4, 138–40

Studies of the Weatherhead East Asian Institute
Columbia University

Selected Titles

(Complete list at: http://weai.columbia.edu/publications/studies-weai/)

Idly Scribbling Rhymers: Poetry, Print, and Community in 19th Century Japan, by Robert Tuck. Columbia University Press, 2018

Forging the Golden Urn: The Qing Empire and the Politics of Reincarnation in Tibet, by Max Oidtmann. Columbia University Press, 2018

The Battle for Fortune: State-Led Development, Personhood, and Power Among Tibetans in China, by Charlene Makley. Cornell University Press, 2018

Aesthetic Life: Beauty and Art in Modern Japan, by Miya Mizuta Lippit. Harvard University Asia Center, 2018.

China's War on Smuggling: Law, Economic Life, and the Making of the Modern State, 1842–1965, by Philip Thai. Columbia University Press, 2018

Where the Party Rules: The Rank and File of China's Authoritarian State, by Daniel Koss. Cambridge University Press, 2018

Resurrecting Nagasaki: Reconstruction and the Formation of Atomic Narratives, by Chad Diehl. Cornell University Press, 2018.

China's Philological Turn: Scholars, Textualism, and the Dao in the Eighteenth Century, by Ori Sela. Columbia University Press, 2018

Making Time: Astronomical Time Measurement in Tokugawa Japan, by Yulia Frumer. University of Chicago Press, 2018.

Mobilizing Without the Masses: Control and Contention in China, by Diana Fu. Cambridge University Press, 2018.

Promiscuous Media: Film and Visual Culture in Imperial Japan, 1926–1945, by Hikari Hori. Cornell University Press, 2018.

The End of Japanese Cinema: Industrial Genres, National Times, and Media Ecologies, by Alexander Zahlten. Duke University Press, 2017.

The Chinese Typewriter: A History, by Thomas S. Mullaney. The MIT Press, 2017.

Forgotten Disease: Illnesses Transformed in Chinese Medicine, by Hilary A. Smith. Stanford University Press, 2017.

Borrowing Together: Microfinance and Cultivating Social Ties, by Becky Yang Hsu. Cambridge University Press, 2017

Food of Sinful Demons: Meat, Vegetarianism, and the Limits of Buddhism in Tibet, by Geoffrey Barstow. Columbia University Press, 2017

Youth For Nation: Culture and Protest in Cold War South Korea, by Charles R. Kim. University of Hawaii Press, 2017.

Socialist Cosmopolitanism: The Chinese Literary Universe, 1945–1965, by Nicolai Volland. Columbia University Press, 2017.

Yokohama and the Silk Trade: How Eastern Japan Became the Primary Economic Region of Japan, 1843–1893, by Yasuhiro Makimura. Lexington Books, 2017.

The Social Life of Inkstones: Artisans and Scholars in Early Qing China, by Dorothy Ko. University of Washington Press, 2017.

Darwin, Dharma, and the Divine: Evolutionary Theory and Religion in Modern Japan, by G. Clinton Godart. University of Hawaii Press, 2017.

Dictators and Their Secret Police: Coercive Institutions and State Violence, by Sheena Chestnut Greitens. Cambridge University Press, 2016.

The Cultural Revolution on Trial: Mao and the Gang of Four, by Alexander C. Cook. Cambridge University Press, 2016.

Inheritance of Loss: China, Japan, and the Political Economy of Redemption After Empire, by Yukiko Koga. University of Chicago Press, 2016.

Homecomings: The Belated Return of Japan's Lost Soldiers, by Yoshikuni Igarashi. Columbia University Press, 2016.

Samurai to Soldier: Remaking Military Service in Nineteenth-Century Japan, by D. Colin Jaundrill. Cornell University Press, 2016.

The Red Guard Generation and Political Activism in China, by Guobin Yang. Columbia University Press, 2016.

Accidental Activists: Victim Movements and Government Accountability in Japan and South Korea, by Celeste L. Arrington. Cornell University Press, 2016.

Ming China and Vietnam: Negotiating Borders in Early Modern Asia, by Kathlene Baldanza. Cambridge University Press, 2016.

Ethnic Conflict and Protest in Tibet and Xinjiang: Unrest in China's West, coedited by Ben Hillman and Gray Tuttle. Columbia University Press, 2016.

One Hundred Million Philosophers: Science of Thought and the Culture of Democracy in Postwar Japan, by Adam Bronson. University of Hawaii Press, 2016.

Conflict and Commerce in Maritime East Asia: The Zheng Family and the Shaping of the Modern World, c. 1620–1720, by Xing Hang. University Press, 2016.

Chinese Law in Imperial Eyes: Sovereignty, Justice, and Transcultural Politics, by Li Chen. Columbia University Press, 2016.

Imperial Genus: The Formation and Limits of the Human in Modern Korea and Japan, by Travis Workman. University of California Press, 2015.

Yasukuni Shrine: History, Memory, and Japan's Unending Postwar, by Akiko Takenaka. University of Hawaii Press, 2015

The Age of Irreverence: A New History of Laughter in China, by Christopher Rea. University of California Press, 2015

The Knowledge of Nature and the Nature of Knowledge in Early Modern Japan, by Federico Marcon. University of Chicago Press, 2015

The Fascist Effect: Japan and Italy, 1915–1952, by Reto Hofmann. Cornell University Press, 2015

The International Minimum: Creativity and Contradiction in Japan's Global Engagement, 1933–1964, by Jessamyn R. Abel. University of Hawai'i Press, 2015

Empires of Coal: Fueling China's Entry into the Modern World Order, 1860–1920, by Shellen Xiao Wu. Stanford University Press, 2015

CPSIA information can be obtained
at www.ICGtesting.com
Printed in the USA
BVHW040212220920
589354BV00014B/881